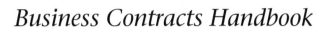

Business Contracts Handbook

To Leika, Emma and Naomi,
Discovering a world of words:
To all who follow them,
And to all who precede them

Business Contracts Handbook

CHARLES BOUNDY

GOWER

Published by
Gower Publishing Limited
Wey Court East
Union Road
Farnham
Surrey
GU9 7PT
England

Gower Publishing Company
Suite 420
101 Cherry Street
Burlington
VT 05401-4405
USA

www.gowerpublishing.com

Charles Boundy has asserted his moral right under the Copyright, Designs and Patents Act, 1988, to be identified as the author of this work.

British Library Cataloguing in Publication Data
  Boundy, Charles
   The business contracts handbook.
   1. Contracts--Interpretation and construction.
   I. Title
   658.1'2-dc22

   ISBN: 978-0-566-08856-8 (hbk)
       978-0-566-09222-0 (ebk)

Library of Congress Cataloging-in-Publication Data
Boundy, Charles
  The business contracts handbook / by Charles Boundy.
     p. cm.
  Includes bibliographical references and index.
  ISBN 978-0-566-08856-8 (hardback) -- ISBN 978-0-566-09222-0 (ebook)
1. Commercial law--England. 2. Commercial law--Wales. 3. Contracts--England. 4. Contracts--Wales. 5. Sales--England. 6. Sales--Wales. I. Title.
  KD1629.B68 2009
  346.4207--dc22

                                                                            2009024522

Mixed Sources
Product group from well-managed forests and other controlled sources
www.fsc.org Cert no. SA-COC-1565
© 1996 Forest Stewardship Council

Printed and bound in Great Britain by
MPG Books Group, UK

Contents

Acknowledgements

Many acknowledgements are due. The first are to those of my family and colleagues who have lived or worked closely with me during the gestation period of this work. Prime among these, especially when having to bear the brunt of those household and other tasks that she had hoped I would finally help with, is my wife, Hazel. At work my PA, Nathalie Coupland, has been a constant support and encouragement and my colleagues, Sinead Martin, Vanessa Milton, Emma D'Cruz and especially Lisa Pickering, have had to live with regular cries of, 'It's in the book!' when a contract issue came up. Paula Neary, who heads our IT team, has read and commented on relevant sections. My former colleagues at Fladgate LLP (www.fladgate.com), David Robinson (corporate), Simon Ekins (dispute resolution), Eddie Powell and Anthony Lee (IP and IT) and Nick Tsatsas (employment) have been especially good at looking at various chapters and sections, and have provided invaluable feedback, as have Richard McMorris (media outsourcing and IT) and Marcus Rowland (TUPE on outsourcing) of Wiggin LLP (www.wiggin.co.uk). Simon Neill, Katherine Kirrage and Amisha Patel of Osborne Clarke (www.osborneclarke.com) have been good enough to review the sections on restrictions and competition law. To all, and others who have helped, very many thanks. Any mistakes are of course entirely mine.

List of Abbreviations

AAA	American Arbitration Association
ADR	alternative dispute resolution
ASA	Advertising Standards Authority
BCAP	British Code of Advertising Practice
BERR	Department of Business Enterprise and Regulatory Reform (*see* BIS)
BIS	Department for Business, Innovation and Skills (formerly BERR)
BPRs	Business Protection from Misleading Marketing Regulations 2008
BSI	British Standards Institute
B2B	business to business
B2C	business to consumer
CA	Companies Act 2006
CEDR	Centre for Effective Dispute Resolution
CFA	conditional fee agreement
CI	confidential information
CIF	cost/carriage, insurance and freight
CISG	Convention on Contracts for the International Sale of Goods (1980)
CMR	Convention on the Contract for International Carriage by Road
CPA	Consumer Protection Act 1987
CPRs	Consumer Protection from Unfair Trading Regulations 2008
CTM	European Community Trademark
CVA	company voluntary agreement
DPA	Data Protection Act 1998
DRM	digital rights management
DTI	Department of Trade and Industry
D2C	direct to consumer
EC	European Commission
ECHR	European Court of Human Rights
EEA	European Economic Area
ETO	economic, technical or organizational reason (under TUPE)
EU	European Union
EULA	end-user licence agreement
EXW	ex works
FOB	free on board
FOIA	Freedom of Information Act 2000
FSA	Financial Services Authority
HMRC	HM Revenue and Customs (Inland Revenue)
HRA	Human Rights Act 1998
ICANN	Internet Corporation for Assigned Names and Numbers
ICC	International Chamber of Commerce
ICDR	International Centre for Dispute Resolution
ICO	Information Commissioner's Office

IP	insolvency practitioner
IP	intellectual property
IP	Internet protocol
IPO	Intellectual Property Office
IPR	intellectual property right
ISP	Internet service provider
IT	information technology
ITT	invitation to tender
IVA	individual voluntary arrangement
KPI	key performance indicator
LCIA	London Court of International Arbitration
LLP	limited liability partnership
NAOMI	Notice on Agreements of Minor Importance
NCO	non-compete obligations
NDA	non-disclosure agreement
NIC	national insurance contributions
OFT	Office of Fair Trading
PAYE	pay as you earn
POCA	Proceeds of Crime Act 2002
POD	proof of delivery
PR	price received
PTO	post-termination obligation
P2P	peer-to-peer
ROT	retention of title
RFI	request for information
RIPA	Regulation of Investigatory Powers Act 2000
RPA	Resale Prices Act 1976
RPI	retail prices index
RPM	resale price maintenance
RRP	recommended retail price
RTPA	Restrictive Trade Practices Act 1976
SGA	Sale of Goods Act 1979 as amended
SGSA	Supply of Goods and Services Act 1982 as amended
SLA	service-level agreement
SME	small or medium-sized enterprise
SMT	scientific, medical and technical
TLD	top-level domain name
TOB	terms of business
TPM	technical protection measure
TPPS	third-party proprietary software
TTBE	Technology Transfer Block Exemption
TUPE	Transfer of Undertakings (Protection of Employment) Regulations 2006
UCC	user-created content
UCTA	Unfair Contract Terms Act 1977
UGC	user-generated content
UNCITRAL	United Nations Commission on International Trade Law
UTCCR	Unfair Terms in Consumer Contracts Regulations 1999

VAR	Vertical Agreements Regulation
VRBE	Vertical Restraints Block Exemption
WIPO	World Intellectual Property Organization

Glossary

Note: The following are general descriptions of how certain words and phrases are used in this book – they are not legal definitions!

acceptance	Agreement that something has been done or delivered as per contract.
account of profits	An alternative to damages in IP claims by seeking a share of the other party's benefits rather than compensation for own loss.
ADR	Alternative dispute resolution – such as a form of non-binding mediation.
agent	A party authorized to act on behalf of another.
agreement to agree	A contract that lacks certainty on a vital term.
arbitration	An alternative to litigation in which the dispute is heard by, typically, one or three arbitrators who will make a decision based on the evidence heard.
Articles 81 and 82	The main anti-competition rules of the European Treaty.
articles of association	The internal constitution of a limited company.
assignment	The transfer of intangible rights/obligations, such as a contract, licence, trademark or copyright.
attest	Witness.
bailment	Lodging of goods by one party with another with an express or implied obligation to look after the goods.
best endeavours	A very high standard of effort.
block exemptions/ specific exemptions	Specific exemptions from Article 81.
blue-pencil test	A test operated by the courts as to whether offending parts of a restrictive covenant or similar term can be deleted.
boilerplate	A contract or clause of general application.
claim	A demand for compensation or other remedy for breach of contract or other civil wrong.
claimant	A party making or threatening to make a claim.

claims handling	The process of making, defending or otherwise dealing with claims.
collateral contract	An agreement running alongside main terms of the contract.
comfort letter	A side letter which may or may not be legally binding.
common law	Judge-made law developed from decisions on individual cases.
conflict of laws	Where there is an international element to a contract and the laws of the countries involved difer on the issue in question.
connected	A specific degree of association between two or more parties, such as associated companies, relatives or those having common interest in a business.
consequential loss	Loss arising from breach of contract, negligence or tort other than the immediate physical or financial damage or injury directly arising.
consideration	Money or some other obligation of value.
constructive dismissal	Resignation of an employee as a result of breach of contract by the employer.
construe (also 'construction' of documents etc.)	Intrepret/decipher the meaning of.
consultancy	Appointment of a person (other than an employee) to assist or advise in relation to a project or business.
consumer	An individual buying products or services in a personal (and generally) non-business capacity.
contra proferentem	The principle that an onerous clause will be interpreted by the courts, in case of doubt, against the party seeking to impose it.
contract	(For the purposes of this book) an agreement which is legally enforceable.
control (of companies)	The ownership of [more than] 50 per cent or the right to direct the affairs of a company.
copyright	The right to prevent another person from reproducing all, or a substantial part of, an original work.
corporate veil	The protection of incorporation given by company law.
counter-offer	A revised offer made on different terms.
counterpart	One of several signature parts of a contract or deed.
course of dealing	One or more previous transactions between the same parties relating to a similar subject-matter.
damages	Compensation awarded by the courts for breach of contract, negligence and other appropriate cases.
deed	A document which is expressed to be and is 'signed as a deed' and witnessed.

defendant	A party defending court proceedings.
del credere agent	An agency where the agent guarantees to the principal that the third-party customer will perform the contract.
de minimis	A low-level threshold, often used in relation to competition law, but also sometimes used in relation to matters such as warranty claims.
directives	European laws required to be implemented by each of the member states in their respective territories.
disclaimer	A contract item or notice seeking to exclude or limit liability for loss (see also exemption clause).
distance selling	Selling (usually to a consumer) without meeting face-to-face – typical of an Internet transaction.
distributorship	Relationship whereby a supplier appoints a distributor to buy and resell the supplier's goods.
domain name	The name used, particularly by an organization or business, to identify itself on the Internet or World Wide Web.
dominant	A business may be dominant in the market if it has the ability in effect to behave to a large extent independently of its competitors.
due diligence	Checking information regarding the other contract party, or details supplied by that party, that are basic to the contract.
drafting	Preparing the written layout and wording of a contract.
EEA	European Economic Area, comprising the European Union, together with the additional states who were previously members of the European Free Trade Association (Iceland, Liechtenstein and Norway).
eiusdem generis	The general proposition will apply to the particular examples given.
end-user	Consumer using a technology product or service.
entire agreement clause	A clause stating that all relevant terms are included in the one contract.
equity	Decisions of the courts of equity initially based on correcting any unfairness of common law, subsequently developing into even stricter rules, now giving the basis for 'equitable remedies'.
escrow	The holding of funds or a document (including details of a computer source code) pending the occurrence of a pre-stated event.
estoppel	The rule that someone is prevented from denying that which they have previously stated or accepted as correct.
European Treaty	The formal constitution of the European Union (formerly the Treaty of Rome).

European Union (EU)   The economic and political union, currently of 27 states, previously the Common Market or the European Economic Community.

exclusion clause   An exemption clause that seeks to exclude certain liability altogether.

exclusivity   A term denoting that one or more parties agree not to take specified action in a specific area.

exemption clause   A clause in a contract seeking to exclude or limit the liability of one or more parties to the contract. (Cf. limitation clause and exclusion clause.)

expert   A person qualified and experienced in a particular discipline, who will make a decision from personal knowledge of the subject in question.

fiduciary duty   A duty to act honestly and in good faith in relation to another party.

force majeure   An event beyond the control of one or more of the parties to a contract.

franchising   The grant of the right to use a brand name and certain other intellectual property rights in relation to an established business format.

frustration   The point when a contract becomes impossible to perform through no fault of the parties.

further assurance   The obligation to take any further action necessary to perfect a contract or deed.

good faith   An honest approach (but not necessarily a legal commitment).

goods   Items which have a physical character (other than money), but which may be specifically defined by individual statutes or regulations.

guarantee   a)   An undertaking that goods or services will perform to a stated level (cf. warranty);
b)   An undertaking from an individual or company to pay money on behalf of another if that other fails to pay.

horizontal agreements/ restraints   Agreements/restrictions between two or more parties operating in parallel, such as competitors in relation to similar products (cf. vertical agreements).

incapacity   Legal inability to do something, such as enter into a contract.

incorporation   a)   The point at which a limited company is legally established;
b)   The inclusion of a term in a contract.

Incoterms   Recognized terms used in international trade, published by the ICC.

indemnity   Requirement in a contract or deed to repay another party for a claim made against them or loss incurred by them.

independent contractor	An individual or firm who provides services to a party but who is not an employee of that other party.
injunction	A court order requiring a person to do something or preventing a person from doing something.
insolvent	Bankrupt or unable to pay debts (including liquidation, receivership and administration.
intellectual property rights	Patents, trademarks, copyright and other non-physical rights given legal protection.
interpretation clause	A clause giving the precise meaning attributed to a word or phrase in the contract.
jurisdiction	The right of a particular court or the courts of a particular country or a tribunal to hear and adjudicate on a particular dispute.
know-how	A process or way of doing business.
legislation	Statutes, regulations and directives.
licence	The right to do or use something, such as intellectual property, for a period of time.
limitation clause	An exemption clause that seeks to limit (but not totally exclude) certain liabilities.
limitation period	The period within which legal action must be commenced.
liquidated damages	A specified level of compensation as an agreed pre-estimate of loss.
liquidation	The point at which a company finally ceases to exist and is wound up.
litigation	A dispute pursued in court.
milestones	Predetermined markers of progress – for example, in a technology project.
misrepresentation	A representation that turns out to be incorrect.
mitigation of loss	Proper efforts to reduce the loss caused by breach of contract.
necessaries	The essentials of life, such as food, drink, clothing, housing, vital medicine and their modern equivalents.
negligence	Breach of a duty of care to a third party, causing loss or damage.
nemo dat	The rule of law that you cannot give what you do not have.
non-compete clause	A restrictive covenant (see below).
non est factum	A document that was not the type of transaction that the relevant party intended or agreed to enter into.
novation	The replacement by one party to a contract of another party.

null and void	Deemed never to have come into existence in the first place.
operative clause	A clause setting out what a party has to do or how the contract works.
outsourcing	Arranging to have carried out externally a business or project previously carried out in-house.
part performance	A situation where a person or company partly performs an agreement which they are led to believe exists.
passing-off	Representing goods or services as being associated with another company or brand.
personal contracts	Contracts which, by their nature, are personal to the original parties and cannot be assigned without the consent of the other party.
privacy	The human right to a private and family life.
privity (of contract)	The principle that only the parties to a contract (or those intended to have a defined benefit under it) may enforce the contract.
public domain	The accepted level of general public knowledge or information.
quantum meruit	Payment of a fair rate for the work actually done (as opposed to a pre-agreed amount).
reasonable endeavours	Commercial efforts to achieve a result but less than best endeavours.
recital	A preliminary clause explaining the background to a contract.
rectification	The legal process of amending a contract to reflect the actual intentions of the parties.
regulations	Statutory instruments and other delegated legislation brought into force by the government as authorized by statutes; also laws passed by the European Commission having direct application in member states.
regulatory body	An official body with powers to oversee certain activities, such as the the Financial Services Authority (FSA) in respect of certain financial dealings.
representation	A statement of fact about goods or services.
repudiation	A fundamental breach of contract by one party which entitles the other or others to treat the contract as at an end.
resale	A subsequent sale – by retail or otherwise.
rescission	Cancellation of a contract as if it had not been in force.
restitution	An order to restore another party to their original position – for example, by returning goods or money to them.

restraint of trade	A limitation on the ability of one or more parties to trade freely.
restrictive covenants	Provisions in a contract preventing one or more of the parties from undertaking certain specified activities.
retention of title	Reservation by the owner of goods to title in them until an event (such as payment for those or other goods) has occurred.
revocation	Withdrawal or revoking an offer.
satisfactory quality	An obligation as to the condition of goods implied by the SGA.
service levels	Stated expected levels of performance of a service with regard to objective criteria.
severance	Deleting words from a contract.
sole remedy clause	A form of exemption clause in which the innocent party's rights in respect of a breach by the other are limited to a specific remedy.
statutes	Laws formally passed by parliament.
statutory duty	A legal duty set out in a statute.
subject to contract	Words used to indicate that there is no intention to enter into a legally binding agreement.
subrogation	The principle that an indemnifying party, such as an insurer, can take action on behalf of the party they are indemnifying.
subcontract	Delegate all or part of a contract to another party.
takeover	Taking control of a company (normally by buying the majority of the shares).
term	a) A provision in a contract (sometimes used by courts to mean a fundamental provision); b) the period a contract is due to run.
termination	The end of an agreement.
time of the essence	Stipulation in the contract that an obligation be performed strictly on time, failing which a material breach of contract will arise.
title	Legal ownership.
tort	A civil wrong, such as negligence.
transfer regulations	Transfer of Undertakings (Protection of Employment) Regulations 2006 (TUPE).
undertaking	a) A commitment to do something. b) An active business (cf. transfer regulations).
undue influence	Exercise by one person of excessive influence over someone else relying on them.

unenforceable	An agreement or deed which the law, for a particular reason, will not be prepared to enforce.
vertical agreements/ restraints	Agreements/restrictions between parties in a vertical relationship, such as supplier and distributor (cf. horizontal agreements).
vicarious liability	Legal liability for another party, such as an employee.
voidable	An agreement or deed which is subject to a defect that can destroy it.
waiver	The effective acceptance by one party to a contract of a breach of that contract by another party.
warranty	a) A guarantee of quality or performance; b) A statement that certain things are, or will be, true at a stated date.
without prejudice	Words used to protect a genuine attempt at negotiation from being produced in court as evidence.
writing	Representing or reproducing words in a visible form.
wrongful trading	Continuation of trading by the directors of a company after the point when insolvent liquidation has become inevitable.

Preface

The Aim of This Book

Almost everyone involved with business deals in one way or another with contracts, ranging from high-profile and complex agreements to the day-to-day. Major deals, such as takeover, business purchase and property transactions, tend to be planned for and negotiated from the outset with specialist help and documentation drafted and reviewed at each stage by lawyers experienced in the field. But, with middle-range contracts, such as terms of business, website terms, outsourcing contracts and agreements for agency, distribution or even critical IT purchases, the process is often haphazard. The tendency is for the contract to be given too little thought and considered too late to be integrated effectively into the negotiation process. Yet these contracts can be just as important to a company's future well-being and may give a nasty and potentially expensive bite when overlooked.

The aim of this book is therefore to provide a practical handbook for all those involved in the contract process, so that they can understand the background, anticipate the issues, plan the structure, identify the key points, negotiate with confidence and ensure that the whole package is properly recorded in a contract that can be relied on. Those who have little prior knowledge will be able to acquire a working background quickly; those with years of experience will still benefit from a checklist – a reminder of what is important and why, and easy reference to up-to-date language and drafting. Even in researching and writing this book, and although I have given regular update seminars on the issues, I was drawn back to a re-examination of a number of legal aspects that I had worked with over the years; there is always more to learn.

This is a book written for, but not solely for, executives and managers. Having had personal experience on both sides of the corporate fence, I know that much of the detail will be relevant to professional advisers, including qualified lawyers, as well as to their in-house or external clients. Commercial law is often the Cinderella of the legal profession, just as business contracts are regularly underappreciated (and sometimes locked away) by those who deal with them. Managers and lawyers could often do much more to develop a really effective working relationship as, too often, time is not put into a proper briefing at the start or effort is wasted on peripheral issues at the cost of more vital ones. One principle of this book is that a dedicated manager should be able to handle most aspects of a company's business contracts, but should also know when to seek help. So practical tips are given throughout on how and when it is advisable to seek specialist support. When that help is called for, the text suggests approaches which, if applied, will save valuable time and could save substantial cost in the process.

Sources of Law

As a lawyer in private practice, I often found that when I needed more guidance there was a lack of variety or suitability in the material available. The top textbooks, such as

Chitty on Contracts, are a wonderful mine of information for helping distinguish the finer points, but tended to absorb valuable time in arcane issues. Student companion volumes were at the other end of the scale, with a strong set of key points but geared to grounding students to answer exam questions. Reported cases have always been fascinating in their own right, especially in terms of human interest and why people go to court, but, as we were always taught at law school, each case depends on its own facts. And, of course, there are always appeals which often seem to confuse complex law yet further. (Non-lawyers should appreciate that the appeal courts concentrate on specific grounds of appeal and do not rehear the whole case; they do not therefore hear the witnesses live, sometimes leaving the reader perplexed as to why either the trial judge or the appeal court reached the decision in question.)

In my earlier years in the law, know-how, being the benefit of expertise and experience, was often locked away in the heads of the senior practitioners who were too busy, and sometimes disinclined, to share it. Over the last 15 years or so, however, law firms have built up their own legal know-how systems through librarians and professionally qualified support lawyers (PSLs), complemented in turn by detailed legal journals such as *PLC* (*Practical Law for Companies*) and specialist legal search and retrieval websites, such as Lexis, Lawtel and Westlaw. In addition there are many excellent works on specialized areas of law or legal practice, mostly written by lawyers for lawyers. Gower books are a notable exception in their management focus. Even then, whilst slices of detail are now much easier to find, it is difficult for anyone in business – lawyer or non-lawyer – to grasp enough of the broader picture and framework of the contracts they deal with to be able to maximize their input into them. Just because nearly everything can be found on the Web does not mean it is correct or up-to-date, and browsing rarely leads to a broad understanding of a subject as complex as contract law. And there is even less on the craft of creating contracts to achieve their desired effect. Those drafting contracts need to be as precise as sculptors moulding clay heads; press too hard in one place and the clay will distort the head in another aspect!

Background to This Book

Faced with this, and wishing to record some of my ideas, I wrote the predecessor to this book, *A Concise Business Guide to Contract Law*, published by Gower in 1998. The Introduction started: 'This book has been written for people in business.' That objective has not changed, nor has my wish to write in an accessible style. What has changed is the move from setting down the principles of contract law to seeking to relay these in the practical style of a handbook with recommended wording.

This process has been accentuated by two things. First, having written the *Concise Guide*, I realized I wanted to know more about the broader issues as to why people react to contracts, and the responsibility that goes with them, the way they do. So, while still a partner at my law firm, I took a part-time M.Phil degree, between a masters and a doctorate, in 'Critical Management' at Lancaster University Management School. The first two weeks left me dazed from trying to master the new language of management and with an introduction to philosophy, sociology, anthropology, psychology and spirituality to explore. The course was an eye-opener to another world, but I remained happy to have the legal grounding. Looking back, my thesis on 'Privacy at Work' seems to have anticipated my move into publishing where the emerging law of privacy has become a major legal growth area.

For the last five years I have been the Group Legal Director of The Random House Group Ltd, one of my former clients and the leading UK consumer book publisher with subsidiaries in several Commonwealth countries. In this role, with an initial sharp focus on publishing risks and agreements, contracts of all kinds from all parts of our business have come across my desk, further accentuated by our development of digital publishing. This has enabled me not only to be even more aware of the business side of contracts but also to have the freedom to approach them in a fully commercial way, without timesheets to complete, and with the 'client' able to walk into my office or book a meeting at any time! The converse is that, with no 'client' paying directly for my time, prioritization and issues of practicality became paramount. In turn, many of the recommendations in this book have resulted from my in-house experience and have often been tested on my non-legal colleagues.

Scope of the Book

The problem with writing a book of this sort of that its scope is potentially vast. This gives two major problems. The first is what to leave out and the second is how to cover reliably the whole of the canvas on which I have chosen to paint. On what to leave out, I have made a personal choice, largely as to what I thought would be most relevant to most potential readers. On the second issue, I have had to research some areas more thoroughly than I would normally need to and shoehorn others, like competition law, into a succinct space. I have enlisted the services of some professional colleagues, acknowledged above, in specialist areas. Any mistakes are, of course, mine alone.

The book covers only English law, but cross-refers where possible to other jurisdictions, with a separate chapter on the international element. It does not tackle land law or company law, although, again, it cross-refers in several aspects. Likewise, it does into go into specialist areas such as consumer finance or bills of exchange or shipping. These points are flagged where appropriate. In terms of layout I have chosen my own format, with five sections: Part 1 starts with the general principles of creating and writing contracts and Part 2 picks up a series of typical key issues found in contracts. There follow two sections on specific types of contract: Part 3 on contracts for goods and services generally and Part 4 on contracts with a technology bias. Part 5 covers the wider world and issues that typically arise after the contract is created, such as transfers, changes of control, breaches and disputes, remedies and termination.

How to Use This Book

A manager faced with a contract issue would do well to read Part 1 either as a general introduction or as a reminder of salient points, such as: how to negotiate by e-mail, when to use 'subject to contract', how to plan cost/ risk and benefit and how these are to be dealt with in the contract and a reminder to keep to the main issues with the 90:10 rule. Part 2 should be checked if there are (highly likely) issues of confidentiality, dealings with companies, damage limitation classes or legal restrictions which might be serious enough to have a competition law implication. These areas all need to be planned carefully up-front, or the damage can all too easily be done. Then the manager can turn to whichever of Chapters 9–16 is most relevant to the subject-matter of the contract, such as the appointment of a marketing consultant (Chapter 12 on 'Contracts for Services'), an outsourcing project (Chapter 13) or a web-design agreement (Chapter 12 and also 16 on Internet-related contracts). If reviewing an existing and now burdensome contract, it may be best to start with Chapter 18 on problem contracts and work from there. There are supporting checklists at the end of chapters.

Clearly, much cross-relates. Dealing with even more typical contracts separately at length might have doubled the length of the book, but the cross-referencing is assisted by a combination of chapter and sub-chapter headings, a comprehensive index and a glossary of technical terms and abbreviations. In addition there are a number of specially written appendices, including some template contract forms.

Limitations

This book is intended as general guidance with wording as sample drafting, but not provided, nor can the author or publishers accept liability for it, as legal advice; readers must take their own legal or other professional guidance on specific issues. The law also continues to change, and current checks should always be made on the latest law and technical developments. Wherever possible I have tried to flag areas expected to change. Although there are one or two references to later developments, the law is generally stated as at July/August 2009 with major developments from then to the end October 2009 being highlighted in the Stop Press! section at the end of the book.

Charles Boundy

CREATING AND WRITING CONTRACTS

CHAPTER 1 *Contract Basics*

Introduction – The elements of a contract – contract essentials – offer, acceptance and certainty – consideration – the need for writing – defective and incomplete contracts – 'subject to contract' and 'without prejudice' – gentleman's agreements and business misunderstandings – some sample cases – summary and checklist

Introduction

If money is the lifeblood of business, contracts are the arteries that help carry that lifeblood around the commercial body. The connections between a business and its suppliers, customers, employees and service providers all rely on contracts. The medical analogy is also a reminder that, whilst contracts may be constructs of law, they are negotiated and acted upon by living people. Understanding and agreement is therefore challenged not just by changing events, but frequently by the hopes, fears and other emotions of those involved, which may also cause them to see contracts as they would wish them to be rather than as they really are.

THE FRAMEWORK OF CONTRACT LAW

Common law

English contract law has no overall statutory commercial code, but relies on a combination of judge-made 'common law' and statute law or regulations authorized by parliament. This common law is further adjusted and supplemented by acts of parliament or regulations (many derived from European Union directives), which are in turn reinterpreted by judges as cases come to be decided under the new laws. And so the wheel turns full circle.

English law in this book means the law of England and Wales. Chapter 17 on the international dimension explores the effect of contracting elsewhere.

What is a contract?

Sam Goldwyn's quotation that 'a verbal contract isn't worth the paper it's written on' is famously misleading. Dictionaries suggest that a contract is an agreement, whether written or spoken, with a person or company to do something on agreed and binding terms. For the purposes of this book, a contract may be simply regarded as '*an agreement which is legally enforceable*'.

Consider the act of buying a newspaper from a shop – a basic purchase contract. There is no written agreement, but a contract is created between the time you walk in the shop and the time you walk out with the paper in your hand. You may well just pick up the paper and take it to the till with your payment without a word being spoken. In law there is an offer to buy and an acceptance of that offer backed by payment of the purchase price. By the time the money is paid and the paper is handed over, the contract has been made and completed, the only written evidence being the till receipt, if there is one.

Contract development

The emphasis in this book is to plan ahead and get the contract as right as possible from the start. Unlike our inherited genetic make-up, we do have the chance to build our own contract. But things don't stand still. Contracts, like bodies, can suffer from inherent defects and from viruses carried by the wind of changed circumstances. Like evolution, the contract that may prove the best equipped for the longer term may be the one that can best adapt to change.

Contract Essentials

An effective contract requires *all* the following:

- offer and acceptance,
- certainty,
- consideration (something of value), and
- intention to enter into a legal commitment.

These are looked at it more detail below, but first there are two important preliminary points – the need for writing and the use of e-mail.

THE NEED FOR CONTRACTS TO BE IN WRITING

The general rule

The general rule is that contracts do not need to be in writing. This is not an absolute rule, because there are some exceptions (see below) and because the law accepts that there are some occasions where special protection is required, such as where there is a material imbalance in the negotiating position of the parties. Even so, a written contract is the best evidence of what the relevant parties actually agreed at the time.

The use of e-mail

For most practical purposes the law treats an e-mail as 'writing' and a contract created or evidenced by e-mail as the equivalent of a written contract. E-mails are so extensively used in business that it is easy to forget that they can of themselves create or evidence a contract, and there will not be the same opportunity to deny what was said as with an unrecorded conversation.

OFFER AND ACCEPTANCE (HAVE WE AGREED?)

Offer and 'invitation to treat'

When is an offer made? Going back to the example of buying a newspaper, there are two possible interpretations of what happens. The first view is that the shop is offering to sell the newspaper at a stated price and you accept the offer by picking the paper up and paying for it. The second is that the shop is merely displaying the newspaper, that you offer to buy it and the shop accepts the offer by selling it to you. Under English law the second analysis is correct – you offer to buy the paper and the newsagent accepts by taking your money. The display of goods is not, in normal cases, an offer capable of acceptance as such, but only 'an invitation to treat', meaning an invitation to a potential buyer to make an offer. As will become apparent, this distinction can be all-important in business.

Acceptance

Acceptance has to be 'communicated' to the person making the offer. This is often instantaneous, as with the newspaper purchase, or with an agreement made face-to-face or over the telephone. But what if the acceptance is sent by post? In the absence of other factors, English law treats posting in an official post box as due notification of acceptance (even if the letter goes astray). Whilst an offer can be withdrawn at any time before it is accepted (though obviously not afterwards), the revocation of an offer must actually be received by the other party before the offer is accepted. Mere posting of revocation does not suffice. To avoid some of these problems, an offer can specify exactly how it can be accepted, in which case the contract will come into existence as and when one of those specified means of acceptance occurs. Any other form of acceptance would then be a counter-offer.

Acceptance by conduct   Acceptance can also be inferred from conduct, such as the handing over of the newspaper by the shop in return for payment.

Auctions   Auctions are generally conducted on the basis that the bidder makes the offer to buy and the auctioneer accepts the best (or desired) bid. The offer is accepted once the auctioneer's hammer goes down. Before then the sale items are merely displayed, but not offered for sale as such.

CERTAINTY (WHAT EXACTLY IS ON OFFER?)

Being precise

Agreements need to be certain to be enforceable. This means that both (or all) parties must agree on what exactly is being offered and accepted. For example, you will want to choose your preferred newspaper. *Sun* readers might not want to accept *The Times* and vice versa. Requesting 'a newspaper' would be too general to create any certainty. Selecting from a display gives certainty by presenting your choice. The same is true of a catalogue with prices. The buyer selects from the range shown and submits an order on the basis of the details set out in the catalogue. The collection or despatch of the goods is the acceptance of that offer.

Following through

If the offer and acceptance do match up, the contract will (in the absence of special factors) be binding. Even if the buyer forgets to mention a specific requirement, the buyer will (usually) have to accept what has been ordered. Conversely, a seller must ensure that all the terms that a buyer does stipulate are satisfied, since the seller will be in breach of contract if the wrong goods are supplied. The seller will then be liable to replace those goods with the goods actually ordered or to compensate the buyer for the failure to do so.

CONSIDERATION (WHAT WILL IT COST?)

'Consideration' means money, the promise to pay money or some other obligation, such as a promise to provide a service, which has some value. The existence of consideration (money, goods or services or the promise of them) must be given by the party seeking to enforce the contract and is the main difference between a legally enforceable contract and a gratuitous promise. There are, however, two main exceptions to this general rule. First, 'negotiable instruments', such as cheques and letters of credit, do not need consideration to be valid; effectively they are the consideration itself. Second, as seen below, a document signed as a deed is enforceable without consideration. The adequacy of the consideration is considered below.

INTENTION TO BE LEGALLY BOUND (DO I WANT TO BE COMMITTED?)

All the parties involved need to *intend* to create a legally binding agreement. This is in contrast to informal domestic obligations or arrangements with friends, which tend to be informal personal arrangements with no expectation of legal commitment. There might be a falling out, but not recourse to law. The bigger issue in a business context is often whether discussions which one party might regard as a commitment were never intended as such by the other. One way of avoiding this is always to make sure that any discussion of detail is made 'subject to contract' or words to that effect.

The next section looks in more detail at the contract essentials just summarized.

Offer, Acceptance and Certainty

AN EXAMPLE OF SIMPLE OFFER AND ACCEPTANCE

Sidney Smith of Smith (Computer Supplies) Limited meets and offers to sell specified equipment to regular customer Ben Braby of Braby Business Machines Limited for £550; Braby accepts the offer by agreeing the goods and the price. A binding contract then exists, even with nothing in writing. Alternatively, Braby could offer Smith £550 for the equipment; if Smith accepts that offer without further conditions, a contract arises.

THE EFFECT OF ACCEPTANCE ON DIFFERENT TERMS

If and when the person to whom the offer is made accepts the offer, the terms are fixed. If the recipient of the offer agrees but specifies different terms, this cancels the original offer and creates a counter-offer on the revised terms proposed, open for the person making the original offer to accept or reject in turn. A counter-offer should be distinguished from a request for information, and, if you want to keep an offer open while seeking more details, it is important to use language consistent with this.

> So, if Braby offers to buy the computer equipment, but only for £500, this would be a counter-offer which Smith could accept or refuse as he chose, but, once this counter-offer has been accepted, a contract would be created. If Braby just asks for clarification, Smith's offer remains open unless and until revoked.

Just occasionally, offer and acceptance do not precisely match but the parties carry on as if they did. In those circumstances a court may (but very exceptionally) decide that a contract does exist.

UNCERTAINTY

Is there a match or mismatch?

> What if Smith offers to sell Braby a piece of computer equipment and there is a fundamental mismatch between the actual equipment that Smith is offering to sell and what Braby thinks he is offering to buy?

A mismatch about the real subject matter of the contract is all too common in business, especially when the equipment is described by product names or code numbers that mean much to the seller but little to the buyer. The buyer may ask for something to perform certain functions, and a seller will offer to sell something described mainly by a product name or number. The buyer assumes that the product will match what he has asked for, and the seller assumes that the buyer is agreeing to purchase the specific equipment identified.

There are two main likely outcomes to the example above. First, if the evidence showed that Smith, the seller, had been clear about what was on offer and Braby, the buyer, had agreed but failed to check the details, there could be an enforceable contract for the product actually sold. Second, if there was a genuine misunderstanding on both sides about what was being bought and sold, there may be no contract at all, because offer and acceptance did not match.

Misrepresentation

Alternatively, if the evidence indicated this, a court might conclude from the evidence that Smith had misrepresented the position to Braby to induce Braby into buying something different from what he wanted. If a seller misrepresents his products, even innocently, and the buyer honestly relies on that representation, the buyer may be able to cancel the transaction and claim damages for misrepresentation.

Being clear

The message is that you must be clear from the outset what it is you are selling or buying. If you are not, you might either not have a deal at all or not have the deal you thought you had. Uncertainty causes distress, potential legal costs and a falling-out in relationships. There is therefore no substitute for getting the basics clear at the outset.

Evidence

These examples reinforce the benefit of putting things in writing. Without a written record, resolving this sort of issue will depend very much on the witness testimony of those involved. This also means that those involved may need to be cross-examined in court on what they said or did not say – an experience with an uncertain outcome and cost and not one to be undertaken lightly.

THE USE OF IMPLIED TERMS

In some circumstances the law will imply additional terms into a contract, either by legislation (such the Sale of Goods Act) or by common law from the circumstances. Typically, such an implication may arise when the term is so obvious that it did not need to be stated or where it is necessary to give the contract commercial effect. Terms may also be implied from a previous course of dealing or implied by custom and usage, as with some specialized trade markets. These situations are addressed in later sections as they arise, but implied terms should never be regarded as a reliable substitute for clear contract wording in the first place.

Consideration

CONSIDERATION AND VALUE

Consideration is necessary for a contract but it does not have to be market value. The law is generally more concerned with the fact that people deal openly – and, with consumers, fairly – than with value. After all, business might otherwise grind to a halt. So far as contract law is concerned, token consideration is usually sufficient, if clearly agreed.

SOMETHING FOR THE FUTURE

Consideration must be something to be paid or done in exchange, at the time the contract is made or in the future. A debt already due will be 'past' consideration and ineffective for this purpose, although an agreement for the future, such as not to sue for an existing debt, can be 'new' consideration if given in return for something else of value.

GRATUITOUS PROMISES

The need for consideration can easily be overlooked. The fact that someone has, for some time, gratuitously permitted you to use their premises or their name or their copyright material, for instance, does not prevent them withdrawing that permission – for the future – at short notice. It is therefore often worth making a payment or performing a service in return for having a legal right for a minimum future period in order to have an enforceable agreement.

CONTRACT VARIATIONS

The same principle can apply to variations of an existing contract. To be enforceable, these generally require new consideration.

SIGNATURE AS A DEED

Consideration is not required where an agreement is in writing and expressly 'signed as a deed'. Accordingly, if there is ever doubt as to whether there is adequate consideration, such as lack of direct payment, the commitment is best captured in writing signed as a deed. A deed may also indicate the existence of a gift or trust or some other legal relationship which is, by its nature, not made in return for consideration nor dependent on offer and acceptance. Deeds are also necessary in some specialized cases, such as in transferring interests in land, granting mortgages and giving powers of attorney. Chapter 2 sets out the details as to how deeds are signed.

The Need for Writing

The example above shows the value of a deed where consideration is in question. In general, although written agreement is highly advisable, most contracts do not need to be in writing to be valid or enforceable. However, there are a number of principal exceptions, and these are briefly reviewed below.

CONTRACTS RELATING TO LAND

Agreements relating to, or dealing with, freehold or leasehold property are likely to be unenforceable (and may be void or voidable) if not in writing in a single document. Property law is a specialist area that is not covered further in this book; you should check that no part of your contract relates to land or buildings and, if it does, ensure that aspect is covered separately. Owners or lessees of property should be especially wary of letting other people or businesses occupy any part of that property, as this may set up a tenancy or other legal rights if not properly prepared and documented before the occupiers move in.

THE TRANSFER OF INTELLECTUAL PROPERTY RIGHTS

Legal assignment (transfer) of copyright and other IP rights is only effective if made in writing. Chapter 14 covers this area in more detail.

GUARANTEES

Evidenced in writing

A guarantee can be enforced only if it is suitably evidenced in writing and signed. This is one of the longest standing legal rules, dating back to the Statute of Frauds in 1677, designed to stop spurious claims against individuals based simply on oral evidence or – as the Act puts it – '[f]or prevention of many fraudulent Practices which are commonly endeavoured to be upheld by Perjury and Subornation of Perjury'. Most of the Act has been repealed, but the majority of section IV remains in its ancient glory from the times of Charles II:

> *Noe Action shall be brought … whereby to charge the Defendant upon any speciall promise to answere for the debt default or miscarriages of another person … unlesse the Agreement upon which such Action shall be brought or some Memorandum or Note thereof shall be in Writeing and signed by the partie to be charged therewith or some other person thereunto by him lawfully authorized.*

The statute does not state that the actual guarantee must be written or signed, but that there must be *written evidence* of the guarantee having been given, which should be signed by or on behalf of the guarantor.

Consideration

As with most other contracts, consideration (or signature as a deed) is also required to make the guarantee enforceable. A company director asked to give a guarantee on behalf of a limited company may do so on the basis of a personal request for credit, generally regarded as good consideration. It is, however, always wise for a guarantee to be expressly signed as a deed because, if the debt being guaranteed is already due and nothing else is being given in return, the consideration will be 'past' and ineffective. See the specimen guarantee in Chapter 6 (p. 100) on dealing with companies.

Indemnities and representations

Unlike guarantees, indemnities and representations do not strictly need to be evidenced in writing, but, of course, have to be proved to have been given. For example, if Ben Braby said to Sidney Smith, 'I give you my word that I'll pay you for any loss if anything goes wrong', this might be enforceable against Braby personally as an indemnity if anything did go wrong. If Braby said, 'I guarantee that I have a customer lined up who will give you another order for the same amount on the same terms', this might be a misrepresentation on which Smith's company could sue if it would not have done the deal at that price otherwise. It is necessary to look at the words and their intention; written confirmation would not be required in either case if other evidence were clear enough.

E-mail guarantees

The case of *J Pereira Fernandes* v. *Mehta* (2006) had to apply these principles to an e-mail. The director of a company offered his personal guarantee of a major debt of the company in return for the creditor's agreement not to press for the company's insolvency. The guarantee was given orally and followed up in an e-mail sent by the director's agent. The e-mail was not signed by the guarantor and just had his name on the header automatically generated by the sending of the email. The trial judge held that the e-mail was not 'signed' as required by the Statute of Frauds 1677, but suggested that the sender's full name or name and initials or even pseudonym at the foot of the e-mail might have been sufficient, giving authenticity to the communication, even if the e-mail was not signed as such. The moral still remains; have a guarantee in writing and duly signed (preferably as a deed).

CONSUMER CONTRACTS

The law regards private consumers as needing special protection when buying goods or services from businesses, especially when it comes to issues such as distance selling, liability limitation clauses and consumer finance. Many consumer finance agreements need to be in writing. Consumer contracts generally are heavily regulated in different ways, considered in some detail in Chapter 10.

EMPLOYMENT CONTRACTS

An employment contract is created by job offer and acceptance. Even starting work can be acceptance. The law does not require that the contract is in writing, but it does state that certain minimum particulars of the terms of employment must be given by the employer to the employee immediately or after the employee starts work. Contracts for services are considered in some detail in later chapters, but contracts of employment as such are a specialist subject, again highly regulated, outside the scope of this book.

Defective and Incomplete Contracts

DEFECTIVE CONTRACTS

A defective contract may conveniently be thought of as one which has all the requirements (offer and acceptance, certainty, consideration and intention to be legally bound) to constitute a contract, but also has some defect (or virus) that could damage or destroy it. The result will depend on the nature of the defect or virus and how serious it actually is. Typically there will be one of four categories. The contract may be:

*   deemed not to have come into existence in the first place (*null and void*); or
*   deemed to have come into existence but to be subject to a defect that can destroy it (*voidable*);
*   valid but unenforceable in law (*unenforceable*); or
*   valid and enforceable (*enforceable*).

Each of these situations can have a different result in law. The subject is also explored further in the 'problem contracts' section of Chapter 18.

INCOMPLETE CONTRACTS

Unless the contract essentials are all fully in place, a legally binding contract will not come into effect. In one sense, the phrase 'incomplete contract' is an oxymoron because the essentials of a contract need to be certain for that contract to be enforceable. The next section looks at some typical cases.

CONTRACTS WITH CHILDREN

Although the age of criminal liability is lower, the minimum age at which someone is legally capable of making a contract under English law is 18 (Family Law Reform Act 1969). The general rule is that contracts entered into by a child ('minor') under that age are not binding on the child unless they relate to so-called 'necessaries' or unless the minor adopts (confirms) the contract after reaching the age of 18. Adoption requires some clear approval or equivalent course of action accepting the contractual obligations. 'Necessaries' are the essentials of life, such as food, drink, clothing, housing, vital medicine and their modern equivalents. It will be up to a supplier to prove that they were necessaries, but the point is rarely contested because, on disclaiming the contract, the child will have to return the products in question. However, even a contract for necessaries must not be oppressive on the child. In practice the best approach, if in any doubt, is to have the child's parents enter into the contract. Note also that the age of majority in Scotland is 16, and the law on contracts with those under that age is also more lenient on the supplier than in England.

Services can be a bigger problem, as seen in the case of Wayne Rooney, the footballer, who was the focus of the case of *Proform Sports Management* v. *Proactive Sports Management* (2006). The judge decided (perhaps somewhat harshly for Proform) that, although the agency contract which Rooney signed with Proform at the age of 15 was beneficial to Rooney, it was not a 'necessary', because ultimately it was Rooney's contract with his football club that paid his wages, and not the agency contract.

Advertising and websites have special rules or codes of conduct, and credit transactions have to be made by parents or other adults on the child's behalf. In some codes, such as the British Code of Advertising (CAP Code), 'child' is defined as anyone under 16, but that does not avoid the basic law on the age of capacity. Legislation is planned to impose duties on those providing services by electronic communications to take all reasonable steps to ensure that age restrictions are observed by consumers.

'Subject to Contract' and 'Without Prejudice'

'SUBJECT TO CONTRACT'

Knowing how and when to use (and not to use) the words 'subject to contract' can save substantial sums in business. If you are negotiating, especially in writing, and you are not yet ready to be legally bound, use the words 'subject to contract', preferably at the head of your letter or proposal. This will prevent a contract coming into existence, although the words cannot undo a contract already created.

'WITHOUT PREJUDICE'

The term 'without prejudice' is appropriate only where there is a genuine attempt to settle a dispute. Marking something 'without prejudice' prevents the relevant offer from being produced in court as an admission or as a sign of weakness. The words are not a general cover, and putting 'without prejudice' on an abusive letter, for example, will not prevent it being defamatory, because there is no genuine attempt to settle a dispute. Likewise, putting 'without prejudice' on a letter of negotiation where there is no underlying dispute, simply confuses the situation – and, perhaps worse, shows ignorance of the principles of negotiation. Bear in mind, however, that a 'without prejudice' offer can be accepted in the same way as any other offer, so that a binding contract may come into existence if offer and acceptance match, and there is consideration.

'SUBJECT TO CONTRACT' AND 'WITHOUT PREJUDICE'

Using the two terms together is useful in the rare case where you are genuinely negotiating and do not want the offer to be accepted without further thought, as it then covers both aspects. But don't make this a standard practice, as it negates the value of both phrases and could have unintended consequences.

'Gentlemen's Agreements' and Business Misunderstandings

GENERAL STATEMENTS

As mentioned earlier, an enforceable contract will not come into existence unless there is intention on both sides to have a binding commitment. If, for example, someone says to a friend, 'If you go into business, I'd be happy to put in £20,000', what does this mean? Is it a statement that an investment of £20,000 will be made if the other person starts up a business or is it a mere declaration of confidence or goodwill? Even if there were a genuine intention to enter into a legally binding agreement (which is unlikely), the terms of the investment (for example, was the money to be capital or loan, what interest or equity would the investor receive in return?) are insufficiently clear to be enforceable.

HANDSHAKE

A handshake may create an expectation, but does not in itself create a contract. It is always worth questioning what, if anything, has actually been agreed rather than making assumptions. Very often, people choose to believe that an agreement has been reached but, when analysed, it can be seen that there was insufficient certainty for a binding contract to exist. In other cases, if one party is later reluctant to honour an alleged deal, and there is nothing in writing, there is the foundation of disappointment and possible litigation. After all, there are times when we hear only what we want to hear and other times when memory fails. So there is no real substitute for having the details agreed and clearly written down *at the outset*.

AGREEMENT TO AGREE/'TO BE AGREED'

Consider the statement that 'Smith will supply Braby with such products at such prices as they may both agree' or even 'You will supply me with computer equipment against purchase orders, with payment to be made within 30 days'. On their own, these statements would be unenforceable because the key elements relating to the number and type of products and the price are omitted. In the absence of such provisions and anything to identify the products, the second 'agreement' is, at best, a framework that if and when specific products are ordered and supplied, they will be paid for in 30 days. At worst, the wording is a mere statement of intent.

'What happens if we don't agree?' is a vital question if any element of the deal is left 'to be agreed'. This can even occur in the middle of a complex agreement, sometimes because the parties have simply not checked or agreed a vital piece of information. At other times, wearied by negotiations, they might just say, 'Oh, we'll agree that at the time'. This temptation is to be resisted, because there could later be a dispute and, at worst, if the missing part is vital to the whole deal, the entire contract could fail.

Reference to a third party or agreed index may be the way forward – for example, by leaving some missing terms to be decided by reference to known external factors, such as a distributors' list price, a quoted commodity price or the retail price index or one of its variants. Obviously, such reference points can only apply to issues where there will be certainty. An alternative is to specify a fair price to be fixed by an expert or an arbitrator (considered later). Remember too, lest we forget, that prices – and indices – can go down as well as up.

UNSIGNED AGREEMENTS AND COMPLEX NEGOTIATIONS

Negotiations can be lengthy and complex, with exchanges at meetings, by e-mail and by telephone to try to reach agreement. Once all material terms are agreed, those terms apply, despite what may have been discussed beforehand or what happens afterwards. This is a key point for negotiators to understand.

Unsigned drafts

Especially in more complex transactions a draft contract may be produced and negotiated, but left unsigned. This scenario is not uncommon (and considered elsewhere), but there will be times where the evidence shows that the agreement terms were agreed and are binding, even if not signed. In other cases, it will become apparent that the written terms were never agreed (and sometimes would never be agreed). Again, uncertainty is liable to breed doubt, dispute and cost.

Starting work early can make the position even more difficult to unravel if negotiations then break down. How will the work done then be valued and paid for? But the fact that one party starts work, and the other encourages or openly accepts it, will strongly suggest that there is some form of contract, and the hunt is then on to find what the relevant terms of that contract might be, leading to more uncertainty.

Fixed fee or *quantum meruit*

The question may then arise as to whether the work was done on a fixed-price basis or on what lawyers call a quantum meruit basis, where the work needs to be paid for at a fair rate for what is done. The difference can be significant if something unexpected (or not thought about) comes to light during the work process. The VHE case discussed below highlights this.

ESTOPPEL AND PART PERFORMANCE

Occasionally, even if there is no contract as such, the actions of the parties may indicate that there is an obligation which they all regard as binding. In such cases one party may be 'estopped' – or legally prevented – from denying that a contract exists if the evidence shows a mutual commitment, that the other party has wholly or partly performed their part of the bargain and that the 'estopped' party has taken no action to prevent this. The *Confetti Records* case referred to below is an example.

Some Sample Cases

CARLILL V. CARBOLIC SMOKE BALL COMPANY (1893)

This famous case, perhaps the only one remembered by former law students, simply reinforces the rules about offer and acceptance. An offer to pay £100 was made 'at large' to any consumer purchasing a Carbolic Smoke Ball who used it as prescribed and nevertheless contracted influenza. The claimant purchased, complied and still got the flu. The Court of Appeal held that the offer was clear enough and could validly be accepted by any purchaser who relied on the promotion. It did not matter that the offer was made to unspecified parties. Once someone had complied with the conditions, the advertisers had to pay up, potentially exposing the Carbolic Smoke Ball Company to a rash of claims. Interestingly, it was suggested that even the inconvenience of taking the supposed medicine as required could amount to consideration, even if no price had been paid!

FISHER V. BELL (1961)

This was actually a criminal case about a flick-knife on display in a shop. If this was 'offered for sale' in a way that any customer selecting the knife and tendering the stated price for it could buy it, such an offer would have been a criminal offence. The court held that the display of the knife, even with a price tag, was only an 'invitation to treat' by the shop. This meant that the display invited the prospective buyer to offer to purchase the knife – an offer which the shop could either accept or, in certain cases especially in respect of those under age, refuse.

VHE CONSTRUCTION PLC V. ALFRED MCALPINE CONSTRUCTION LTD (1997)

This is one of very many cases to come to the courts regarding construction contracts. Whilst construction law is itself a specialized subject beyond the scope of this book, the case is a good example of the sort of issues that any contract dispute might involve. Indeed, the judge commented that:

> 'On projects involving thousands and sometimes millions of pounds, when a dispute arises about payment, the first issue very often is to decide whether there was a contract and if so what were the terms of that contract, if any.'

The judge made a careful analysis of the facts in the case and concluded that a contract had indeed been entered into. He identified the precise time at which agreement was reached during a specific telephone conversation between managers on each side, reaching consensus on the last outstanding item. The terms of the contract were those which applied as common ground between the parties at that time. In this case, as a contract had been created at an agreed price, that contract price applied and the subcontractor had to bear the cost of the major additional work which became apparent only later.

CONFETTI RECORDS V. WARNER MUSIC UK LTD (2003)

Background

This case is a fascinating insight into the world of garage music, virtual groups and record industry practice at that time, all ending up in a court battle over whether copyright in a musical track had been infringed. It demonstrates what can go wrong in creative industries and how acceptance of an offer can be inferred from the conduct of the parties. It also shows when and when not to remove the heading 'subject to contract'.

Warner wanted to use a music track on a compilation album produced by Confetti, an independent record label. There was a deal memorandum which Warner amended and faxed back to Confetti with a 'subject to contract' heading. (The person handling the paperwork admitted in court that the words were on the company's standard 'deal memo' paperwork, and she had no idea what they actually meant!) Confetti in turn signed and faxed this back to Warner. Confetti followed this up by sending Warner a label copy, a CD of the original track mix and an invoice for the 'agreed' copyright permission payment. Later on, Confetti changed its mind (possibly because a rap line had been added to the mix by Warner) and requested that the track be withdrawn, but Warner had by then recorded, mixed and manufactured its own version.

Decision

The first question was the status of the 'subject to contract' wording. Here the court held that this was effective in preventing the signed deal memo from being a binding offer or acceptance. However, Confetti's action in sending Warner the label, CD and invoice amounted to an offer which Warner was entitled to accept by going ahead with its own production processes. Moreover, the signing of the deal memo and the sending of the track and invoice had amounted to a representation by Confetti that licence had been granted, and Confetti was prevented (or 'estopped') from denying the grant of a licence.

Summary and Checklist

Certain fundamental ingredients need to be present for a contract to have legal effect. It may be necessary to follow through the sequence of the negotiations to decide which terms were actually incorporated into the contract by the point that binding agreement was reached. Although some contracts must be in writing or signed, in most cases a contract can be created by the spoken word or e-mail exchange, but it will still be necessary to prove what the agreed terms were. Care should therefore be taken to ensure that the terms are fully thought through and put in writing and that there is 'consideration' or that the contract is signed as a deed.

Consider the following in relation to a contract you have just made or are about to make:

- Are there two or more parties who are each correctly identified?
- Is the agreement intended to be legally binding?
- Is each party agreeing to do something of value for the other/others?
- Have all relevant terms been agreed, including everything the other person is to do?
- Are the products/services involved clearly identified and understood?
- Are all the material terms certain?
- Was everything agreed before the contract was finalized?
- Is the price clearly established? When and how is it due?
- If not, what mechanism exists for establishing the price?
- Are there any assumptions you rely on and have these been checked?
- Do all the agreed terms make sense and are they consistent?
- What do *you* need to do to make it work and are you able and committed to do it?
- Have you got all these points agreed in writing and signed?
- Should you mark anything 'subject to contract'?
- Does the agreement need to be signed as a deed?
- Is there any personal guarantee involved?

CHAPTER 2 *Reaching and Recording Agreement*

Introduction – getting started – negotiating contracts by e-mail – structuring the contract – the language of contracts – summary and checklist

Introduction

This chapter explores how businesses reach – and record – agreements. Apart from one-off sales on standard forms, reaching agreement is rarely a one-shot event. Maintaining focus on key essentials, as well as detail, involves inquiry and challenge, coupled with a constant recapping of the main ingredients of the deal to check that you are remaining on track and in line with original objectives.

In an ideal world, negotiating and recording contracts would perhaps be done on a totally rational basis, but that is perhaps a contradiction in terms. Total rationality is not the normal human state, and the totally rational word might be a world of automatons, which would extinguish the essence of humanity. In the so-called real world, people are fully human, with the mix of ambition, fear and other emotions that characterizes us as human, and underlies most negotiations. So 'getting to go' is often a far more complex process of managing facts, opinion and emotion than is generally recognized. In that process 'being right' can sometimes seem more important than being sensible, and our emotional attachment to our version of the truth can prevent us being able to listen to where we might have gone wrong.

Getting Started

In his books Richard Branson describes how being dyslexic decreased his reliance on written detail and sharpened his mental grasp of key issues as well as his willingness to challenge the status quo. These are good attributes to bring to any negotiation, and the first step is to focus on the key objectives of any deal. The detail will, however, need to follow and, for most people, the easiest place to start is with pen and paper – or the computer keyboard.

WRITING IT DOWN

Putting it off

Putting it off is a favourite tactic. Many of those in the front line of business, especially those who relish the product-sourcing and the cut and thrust of a negotiation process, often have little appetite for the written side of business. Faced with a blank sheet of paper or computer screen, their confidence is drained and they will make another phone call or do anything else rather than write down the deal. Or they will be tempted to knock out a fast and sparse draft and send it off before it is seen by anyone else. They may also find it difficult to risk what they believe is a good deal or a good relationship by raising or following up an issue that they have recognized – or they anticipate – as sensitive. Relationships, after all, take a long time to build and are fragile. But so are businesses. Failure to go the extra step to get all the key terms identified, expressed and agreed can be a critical mistake.

No protection for lack of application

Contract law is not there to protect businesspeople from themselves or from making a bad bargain. As many examples in this book show, it pays to do the groundwork thoroughly. The courts treat those in business differently from consumers and, whilst protecting business people from some overtly unfair practices, will not readily give them much leeway for failing to follow up on matters that should have been apparent at the time. As with everything else, writing complex contracts takes time, experience and practice. This chapter aims to help you get started, and later chapters look at more detailed and specialized situations.

Negotiating Contracts by E-mail

In most cases, little formality is required; a letter or e-mail can be sufficient. The first thing is to get the basics down: who is writing to whom, and what is it that they need to cover. Taking the example from Chapter 1, assume that, after various discussions and a meeting, Ben Braby, the buyer of computer equipment, decides to take the initiative and e-mail Sidney Smith. As a minimum, Ben will want to cover the following basics:

* *what* are precisely the products he wants to buy
* *how* the products are described
* *how many* products he wants
* *how much* is the price and when it is payable
* *when* delivery will be and at whose cost.

A BUYER'S OFFER – AN EXAMPLE

Dear Sid

Thanks for our meeting on Monday. I like the look of your new range and write to confirm that you will supply 50 of your F502/zt computers as set out in your quotation number 657/9. So that we are clear, these are the machines which you showed me when we met and as described on page 52 of your Spring brochure.

Based on this quantity, we agreed a price of £465 each, exclusive of VAT and delivery. You will deliver between 1st and 31st August this year, giving us at least five days' prior notice of delivery, at a delivery cost of £65 + VAT overall. You will invoice us for the machines on delivery and we will pay in full by the end of the month afterwards.

We will see how they sell before making further plans!

If you agree that covers everything please confirm by return e-mail.

Regards

Ben Braby

For and on behalf of Braby Business Machines Limited

A closer look

It is worth looking at the e-mail in more detail, first to see how it deals with the checklist issues in Chapter 1.

- There are two parties, each correctly identified (assuming correct full company names are used – see Chapter 6).
- The actual contract will be made only when intended, either at the meeting referred to or later, when confirmed by e-mail.
- The products and price are clearly identified, and all relevant terms have been recorded.
- Braby's assumption that the machine number tallies with inspection and catalogue has been expressly referred to.
- On the face of it there is nothing else obvious that a normal businessperson need ask to understand the whole bargain. (The question of the actual performance capabilities of the machines is a matter dealt with later.)
- Smith needs to be confident that he has, or can get, the right equipment in time and Braby that he has the means to pay for the order.
- The exchange of emails will be clear evidence of the contract.
- There is adequate consideration in the promise to pay.

There is no particular magic formula in the way the letter is expressed, provided it deals with the basic issues and avoids muddying the waters. For example, anything suggesting the deal was uncertain or incomplete, such as 'we are thinking of ordering ...' or 'before confirming our order I just wanted to confirm what we discussed ...' would raise doubt on their being a binding contract. Equally, these are the sort of phrases that Braby could, if he wanted, use to avoid a binding contract coming into force. He may wish to check his would-be sub-purchasers are ready and able to go ahead before committing himself, because, once he has ordered without any sale or return provision, he will not be able to back out or return any unsold products to Smith. Instead, he would probably have to sell them on elsewhere at a reduced profit or even at a loss.

THE SELLER'S RESPONSE TO THE BUYER'S OFFER

If Smith e-mails back to confirm agreement without further comment, a contract will have been made (or confirmed) on the terms set out in Braby's e-mail. If he e-mails back to agree most points but reject some, this creates a counter-offer. If he merely queries some points, but does not reject them, this leaves the issue open. The advantage to Braby in writing to Smith first is that Braby has the first shot and Smith may overlook the fact that there is no reference to terms of business.

A SELLER'S OFFER

If, on the other hand, Smith, as the seller, is first off the mark, his e-mail might look like this:

> Dear Ben
>
> Further to our meeting on Monday I write to confirm your order as follows:
>
> 50 (fifty) F502/zt computers in accordance with our quotation number 657/9, which incorporates our standard terms of business.
>
> Price – £465 each, exclusive of VAT and delivery. You will accept delivery to your store in High Street provided we give you at least two days' notice, at a delivery cost of £65 + VAT overall.
>
> Payment terms are 30 days from end of month.
>
> Please sign and return the attached order confirmation.
>
> Regards
>
> Sidney Smith
>
> Smith (Computer Supplies) Limited

Smith would do well to attach the quotation with his terms of business (TOB), probably in PDF format if an e-mail is sent. Alternatively, he might refer to the TOB set out in a previous letter or on his company's website. What is important is that the terms will have been notified to Braby *before* the contract is made. Otherwise the TOB will not be effectively incorporated into the contract and will not apply.

THE BUYER'S RESPONSE TO THE SELLER'S OFFER

Analysing the offer

Ben Braby might look at this, check that it covers what he wants and be tempted to sign the confirmation form and press on with the next job. Or he might look to see what is hidden in the note and what's missing. The main point in Smith's approach is that he has built in reference to his standard terms. If Braby then signs, having received the TOB on the front or back of Smith's quotation form, he will be bound by those terms, whether he has read them or not. The same would apply if Braby had referred to the TOB in another document which was readily available.

What's missing?

What Smith's note does not cover is linking his technical product numbers to the catalogue and what Braby has actually seen, so Braby needs to be absolutely sure he is ordering what he wants. There is also no commitment to a delivery date, the onus instead being put on Braby to accept delivery on two days' notice (possibly a holiday or at the weekend!) If Braby has customers for the equipment, he may want to specify a latest delivery time or build in a cancellation right if delivery is late. The payment terms are not entirely specific either. It is quite normal for payment terms to be 30 or 60 days from end of month, as many accounting systems run on a month-end basis. Although the language used by Smith is common, it implies that the goods will have been delivered before the invoice is sent without actually stating so. Hard-pressed sellers can occasionally send out their invoices before the month-end, with the goods being shipped only the following month, thus gaining payment a month early.

The buyer's response

So there are a couple of points that Braby will want to consider before he responds to Smith. Whether he raises these by way of queries or suggests actual changes, Smith will need to agree any changes before a binding contract is created (again assuming that this was not actually at the meeting referred to.) Braby might accordingly reply on the same e-mail string:

Sid

Thanks for this. I just wanted to clarify a few points. Please confirm that:

1. The machines are the ones you showed me when we met;
2. You will deliver between 1st and 31st August this year, giving us at least five days' (rather than two days') prior notice of delivery, as I will have customer delivery obligations;
3. Payment is 30 days from later of delivery and invoice.

Regards.

Ben

THE SELLER'S COUNTER TO THE BUYER'S RESPONSE

The seller's counter-response

Smith then has to decide if he is happy with these points. Point 3 (payment) is straightforward. Point 1 (which machines) raises a degree of uncertainty, because there could always be an argument over which products Braby actually saw. Point 2 (delivery) also raises the question of what would happen if Smith failed to deliver during August.

The importance of timing

The general rule is that a buyer cannot withdraw from a deal because of delayed delivery unless time (of delivery) is expressly made 'of the essence' or the circumstances imply this, such as in the case of perishable foodstuffs. Braby has flagged that he will have customer obligations and will be relying on delivery by the end of August, so – if in any doubt as to his ability to source and deliver the goods – Smith will be wise not to commit absolutely to the date. If Braby had been relying absolutely on the delivery date, he would want to amend point 2 to read:

> ... you will deliver between 1st and 31st August this year, giving us at least five
> days' (rather than two days') prior notice of delivery; as I will have customer delivery
> obligations I must require time to be of the essence as regards this delivery period;

So Smith might reply:

> Ben
>
> On your numbered points:
>
> 1. I showed you several machines and we do need to be clear on this. The ones we are
>   talking about are the F502/zt, which you can check out in our Spring catalogue on
>   page 52 or on our website. If you are still unclear please feel free to come and have
>   another look.
> 2. I will do my best, but cannot guarantee delivery dates as we are also in the hands
>   of our suppliers.
> 3. Confirmed.
>
> Please let me know if we are now agreed.
>
> Regards
>
> Sid

THE BUYER'S REACTION

Decision time?

It is probably now make-your-mind-up time for Braby. He has agreement on the payment and understands that Smith recognizes that timing is important. Braby will therefore have to be clear with his own customers that the same provisions apply and he cannot himself commit to an absolute date with them. If this is still an issue, it might be possible to build in the right to cancel if delivery is not by, say, 15 September, since otherwise Braby could not source the machines elsewhere without being at risk of having to pay Smith as well when his machines arrived. This long-stop date can be a useful arrangement, but really has to apply the whole way through the supply chain to avoid anyone being left with unwanted goods when the pass-the-parcel music stops.

Terms on websites

Reference to products or TOB on websites is increasingly used, but websites can change overnight. A catalogue does give a written record but if a website is used, the record may be lost. Some evidence, such as a printout with time and date showing or a timed screenshot of the relevant website details, may therefore be a useful precaution. After all, many terms and conditions (perhaps also on the website) will say that product specifications may change without notice.

Structuring the Contract

As seen above, a contract can be expressed in simple e-mail or letter form, but more complex issues call for a more formal structure. A typical contract structure, looked at in more detail below, would be:

- *Parties* – names and details.
- *Introduction* – a summary of the background and intention of the document (known as 'recitals', in older contracts, often prefaced by the word 'whereas').
- *Definitions* – in a separate clause or glossary if applicable.
- *Operative clauses* – the heart of the contract, setting out the main obligations of each of the parties to one another.
- *Termination provisions* – how and when the contract ends, and what happens after this.
- *Boilerplate clauses* – of general application (see Chapter 4).
- *Schedules or appendices* – giving more detail on specific aspects if applicable.
- *Signature provisions*.

NAMES AND DETAILS OF THE PARTIES

Who are you dealing with?

A fundamental, but surprisingly often overlooked, aspect of doing business is to know exactly who you are dealing with. Once the outlines of a deal become clear, it is time for some basic 'due diligence' on your counterparts across the contractual table. The first stage is to know who you are dealing with, that you have the right person or company and that they are who they say they are. If they are not, the contract may prove to be worthless – or worse. Contract law case books are full of examples of what can go wrong even at this level. Until relatively recently, people could fraudulently sign away their own and other people's property fairly easily, and it was only with the coming of the money-laundering laws that identity has regularly checked. These 'compliance' checks can be frustrating, but the inconvenience needs to be balanced against the value of the precaution when entering into business contracts. For example, an address is really part of identifying that you have the right person or company. There may be many men called Ben Braby, for example, but probably only one who now lives at that particular address.

Who is taking responsibility?

The starting-point is to be clear who is taking responsibility. This means getting the full name and home address of any individuals (including driving licence, passport or similar evidence if the person is new to you) and whether this is just the one person or more. In business you will often be dealing with a private limited company, rather than a partnership or an individual trader. Chapter 6, 'Dealing with Companies', contains some useful suggested precautions, starting with a search of registered company names to check the correct (and complete) company name and number.

Finances and reliability

Once you are sure of the individual or company, consider what you really know about their business history and finances, what checks and searches are available and whether these have been done, so that you have as full a picture as possible of your opposite number (as they should have of you). It is always as well to remember the reality check. As we should all know since the credit crunch turned into massive recession, if something looks too good to be true, it probably is. If you are in doubt about the other party's finances, what additional financial security can you obtain? This might range from tighter credit terms or even payment on delivery through to seeking personal guarantees. Part of the equation might also be a discreet test on the other party's business integrity: are they doing what they say they will do? If they show little integrity in negotiations, what might happen after the contract is signed?

The individuals involved

Then there is the question of the individuals with whom you may be dealing. Do they have the authority to make a deal with you? Are those with whom you are negotiating the ones who will also be directly involved in performing the contract? If not, you could meet resistance at the implementation stage if there has been no buy-in from those due to carry out the work. Even then, how long might those people remain on the project and how vulnerable would you be if they left? Few companies like to have third-party contracts dependent on specific employees, because of the leverage that gives those employees, but occasionally a particular person may be so critical to the deal that you will want the right to terminate the contract if they are unavailable. But bear in mind that you might be asked to agree the same.

INTRODUCTION ('RECITALS')

Recitals

A recital is a preamble or introduction to the background and intent of an agreement, traditionally preceded by the word 'whereas', such as: 'whereas the Seller is a manufacturer and has agreed to manufacture and sell and the Buyer has agreed to buy ...'. European directives have lengthy recitals as to the background and intention of the regulations, which are key part of their correct interpretation. In England such recitals were (and sometimes still are) used in property documents – for example, to describe where a larger piece of land has been carved up into smaller pieces, so that the 'chain of title' to the individual plot of land can be more easily identified.

Using recitals effectively

If they are to be used, recitals should add some value. In commercial agreements they may be a useful drafting aid in that they lay out the background and introduce the key objectives of the contract. They should then be checked at the end to ensure that the flow has been maintained and the drafting objectives realized. They may still remain a useful introduction, and can sometimes be called on to resolve ambiguities in the later drafting. They may also be a useful and informal way of bringing in definitions, as seen in the following section, but should not be used as operative clauses in the contract. What is critical is that recitals, when used, do not conflict with the operative provisions of the contract; whilst generally the operative part will prevail if it is clear, obvious inconsistency could indicate a mistake in the drafting and even support a case for rectifying the contract.

DEFINITIONS

When to define a term

Words in a contract will be given their ordinary and natural meaning, but some, especially technical terms or phrases used several times in a document, may be worth defining, so that subsequent references will avoid repeating the same information. Definitions are also a useful way of specifying some of the key terms at the outset, such as the range of goods to be sold or the services to be provided or the price to be paid. Definitions can also help ensure consistency throughout the contract. The corollary of this is that any change in a defined term during redrafting should be checked carefully against the use of that term throughout the rest of the agreement. Once defined, such terms should start with a capital letter when used in the document; terms not defined should not use capitals unless they are proper names or similar.

Where to define a term

Definitions are often set out in a definitions section or schedule or a glossary. The subsequent use in the text of a capital letter at the beginning of a word (other than proper names or similar) will then indicate that the term is defined later in the document. Alternatively, definitions may be introduced through the recitals or introductory section, such as the following:

> The Seller has offered to sell to the Buyer fifty (50) F502/zt.computers (**Products**) for the sum of four hundred and sixty-five pounds each (exclusive of VAT and delivery) (**Price**) payable on 17 January 20XX (**Completion**).

OPERATIVE CLAUSES

Individual clauses set out the parties' positive and negative obligations and other main terms. Ideally, these should be grouped logically, so that similar issues are dealt with together in one clause before moving on the next. These are the heart of the contract and considered in more detail later.

TERM AND TERMINATION

Unless the contract relates to a one-off order (see the example later in this chapter), you should always consider how long the contract is expected to last and what might bring it to an end and when. This may range from mutual no-fault termination by a set period of notice to termination for breach or other possible eventualities.

SCHEDULES OR APPENDICES?

It is really a matter of style as to which of these words is used. The concept is that some information is more clearly set out in schedule or appendix form than fitted into the detailed contract wording. This might include the technical specification of goods or a detailed statement of specific services or a list of agreed customers. Anything that breaks up the smooth flow of the agreement might be considered for inclusion in a schedule or appendix.

CONTRACT SIGNATURES

Simple signatures

A contract worth writing down is always worth having signed, and all the parties need do is actually sign. What matters is that the signatures are those of the parties themselves or someone authorized to sign on their behalves. Old style wording, such as 'the parties hereto have hereunto appended their hands', is now unnecessary.

Signing on behalf of a party

Many straightforward contracts are signed by an individual on behalf of another. In the case of a limited company a single director may sign; with a partnership or limited liability partnership (LLP – see Chapter 6) a partner or member can sign. If the document is signed on behalf of another party it is best signed above a line stating 'signed for and on behalf of ...' with the name of the relevant party set out in full. For the signatory, this makes it clear that they are signing on behalf of another, but at the same time the person signing is deemed to warrant that they are that person or have authority to sign on their behalf. If the person signing has no formal status in relation to the party for whom they sign, difficult questions may arise as to the authority of the signatory and whether the contract is binding on the party named.

A *witness* is advisable to attest the signature – meaning that the witness sees the signature and signs alongside to confirm this – but is not a legal requirement for most contracts (unless signed as a deed). Ideally, the witness should be independent (not related to or a business associate of the parties) and one who knows the parties signing so as to be able to attest, if ever called upon, that each was who they claim to be, that they did in fact sign as indicated and that the signatures appeared to be voluntary.

Electronic signature is officially recognized by the Electronic Communications Act 2000 and the Electronic Signatures Regulations 2002. An organization can also add a digital certificate to authenticate signature on its behalf. Even clicking on an 'I accept' button may be equivalent to an electronic signature. The Business, Innovation and Skills website[1] may be worth checking for the latest guidance.

SIGNING AS A DEED

Signing as a deed is advisable if there is any doubt whether there is adequate 'consideration' (see earlier) or if the document is one of a limited type requiring to be signed (or 'executed') as a deed. Business contracts do not, as a rule, require to be signed as a deed because they specify a price to be paid or other consideration, but some other documents do need signing as a deed, notably the following:

- *property (real property) transfers* (but not property sale contracts as such – although these do need to be in writing and signed)
- *powers of attorney*
- some formal *documents required by other jurisdictions* (which may also require notarizing).

Wording

If the document needs to be a deed, s. 1(3) of the Law of Property (Miscellaneous Provisions) Act 1989 requires execution in the presence of a witness and delivery as a deed. Technically, the Act requires that a deed requires to be: a) signed by an individual in the presence of a witness who attests the signature; or – in very exceptional cases – b) signed at the direction and in the presence of an individual and in the presence of two witnesses who each attest the signature; and – in either case – c) delivered as a deed by the individual or a person authorized to do so on his behalf. Section 1(4) states that the 'sign' includes 'making one's mark on the instrument'.

The wording need simply state:

Signed as a deed by [ABC]' or 'Signed by [ABC] in the presence of [XYZ] and delivered as deed.

With companies, assuming the old-style common seal has been dispensed with (it is still legal to use it), execution as a deed may take place either by the signature of two directors or one director and the company secretary, without the need for a witness, or, since the Companies Act 2006, one director in the presence of a witness attesting the signature.

'Delivery' is necessary for a deed to be effective. Sometimes a deed may be signed in anticipation of the happening of a certain event, such as the signing of related documents

---

1   The new 'super' department created in 2009, formerly the Department of Business, Enterprise and Regulatory Reform (BERR) at: http://bis.gov.uk.

or payment of money. The deed is signed but held in suspense (known as 'escrow') until the specific event occurs, when it is deemed 'delivered'. This is why some longer signing provisions will state:

Signed by ABC but not delivered until [stated event] ...

The Language of Contracts

It is tempting to quote the *Alice in Wonderland* principle that 'words mean what I want them to mean'. That is, in fact, how some approach the question of contract drafting, but it is about as reliable as Alice's philological approach: it may work, but don't count on it!

WHAT THE LAW SAYS

There are exceptions that are considered in more detail in later chapters, but the general legal principle of 'construction' (that is, understanding the real meaning) of an agreement is that if the contract terms are clear and the issue comes to court, the court will honour and seek to implement the stated terms if – and to the extent that:

- there is a valid contract and not, for example an 'agreement to agree'
- the language and main terms of the contact are clear
- there is no fraud or misrepresentation or other defect
- there is no 'inequality of bargaining power' and the terms are not unfair
- there is no illegal or unreasonable restraint of trade
- there are no other material defects or 'viruses'.

If you have just forgotten to put in a provision that you intended, and all else is clear, the courts are unlikely to step in and rescue you (although they, like everyone else, continue to surprise us). If, however, certain aspects of the language are unclear but all other provisions are valid, the courts will consider what is required for 'business efficacy', meaning that they will try to find what is needed to make the contract work to achieve its commercial intention. In considering this, the courts will also consider what the hypothetical 'innocent bystander' would ask at the time the contract was made – and what the parties to the contract would have answered.

THE PRINCIPLES OF 'CONSTRUCTION'

Where the main terms are clear but there is some uncertainty on specific provisions, the principles are as follows:

- A contract will be interpreted according to the *meaning it would convey to a reasonable person with the background knowledge* that the contracting parties would have had at the time they made the contract (see the leading case of *Investors Compensation Scheme* v. *West Bromwich Building Society* (1997)).

- This includes anything that would affect *the way in which the language would have been understood by the reasonable person* at the time, interpreting what the parties appear to have intended to say at the time.
- *Dictionary definitions may be helpful*, but courts will allow for the fact that the parties may have used words or syntax which later seem to be wrong in the overall context; judges do not have to follow precise wording which attributes to the parties an intention that they clearly could not have had.
- Except in extreme cases (such as those mentioned below) or in an action for rectification (see Chapter 18), the court will *not* look at the *declared intentions or previous negotiations* of the parties outside the signed contracts (the so-called 'exclusionary rule' – see *Prenn v. Simmonds* (1971)).
- *Missing terms* will not be implied into the contract except to the extent required to give the contract business efficacy.
- *An interpretation* that makes the contract effective and enforceable is to be preferred to one that results in it being void.
- *The court* will prefer an interpretation which produces a result that the parties are likely to have agreed over an improbable result.
- For most purposes, what happens after the contract is made is irrelevant; it is what was agreed at the time the contract came into existence that matters.

Proforce Recruit Ltd v. *Rugby Group Ltd* (2007) was a classic case, which went through three courts in order to decide the meaning of the term 'preferred supplier', used in a contract between the parties, but not defined. The question concerned not only what it meant but also how much evidence could be produced of previous negotiations to decide what it meant. Proforce, a cleaning contractor, claimed that being a 'preferred supplier' in a two-year agreement meant that all Rugby's cleaning work had to be offered to Proforce. Rugby disagreed. The Court of Appeal decided that there was more than one reasonable view as to what the term actually meant and what obligations it imposed. It therefore sent the case back to another judge who decided that 'preferred supplier' in these circumstances meant little more than an approved supplier and did not grant any exclusivity as Proforce had claimed. The dispute is a reminder of the need to clarify key phrases which may be often used in an industry, but are not necessarily clearly understood by everyone the same way! It is better not to assume, and to spend the time agreeing a definition, than to go through the agony of protracted litigation.

Another case was decided by the House of Lords in July 2009. In *Chartbrook Ltd v. Persimmon Homes Ltd*, a 'grammatical ambiguity' existed in the drafting of an 'overage' clause on a land development deal which gave an answer varying from close to £900,000 on one interpretation to nearly £4.5 million on another. The highest UK court overturned the strict approach of the Court of Appeal by saying that once 'something had gone wrong' with the language, the court could take into account 'the background and context' of the events leading up to the ambiguous calculation. Taking a commercial view of what had occurred, the court decided that good business sense must prevail and awarded judgment for the lower amount. There is obviously a fine line here between ensuring that good sense prevails and reopening the principle of the exclusionary rule.

LEGALESE

Contracts need clarity – in purpose and expression – but these days there is no justification for legalese. This is the language of traditional legal documents, originally designed to give certainty of legal interpretation, but increasingly used as a badge of legal pedigree and sometimes even to cloud commercial clarity. Take, for example, the following clause, inserted in a sale and purchase agreement for goods, after a summary of what the contract is trying to achieve:

> *Now pursuant to the foregoing and in consideration of the sum of one hundred pounds (£100) (receipt of which the Transferor hereby acknowledges) and the undertakings of the Transferee hereinafter contained the Transferor hereby agrees and undertakes to transfer to the Transferee the Goods hereinbefore more particularly described to hold unto the Transferee absolutely.*

This may sound very impressive, but let's first consider what it means and why the language is used.

- '*... pursuant to the foregoing*' refers back to the introduction to the agreement explaining the purpose of any recitals or introduction. It means that you have reached the point where the intention is to be carried through into legal obligations or actions. In most cases, it really adds nothing to what follows.
- '*... in consideration of the sum of ... acknowledges ...*' states the consideration in terms of how much is to be paid or what is to be done in return for the transfer of the goods. Consideration is necessary, but anything beyond stating the price and when it is to be paid – or what else is to be done – is unnecessary. The reference to receipt of the amount is evidence that it has been paid, which is useful if there is a token payment, in case there is future argument as to whether the amount was indeed paid or not.
- '*... the undertakings of the Transferee hereinafter contained ...*' is a further reference to consideration and does not need to be stated so long as there is something of value being given. It is enough that payment is made, even if token, or that the Transferee commits to do something of value in the document, and it does not need stating again.
- '*... the Transferor hereby agrees and undertakes to transfer...*' is tautologous because an undertaking is an agreement anyway. There is another and bigger issue, however; the wording refers to an agreement to transfer, whereas if the price had indeed been paid, as the wording suggests, there would seem no reason why the goods should not actually be transferred. If there were some licence or certificate that needed to be obtained first, the buyer would not expect to part with the cash until the transfer was certain. The drafting may just be unnecessarily cautious, but the difference between agreement to transfer and actual transfer is that between the right to something and actually possessing it.
- '*... the Goods hereinbefore more particularly described ...*'. There are alternative approaches here; it would be enough to state 'the goods described above'. Alternatively, the goods could be defined the first time they are mentioned, with reference to the quantity and the essential features to identify them precisely (see the product sale agreement example in Appendix B).

- '*... to hold unto the Transferee absolutely ...*' is language borrowed from property documents and, again, unnecessary in the case of goods.

Since this is essentially a sale and purchase transaction, it would be much clearer to use everyday expressions such as 'Seller' instead of 'Transferor' and 'Buyer' rather than 'Transferee'. So, assuming that goods and price have already been defined, we could reduce the language to the following:

> *On Completion the Buyer will pay the Price to the Seller and the Seller will transfer the Goods to the Buyer.*

'Completion' would need to be defined but this is 21 more readily comprehensible words instead of 54! Note that this is still an agreement for sale and purchase. Most actual sales are completed by delivery in return for payment or the promise to pay on a stated date.

INFORMAL LANGUAGE

Many contracts are now written in an even more direct style, particularly in the use of 'you' and 'we' language instead of a formal definition of the parties. So the previous example might read:

> *As soon as you pay us the Price we will transfer the Goods to you.*

This reduces the original 54 words down to 15, and offers complete clarity of meaning. This type of language, reflecting the style of the letter or e-mail, can be suitable even for lengthy contracts. However, if 'we' or 'us' is defined to refer to one party, extra care in drafting is required when 'we' is intended to refer to both parties!

Nevertheless, informality should ideally not descend to the level of colloquialisms or abbreviations that might cause confusion later on. Useful though text messages may be, it is also probably best to avoid cryptic abbreviated texts as evidence of contract terms!

ARCHAIC LANGUAGE

The use of language is, to some extent, a personal preference, not necessarily shared by all lawyers, and the following comments should be seen in that context. A list of archaic language and suggested alternatives is set out in Appendix A, but the following – in my view – should definitely be avoided.

Shall and will

There is little reason for Biblical-type language, as, for example, 'The Seller shall deliver the Goods to the Buyer'. 'Shall' is not normal language; 'will' works perfectly well and is the word used in normal speech. It imposes just as much of a legal obligation as shall (although grammar purists may still wish to use the conjugation 'we shall').

Hereunto, hereinbefore and the said

Similarly, we don't use words like 'hereunto' or 'hereinbefore' or 'the said' in normal language, and they can all be avoided in sensible drafting. 'Hereunto' is often a qualification to 'the parties hereunto', meaning the parties to the agreement. It will generally be clear who the parties are (which is – despite the fun made of the term by Groucho Marx – a useful legal term for the people or companies entering into the contract). If not, a simple definition will suffice (see the various examples in this book). 'Hereinbefore' can be replaced by 'above' or, for greater clarity, reference to 'clause x', with the clause being defined, if appropriate, as 'a clause in this agreement'. This will distinguish it from a clause in any other agreement and avoid the distraction of the words 'in this agreement' being inserted every few lines. Likewise, 'the said' becomes unnecessary if definitions are used or the drafting is clear.

Latin

Similar considerations apply to Latin, and indeed other languages, still much beloved of many traditional lawyers. Business contracts need neither the erudition nor the distraction of Latin where a perfectly adequate English phrase is available. Some terms, whether of Latin, German or French origin have, however, become part of everyday business language. One example is the phrase 'force majeure', which may be both more accurate and more readily accepted than the traditional 'act of God' – a phrase that nowadays may carry many other connotations.

UNNECESSARY LANGUAGE

Unnecessary phrases easily creep into drafting. Wording such as the superfluous 'now it is hereby agreed and declared' has already been mentioned. Another classic is: *'in the event that'* which can be replaced by the simple two-letter word: 'if'.

TECHNICAL, INDUSTRY OR COLLOQUIAL TERMS

Many types of business develop technical terms that are understood in that industry, even if they are not generally in use elsewhere. Sometimes, however, these terms move far away from their original meaning, and can have different interpretations in different parts of the industry or even in the same area of business. The disastrous use of the undefined term 'preferred supplier' has already been mentioned (see *Proforce Recruit Ltd* v. *Rugby Group Ltd* above). Another example is the acronym OEM, derived from 'original equipment manufacturer', but increasingly used in other, often contradictory, ways (as a browse at the Wikipedia entry for the initials will disclose). If you want to use technical or even colloquial terms, even if they seem to have a common understanding, it is worth checking that they are indeed understood by all involved in the same way. Otherwise, confusion tends to create dispute – and disputes can easily lead to litigation. If in doubt, don't be afraid: it is better to define the meaning of such terms in the contract than not.

PUNCTUATION

Full stops and commas can be very useful and are not illegal! The example under the 'Legalese' section above has no punctuation, and for many lawyers and others there is still a fear of using punctuation, especially commas. It may be that a misplaced comma can change the sense of a piece of text, but *lack* of punctuation can have the same effect. Punctuation is designed to clarify meaning. There are many uses of a comma, including indicating a pause between different parts of a longer sentence, the introduction of a qualifying phrase, the separation between parts of a list (such as 'men, women and children') or separating adjectives describing different facts, such as 'long, cold winter'.

SENTENCE CONSTRUCTION

Whilst it may be pleasant to have a contract that reads well, the essence is to have one that covers the relevant issues in language that is as clear and concise as possible. Short sentences are a great aid to achieving this. Where possible, make the point and move on.

CLAUSE NUMBERING

Numbering style

One of the great frustrations of dealing with some traditional contracts, publishing contracts being a notable example, is to find the relevant clause. A paragraph marked, for example '(vii) (a)', can leave the reader struggling and having to scroll back several pages to find the rest of the reference before finding that this is in fact part of clause 5. It would have been so much clearer if it had been numbered 5.7.1 from the outset! Most automatic numbering functions on computers can manage this (some with a little prompting), and can adjust automatically to changes when the clauses are edited. This is a matter of preference. There is, of course, nothing legally wrong with '5 (vii) (a)', but why add the complexity?

Managing the numbering

A useful rule is to avoid more than two sub-clauses, so that it never gets, for example, to 'clause 5.7.1.2'. At this point, it is probably much better to review the drafting and start a new sub-clause. This sort of problem typically occurs when the person drafting a contract tries to put too many qualifications in one clause. It is better to break the clause up into parts as shown in the following section.

PROVISOS AND OTHER CONDITIONS

'Notwithstanding the foregoing' is a classic legal phrase, meaning 'despite what has already been stated'. It therefore presages an exception to a previous statement. An alternative is the phrase 'provided that', often in capitals, followed by a list of exceptions. Neither of these approaches, though long beloved of lawyers, is ideal. It is normally better to say at the start of a clause if there will be exceptions to it, and then list those exceptions in a separate sub-clause. This also deals with the legal principle of understanding contracts (known as the 'construction' – from construing – of contracts) that the earlier clause takes precedence over the later clause if the two are in conflict.

Example 1:

2. The price of the goods will include the delivery thereof to the premises of the Buyer provided however that where the Goods are delivered to the Buyer other than on the mainland of Great Britain the Seller will charge and the Buyer will pay the additional costs of delivery so incurred by the Buyer.

Example 2 – which is a much clearer alternative:

2. The Price includes the cost of delivery of the Goods to the Buyer's premises in the mainland of Great Britain and the Buyer will pay the additional costs of the Seller incurred in any deliveries required by the Buyer outside that area.

The same concept could be split into two sub-clauses, which may be more helpful if there were to be a number of other qualifications added.

Example 3:

2.1 Subject to clause 2.2, the Price includes the cost of delivery of the Goods to the Buyer's premises.
2.2 The Buyer will pay the additional costs of the Seller incurred in any deliveries of Goods outside the mainland of Great Britain.

Here the basic principle is first clearly stated, and then the exceptions. In fact, in a simple example such as this the same effect could be achieved in one clause:

Example 4:

The Price includes the cost of delivery of the Goods to the Buyer's premises, except for delivery outside Great Britain. The Buyer will pay the additional [third-party] costs of the Seller incurred in any deliveries of Goods outside Great Britain.

Whichever way is chosen there is no need for provisos or 'notwithstandings'.
'Subject to' is another common phrase, as seen in example 3 above, but it needs to be used carefully, especially used with 'notwithstanding' or any similar qualification in an adjacent clause. Consider the effect of example 3 with 'notwithstanding' added to clause 2.2 as follows:

2.1 Subject to clause 2.2, the Price will include the cost of delivery of the Goods to the Buyer's premises.

2.2 Notwithstanding clause 2.1 the Buyer will pay the additional costs of the Seller incurred in any deliveries of Goods outside the mainland of Great Britain.

It is clear from the drafting that 2.1 is subject to the variation of 2.2 but the addition to 2.2 puts doubt on which clause takes precedence over the other. Even worse would be to have clause 2.2. 'subject to' clause 2.1!

WORKED EXAMPLES

A worked example – for instance of a price adjustment formula or a net proceeds calculation – can be a useful addition to a contract. The draft should then make it clear whether the example is just of the calculation set out in the clause or whether the formula shown by the worked example is to take precedence over the wording of the written clause.

'For the avoidance of doubt'

This phrase deserves special mention, as it indicates the point where there may be a doubt in the first place. It is essential that doubt is not then increased by what follows! The first point to consider is why there should be a doubt and whether it can be more simply dealt with by clarity in the original drafting. Very often the doubt can be resolved by a clear definition of a particular term. If not, check whether the issue is in fact an exception to a previous principle rather than a clarification of it. For example, with the delivery scenario above:

> *The Price will include the cost of delivery of the Goods to the Buyer's premises. For the avoidance of doubt the Buyer will pay the additional costs of the Seller incurred in any deliveries of Goods outside the mainland of Great Britain.*

In this example there was no doubt in clause 2.1. Clause 2.2 is an exception, not a clarification, and should be dealt with according to the previous example. If this warning can be followed, however, the phrase can have its uses, such as in taking a specific example that might be of especial relevance to the parties and explaining how this would operate. In that sense it is somewhat akin to a worked example as mentioned above.

Example – a product sale agreement

Taking these principles into account, the contract set out in correspondence earlier in this chapter has been reproduced in a slightly more formal style as a product sale agreement in Appendix B. The advantage of this approach is to have a single document for certainty and easy reference. Although it is as legally binding as an exchange of correspondence setting out the same terms, there may also be a greater sense of conclusion and commitment to this sort of signed format.

Summary and Checklist

ESSENTIALS

For anyone in business, it's worth building confidence in your ability to prepare a sound contract, and this takes practice. The trick is to get the essentials written down. The basics are:

- *what* you want to buy/sell
- *how* the products are accurately described
- *how many* products are wanted

- *how much* is the price and when it is payable
- *when* delivery will be.

WRITING IT DOWN

You then need to decide how you want to document your contract, the choice generally being between e-mail, letter and formal agreement. If all the essentials are there, e-mail works perfectly well. Whichever way is chosen, there are some principles to follow:

Preparation

- *Due diligence* – do you really know who you are dealing with?
- *Creating or recording agreement?* – is the agreement already made or not?
- *Terms of business* – do they apply and whose apply (see also Chapter 9).
- *Driving the contract process* – who is responsible for this?

Drafting

- *Legals* – are all the contract essentials included?
- *Recitals and definitions* – are they clear and consistent and followed through?
- *Technical terms* – are they clearly defined?
- *Check* – against the project plan (has anything slipped into or out of the 'agreed' terms?)
- *Avoid ambiguity* – define the products and any terms that may be uncertain.
- *Simple language* – and short sentences for clarity.
- *No vagueness* – around commitments.
- *Details* – are they covered in sufficient detail?
- *Obligations* – have you included what each party must do and must not do?
- *Principles first* – exceptions afterwards.
- *Is the contract complete?* – check there's nothing vital missing.
- *Is it intelligible?* – try to have someone else in your business sense-check the document.

Afterwards

- *Follow through* – make sure it gets agreed, signed and dated (in all relevant places) – and witnessed if necessary.
- *Deed* – does it need to be signed as a deed?
- *Follow up* – afterwards and stay on track with the agreed terms.
- *Perform* – what you've said you will do.
- *Hold* – the other party to what they have undertaken.
- *Template or pro-forma* – would this document be useful to adapt for use subsequently?

3 *Planning More Complex Contracts*

Introduction – planning the deal outlines – internal and external teams – planning the contract documentation – planning for change – the length and complexity of contracts – summary and checklist

Introduction

As circumstances become more complex, so more time and attention needs to be put into the earlier stages of planning both the framework of the contract and the involvement of others to try to ensure that the right issues are being addressed in the right way by the right people at the right time.

Planning the Deal Outlines

No one would deny that military campaigns may be won or lost in the planning, and, without taking the analogy too far, contract campaigns may also be badly compromised if those involved fail to think through all the issues in good time and organize their forces to best advantage. At a more logistical and less adversarial level it can be helpful to think of planning a business contract like a trip abroad – as a packing list.

A pro forma 'packing list' contract planner

- *The subject* – where are we going and how are we going to get there?
- *The object* – why are we going there and how will we know we have got there?
- *The benefits* – what are we aiming to get out of this trip longer term and how will we evaluate that, if at all?
- *The cost* – what will the whole thing cost and have we factored in all the incidental things, such as the equivalent of currency exchange, airport transfers and taxes, insurance and gratuities?
- *The risks* – what are the main risks, how are we going to keep these to a manageable minimum and what insurance should we have in place?
- *The effects* – what will be the result if this all works out? What are we likely to want to do next and should this be built in now?
- *Tolerance* – have we built in enough margin for delays or problems (or time out)?

An example of the planner

Here is an example of client use of the planner in the context of an IT project. This will then feed through to the rolling memorandum, as seen below, and the framework and content of the agreement, as shown in Chapter 15 on technology contracts.

Subject – New software system to handle order processing, designed externally to our requirements (schedule to be prepared and attached).

Object – Effective order processing measured by a) ability to handle current volumes of [...] customer orders with expansion up to [...] orders with b) average 24-hour maximum turnround on average staff complement of three accounts staff and c) 99.9 per cent accuracy – initial measure after four weeks' operation and regular reassessment each quarter.

Benefits – Ability to process customer orders within three working days and invoice immediately, leading to greater customer satisfaction and average invoicing one week earlier than current levels, giving improved cash flow and ability to negotiate early payment discounts with suppliers.

Cost – Fixed cost (budget figure £x) to satisfactory implementation with annual support and maintenance contract with guaranteed 24-hour response (budget figure £y).

Main risks and suggested actions –
- *Choosing wrong supplier: carry out effective due diligence.*
- *System non-compliant: specify performance/acceptance tests.*
- *Delays caused in commissioning process: clear timescale with price adjustments.*
- *Failure after implementation: workable but not to specification – price adjustment.*
- *Failure after implementation: non-workable – need to terminate – build in parameters and termination right.*
- *System works but maintenance poor: need to find a new maintenance provider (will anyone else have the knowledge?) but not to lose system – due diligence and contract provision to permit change.*

Effects – If successful, we will want it long term and to have capacity for upgrades.

Tolerance – Ensure we have sensible timescale and fall-back position for possible downtime.

THE ROLLING MEMORANDUM

Keeping track

As negotiations continue, it can be difficult to keep track of where you are. The biggest danger is that one of the original objectives or concerns gets lost in the detail of particular points. To prevent this, the original planner – or packing list – can be usefully developed into a document that you can keep updated, incorporating an action list for the project team. This will be of great help when drafting or reviewing the contract and, as the chances are that the terms finally agreed will have moved some way from the original planner, the rolling memo gives the chance to compare directly where you finish up against where you started – before you sign the contract! An example, following on from the IT contract planner above, is set out in Appendix C.

An aid to communication

The rolling memo could then trigger a separate note to the other party to the negotiations – the system supplier in the example – summarizing the agreed and outstanding issues. Their response would then be fed back into the memo until all everything is agreed, at which point the memo would become a guide to preparing or checking the contract itself. The memo could also be used to keep the rest of the implementation team updated.

ATTITUDES TO RISK

Assessing the risk

Risk goes hand-in-hand with cost and benefit. If you don't get what you ordered, what are you likely to lose? A short-term computer failure could be a blow, but what about the effects of failure of the computer system altogether or – at an extreme – the collapse of a hydro-electric dam? One failure to mend a computer fault may have limited effects, but a full system crash or the failure of one vital component might make a complete system useless for its intended purpose. It could also cause major loss of data, enforced downtime and perhaps a resulting breach of the affected company's obligations to a customer. This becomes even clearer with a hydro-electric dam, whose construction is as strong as its weakest part. Here there will be massive power and property interests, and human life potentially at risk. In such cases, the risk factor may outweigh all others and will influence the entire process of selecting and agreeing terms with designers, engineers and contractors.

Limiting the risk

Contracts are not playing cards, and should not be a gamble. For the supplier or provider planning a commitment with a high potential downside, it pays to think at an early stage how that risk can be limited. This may include tighter contract terms, limitation and exclusion clauses and insurance. These are all increasingly important and complex issues, considered in more detail in Chapter 7, and they fundamentally affect the way in which the contract is planned and drafted.

Internal and External Teams

Armies need supply lines. Without the right equipment and ongoing supplies of ammunition, clothing and food, the army will be unable to continue in the field. Supplies require excellent lines of communication and support throughout the whole task force.

INVOLVING THE RIGHT PEOPLE INTERNALLY

In the same way, businesses need to ensure that all those likely to be involved in the supply or purchase chain or the implementation process know what is going on that affects their area and have the chance to feed into the process in good time. Any complex negotiation benefits from being run in parallel with an implementation group. A classic area is outsourcing – the contracting-out to an external specialist of a defined function or part of the business, considered in more detail in Chapter 13. A contract drawn up and signed without reference to those who will need to put it into effect is liable to create all sorts of problems including delay and frustration and, quite possibly, breach and termination. So the advice must be to consider at the outset who has the knowledge and experience to feed into the project and who will need to be fully briefed as to implementation. Without needing to swell the size of the actual negotiation team, this should help ensure that all others who will help formulate and make the project work are – and feel – involved from the outset.

INVOLVING LAWYERS

When to use a lawyer

Business people enter into contracts every day without feeling the need for a lawyer, and this book supports that proposition, but there will come a point when specialist support should be sought. It can be as critical to work out how and when to involve a lawyer as it is whether to involve one. The right planning process will help highlight the issues that will need professional support and when this is best obtained. As a private-practice lawyer, I always felt that clients often tended to leave it too late to instruct me, but, as my experience developed, the clients I had worked with increasingly gave me at least an initial brief at an early stage. This enabled issues such as potential competition law problems to be identified and addressed early on, these often being material in deciding not just what could be negotiated, but also the basic framework of the draft contract itself. As an in-house lawyer, my focus is somewhat different with the acid tests being to balance priorities of overall in-house workload and expertise against the cost and value of external advice. The in-house legal team will know its industry well, so external advice has to be in tune with, able to build on and add value to that knowledge.

The importance of a clear brief

Any lawyer will need a brief; the clearer the brief, the better the outcome is likely to be. The old computer adage 'garbage in, garbage out' applies to contracts too, and if the brief is muddled, the drafting is liable to reflect this. A good lawyer will, of course, know the most appropriate questions to ask and will add value in the formation process, not just to the drafting. If you are using a lawyer, allow adequate time and scope for this process. There is no substitute for spending some time in working through the issues at the outset.

Being realistic

Lawyers will be familiar with the 'could you just?' request, as in 'Could you just give this the once over?' Often this is requested without any background as to the deal, objectives or main risk areas. To best manage cost and the lawyer relationship, send your lawyer the key documents – and the draft contract if there is one – and then book a meeting to run through it. That meeting may be all you need in order to flush out the main issues and raise and address up-front any key questions not in the initial brief. It can also save time and cost, avoiding lengthy correspondence and unnecessary redrafting. Yet all too often this stage is missed, with the lawyer starting with limited information and an unrealistic timescale. Lawyers are professionally risk-averse and need to be told what level of risk clients will and don't want to accept. Otherwise, they will try to cover them all!

The relationship with your lawyer

Working regularly with a lawyer who knows you and your business is an enormous advantage. Spending time at the outset of the relationship, with updates from time to time, pays dividends, allowing your lawyer to develop the quality, speed and relevance of their advice as their knowledge of your business increases. Most commercial lawyers will respond well to such opportunities and the prospect of building a lasting relationship with a valued client.

Confidence and confidentiality

Confidence in your lawyer is vital in the longer term. If you don't feel that confidence, think about a change. Try to find someone that you respect personally and can get on with, as well as instruct, as they are more likely to go the extra mile for you at critical times. If, however, you are consistently disappointed after using several different lawyers, it may be worth thinking about your own expectations and approach to the relationship! Some businesspeople are actually reluctant to recommend their lawyers to anyone else because they don't want their adviser distracted by potentially competing clients. Others will happily recommend their lawyers, but consider confidentiality. If your lawyer acts for many of your friends or competitors, how confidential will they really be able to keep your own plans?

Challenge

It's also worth encouraging your adviser to challenge you occasionally. There will be times when you are intent on doing a deal that is fundamentally flawed or exposes you to a major degree of risk with limited upside. This is when you need someone working with you who will question you before it's too late. It is a delicate task, but can sometimes make the difference between success and failure at a critical time. But it is not the lawyer's job to make your decisions, and the external professional who seeks to run your business probably either needs to be brought on board or replaced. Independence is important, and both lawyer and client must have the ability to walk away from a relationship in which trust and confidence has been lost.

Managing legal costs

However you choose a lawyer the issue of hourly rates soon comes up. Comparing hourly rates is a factor, but can be misleading, as it is the rate for the job that will often matter. The approach mentioned in this section can help keep fees down. It's always worth asking for a fixed fee, or at least an estimate based on assumptions which the lawyer can spell out. Good lawyers will work to that because they know that managing client expectations is vital. But clients need to be realistic too, and, if the deal becomes more protracted than expected, should not expect their lawyer to put in the extra time for no extra reward. Most lawyers do work under pressure and don't rack up extra hours unnecessarily (though there are exceptions). The greater risk is to pretend that the issues are simple, leading to work being passed to junior lawyer with the technical legal knowledge but without the experience to see the wood for the trees and separate out the possible from the probable. You then pay for their work and the partner supervision time to sort it out.

Specialization

Sometimes you will choose a lawyer who has broad experience, even if not necessarily detailed knowledge of your own business. This can involve a learning process, the cost of which the chosen lawyer may be prepared to share with you for building a longer-term relationship, but does give you the added benefit of the lawyer's experience from other kinds of business. Although there are a few exceptions, your conveyancing or matrimonial lawyer is – these days – unlikely also to have the legal expertise you need for business contracts. Even with a general commercial lawyer, there may be times when a specialist in a particular subject needs to be brought in. Your lawyer should suggest when this might apply, but occasionally lawyers do take themselves beyond their own area of expertise, fearing to disclose the limits of their knowledge in case they risk losing you as a client. Ideally, this is the point at which you should encourage your lawyer to be up-front and accept that there is more to be gained from honesty than from trying to sort out unnecessary mistakes afterwards.

Planning the Contract Documentation

It is easy to leap from agreement on the outlines of a deal straight into detailed contract drafting. Once the framework of the written contract is set, it can assume a life and resilience independent of its original creators The aim must be to draft business contracts designed to give the best chance of the contract serving its intended purpose and the minimum risk of its becoming an agent of destruction. In extreme cases, the contract draft becomes Frankenstein's monster, threatening to destroy the original basis of agreement.

SOME INITIAL CONSIDERATIONS

Type of transaction

The first step is to consider what kind of transaction is proposed and what sort of document would be appropriate for that transaction. An agreement covering a period of time and/or a mix of goods and services will require much more thought and planning than one for a single transaction.

Precedents are useful but should be used with caution. Contracts are often prepared against tight time deadlines; there is a tendency just to grab a familiar format or the last similar agreement, change the names of the parties and make any other obvious amendments. But the new deal may be significantly different or the last precedent may have been specifically adapted, with some normally vital clauses omitted, so it pays to start from the right point. Shoehorning a deal into the wrong template ultimately serves no one.

SATISFYING CONDITIONS OR REQUIREMENTS

Conditions

Some agreements set out conditions, either 'conditions precedent' to the rest of the contract coming into force or 'conditions subsequent', to be complied with during the contract. In other cases there may just be a requirement to do something to a given level, such as acceptance testing in technology contracts. These conditions or requirements then need to be 'satisfied', either in order to engage the rest of the contract or to establish that the relevant party has complied with its specific obligations. If so, it is essential that the conditions or requirements are clearly expressed so that whether they have taken place can be objectively verified. Where there is the need for the consent of a third party, such as licensor consent, this can most clearly be demonstrated by a signed form or letter. Where there is unlikely to be such a clear-cut position, the contract should, if possible, specify how it will be established that the condition has been met.

'Satisfactory'

Sometimes the contract will require that something is done to the satisfaction of the other party. Whereas 'satisfactory quality' can be objectively judged in sale of goods issues (see Chapter 9) and 'reasonable satisfaction' can ultimately be judged on the principles of reasonableness already mentioned, the requirement to do something to the 'satisfaction' of the other party is normally best avoided. If confirmation is given, well and good but, if not, it is difficult to imply and, if someone is not satisfied, there is no objective standard against which to judge their view (see *Stabilad* v. *Stephens & Carter* (1999)).

MAKING ASSUMPTIONS (SEE ALSO 'WARRANTIES', P. 62 IN CHAPTER 4)

'Don't assume anything' is a useful golden rule in negotiations. This is not meant as a negative, but as a reminder to check every assumption. Experience shows that many problems could have been avoided by sensible checks at the outset. Many of the potential problems outlined in this book could be identified by a thorough checking process. Of course there are leaps of faith to be made, but better an informed leap than a blind leap into the unknown.

Due diligence (both ways)

Whilst there is always a practical, as well as a theoretical, limit to the extent of 'due diligence' that can be undertaken on any project, there is much that can be done quickly and easily (see the comments in the previous chapter). If you find you are making assumptions that have not been tested, then it's worth going back and making the checks. In addition to the fundamental questions below, 'who' and 'why' are always worth extra thought. Part of that process might usefully include revisiting your own attitude to the other parties. Sometimes their motives may not be what they appear. Equally, on reflection, you might find that your own attitude and performance could be giving the other parties real doubts as to your integrity and commitment. So it pays to try to look both ways.

THE ST ALBANS CASE – RISK, LOSS AND LIABILITY

The leading case of *St Albans City and District Council* v. *International Computers Ltd* (1996) is worth referring to here as it highlights many issues of contract planning. In brief, ICL provided software which failed to do what the contract said it would do. As a direct result, a substantial loss was incurred by the council which successfully sued ICL. The case is referred to several times in this book. In planning terms, two points are especially worth noting here:

- *Specification/whose terms?* – In *St Albans* the specification requirements were set out in the council's invitation to tender (ITT) and ICL agreed to produce 'a system to cope with all statutory requirements for … the community charge'. It therefore undertook not only to supply the goods, but also in effect to ensure the result, directly increasing its own risk as provider and reducing risk for St Albans as buyer. If the specification had been based on technical performance and not on actual functionality, the outcome might have been different.
- *Limitations on liability* are really key commercial terms. The contract, although including St Albans' specification, incorporated ICL's standard terms of supply. These limited ICL's liability to £100,000 or the amount of the contract price, whichever was the less. The £100,000 bore no relation either to the contract price (c. £1.3 million) or the council's possible loss. As explained in Chapter 7, this limitation was held to be unreasonable and ineffective, exposing ICL to the full amount of the claim.

Planning for Change

TOLERANCE FACTOR

In engineering, even main supporting structures are designed to move. If they did not, the tension in their construction would break them apart, either slowly or dramatically, when the stresses of their environment proved too strong for the rigidity of their framework. This is even more critical where the risks are high. Buildings in known earthquake zones are now constructed to withstand minor tremors and to cause less destruction if they collapse. Yet businesses often seek to contract on strict terms and time limits with no tolerance built in for inevitable commercial strains.

PEOPLE AND EVENTS

Both circumstances and people may change. The person with whom you negotiated and worked well may suddenly leave and be replaced by someone else with no understanding of the background. Worse still, the new agenda may be completely different. You may have trusted those with whom you were dealing (and their ability to remember all those unwritten promises!), but they may suddenly not be there when the chips are down.

CHANGE CONTROL CLAUSES

Many business contracts (outsourcing being a prime example) now build in clauses dealing specifically with the management of changes to the contract. (The reference to 'change control' is somewhat misleading and not to be confused with 'change of control'.) These typically involve a summary of the likely provisions that may be changed, the procedure and timetable for discussion, a resolution mechanism in the absence of agreement on the change and a process for documenting the change.

A PRACTICAL EXAMPLE OF CHANGE

The background and intention

These last two points can be illustrated by an actual case in which I was involved when in private practice. My then clients were selling their bakery production business, basically getting out of production to concentrate on the business of selling bakery and other food products. To secure the ongoing value of the production business, they were, at the same time, agreeing an exclusive distribution agreement with the buyer of the production business to distribute their products into specialist markets. Quality, consistency, freshness and speed of delivery of the products were all vital to compete effectively in this market. To secure the sale of the production business, the sellers had to undertake that, for a specified period after completion of the sale, not only would they not compete in producing the same type of bakery products, but also that they would not buy those products from anyone else. We argued on behalf of the clients that they needed the right to buy bakery products elsewhere if the new owners of the production business were unable to supply on time or to quality standards. The prospective new owners insisted in negotiations that the exclusivity in the agreements was absolute in the restriction period, even if they themselves were unable to produce and deliver the right quality products on time. The sellers, whilst having misgivings, considered the importance of selling the business to be paramount and went ahead on this basis.

What actually happened

The buyers may have started with good intentions but, first, the bakery production manager had not been enrolled into the agreement and, second, the new owner's sales team brought in much more business from other sources than had been expected. There was then a change of personnel, with the new team having no allegiance to the original deal. The quality and reliability of the deliveries started to suffer, but the bakery, now run by the new owner, refused to let our clients go elsewhere for supplies or, even temporarily, to produce the food itself. When customers started pulling out, something had to give. In the end both parties suffered through customer loss and legal costs because, however apparently justifiable, there was no tolerance allowed in the contract for this outcome, even though the outcome had been predicted at the outset.

PRICE CHANGES

Price changes in long-term contracts

Another area that is largely predictable, and where many longer-term contracts come under strain, is price. The ideal for providers of goods of services is a price that they can change (normally increase) at will; the ideal for buyers of those goods or services is a price that is fixed, or even one that will reduce if costs go down. Contracts need to find a viable route between these extremes.

Legal implications

As seen earlier, except for rare cases where an obligation is implied to make a contract work at all, the courts will not fill in the blanks where the parties have simply left open – or agreed to agree – a crucial issue, such as the price (or the quantity or the delivery date). The exception here is where the parties have set up in advance a clear procedure or machinery to resolve the issue. This may be by means of reference to an agreed price index or a third-party arbitrator or expert.

Planning ahead; the short-term approach

The temptation to put the issue off should be stoutly resisted, unless both parties accept that, if they don't agree, the contract can be terminated at short notice and without penalty. This is often the best approach but, clearly, would not work in the bakery example above, since a long-term supply agreement underpinned the whole value of the business. A short-term deal will, however, help keep both parties on their commercial toes and enable quality and service issues to be dealt with quickly if they wish to keep the relationship alive.

Planning ahead: the longer-term approach to price changes

Where there is material up-front investment (or a discounted up-front price) and where a long-term support commitment is required for that investment to pay off, a different approach is required, and sustainable pricing is likely to go to the root of the deal. The following questions are then worth considering:

- *Acceptance tests* – Where payment depends on a satisfactory working installation, as with computers or software, is there an adequate acceptance test process? (For example, see Chapter 15, 'Technology Contracts'.)

- *Market price* – With raw material or product prices, is there an active market which can be used to establish market value at any time? Ensure you have the right details and a fall-back position if that market ceases to be viable.
- *Raw materials* – In a manufacturing agreement should there be price adjustments in line with changes in raw materials costs and, if so,
  - how are these costs to be assessed?
  - how much advance notice of a price change should be given?
  - will increases be permitted at any time or only at certain times of the year?
  - should there be a maximum increase or a maximum number of increases in any year?
  - are retrospective rebates appropriate, based on the volume of business conducted in the period?
  - what about *reductions* in raw material costs, especially if these are at an historic high at the time the deal is negotiated?
- *Labour and overheads* – What about these – do the same principles apply?
- *Maximum change* – Should the parties be able to terminate the contract if price changes go beyond agreed levels?
- *Inflation* – Is the rate of inflation relevant and, if so, which index should be specified in the contract? How far is it safe to predict inflation in view of past volatility, and should there be a cap or maximum on the amount of any increase? The wide disparity in recent years between retail and consumer price increases, let alone raw material costs, shows that a simple inflation measure is insufficient. Indeed, such indices have shown some retail prices falling sharply as others have increased, so that prices of imported consumer goods, for example, might bear no relation and might actually be moving in the opposite direction to prices for fuel and power or wages or home-produced goods directly affected as a result.
- *Termination* – If there were to be a spectacular change in circumstances, producing a fundamental shift in the economics of the contract, might there be an exceptional right for either party to terminate? Such a change might be difficult to define, but the financial disasters of 2008–09 suggest that the collapse of a major international bank ('the Lehman's effect', as some have called it) or the plunging in value of specified stock markets or currencies might be indicators of such circumstances.

PLAN FOR SUCCESS (AS WELL AS FOR RISK AND FAILURE)

What will happen if you succeed?

With all the risk analysis and fear of adversity, it is easy to forget that success can be as great a problem as failure. In a way, the example of the bakery business ('A practical example of change' – see above) shows what can happen when a business is too successful. As another example, imagine that you run a house-building company and are looking for appealing new house designs. Market research indicates that converted railway stations have great appeal as homes, so you engage designers to prepare plans of new houses that look like converted railway stations. The houses are popular, and your competitors want to get in on the act. What could be easier than for them to go to the same designers and ask for the same design? There will normally be no breach of copyright because the copyright belongs to the designers and not the client (see Chapter 14), so the designers are free to reproduce the design, with or without amendments, for your competitors.

The Cala Homes case

This is not a fanciful scenario, but substantially what led to litigation in *Cala Homes* v. *Alfred McAlpine (No. 1)* (1995), with the added factor that the managing director of Cala left to join its competitor, Alfred McAlpine, complete with the house design idea. Cala took McAlpine to court but had the difficulty that, although the McAlpine design was effectively a copy of the Cala house design, the architect's copyright in the actual design had not been assigned to Cala. Although the whole point of the design was to obtain business advantage for Cala, there was nothing in the contract with the designers to protect the design. In the event, the court took a practical approach to the situation and held that Cala had effective editorial control over the drawings and such an input into the design through their employees that the copyright was owned jointly between themselves and the designers. Cala, as joint copyright owner, had not consented to the licence to McAlpine and could therefore prevent McAlpine from copying the plans. So Cala finally succeeded, but this result necessitated court action and – to some extent – a creative legal interpretation to achieve. The moral is that the effect of success, and not merely the effect of failure, needs to be considered in advance.

Success and exclusivity

Basic economics tells us that the fulfilment of any demand may stimulate more demand, and this can often be anticipated from the outset. That success can, in turn, lead to suppliers or main customers attempting to tie in the successful party. If the baker finds a magic new product or ingredient which starts to sell superbly, its main distributor may seek exclusivity for that product, particularly if the distributor had originally established the product by its effective marketing. For its part, the baker will want to protect the recipe and prevent the distributor from setting up its own bakery or obtaining equivalent, but cheaper, supplies from someone else who has not made the same investment. Exclusivity in contracts, looked at in more detail in Chapter 8, is a particular problem in relation to competition law and needs careful planning. It might best even be avoided unless a clear business case can be made out, which could not adequately be achieved in another way. Where exclusivity is appropriate, it could be conditional on satisfactory ongoing performance by the party benefiting from the restrictions. In the bakery example, the seller who became the customer could have been allowed to buy elsewhere, without detriment to the new owner, only if the latter was unable to produce on time and to quality standards.

The Length and Complexity of Contracts

Having set out many aspects of what to plan for, it is important not to lose sight of practicalities. Every business transaction carries a risk, and a key reason to have a written contract is to set out who is responsible for what, and what the consequences would be if those responsibilities were not followed through. In a simple sale and purchase of goods, the major risks can be fairly quickly identified. But if the transaction is more complex, how many more issues might arise, and how far should the contract cover all these risks? This is where those negotiating the deal need to decide how far the contract should concentrate on probabilities, rather than distant possibilities, and just how complex the contract should be. Every different possibility can create several new pages of drafting if care is not taken.

The 90:10 rule

In this context my version of the 90 per cent rule is as follows:

> *Rule 1*: In an average contract, 90 per cent of the substance of the transaction will be covered by 10 per cent of the content of the document. The remaining 90 per cent of the document content will deal with things that require clarification, are unlikely to happen or are just irrelevant. So, in an average 20-page document, two pages will cover 90 per cent of the substance.

> *Rule 2*: If you start with a two-page document covering 90 per cent of the substance, each 1 per cent increase above 90 per cent will double the length of the document from what it was before. So 91 per cent will involve four pages, 92 per cent eight pages, 93 per cent 16 pages, 94 per cent 32 pages and so on, so that a 20-page document will probably only reach about 93 per cent cover.

> *Rule 3*: You will never actually achieve 100 per cent. There is no such thing as an infallible document.

The packing list principle

So, if you want a short document, think of it as a matter of choice as to what to put in and what to leave out, like having a limited amount of space in your suitcase. What are you most likely to be doing on your journey and what is the weather likely to be? You may want one sweater, but there's no point in packing several for a warm climate. Likewise there is no reason to have extensive default provisions if the business arrangement can be cancelled at short notice without fault on either side. Will there be laundry facilities? The equivalent might be regular meetings built into the agenda to assess how the project is developing and to give an early opportunity to deal with any problems that arise. Or is this a long-term multi-continent expedition where you really have to provide for a full range of possibilities? Even so, you might be going somewhere where local supplies are cheap and plentiful. The analogy has its weaknesses of course, but the danger lies in thinking that the contract is an ever-expandable suitcase, with the result that it becomes harder to choose (and can cause friction) as to what to put in it and much harder to carry from place to place once you have finally finished packing. Sometimes the tendency to want to forget the over-heavy contract is as great as the tendency to leave the over-heavy suitcase behind and travel light.

Summary and Checklist

Planning can be half the battle. A packing list approach and/or a rolling memorandum can help focus attention and negotiations; it may also prompt involving the right colleagues at an early stage.

Lawyers can add clarity, independence, experience and drafting skills to the mix. The project team needs to do the initial planning and appraisal first, but should know who to bring in to support them and when. The process can be planned so as to maximize added value and manage cost effectively.

Achieving the right contract may, at this stage, begin to look daunting! But the right contract is the right contract for the occasion, not the definitive draft for all occasions. The comprehensive document designed to cover all eventualities and fiercely protect its own corner is rarely agreed, more rarely signed and, if signed, hardly ever observed. The negotiation process itself can become like an emotional tug-of-war. Similarly, no two sets of circumstances are the same, and time does not stand still, so templates need regular updating. You would not take the same precautions for a walk in space as for a walk in the park. They are both excursions, but are utterly different in objective, technical difficulty, cost, overall importance and risk. Despite this, there is tendency to prepare similar contracts to cover entirely dissimilar situations.

A *sense of proportion and relevance* goes to the route of contract planning. If you asked a lawyer for an infallible contract for your spacecraft you would never take off, as no contract can cover everything that might go wrong. A balance needs to be achieved between action and protection and it is primarily up to you, as the person who knows the business, to decide what sort of document you want. The 90:10 rule applies: more comprehensive documents are longer – longer in length, longer to prepare and longer to negotiate. The decision needs to be made at the outset as to what is appropriate, since the mould is set by the first draft.

The emphasis should therefore be on what is important to make the contract reflect the *essential obligations* of the parties, what is needed to make it work and what should happen if it does not. When that foundation and load-bearing structure has been established, the detail can then safely be added. The process of identifying subject, object, benefit of the contract, cost, risks and the tolerance factor should all help in planning that foundation and structure for the relevant terrain.

Key planning points to consider include:

- What is the subject of the contract and is it clearly covered – for example, by a detailed specification?
- What are the objectives of the agreement? Are they measurable and what are the conditions of achievement?
- What will be the benefits of the contract being carried out and what new pressures might this produce?
- Have you worked out all the cost implications and covered these in the contract as far as possible?
- Have all assumptions been checked and recorded in the contract?
- What are the risks and how are these dealt with? Are there exclusion or limitation clauses to be negotiated? Is suitable insurance cover in place?
- Has some tolerance been built in to the equation?
- Will the deal work in practice and have you done all that is required to integrate the necessary processes to make it work as effectively as possible?
- What areas of uncertainty still exist and how far can these sensibly be covered?

4 *Common Contract Terms and Clauses*

Introduction – commonly used words and phrases – key common clauses – boilerplate clauses – summary and checklist

Introduction

This chapter deals with commonly used words and phrases and those provisions often collectively called 'boilerplate' clauses.

Commonly Used Words and Phrases

The first step in reviewing words and phrases commonly used in contracts in to start with that (supposedly) well-known British quality – 'reasonableness'.

REASONABLENESS

The reasonable person

The classic English common law standard is that of 'the reasonable man'. This is a theoretically normal person of average intelligence, with 'reasonableness' being a theoretical norm of behaviour and judgement, against which the courts can decide whether action or inaction was within a range of reasonableness. The traditional legal figure was the hypothetical 'man on the Clapham omnibus', a phrase variously attributed to Walter Bagehot in the seventeenth century and judicially to Lord Bowen, quoted in 1903 by Collins MR in *McQuire* v. *Western Morning News* (at 109). Nowadays we perhaps need to think of a modern, gender-neutral and status-neutral successor individual.

Alternative approaches

Some tests of behaviour for company directors have a dual standard – of both a competent director and a director having the skills and professional expertise that the director in question has (or should have). The more qualified the director, the higher the standard expected. So if the standard of the attitude required is important, it might be better to specify a more precise test than 'reasonableness'.

Consent 'not to be unreasonably withheld' is a tried and tested formula that works well in most cases. The statement that: 'X will not [assign this agreement] without the

prior written consent of Y, such consent not to be unreasonably withheld or delayed'
has the double test as to whether consent is being actually withheld and/or whether it is
being delayed to an unreasonable extent to forestall the argument that a failure to answer
cannot be a refusal.

BEST/REASONABLE ENDEAVOURS

The phrases 'best endeavours' and 'reasonable endeavours' are in regular use and have
been – and continue to be – much interpreted by the courts, and it is important to know
how and when to use them.

Case law on best endeavours

The classical statement on best endeavours was set out in *Sheffield District Railway* v. *The
Great Central Railway* (1911) when the court held that the phrase meant – subject to some
limit to the costs to be involved – that 'no stone should be left unturned'. 'Best' endeavours
did not mean 'second-best' endeavours. This robust principle has been somewhat watered
down by later cases. In *Rackham* v. *Peek Foods* (1990), for example, the requirement to use
best endeavours to procure shareholder approval did not require the company's board of
directors to give bad advice to its shareholders or override their fiduciary duties.

Case law on reasonable endeavours

In *Yewbelle* v. *London Green Developments* (2008) the Court of Appeal, in considering
'reasonable endeavours', asked whether the action proposed would, if taken, offer a
'significant chance of achieving the result aimed at' (*Yewbelle*, para. 13). Then in *Rhodia
Int Holdings* v. *Huntsman Int* (2007), a case regarding a business sale with an obligation
on the parties to use their 'respective reasonable endeavours to obtain all requisite
consents or agreements of [third parties to contract assignments]', the judge suggested
that reasonable endeavours '... probably only requires a party to take one reasonable
course, not all of them'. On the other hand, he commented that an obligation to use
all reasonable endeavours requires a party to take all the reasonable courses available
(*Rhodia*, paras 30–35).

Case law summary

The cases suggest that 'best endeavours' might involve the need to take unreasonable
action, such as action against the commercial interests of the relevant party, so long
as this was not in breach of that party's other legal duties, but 'reasonable endeavours'
probably – by definition – does not go that far. However, if the contract specifies specific
steps, these will have to be taken even if they are against the relevant party's commercial
interests. The broad position might be summarized as follows:

* *'Reasonable endeavours'* indicates that some effort or action must be taken to achieve
  the objective in question. That effort is somewhere beyond trying without enthusiasm
  or only trying once, but less than leaving no stone unturned.

- *'Best endeavours'* normally involves something more, such as repeated attempts and different approaches. It has even been suggested that best endeavours might involve taking a case to court or a decision to appeal.
- *'All reasonable endeavours'* normally means something more than 'reasonable endeavours' and may mean as much as 'best endeavours'.
- It is not always appropriate to press for – or to agree to give – *best* endeavours, as the obligation is such a strong one, although occasionally it is justified and appropriate.
- US expressions 'best efforts' and 'reasonable efforts' seem to have similar meanings to the English 'best endeavours' and 'reasonable endeavours' respectively.

Endeavours and good faith

It is generally best to avoid mixing endeavours with 'good faith' obligations to agree or negotiate, which are generally unenforceable in English law. As can be seen from the comments on good faith on page 56, the two tests arise from very different standpoints.

Endeavours and absolute obligations

An obligation to use endeavours, whether best or just reasonable, is not a proper substitute for an absolute obligation. When one party's commitment or undertaking is meant to be absolute, it should not be expressed as best or reasonable endeavours but with phrases such as 'X will sell/purchase/provide ...' or 'X undertakes to do the following ...'.

Drafting 'endeavours' clauses

When preparing contracts, try to be more specific where the issue may be important, such as by specifying the required approach. This might include clarifying: a) whether or not either party can be forced to act against its own commercial interests; b) whether court action needs be taken or not; and c) whether there is need to appeal any formal decision, as in the following example.

Example   Assume that there is a contract between Seller (S) and Buyer (B)), but that the consent of a third party, Z, is necessary to enable the S and B deal to go ahead – for example, because S has a contract with Z that B wants to take over, but which cannot be assigned to B unless Z agrees.

This agreement is subject to the written consent of Z to the assignment of the [Reserved Contract] to the Buyer ('Z Consent'). Buyer and Seller will use their respective reasonable endeavours to obtain the Z Consent as soon as practicable, including (but not limited to) a joint written application to Z with regular follow up by letter/e-mail and telephone, each of Buyer and Seller liaising closely with the other and acting consistently but without obligation on either Buyer or Seller to threaten or take legal action against Z if Z fails or refuses to grant the Z Consent. If, notwithstanding such efforts, the Z Consent cannot be obtained by [latest date] either party may terminate this agreement (with immediate effect) by serving on the other written notice to such effect with specific reference to this clause.

REASONABLE NOTICE

What is reasonable can depend on many factors. What, for example, if there is only an oral contract or there are no provisions for termination even though the contract, by its nature, is clearly intended to be terminable? One of the few reported cases on the subject, *Alpha Lettings Ltd* v. *Neptune Research* (2003), concerned the termination of an exclusive agency at common law, in the absence of a formal written contract. The Court of Appeal held that the right range of notice in the circumstances was three to six months. The factors they took into account were: a) there had been a 15-year relationship between the parties; b) there was no restriction preventing the agent from dealing with the principal's competitors, so the agent should be able to fill the void quite quickly; c) the principal's business produced only about 20 per cent of the agent's turnover, leaving the remaining 80 per cent still available to the agent; d) the agent was still obliged to use best endeavours to sell the principal's products during the notice period. Overall the court decided here that four months was a reasonable notice period.

GOOD FAITH

Some contracts specifically require 'good faith negotiations' to take place in certain circumstances, such as negotiations for potential renewal after the initial contract term or where there is a potential disagreement or lack of consent to an issue. Such a provision may have advantages in management terms by setting a timescale for discussion, but is unlikely to be binding in English law. Although it may well be legally effective in other, especially continental, jurisdictions, a pure obligation 'to negotiate in good faith' should not be relied on in contracts under English law. The principle was repeated in *Walford* v. *Miles* (1992), where the House of Lords robustly held that:

> ... *a duty to carry on negotiations in good faith is inherently repugnant to the adversarial position of the parties when involved in negotiations. Each party ... is entitled to pursue his (or her) own interest, so long as he avoids making misrepresentations.* (Lord Ackner, Walford, at para. 138)

Where there is evident display of bad faith, on the other hand, a legal remedy may well be available.

'INCLUDING, BUT NOT LIMITED TO ...' OR 'INCLUDING, WITHOUT LIMITATION ...'

This phrase can be seen dotted around legal documents (including examples in this book). It stems from an ancient judicial tradition (the *eiusdem generis* rule) of assuming that, where there is a general proposition in a legal document with a list of examples, the general proposition covers issues of the same type as those set out in the list. For example, giving a list of possible force majeure events followed by the words 'or other event beyond the control of the parties' would limit those later words to events similar to those previously specified and not a completely different type of event altogether. A phrase such as 'including, but not limited to ...' seeks to displace the application of the rule, but is far from infallible. It is therefore best to be as precise as possible in anticipating specific circumstances.

Key Common Clauses

This section considers many common contract clauses, drafted here in plain English and deliberately short-form in keeping with the spirit and intent of this book. Every lawyer has pet wording (and probably pet hates) in drafting, and these comments and samples are intended to be illustrative rather than definitive, either as to law or as to possible variations.

LENGTH OF THE AGREEMENT

In most business agreements the 'term' of the agreement – that is, how long it should last – is a central issue, coupled with what might bring it to an end. Commercial agreements covering more than a one-off transaction tend to have a fixed initial term which may then run on for successive periods until terminated by notice. How long, then, should an agreement last? There are many factors to consider, including:

- *Project length* – what is the likely minimum and maximum time the project will take to come to a conclusion?
- *Two or more stage deals* – should there be separate time periods, such as a primary and secondary term, and, if so, what notice or other step, if any, should be required to continue or terminate at the end of each period?
- *No-fault termination* – should either or both parties have the right to terminate the agreement early – other than for default? The right to terminate and the length of notice required to do so are closely linked to the term of the agreement. Take, for example, a five-year contract term. This is lengthy in some circumstances, but if there is the right for either party to break (terminate) at any time after one year by giving six months' notice, there would be effectively a minimum commitment to only 12 or 18 months (depending on the wording), giving a very different flavour to the contract. If the relationship works, it carries on and there is no need to rush to prepare another agreement. If it does not, or the terms have to be adjusted, notice can be given and any appropriate negotiations can take place.

RENEWAL

Renewal is the converse of termination, and is therefore more likely to be an issue if the original contract term is short.

- *Renewal rights* – Should either or both parties have the right to renew the agreement, and, if so, can the terms of renewal be decided now?
- *Renewal terms* – If the renewal terms cannot be decided now simply because of price or cost factors, is it practical to include reference to some form of third-party reference, such as a national or industry index or independent arbitration to define pricing or cost?

- *Minimum conditions for renewal* – Are there any conditions, such as target levels of turnover or even due and timely performance of the contract to date, which need to be satisfied for the arrangement to continue?

NOTICE TO TERMINATE

The notice period, probably between three and 12 months, needs to be carefully considered in each case. What needs to be achieved within the notice period, and is the period appropriate? For example, does this give adequate time to complete current work in progress? What about stock in hand at the end? Can this be sold-off within a further six or 12 months, after termination of the main agreement?

DATING (AND BACKDATING) AGREEMENTS

Documents should be dated the day they are signed by the last party to sign, or any later date they are handed over ('delivered') unconditionally. They should not be backdated or forward-dated, as this could be false accounting or a false statement under ss 17 and 19 of the Theft Act 1968 (if the changed date falls in a different tax year, for example) or even forgery under the Forgery Act 1913, which is essentially issuing a false document. Of course, nothing improper is usually intended, but if the agreement is intended to take effect or the term to start running from a different date than the date of the contract, this should be expressly stated.

TERM AND TERMINATION – DRAFTING POINTS

Start date

It is accordingly best to define a start date for the contract ('Commencement Date' or 'Start Date'). Leaving the term to run from the date on which the contract is signed can create uncertainty (even more so if the contract is never dated!) and, as stated above, the contract date should not be 'manipulated' to achieve this.

Termination

Make sure that when and how the contract may be brought to an end is made clear. Check, for example, that the following are clear and unambiguous:

- When is the earliest/latest date that notice to terminate can be given?
- Does notice have to be in writing? (Highly advisable for certainty.)
- Is there a date when notice must be served?
- When is the earliest/latest date that the notice will expire (termination take effect)? Bear in mind that this may be on an anniversary date of the contract or the commencement date, which may mean that notice is actually longer than the period specified (see 'Example 1' opposite).
- Could there be any doubt as to what is meant by 'day' (any day or a defined 'working day' or 'business day', for example), month (normally calendar) or 'year'?

- Is the date of service of the notice to be excluded (as may happen with notices of short duration, such as ten days or less)?
- Have you unintentionally created a perpetually renewable contract (see Example 2 below).

Examples of drafting termination dates

Example 1

This agreement is for an initial term of two years commencing on [Commencement Date] and will continue in effect after that period unless and until terminated by either party on six months' written notice to the other, such notice to expire on the second or any future anniversary of the Commencement Date.

This means that the earliest date for termination of the contract is the second anniversary of the commencement date *and*, in order to terminate, the notice must have been correctly served six months earlier. But there is a further trap in the drafting here. The reference is to *'six months' written notice'*. This means what it says – six months exactly, no more or less. Moreover, the notice has to expire on a stated day. It is therefore very tricky to get the right notice served on the right day. If you are faced with this terminology, amend the wording to *'not less than six months' written notice'* (or 'no fewer than six months') or *'at least six months' written notice'* or redraft to provide that six months' notice can be given to expire at any time, specifying whether this applies during or only after, or so as to expire after the end of the original term.

Example 2

This agreement is for an initial term of two years commencing on [Commencement Date] and will continue in effect after that period for successive periods unless and until terminated by either party in accordance with clause 13.

The key is to check what clause 13 says. If it covers only termination for breach, the contract becomes what lawyers call a 'perpetually renewable contract', because it can only be brought to an end by a breach which the other party chooses to act on. Any other termination could trigger a large claim for damages because of the long-term nature of the agreement! Such wording should be challenged and changed.

PAYMENT PROVISIONS AND CHARGING INTEREST

Being clear

It pays to be clear as to when payment is due, especially where this affects other aspects, such as when and how risk and title in goods pass to a buyer (see Chapter 9).

Late payment can trigger the default provisions in the contract. It is often sensible to have a few days' latitude in payment, despite the risk that this can be abused. Normally, late payment would not be a material default and would be remediable. If late payment is likely to become a regular event or could cause major inconvenience, the contract might specify that persistent default (including, but not limited to, delayed payment) is irremediable and grounds for termination. In such cases, it would be best to specify how many delays in any given period of time would constitute 'persistent'. Those paying late should also be aware that such defaults, even if not acted on at the time by the other party, could debar them from exercising any option or similar right under the contract. The law regards options and the like as privileges, capable of being lost if the contract terms are not strictly observed.

Interest can be charged if payment is late. The Late Payment of Commercial Debts (Interest) Act 1998 was introduced to try to protect smaller businesses from suffering at the hands of large corporations that abuse agreed payment terms. Unfortunately, the interest terms in the Act are so punitive (currently 8 per cent above the Bank of England base rate) that invoking the Act is likely to be terminal for the business relationship. Nevertheless, the Act will apply if there are no alternative interest provisions in the contract, which must specify a sufficient rate to give a 'substantial remedy' for the payee. It can therefore be in the interests of both parties to have a suitable interest clause included, possibly specifying (in business-to-business (B2B) cases) that notice must be served before interest can be charged, such as that given in various examples in this book:

> *We may charge you interest, calculated on a daily basis, at three percentage points above [...]*
> *Bank base rate (or its then equivalent) on any amounts unpaid after [seven days' written notice*
> *from you following] the due date for payment.*

POST-TERMINATION

There is often some form of life after termination, and this needs to be thought about in advance. For example:

- *Post-termination limitations* – Restrictive covenants intended to apply after termination will be relevant, as will ongoing obligations of confidentiality, but will there be other issues also, and, if so, for how long?
- *Other provisions* – What other provisions of the agreement may be expected to continue in force after termination? An example would be a suitable sell-off period for stock.

BREACH AND OTHER EARLY TERMINATION EVENTS (SEE ALSO CHAPTERS 6, 19 AND 20)

- *Termination for breach* – What period of notice for termination on breach should be given (if any), and should the party in breach be given the opportunity to remedy the breach before final termination?
- *Material breach* – Should the opportunity to terminate be limited to 'material' breach and, if so, what does that mean? Material breach is generally regarded as something that has, or is likely to have, a serious consequence, in terms of money, reputation or inconvenience or the like, to the person suffering, often denying them a significant part of the contract benefit. Missing a due date on its own is unlikely to be material for this purpose unless otherwise specified or obvious from the circumstances.

- *Persistent defaults* – Can one party terminate because the other persistently defaults (for example, is always late on payment) even if these defaults are not individually material?
- *Change of control* – If one party sells out (normally the company, but possibly also the business), will this enable the other(s) to terminate?
- *Insolvency* – Will there be automatic termination on insolvency, and how will insolvency be defined?

Examples (short-form clauses but covering the essentials)

Either party may terminate this agreement at any time by serving written notice on the other party if the other party:

3.1   is in [material] breach of this agreement and fails to remedy such breach within [14/21] days of written notice specifying the breach and requiring its remedy; or

3.2   becomes insolvent [or Insolvent if defined elsewhere] or unable to pay its debts as they fall due; or

3.3   undergoes a change of Control.

DAMAGES – DRAFTING ISSUES (SEE ALSO CHAPTERS 7 AND 19)

Damages

If there is a breach, the 'innocent party' may have a claim for damages for any loss it suffers arising from the breach. The damages issue is considered further in later chapters, but the drafting point here is to consider the potential level of loss and how possible it will be to calculate this.

Liquidated damages are worth considering where the loss calculation may be difficult. This is a clause where a specific level or scale of damages is agreed by the parties and written into the contract at the outset as payable if the contract is breached in certain specific ways. Such provisions can be especially useful in certain types of agreement, such as construction and IT contracts, where the risk is apparent but the level of damages can be hard to calculate. To avoid lengthy disputes as to the actual extent of loss there may be a pre-agreed rate payable either overall or for each day or week that completion is delayed because of the breach. The contract should generally make it clear that the amount specified is payable to the exclusion of other financial claims directly arising from *that* breach of contract, although it need not preclude other remedies (for example, termination if the breach were fundamental) or damages for other breaches. It is also useful to state that the amount is recoverable as a debt, so that it can immediately be set off against any sums due the other way.

Genuine pre-estimate of loss

Liquidated damages must be 'a genuine pre-estimate of loss'. Recent statements of this have indicated that this can be assessed, judged objectively at the time the contract was entered into, by asking whether the amount specified was designed to deter a party from breaching the contract, which is likely to be an unenforceable penalty, or to compensate the innocent party for the loss caused by the breach, which should be recoverable (see, for example, *Lordsdale Finance* v. *Bank of Zambia* (1996)). The courts are now predisposed to uphold a liquidated damages clause to give commercial efficacy to a business contract. The essential question is whether the calculation or estimate was objectively reasonable. If the estimate was hopelessly inaccurate, even if genuine, it is unlikely to be enforceable. The higher the amount is negotiated, the more likely it is to be upheld. An example of a case which went wrong for the party seeking to enforce liquidated damages was *CMC Group* v. *Zhang* (2006), where there were really two major failings, both contained within the wording that breach of the agreement would 'render [defaulting party] liable to [claiming party] for the sum of $40,000' together with costs 'in addition to a claim for damages in relation to loss of business'. The clause failed because $40,000 applied irrespective of the seriousness of the breach and the claimant reserved the right to seek damages additionally for breach of the same clause.

Cumulative remedies

To limit disputes on the issue it may be wise to add a clause to the effect that:

> *The rights and remedies in this agreement are cumulative and except as otherwise stated do not exclude any other rights or remedies.*

WARRANTIES AND INDEMNITIES

Warranties and indemnities, mentioned several times in this book, are essentially ways of managing assumption and risk, and they need careful thought and drafting to suit each deal. Some principles are set out below and more detail is given in chapters on specialized contracts and in the various examples and templates.

A *warranty* for this purpose is a statement that certain things are, or will be, true at a stated date (distinguished here from guarantees as to quality of performance). For example, there will often be a warranty by each party that it is legally entitled to enter into the agreement in question, or a trademark licensor will normally warrant that it is the registered owner of the relevant trademark. Unlike an operative clause, a warranty does not require any action. Some warranties are implied by law, such as under the sale of goods legislation (see Chapter 9), but in most cases they need to be expressly set out in the contract. Beyond the basics warranties are matters for negotiation.

Breach of a warranty gives rise to a claim for damages. The party claiming damages must prove, 'on the balance of probabilities', first that the loss in question arose because the warranty was breached (that is, the warranty was untrue), second that the damages claimed are a fair reflection of that loss (where the actual loss might be difficult to establish) and third (as with other contract claims) that the claimant has taken whatever reasonable steps were available to that party to mitigate the loss.

An indemnity, on the other hand, is an obligation to compensate for or make good any loss caused by the event described, irrespective of any mitigation that might have been available. If the seller of an IT system, for example, agrees 'to indemnify the buyer against any third-party claims made against the buyer relating to [the IT system supplied]', the seller would have to pay up on any third-party claim even if the system turned out to have many other benefits that the buyer had not expected or paid for and, in this example, even if the claim was ultimately defeated or settled. It is often described as a *'hold harmless'* clause because it passes the full responsibility over to the indemnifier to ensure that the innocent (indemnified) party comes to no harm from the claim. It can thus be seen that an indemnity is a potentially powerful weapon not to be given lightly or valuable protection against the unexpected, depending on which side you are on. Where it is given, it is sensible to consider a suitable claims-handling clause.

Claims handling is the process setting out what happens if a claim is made. Imagine that a third party makes a claim against the buyer of an IT system that the system infringes the third party's rights. If the sort of indemnity mentioned above exists, the buyer will look to the system seller to cover the claim. The clause aims to give the seller notice of the claim, with all relevant details, as soon as the information is available and may require that the parties work together to secure the best outcome. The seller, having given the indemnity, might then insist on handling the claim itself, but either way there may be provisions about consultation and possibly for consent, not to be unreasonably withheld, to be given to any settlement.

DEFINED TERMS AND INTERPRETATION CLAUSES

Defining terms

Interpretation clauses define terms which are used in several places and set down other rules of interpretation. They can avoid tortuous repetition of the same words, but need time in both drafting and reviewing a contract, both as to what they mean and as to consistency of use. Contracts drafted poorly, or by several people. all too often define a term in one place and then ignore or muddle that definition in another. For example, the definition of 'Products' may be all important in agency, distribution and similar agreements, but may then have to be differentiated from 'products' (small 'p') as an undefined term, such as when used in 'other products'. Provisions as to terms relating to finance, such as 'accounts', 'turnover' and 'profits', will also need considerable scrutiny by both accountants and lawyers.

Location of the interpretation section

As seen in the previous chapters, defined terms can be introduced as they arise, but are often more extensive and better suited to a clause or schedule of their own, either in the first schedule at the back of the agreement or in the first clause or even a glossary at the front. Either way, the glossary or schedule should be clearly incorporated by reference into the main agreement.

GROUPS OF COMPANIES (SEE ALSO CHAPTER 6)

- Is one of the contract parties a company which is part of a larger group of companies? If so, check the group structure and that the right company is party to the contract.

- If any of the rights or obligations in the contract are to be shared by other members of the group, should they be parties to the contract or third parties? (See 'Third-party Rights' oppposite.)
- If there are definitions of 'Group', 'Holding Company' and 'Subsidiary', have you checked that they are used consistently throughout the agreement?
- If there are references to 'Affiliate', prevalent in US contracts and often undefined, have you checked whether these are appropriate? The term is not generally defined in under English law.

CHANGE OF CONTROL CLAUSE

The relevance of control is considered further in Chapter 6. 'Change of control' in most cases will mean a takeover. Headline and drafting issues to consider include the following:

- The takeover of a company that is party to a contract can, and often does, change both the direction and the finances of the company that is taken over. Worst of all, the new owner may be a direct competitor of the other contract party or a company of poor repute.
- If you are or are dealing with a group company, have you considered what would happen if your company or the company with whom you are dealing left the group and joined another or became independent?
- Alternatively, a company with a strong balance sheet can be taken over and have its assets leveraged to raise finance for its new holding company. After the credit crash of 2008, we should have few illusions about what can happen, and it can happen overnight.

Defining control

In these cases, a suitable change of control clause should be considered. The definition of 'control' can, however, create problems. It is not defined by the Companies Act 2006 as such, and the definition in tax statutes is highly complex. Because reference has to be made to another source, and even then the definitions can cross-refer to several other definitions, the real meaning can be very difficult to decipher. One definition of 'control' used in some template agreements in this book, following the 90:10 rule, states simply:

> Control *means the legal or beneficial ownership of [50 per cent or more/more than 50 per cent of] another entity or the power to direct the affairs of another entity.*

This is certainly a wide definition of control, especially if the words in square brackets are omitted. The statutory definition requires the ability to have a majority, effectively either of voting rights or directors, which would exclude a 50:50 deadlock-type joint venture, which is why the 50 per cent equivalent is added here. Also, the definition concentrates on the 'power' to control the affairs, which may be exercised, for example, by a shadow director, whereas the Companies Act definition concentrates on formal structures.

Boilerplate Clauses

The function of boilerplates is to help hold the framework of a construction together and, although the word suggests something mundane, boilerplate clauses are integral to the construction and meaning of the contract and should be accorded due care and consideration. For example a restrictive covenant could be wholly unenforceable if it goes too far and there is no 'severance' clause, a valid 'entire agreement' clause could exclude a previous agreement and a notice served outside the terms of a notices clause could be entirely ineffective, possibly losing vital renewal or termination rights. The expression 'boilerplate' typically includes the following types of clause.

ASSIGNMENT AND SUBCONTRACTING (SEE ALSO CHAPTER 18)

The general rule is that a contract may be assigned (that is, transferred) to another party unless the contract is in the nature of a personal contract.

Personal contracts are those where the identity of the parties to the agreement is essential, such that no assignment is contemplated. For example:

> *Assignment: This agreement is strictly personal to the parties and may not be assigned or subcontracted by either.*

Assignment with consent

More often, the contract is potentially assignable, but the other party should have the right to object if they consider their interests may be prejudiced. For example:

> *Assignment: Neither party may assign or transfer its rights or obligations under this agreement without the prior written consent of the other party, such consent not to be unreasonably withheld or delayed. This clause will not prevent the assignment or transfer of rights or obligations to [an Associate/a Group Company].*

THIRD-PARTY RIGHTS

Privity of contract

At common law, only parties to a contract could enforce its terms. So if Andrew agreed with Brian to make a gift to Clare, and Clare was not a party to the contract, Clare would be a 'third party' and could not enforce the contract (unless by historical quirk it was a dowry payment) That rule, known as 'privity of contract', was changed in 1999.

The Contracts (Rights of Third Parties) Act 1999 provides that Clare can enforce the contract if either a) the contract states that Clare can enforce it or b) the terms confer a direct benefit on Clare, *and* she is identified by name or class. In this respect, a direct payment is something the person is entitled to in their own right, whether they are referred to by name or described clearly – for example, by Andrew referring to Clare as 'my eldest niece'. However, if the contract were merely to pass a payment through Clare, without identifying whether or how much benefit she was entitled to, it is unlikely to attract the protection of the 1999 Act.

Inclusions and exclusions

There are some exclusions from the ambit of the Act, such as negotiable instruments, company constitutions, employment contracts or international carriage of goods contracts, but there was an interesting example of where the Act nearly applied in the 2008 case of *Prudential* v. *Ayres*. A clause in a deed between landlord and tenant limited certain aspects of the landlord's claims to the current tenants 'and any previous tenant', without expressly stating that previous tenants could rely on it. The first instance decision that previous tenants could rely on the clause by virtue of the 1999 Act was, on the wording, overruled by the Court of Appeal.

Practical steps

Consider whether you want the Act to apply or not. If it does apply, taking the example above, Andrew and Brian could not change their minds and redirect the gift to Deidre without Clare's agreement. If they did redirect the gift, and Clare could prove the original deal, they could finish up having to pay both Clare and Deidre. In business contracts, the right may be important for group companies (for example, the benefit of supply obligation or restrictive covenants) or enforcement by licensees/end-users. A short-form sample clause might read as follows:

> *Rights of third parties: The parties intend that no term of this agreement may be enforced by any person who is not a party to it.*

Alternatively, a positive clause (using predefined terms) might read as follows (the words in square brackets may be added for extra certainty):

> *Rights of third parties: The parties intend that this agreement is for the benefit of and enforceable by the Licensee and each Subsidiary and any permitted sub-licensee of the Licensee [in accordance with the provisions of the Contracts (Rights of Third Parties) Act 1999].*

CONFIDENTIAL INFORMATION

The principles are set out in more detail in the Chapter 5, together with a fuller clause. However, a sample short-form clause might read as follows:

> *Each party agrees to keep confidential the financial and other provisions of this agreement and the negotiations leading to it together with all information relating to the business or affairs of the other party and not to disclose any such information without the other party's prior written approval.*

NOTICES

Notices in writing

Many contracts specify that notices must be in writing and how they should be served. When serving notices, care must be taken to follow strictly the terms of the notice clause, and this should always be carefully checked and complied with. Fax is still sometimes used as an acceptable means of serving notices, but the issue now is more likely to be whether to permit service by e-mail, on which there are mixed views. Here is a sample clause:

> *Notices: Any notice or other communication given under this agreement must be in writing delivered personally, or sent by first-class post, or sent by e-mail with a delivery receipt, to the relevant party's address specified [in this agreement/ set out below] or to such other address and e-mail address as either party may have last notified to the other. Any notice or other communication is deemed to have been duly given on the day it is delivered personally, or on the second day [or Business Day, if defined] following the date it was sent by post, or on the next working [Business] day following transmission by e-mail.*

> *[Name*
> *Postal address*
> *E-mail address*
> *With a copy of any notice under clauses … or … to*
> *Firm/address*
> *Attention of*
> *E-mail address]*

Keeping track

There can be serious consequences from failing to serve and/or pick up and deal with a formal notice duly delivered under the terms of a contract, so the notices clause in contracts should be carefully worded and carefully checked. For the same reason, having notices (especially in case of breach or termination) addressed and/or copied to a specific person (as above) (another executive or perhaps the party's solicitor) is a useful additional safeguard and prompt to action, but (and it is a big 'but') failure to send the copy can invalidate the notice, so it might be better to make this a request rather than an obligation. Remember to include details of the other parties to contracts in your lists of those to be notified if your business moves. It is also essential to note the other party's last address notified to you, since otherwise the notice served at their old address might be ineffective.

Time for service

Adequate time must also be allowed for service abroad, and it is often useful to specify and define delivery after a certain number of 'working' days (often included as a definition of 'Business Days' based on whether banks are open for business in the country of receipt or service during 'business hours' in that country or place). Many other countries require specific types of service and do not recognize the first-class post concept. It may also be an advantage for the contract expressly to permit service of any legal proceedings on a representative in the home country of the party serving notice, which can avoid complex procedures and delays in service in another territory.

FORCE MAJEURE/ACT OF GOD

'Force majeure' is a phrase from the French Napoleonic Code which may be regarded as more precise than 'Act of God'. The intention is to identify a situation that prevents a party being in breach of contract if events preclude their being able to perform their obligations, either permanently or for some time. Otherwise, English law gives relief only if the contract becomes impossible to perform. A simple force majeure clause might read:

> *Neither party will be liable to the other for failure to perform any obligation under this agreement if and so long as the failure is caused by any factor outside the reasonable control of that party.*

Continuing effects

A secondary, but important, issue is to cover what happens if the situation continues for more than a brief period of time. If a key building is heavily damaged or destroyed by fire, for example, it is unlikely that the client in a storage contract can simply wait until rebuilding is complete. This may lead to a rather fuller obligation, such as:

> *Force majeure: Neither party will be liable for any failure to perform or delay in performing any obligation under this agreement by reason of any circumstance beyond its reasonable control providing that it promptly notifies the other party of such circumstance and uses its reasonable endeavours to mitigate the effect of such circumstance on any affected obligation. If such circumstance continues to prevent performance for more than 60 days, either party may terminate this agreement on 30 days' written notice.*

Drafting issues to look out for

Many clauses go into much more detail and cover such disparate events as war, acts of terrorism, riot and civil disturbance, fire, explosion, flood, theft (of goods), malicious damage, strike and new acts or regulations of government. There are various optional extras, such as: fog or bad weather (to be used carefully since such excuses may easily be invoked and are difficult to define); inability to obtain fuel, power or even raw materials; malfunction or breakdown of machinery; and denial of export or other essential licences. What these events should all have in common is that they are not expected to happen and are beyond the reasonable control of the party seeking the protection of the clause. A strike caused recklessly by an intransigent employer or an equipment breakdown resulting from poor maintenance should not give rise to protection. Where services rely on technology the possible effects of outages of power or essential internet connection may need special attention.

Force majeure and risk planning

As part of the planning process it is sensible to consider which force majeure events should be within the contemplation of the parties, what the effect of those events occurring would be and who should bear the risk. In appropriate cases, such as an order for products where time is critical, the time period for termination if the force majeure event continues may need to be very short, and care should be taken that an apparently innocuous force majeure clause does not shift the careful balance of risk planning elsewhere.

ENTIRE AGREEMENT AND NO VARIATION CLAUSES

Entire agreement clauses aim to establish that the parties can rely only on the terms actually set out in writing in the contract. The parties will therefore give up any claims they may have for anything which went before the contract and confirm that they are not relying on any pre-contract representations. Such clauses are common, but run the risk of being adjudged as another form of exclusion clause and thus subject to the unfair contract terms legislation, as considered further in Chapter 7. The following is an example:

> *Entire agreement: This agreement and the documents referred to in it constitute the entire agreement between the parties, and supersede all other agreements or arrangements between the parties (whether written or oral, express or implied), relating to the subject matter of this agreement.*

Changes to contract terms can also give rise to problems. If the contract says one thing, but the parties habitually do something else, does this vary the contract? A *no variation clause* will seek to prevent this. In practice, many agreements are varied by letter, and it will generally suffice for the clause to permit the contract to be varied in writing, signed by a duly authorized director or representative of each of the parties. For example:

> *Variations: No variations of this agreement are effective unless made in writing signed by the parties or their authorized agents.*

Product variations are a different matter. Consider:

> *Our policy is one of continuous improvement and we reserve the right to change the detailed specification of our products at any time without prior notice.*

Quite apart from questions as to the validity of such a clause under consumer laws, a buyer faced with this wording would do well to add qualifying words to temper the extent of the seller's power. The wording will depend on the circumstances, but could be as follows:

> *... but so that no such change will affect the basic form, fit, function, [colour], performance or key features of the products or their suitability for the purpose for which the buyer is acquiring them as previously notified to the seller.*

COUNTERPARTS

Where there are several parties to an agreement, it may be convenient to have each sign at a separate location and to create the contract by having separate copies – or counterparts – each signed by only one of the parties. This can work perfectly well provided that each of the parties ultimately signs at least one counterpart. In these cases, it is obviously essential that all copies are identical apart from the signatures, and it is sensible to include a 'counterparts' clause such as:

> *This agreement may be signed [or executed as a deed] in any number of counterparts, each of which is deemed to be an original, but all of which together constitute a single agreement.*

OTHER TYPICAL BOILERPLATE CLAUSES

No agency, partnership or joint venture

This is designed to make it clear that the parties do not intend the agreement to be regarded as any of these particular legal relationships. This is no more than a statement of intention and will not, for instance, prevent a true commercial agency agreement from being regarded as such by the courts if a dispute arises.

Further assurance

There may be other documents to be signed or help to be given to enable the parties to perform their obligations or receive their full entitlements under the contract. This is not permission to renegotiate the contract and seek to add new terms! An example is:

> *Each party will if and when called upon by the other execute any further documents or take such action as may be reasonably required to give full effect to the provisions of this agreement.*

Illegality and severance

Contract provisions which are against the criminal law are liable to 'taint' the whole contract so badly that the entire agreement will fail. Where the offending provisions are more minor, however, the courts may delete (or, in legal language, 'sever') from a restriction words which make it unlawful or unreasonable. They cannot add words or rewrite the clause, so if the deletion leaves something incomplete or incoherent, then the whole clause or restriction will fail. This is called the 'blue-pencil' approach. For example, the courts might delete a restriction against pure competition while leaving intact restrictions preventing poaching of existing customers and staff. But if there was only one clause against competition, then deleting that clause would remove all restrictions. It is therefore accepted practice to set out restrictions separately and to ensure that the time period in each case is reasonable for that instance, care being taken not to include greater or lengthier restrictions than are reasonably necessary to protect the interest in question. Some international contracts (not to be relied on under English law) go further and provide for the parties to negotiate in good faith the nearest alternative clause that would be valid. A typical English-law short-form clause would be as follows:

> *Severability: Any provision in this agreement which is held by any competent court or tribunal to be illegal or unenforceable will to the extent necessary be regarded as omitted from this agreement and the enforceability of the remainder will not be affected.*

No waiver

A no-waiver clause can be a useful way (for both parties) of making the point that failure or delay by one party to enforce rights under the contract against another will not automatically be held to release those rights. This is not a foolproof remedy for inaction however (see Chapter 18.) A basic example would be:

> *No party will be prevented by reason of delay in taking action or forbearance from subsequently enforcing any provision of this agreement.*

Non-merger

The legal assumption is that completion or termination of an agreement means that the obligations of the parties come to an end. In practice there may be several clauses intended to have, or continue in, effect after termination (see also 'Post-termination' above.) An example is:

> *Notwithstanding completion or termination of this agreement the obligations in this agreement expressed or intended to have effect after completion or termination (as appropriate), including but not limited to clauses … and …, will continue in force.*

Choice of law/jurisdiction

Examples are given in the templates in the appendices, but the subject is considered in more detail in Chapter 17.

Summary and Checklist

It is important to be clear on the meaning of *words and phrases* commonly used in business agreements and that they are used in the right way in your own contract. For example:

- *Reasonable/ness* imposes an objective standard – is it appropriate with this contract?
- *Reasonable and best endeavours* are not substitutes for an absolute commitment to do something, but do carry specific meanings and can be material obligations.
- *Reasonable notice* is best specified more precisely.
- *Good faith* obligations can be useful where there is clear evidence of bad faith, but are not necessarily a legal commitment to do anything specific.

Key common clauses in business contracts include:

- the length – or term – of the agreement
- any conditions for renewal
- the length and conditions for notice to terminate (note the importance of being clear when and how notice to terminate can be served)
- when and how payments to be made and default provisions for late payment
- what happens after termination
- breach and ability to remedy
- damages and liquidated damages
- warranties and indemnities
- defined terms and interpretation clauses
- terms relating to groups of companies
- change of control issues.

Boilerplate clauses include:

- limitations on assignment and subcontracting
- inclusion/ exclusion of third party rights
- confidential information (see Chapter 5)
- notices
- force majeure/Act of God
- entire agreement and no variation
- counterparts
- further assurance
- illegality and severance
- no waiver
- non-merger
- law and jurisdiction.

KEY LEGAL ISSUES AFFECTING CONTRACTS

5 *Confidentiality, Privacy and Data Protection*

Introduction – confidentiality – sample confidentiality clause – non-disclosure agreements – employee restrictive covenants – privacy – Data Protection Act 1998 – Freedom of Information Act 2000 – summary

Introduction

The boundaries between what is public and what is private or confidential have probably never been more challenged than they are now, and we face a long and protracted debate that will engage some deep-rooted issues. Questions as to the need – and the right – to know go back to the Garden of Eden, but we now struggle to cope with ever greater knowledge, not just about one another's lives and habits, but also about our own genetic make-up and potential future health. Once made available, knowledge cannot easily be removed; and who owns and controls that information, let alone how we cope with it, becomes of more pressing concern. Those concerns, in turn, impact on business.

Confidentiality, privacy and data protection are not subjects normally grouped together in legal books. The law of confidentiality (or 'confidence' as it is sometimes referred to in legal cases) has deep roots in England, but data protection and privacy laws have much more recent and different origins. As times and laws have changed, however, the three areas have come to overlap, and it now seems sensible to consider them together. For example, using or revealing details of living people may create liability in all three areas.

Confidentiality obligations are often included in contracts, but can exist independently of formal agreement. Privacy and data have their own entitlements to protection irrespective of contract, but need to be considered where contract duties involve handling personal information of any kind. Contracts will therefore need to identify and deal with such duties and may add further sanctions where they are breached.

Confidentiality

Below the surface of a business there are normally fairly clear lines between information that is (or you would expect to be) publicly available (*public information*), information that relates to the financial details of the business (such as profit margins and detailed budgets), proposed new products, secret ingredients or formulae and other unpublished data unique to the business, regarded as confidential and limited to those who run the business (*trade secrets*) and information held by and about individuals, likely to be private or personal to them (*private information*). A quick 'litmus test' might raise the following questions:

- What confidential information does your business have that it needs to protect?
- Are you treating the information as confidential and, if so, how?
- Who has/might have access to that information?

THE OUTLINES OF LEGAL PROTECTION OF CONFIDENTIAL INFORMATION

English law implies a duty of confidentiality in certain cases, and we might further distinguish information:

- amounting to commercial or business secrets (*trade secrets*)
- expressly given on a confidential basis (*explicitly confidential*)
- implicitly confidential from the circumstances (*implicitly confidential*)
- that is essentially private or personal (*private information*)
- protected by the Data Protection Act 1998 (*personal data*).

The traditional three-part test for the protection of confidentiality is set out in the case of *Coco* v. *A.N. Clark* (1969). Although it is no longer complete law since the development of privacy and freedom of expression under the Human Rights Act (see below), the case is still a good reference point. To be protected, information must generally:

a) have a 'necessary quality of confidence about it';
b) have been communicated in confidence; and
c) be such that unauthorized use of it may be detrimental to the party to whom it relates.

Questions for business to consider include:

- What confidential information may be disclosed in the course of negotiations or performance of the contract?
- How closely should circulation of the confidential material be constrained?
- How is the information best kept confidential?
- What announcements are to be made about the deal covered by the contract and by whom?

The benefits of written agreement

Without a written agreement it will be more difficult to:

- establish that relevant information was protected at law;
- decide how confidential it was;
- determine who is liable for any breach of confidence;
- obtain an adequate remedy.

Confidentiality agreements (see below) can help by setting out expressly what is confidential, how it is to be kept so and what remedies are available in case of breach.

Loss of data

There are seemingly never-ending reports of loss by public bodies, official organizations and businesses of disks, memory sticks or other data containing personal information. Sometimes this results from breach of trust, such as identity theft or computer-hacking, but often the information is on a device simply left on a train, stolen from a car or lost by a third-party carrier. Each of these losses are likely to constitute a breach of the security aspects of the Data Protection Act (see below), and misuse of the data could be an infringement of privacy, so far as living people are concerned. However, the law of confidentiality goes further by covering not just individuals, but also businesses and other organizations, sometimes even in the absence of a contract.

Other parties

While you are considering the business contract, you may also want to consider whether you are adequately protected in respect of staff – both your own and the other parties' employees. What confidential information do they have, and might they be encouraged to jump ship at some stage during or after the deal? This may be a matter for suitable contract provisions with the other business and suitable employee restrictive covenants.

A somewhat bizarre example of how a duty of confidentiality might arise and be breached was examined by the House of Lords in *Jackson* v. *RBS* (2005), a case on the improbable subject of dog chews. These were imported from Thailand into UK by Jackson, who then sold them on to a UK company called Economy Bag. By chance, RBS was banker to both Jackson and Economy Bag. In 1993 (note the timescale) RBS sent to Economy Bag, instead of Jackson, documents showing the (high) level of Jackson's mark-up on invoices from the Thai suppliers. On learning this, Economy Bag cut out Jackson and went direct to the Thai suppliers. Jackson sued RBS, claiming damages for breach of confidence. The House of Lords held that there was a duty of confidentiality owed by RBS to Jackson by virtue of the circumstances (and even without a written agreement to that effect). The case is a cautionary tale on the importance of confidentiality itself and is looked at further in Chapter 7 regarding the extent of loss. On the facts, because of the bank's knowledge of the circumstances, including both accounts, the court held it liable for Jackson's loss of profit on *future* orders reasonably expected to come from Economy Bag.

Other, and perhaps more fundamental, issues of confidentiality arose as the more commercial dealings of banks started to emerge in 2009, following the banking crisis. See, for example, the High Court decision in *Barclays Bank plc* v. *Guardian News and Media Ltd* on 19 March 2009. This case was an example of banks' wish to keep sensitive information out of the public eye and various newspapers' attempts to publicize banks' inner workings. Judges are forced to balance respect for the law and the principles of confidentiality against the need for ultimate disclosure of matters of public interest and the need for accountability. This is especially difficult where there has already been disclosure on the Internet. We are beginning to see increasing judicial recognition of the difficulty of shutting off Web dissemination of confidential material, but it must be an open question as to whether and how long print will be restrained where the Internet is not.

SOME OTHER CONFIDENTIALITY ISSUES

There are many references to confidentiality throughout this book and many circumstances in which the issue should be considered. Examples include:

- *patents* – where confidentiality is vital to registration (and to commercial protection) – see Chapter 14;
- *know-how* – where the protection of know-how is essentially through the law of confidentiality – see Chapter 14;
- *website/Internet sales* – where a privacy policy is required – see Chapter 10.

Sample Confidentiality Clause

The following clause is an example, and variations of it are also seen in other versions in this book:

3   *Each party agrees to keep confidential the [financial] provisions of this agreement and the negotiations leading to it together with all information relating to the business or affairs of the other party and not to disclose any such information except:*

3.1   *with the other party's prior written approval;*

3.2   *where required by law or by a regulatory body having jurisdiction over it (and then after prior notification to the other party so far as the law allows); or*

3.3   *to its own professional advisers on a 'need to know basis' and on terms of strict confidentiality.*

4   *The provisions of clause 3 will not apply to any information that is or comes into the public domain where this does not occur through breach by either party of the provisions of this clause or apparent breach of a duty of confidence owed to any third party.*

The first issue is whether it is sufficient to keep confidential just the financial provisions of the contract, notably who pays what to whom. Clauses prohibiting *any* information regarding the contract from being passed on can be unnecessarily restrictive if third parties need to know the relationship. Clauses which go into detail about what constitutes confidential information may be helpful, but there is still the danger of omitting something vital. The example above is a broad restriction, but subject to clause 4 which excludes information 'in the public domain', provided it did not get there because one party breached its obligations of confidentiality! Clauses 3.1 and 3.3 are self-explanatory (some clauses limit employees' access to a 'need to know basis'), but clause 3.2 is worth comment. A regulatory or formal request as part of an investigation will take precedence over the contract terms, but the draft requires due notice to the other party, if possible, so that, if their own information is affected, they have the chance to make their own representations, especially where Freedom of Information Act requests are made (see below).

Non-disclosure Agreements (NDAs)

OUTLINES

Non-disclosure agreements, or NDAs, are designed to clarify exactly what is to be treated as confidential, by whom, to what extent and for how long. This may, in some cases, make the difference between information being misused or not and is likely to give an express right of redress against those misusing the information. NDAs are normally used in cases of potential new transactions where one or both parties will need, or will be expected, to disclose confidential information, probably in the nature of trade secrets, such as regarding a prospective:

- business purchase
- distribution, outsourcing or technology contract
- joint venture
- new business concept
- book, film, recording or other media idea or exploitation
- invention.

NDA CHECKLIST

Definitions

> Discloser: the party providing the information.
> Recipient: the party receiving it.
> CI: Confidential Information (as defined).
> Purpose: the purpose for which the confidential information is required.

The main issues

- *Who are you dealing with?* Check the other party's full company name and address.
- *Purpose* – be clear about this.
- *Confidential Information* is best defined, such as:
  - 'any unpublished information regarding the business or business plans of the Discloser disclosed to Recipient in relation to the Purpose [following the signature of this letter].'
  - This wording would limit the CI to what is: a) unpublished, b) actually disclosed following the NDA in the expectation of confidence, and c) related to the Purpose rather than anything else. A problem could, of course, arise if the CI had been disclosed before the letter was signed – and some NDAs expressly seek to cover this.

Recipients

- *Who is to receive the CI?* If the Recipient is a company, should the ability to see the CI and the terms of the NDA apply to all employees of the company? Normally it would be restricted to those of the Recipient's senior managers and executives who have a need to know for the Purpose, and who would accordingly be bound by the NDA.

- *Is the Recipient likely to need to circulate the CI outside the company?* If so, are others who may receive the CI covered by it?
- *Will the Recipient be liable* for any breaches on the part of those others?
- If so, *does the Recipient have sufficient control over them*, or should the obligation be limited in some way? (This may not be acceptable to the Discloser.)

Mutuality

- *Is there a mutual exchange of confidential information?* If so, provide for the same terms to apply to both parties.

Restrictions (sometimes NDAs also contain restrictive covenants)

- *Are there any restrictions?* If so, ensure that these are suitably limited in scope and time.
- *Do any restrictions cover 'pure' competition with the Discloser in any aspect of business?* If so, such restrictions should be firmly deleted.
- *Do any restrictions prevent the Recipient recruiting staff from the Discloser?* If so, the restrictions should be limited to staff actually involved in the Purpose.
- *Are any such restrictions limited to non-solicitation?* If so, the Recipient may wish to 'carve out' an exception for staff responding to a general advert placed by the Recipient.

Try to renegotiate any restrictions preventing the Recipient actually *employing* any of the Provider's staff at all, as there are many reasons why staff might want to move.

See also the section on 'Employee restrictive covenants' below.

FORMS OF NDA

There is a danger sometimes that NDAs become too complex, taking days to negotiate and often getting matters off to a bad start. There is much therefore to be said for a shorter-form document concentrating on the main issues (on the 90:10 rule basis). Two alternative examples are set out below, the former being shorter, but the latter also being concise. Each concentrates on different aspects, and neither has all the provisions of the other, so it would pay to consider which is likely to be more appropriate to the particular case. As elsewhere, square brackets are used to denote variable or optional text.

A sample short-form confidentiality letter

[Date]
Dear [Name]

RE [Outline details of what is disclosed]

1. In consideration of [A Ltd] (**A/we/our/us**) providing to [insert name of company] (**you/your**) certain confidential information (**Confidential Information**) in

connection with [description of the purpose, e.g. investigation with a view to a joint project] (**Purpose**) you undertake with us as follows:

   a)   you will keep all parts of the Confidential Information (which in this letter includes any extract, summary, analysis, compilation, study, data or documents you prepare derived from such Confidential Information) secure and confidential;

   b)   you will not make any copies of or otherwise disclose in any way the Confidential Information or any part of it [except for the Purpose and will use any copies so made only for the Purpose];

   c)   you will not permit any person to be shown any part of the Confidential Information or given any information relating to it other than the individuals whose names have been notified in writing to us, [whom we have first approved in writing to receive the information] and who have been made fully aware of the confidentiality and the terms of this undertaking.

2.   The terms of the above undertaking do not prevent your disclosure of any part of the Confidential Information as may be strictly required by law, provided that you first notify us (so far as the law allows) and give us the opportunity to take such action to resist disclosure as we may be advised.

3.   If we suffer or are likely to suffer material financial loss from your breach of this agreement, you understand that we may seek compensation for any loss or damage caused to us together with all costs and expenses which we may incur as a result of your breach of this undertaking and, if appropriate, a court injunction to prevent any or further breach of this undertaking.

4.   You will if and when so requested, return to us all Confidential Information (including copies) supplied to or held by you and remove from access by any person all such items as are held by you in electronic or other non-written form.

5.   Any amendments to this letter are to be effective only if in writing and signed on behalf of both you and us.

6.   This letter is subject to the laws of England and Wales and the exclusive jurisdiction of the English High Court.

Please confirm your acceptance of these conditions by returning a countersigned copy of this letter to me.

Yours sincerely
[Signed and countersigned for and on behalf of each party]

An alternative form

[Date]
Dear Sirs,

A Limited (**A**, **we** or **our**) has at the request of B Limited (**B**, **you** or **your**) agreed to supply you with certain confidential information (**Confidential Information**) relating to aspects of our business (**Business**) in connection with your wish to consider such information to evaluate (**Purpose**) [e.g. a potential joint venture/outsourcing agreement relating to …] (**Transaction**) on and subject to the following terms:

1. Undertakings

In consideration of receiving the Confidential Information, you undertake with us as follows:

1.1   to keep the Confidential Information confidential including, without limitation, exercising no lesser degree of security and care over it than you would apply to your own confidential information and keeping all documents and other materials containing any Confidential Information separate from all your other documents and materials;

1.2   not to use the Confidential Information except for the Purpose;

1.3   not directly or indirectly to disclose the Confidential Information or any part of it to any person or third party and to use your [best/reasonable] endeavours to [seek to] prevent any such disclosure except as may be permitted under clause 2;

1.4   inform us immediately if you become aware that any other person or party not authorized to receive it has become aware of any Confidential Information;

1.5   not to disclose, without our prior written consent, that the Confidential Information has been made available to you, or that we have entered into discussions with you in connection with the Transaction.

2. Disclosure

2.1   You may disclose the Confidential Information only as follows:

    2.1.1 with our prior written consent;

    2.1.2 to your directors, employees and professional advisers to the extent that they reasonably require such disclosure for the Purpose;

    2.1.3 to the extent that the Confidential Information becomes public through no fault of yours or anyone acquiring it from you or (so far as you are aware) the default of any other person; or

    2.1.4 where disclosure is required by law, by a court of competent jurisdiction or by another appropriate governmental or regulatory body, provided that before doing so you will, so far as permitted by law, give us reasonable advance notice of such intended disclosure.

2.2   You will [use your best/reasonable endeavours to] ensure that any person to whom you disclose any Confidential Information under clauses 2.1.1 and 2.1.2 complies with the terms of this letter as if such person were a signatory to this letter.

3. Term and termination

3.1   This letter will take immediate effect and continue in full force until completion of the Transaction, or, if the Transaction is not completed, until two years from the date of this letter.

3.3   As soon as practicable following receipt of a written request from us you will destroy the Confidential Information (and all documents or material incorporating or referring to the Purpose or any Confidential Information) in your possession or that of any person receiving it from you by confidential shredding or similar means or, to the extent practicable in relation to information held electronically, by permanently erasing it, and will provide us with written confirmation that this has been done.

3.4   This letter sets out our entire agreement and supersedes any other arrangements, understandings or previous agreements relating to the Confidential Information.

3.5   Neither this letter nor the supply of Confidential Information constitute an offer and do not impose any obligation on either party to continue discussions or negotiations with the other in connection with the Transaction.

3.6   We accept no liability to you or to any person to whom you disclose any Confidential Information and make no representation or warranty as to its accuracy or completeness.

This letter is governed by English law and the parties submit to the exclusive jurisdiction of the courts of England and Wales.

Yours faithfully,
[Signed and countersigned for and on behalf of each party]

Employee Restrictive Covenants

This is a complex and continually changing area of law belonging in fact to the field of employment law, but one worth mentioning in passing because of its relevance to confidentiality. Whilst English law generally dislikes restricting someone from pursuing legitimate job opportunities, the courts recognize that there are circumstances where sensible restraints are appropriate to protect the existing or previous employer. The acid test is whether the employee has confidential information that could be of benefit to the new employer, the disclosure of which could be detrimental to the old. The basic concept is that:

a)   the old/current employer must have a legitimate business interest to be protected; and

b)   the employee must be aware (on a reasonable basis) that the information is confidential; and

c)   the restrictions must go no further than reasonably necessary to protect that legitimate business interest.

The law will imply only limited duties of confidentiality in circumstances where fair dealing requires it. Otherwise express clauses must be included within the contract. As stated above, they should go no further than is necessary to protect the business in question, and if they do go too far, they will be unenforceable. However, even in the absence of express restrictions, such acts as an employee handing over to a new employer customer lists developed in the ordinary course of the previous job and held on the old employer's computers is likely to be in breach of the employee's implied duty of confidentiality as well as in potential breach of copyright and, possibly, database rights. Of course, an express contract prohibition would make the old employer's case much easier!

The following questions therefore arise for businesses:

• Do your contracts contain confidentiality and non-competition clauses?

- When were these clauses last reviewed, and are they still suitable?
- How wide a geographical area (typically by radius, county or country) and extent of business (such as hairdressing, accountancy, welding equipment, manufacturer or as appropriate for the business to be protected) is restricted?
- How broad are the separate restrictions relating to existing customers and against canvassing?
- How long is the notice period and the restrictive covenant period, and is this long enough to protect you but no longer than is reasonably necessary?

Privacy

The right to respect for private and family life, commonly known as the right of privacy, was largely a twenty-first century addition to English law. The relevance to business is explored later, but it is worth noting here that not just the media, but any business dealing with information about people, including data, articles, photographs, films, video clips and other material featuring identifiable individuals, will need to have regard to both data protection and privacy laws. To put the subject into perspective, we should first review the Human Rights Act, especially its relationship to the right of free expression, and to note the rapid developments since its enactment.

THE HUMAN RIGHTS ACT 1998 (HRA)

The HRA came into force in the UK on 2 October 2000. It incorporated directly into UK law the European Convention on Human Rights and, as such, brought many European concepts into English law, leaving much to be decided by cases. The thrust of the HRA is that, when interpreting any question which has arisen regarding Convention rights, any UK court or tribunal must take into account the principles of the Convention and the decisions of the European Court of Human Rights (ECHR) and even opinions of the Commission. Further, all existing national legislation is to be construed, so far as practicable, to allow for Convention rights. It was soon accepted that the Convention rights had to be applied in all decided cases as well as in future legislation.

The main Convention rights that might arise in business dealings are:

- the right to liberty and security (art. 5)
- the right to a fair trial (art. 6)
- no punishment without law (art. 7)
- respect for an individual's 'private and family life, … home and … correspondence' (art. 8)
- freedom of thought, conscience and religion (art. 9)
- freedom of expression (art. 10)
- freedom of peaceful assembly (art. 11).

It follows that if any of these fundamental freedoms (as they are also known) is constrained, by contract or in the course of a business, that restraint is likely to be unlawful and unenforceable. That constraint or any breach of the right may in turn be actionable in damages and possibly by a court order to restrain further continuance.

HOW PROTECTION OF PRIVACY HAS DEVELOPED

Article 8 of the Convention (privacy) refers to a 'right to respect for ... private and family life'. Privacy is a two-sided coin. One side protects those parts of our lives that we don't want publicly exposed; the other prevents our looking closer into the private lives of others. This duality is at the heart of the balance between privacy and freedom of expression. The rush of prior cases from 2003 onwards – Princess Caroline (*Von Hannover* v, *Germany*), Naomi Campbell (*Campbell* v. *MGN*), the Hollywood Douglases (*Douglas* v. *Hello!*) and Loreena McKennit (*McKennit* v. *Ash*) – established two basic privacy principles. First, even in public, individuals are likely to have a 'reasonable expectation of privacy' in going about their private and family lives. Second, photographs are generally more invasive of privacy than words. Thus J.K. Rowling was able to defend her young son's privacy in mundane and public activities (*Murray* v. *Big Pictures (UK) Ltd*). These article 8 rights continue to be extended in cases such as the European Court of Human Rights decision in *Reklos* v, *Greece* (2009) where even the taking of a photograph of a newborn baby without the prior consent of his parents (and without any publication of the photo) was held to be a breach of the child's' privacy.

Max Mosley has prompted judicial clarification that even admitted sexual adventures are entitled to protection under article 8, if carried out in private between consenting adults in circumstances of express or implied confidentiality (*Mosley* v. *Group Newspapers Ltd (2008)*). Mosley believed that his success in the case came at too high a price and that the media should be compelled to notify individuals *before* private information is published about them. The Mosley judgment did not change the (new) law as such, but gave a major warning against publishing details that may titillate but which do not reveal matters of genuine public concern. Even where there may be an issue of public interest, the article 10 right of free expression is unlikely to extend to intimate details and even less likely to permit publication of intimate photographs.

Douglas v. *Hello!* (2007) was also a dispute between the two competitors, *OK!* and *Hello!* magazines and concerned the extent to which one could publish pictures obtained in breach of confidence as a 'spoiler' to the other. The various appeals, culminating in the House of Lords, also specifically establish that, although privacy is a human right, celebrities can sell their rights to private information (a form of 'publicity' right), and purchasers of those rights are entitled to legal protection from others abusing the privacy of that information. (See also 'Economic torts', p. 359 in Chapter 19.)

Privacy thus has a potentially wide-ranging ambit, affecting in particular new media and Internet exposure of people's private lives. The issue (touched on further in Chapter 16) needs to be kept closely in mind by any business handling or in any way exploiting the personal lives of anyone who wishes to keep their personal life private.

EQUALITY AND NON-DISCRIMINATION

Whilst not strictly a privacy issue in the conventional sense, equality and non-discrimination legislation is designed to protect the dignity and feelings of individuals in much the same way as article 8 protects their right to respect in relation to their private and family life. Business attention is specifically drawn in this context to section 46 of the Equality Act 2006, which states that it is unlawful for someone providing goods or services to the public to discriminate against a person seeking to obtain those goods or services by refusal to supply the same or similar services as supplied to others or on similar terms.

This prohibition especially relates to access to public premises, accommodation services, financial services, transport and professional services. There are limitations as to who can bring actions under the Act. This Act thus extends the range of previously existing anti-discrimination legislation to a very broad-based personal right, which needs to be kept in mind by all those in business.

The Data Protection Act 1998 (DPA)

The Data Protection Act 1998, as updated and with regulations made under it, applies to the collection and use of personal information. All UK-based businesses need to comply with it and should have a formal policy enshrining the data projection principles and how they apply in the relevant organization. Companies of any size should have one or more key employees trained in these principles and able to deal with issues arising. The DPA is likely to be relevant in making contracts and fulfilling many business contracts where personal information is or may be taken by a business. Website sales to consumers, for example, will inevitably involve obtaining and using personal information within the ambit of the DPA.

This section seeks to give guidance on some of the main areas for business. Further, regularly updated information can be found on the Information Commissioner's website at www.ico.gov.uk. The British Standards Institute (BSI) also publishes guides on the management of personal information (BSI 10012 – www.standardsuk.org) as do other organizations, such as the British Computer Society (www.bcs.org).

DPA – THE BASIC PRINCIPLES

The basic principles can be summarized by saying that the DPA:

- applies to all information relating to a living individual held or processed in or through some form of organized system, whether electronically or even manually (such as a card index system);
- gives those individuals certain rights in relation to that information – including the right to know what information is held about them – and insist that any errors are corrected;
- requires the business to submit a notification to the Information Commissioner's Office (ICO) as to the type of information it holds and/or processes.

Thus the DPA would probably not apply to a casual heaping together of information in a pile, whose secrets are known only to the person to whom they were sent (or their PA!).

SOME DATA PROTECTION DEFINITIONS

Inevitably the devil is in the detail, and one of the ironies of the DPA is its use of such abstract language that it effectively depersonalizes the very people it seeks to protect. Here are some of the key terms used in the application of the DPA:

- *Personal data* is data relating to a living individual who can be identified by reference to that data.

- *Data subject* is the living individual to whom the personal data relates.
- *Sensitive personal data* is information in relation to the individual (data subject) which relates to his or her: a) racial or ethnic origin, b) political opinions, c) religious beliefs, d) membership of a trade union, e) physical or mental health or condition, f) sexual life.
- *Processing* is wide-ranging, covering not just the obtaining of the data, but also any form of recording or holding it or carrying out any operation on it (such as organizing it into a system, changing or adapting it, consulting or using it, disclosing it or even restricting or destroying it).
- *Data controller* means the person or persons who decide how and why personal data is processed.

WHAT DATA IS COVERED BY THE DPA?

A 2009 ICO guide seeking to clarify what information is 'data' for DPA purposes ran to 25 pages of A4, but perhaps two main issues can be extracted:

- *Is the data processed automatically?* If so, it is probably within the Act. Most kinds of computer-entry or form-based system are likely to be an automated process for this purpose.
- *Is the data recorded as part of a filing system?* If so, is the filing structured or systematic? If so, it is likely to be within the DPA (although if the system is structured in some way other than through names or criteria of individuals, it is possible it may not be caught). There may also be particular issues with microfiche records and the storage of sound or image records.

THE EIGHT PRINCIPLES OF DATA PROTECTION

To avoid committing an offence under the DPA, any processing of personal data must comply with the following eight principles, being that the personal data is:

1. *obtained and processed fairly and lawfully* (and particularly with the consent of the data subject);
2. *held only for specified purposes* and processed only in a way that is compatible with that purpose;
3. *adequate and relevant but not excessive* in relation to the purpose for which the data is processed;
4. *accurate* and where necessary, *kept up-to-date*;
5. *held* for no longer than is necessary for the specified purpose;
6. *processed* in accordance with the data subject's DPA rights;
7. *protected* by appropriate 'technical and organisational measures' against unauthorized or unlawful processing and/or accidental loss or destruction;
8. *not transferred* outside the European Economic Area (EEA) unless the country or territory to which it is exported ensures an equally adequate level of protection.

BUSINESS USE OF PERSONAL DATA

Businesses supplying products to consumers will almost inevitably use personal data and may only do so for the purpose for which it was obtained – typically to process payments, handle/deliver orders and to contact customers where necessary. Thus the personal information should be limited to what is necessary to achieve this and only so long as the purpose continues (which might include a suitable period to cover any warranty issues or even product recall). Businesses will also tend to hold personal data on their employees (and possibly) external job applicants and should do so only to the extent and so long as is reasonably necessary.

Processing personal data is extremely widely defined and interpreted. Businesses should assume, unless they check and find to the contrary, that most uses of data can fall within the ambit of 'processing'. As mentioned earlier, even taking a photograph of a living person can be processing of personal data, quite apart from the implications for privacy rights under the Human Rights Act.

COLLECTING PERSONAL DATA FROM A WEBSITE

The key point for those operating websites is to ensure that individuals providing personal information know: a) the identity of the organization collecting the information; b) what this will be used for; and c) how this will be done fairly if the information will be shown to third parties. Privacy statements and policies are covered in more detail in Chapter 10 on consumer sales. There are also restrictions on using other aids, such as 'cookies', where these are linked to private individuals. The same applies, at least in theory, to IP (Internet Protocol) addresses. The ICO advises website operators to take care in this whole area, as putting an Internet address forward for one purpose does not imply that it can be used for other purposes. Information regarding children is especially sensitive, and the latest codes of practice on website dealings with children should be consulted where the products in question are directed at, or likely to appeal to, the under-18 age group.

SECURITY OF PERSONAL INFORMATION

As seen above, the data protection principles include taking proper measures to protect against loss of data, including higher standards, including possible password protection and encryption in the case of digitally-held information and need to know, and locked doors/drawers and higher-level training for physically-held information.

TRANSFERRING DATA

Customer data is a frequent issue in commercial contracts, including the extent to which this can be collected and made available to third parties. The DPA is not an automatic bar. Take the case of a franchisee required under the franchise agreement to make customer information available to its franchisor. This would constitute 'data processing' by the franchisee as 'data controller'. This was the situation in the case of *Grow with Us Limited* v. *Green Thumb (UK)* in 2006 and illustrates a perhaps not untypical situation. The franchisor wanted the information to monitor the business, but the franchisee had failed to provide it as required by the franchise agreement, later claiming that it was unable to comply because of the DPA. The court decided that the franchisee could have complied, but had in effect chosen not to do so, and should not be protected from its breach of contract.

The position becomes even more complex when a business seeks to transfer customer databases as a whole, such as when the business is sold or, indeed, for outsourcing purposes. The ICO issues useful guidance notes on the issue. Clearly, a key question is whether the individual's consent to the use and transfer of the data was obtained at the time the data was collected. If so, transfer is likely to be acceptable. If not, transfer may still be possible if:

- there is a legitimate business purpose; and
- the use by the transferee is the use to which the individual originally consented;
- the buyer of the database knows that this is the case and agrees not to exceed that use without the consent of the individual concerned; and
- the transferee notifies the individual of the transfer and the transferee's details;
- the transferee gives the individual the opportunity to opt out.

Whether express consent to transfer was obtained or not, the transferee should also delete any information which is not relevant to its proper business needs, in accordance with the DPA principles above. Of course, the parties must also notify the ICO with the appropriate details.

Transferring data abroad is subject to further safeguards, especially if the destination country is outside the similar DP regimes of the EU/EEA.

SUBJECT ACCESS REQUESTS

Individuals have the right to access DPA-protected personal data relating to them in the form of a written 'subject access request'. The business may charge a modest administrative fee (£10 is often used as a benchmark – both as a reasonable fee and a reasonable deterrent against frivolous requests) for each time information is requested. The information must then be supplied within 40 days. A subject access request may, of course, also be a forewarning that other issues or claims are in the offing.

COMPLIANCE

The DPA gives personal rights to those affected. Complaints can also be made to the ICO regarding failure to comply, and this can lead to enforcement action and, in some cases, criminal proceedings against a defaulting company and its officers personally.

PRIVACY AND ELECTRONIC COMMUNICATIONS REGULATIONS 2003

These regulations are an extension of the protection of personal data regime, designed to prevent unwanted 'spam' e-mails. The rules require an 'opt in' from a consumer before direct marketing e-mails can be sent. Even then the consumer must be given an opt-out option with subsequent communications. The sender of the e-mail must be made clear, and the consumer must be fully informed about any 'cookies' on the website.

DATA RETENTION (EC DIRECTIVE) REGULATIONS 2009

These regulations bring into force, from April 2009, the requirements of the EU Data Retention Directive of 2006, and actually increase and standardize data storage requirements in relation to Internet data as well as earlier fixed and mobile telephony. The intention is to facilitate investigation of crime, especially terrorism, but the regulations will mean that all affected businesses (though not providers to wholly private networks) will need to keep sufficient details for 12 months to identify the source, destination, time, date, duration and type of communication and equipment used, although not the content of the communication.

REGULATION OF INVESTIGATORY POWERS ACT 2000 (RIPA)

This Act was passed mainly to set out the rights of, and limitations on, various public or quasi-public bodies to exercise surveillance and intercept communications to members of the public, but also – in ss 1 and 2 – sets out some basic rules to outlaw any unauthorized interference with postal or telecoms services. It may become relevant when any kind of disruption or bugging of such services is or may be encountered from private individuals or organizations.

Freedom of Information Act 2000 (FOIA)

Although not strictly a personal right, this is the counterpart of consumer protection in the sense that it is designed to protect members of the public by making official dealings on their behalf transparent by being open to inspection. The provisions of this Act came into force in UK in 2005. Although the intent is to make available information held by public authorities, the wide definition of those authorities means that there is a good chance that information may also be held by them that would normally be regarded as related to private commercial dealings. Thus any contract that a business may have with any local authority or governmental entity, including outsourcing contracts and the like, is potentially subject to public scrutiny. The contract may well contain sensitive information as part of the invitation to tender or contractual process – for example, in relation to company results or staff terms of employment for employment transfer regulations TUPE purposes. As the Act extends to central and local authorities, schools, police, parish councils and many others, it pays for businesses to consider what information they actually need to give. The row over MPs' expenses in 2009, causing much embarrassment and several resignations, and which then spilled over into other public bodies, shows just what can happen when information thought to be private is suddenly released to public scrutiny following an FOIA request.

There are a huge number of exemptions under the FOIA (seven absolute and 17 qualified, according to the circumstances), but these are best not wholly relied on. The practical advice here is, first, to seek to limit the information given to the public authority at the outset so far as possible consistent with getting the job and getting the job done and, second, if a request is made under the FOIA, to require that you are given written notice of the request and the chance to redact (that is, remove from the copy supplied in answer to the request) sensitive commercial material. These provisions can usually be negotiated into the relevant contract. It is also worth noting that, because they are statutory requirements, the information would not be protected by an NDA.

Summary

There is a constant reassessment of what is public and what is private, especially at the interface between press freedom and individual entitlement to privacy and, although much is a matter of law, it is important for contracts to make it clear as to which party has responsibility for which actions, so that the law can be observed and liability for non-compliance duly allocated.

Confidentiality is implied in certain cases, but is best reinforced by appropriate written agreements so that it is clear what is to be regarded as confidential and how such information should be protected. These can include confidentiality clauses in fuller contracts and specific non-disclosure agreements (NDAs). The latter can come in many different forms and require careful consideration to preserve a sensible balance. This principle also applies to restrictive covenants that seek to prevent ex-employees from disclosing business secrets of their former employers.

Privacy is now a human right under English law in accordance with article 8 of the European Convention. Whilst the boundaries between personal privacy and the freedom of expression of others are now fairly clear, they continue to be challenged. The issues will affect many business agreements, especially anything with a media or communications element.

Data protection is, in many ways, a specific form of privacy right, which is now highly regulated. Since personal data is captured by many organizations for a range of purposes, an understanding of the law and what is permitted is important, as is clarity of responsibility for compliance between the parties to a contract.

Any of these issues, especially the publication of confidential business information, may in turn be affected by the disclosure requirements under the Freedom of Information Act.

6 *Dealing with Companies and Partnerships*

Introduction

When dealing with business contracts, the legal status of the businesses involved may well affect the operation of the contract – a point that is often overlooked. This chapter therefore explores some of the issues arising in this context.

Main Types of Business Organization

Business organizations can be divided into two types: unlimited liability and limited liability. Unlimited liability business set-ups typically comprise:

- sole traders – individual traders, such as *Ben Braby trading as Braby Business Machines*
- partnerships, such as *Ben and Eileen Braby trading as Braby Business Machines.*

  The main limited liability businesses are:

- limited liability partnerships, such as *Braby Business Machines LLP*
- private limited companies, such as *Braby Business Machines Limited*
- public limited companies, such as *Braby Business Machines PLC.*

UNLIMITED LIABILITY ORGANIZATIONS

Trading name

Sole traders, like John Smith, should enter into contracts as 'John Smith trading as John Smith Associates'. Small partnerships should ideally contract in a similar way, such as 'John and Jane Smith trading as Smith Associates', so that it is clear who the partners are. Many partnerships use just their trading name, such as 'Smith Associates'. In the absence of a central register of business names, a partnership must display on its business correspondence either the names of the partners or where their names may be obtained. With larger partnerships, such as professional firms, it is easier to supply a list of the names of partners on request.

Effect of unlimited liability

Sole traders and simple partnerships have unlimited liability for the debts and other obligations of their respective businesses. This means that, if the business becomes insolvent, the sole trader or partners are legally liable for all its unpaid debts. This could lead to loss of the home, especially where the debts of the firm are secured by a second mortgage, and/or personal bankruptcy of the business owners.

Joint and several liability

With a traditional partnership the partners are jointly and severally liable for the firm's debts and other liabilities, so that if one partner cannot pay their share, the others must do so. If it comes to it, a creditor can force just one of the partners to pay in full, leaving that partner to recover their due shares from the other partners. Unless there is a binding partnership agreement to the contrary, each partner is liable for an equal share of any losses. Because of the potential impact of these rules, especially in times of uncertainty, many businesses prefer to incorporate with some form of limited liability.

LIMITED LIABILITY COMPANIES

The principles

Limited liability companies initially derived from the wish to encourage investment by enabling those who provide business capital to limit their liability for losses in that business to the capital they put in, leaving the business to be run on their behalf by those with the knowledge and experience to do so. The former became the holders of shares or shareholders and the latter the directors of the business. As time went on, and capital became more freely available, more people started their own business, thus becoming shareholders and directors, and probably also employees, of their own company. These different roles overlap, but much of company and employment law preserves the distinction. The following principles stand at the heart of company law:

- Shareholders should not be personally liable for the defaults of directors.
- Shareholders' liability should be limited to their investments in shares.
- Creditors need to be protected from having their debts used to subsidize the company.
- Directors have high levels of responsibility to both shareholders and creditors.

Owner-managers

Even if the same persons are directors and shareholders, they owe a duty to themselves as shareholders and to all creditors; if there is a conflict between the two, the interests of creditors will normally come first when there is any material risk that all creditors might not be paid in full. One effect of this principle is that there is a sub-set of rules designed to ensure that shareholders may not reduce their capital in a company to the detriment of creditors. The onus falls on the directors to ensure that their duties are understood and properly balanced. This is explored further later in this chapter.

LIMITED LIABILITY PARTNERSHIP (LLP)

A hybrid

The limited liability partnership (LLP) is a hybrid, combining many of the benefits of a partnership with the limited liability of a company. LLPs, permissible in the UK since 2001, have the twin benefits of being taxed as a partnership and having the limited liability of a company. This has led to a major take-up of LLP status by accountants and solicitors, but in fact the model can work well for other businesses too. The Limited Liability Partnerships Act 2000 and Limited Liability Partnerships Regulations 2001 govern the legal position, but are very difficult to follow as they largely cross-refer to other legislation. This is made more complex by the consolidation of the old Companies Acts into the new 2006 Act, reinforced under the Limited Liability Partnerships (Application of Companies Act 2006) Regulations 2008 – a title which shows how complex things are.

Note also that a limited liability partnership is itself different from a limited partnership, which requires registration under the Limited Partnerships Act 1907. Under this Act there can be a partner whose liability is limited to a stated level of capital, but there must also be a general partner who manages the business and whose liability must be unlimited. The proposed (at the time of writing) Legislative Reform (Limited Partnerships) Order 2009 will clarify some of the registration processes.

LLP basics

LLPs are independent legal entities, like limited companies, able to enter into contracts and hold land in the same way as limited companies. The LLP must intend to make profits, which means that not-for-profit organizations are not eligible to hold this status. Incorporation as a LLP is simple. At least two 'members' (often referred to as 'partners'), must act as 'designated' members, with functions similar to those of a company secretary. Details of these and subsequent members must be lodged at Companies House (as with directors, but unlike partnerships). The LLP name must go through the same vetting process as a limited company, so cannot be identical to any limited company or other LLP name or be a 'sensitive' name (such as 'Royal' or as specified by Companies House from time to time). Like limited companies, each LLP has a unique incorporation number which does not change even if the LLP changes its name.

The need to file accounts

Incorporation with limited liability is seen as a privilege, and one of the costs for this is that 'true and fair view' accounts must be lodged at Companies House, much as with limited companies and subject to similar concessions. This means that LLP accounts can be inspected by those dealing with the firm. There are also potential sanctions against members who permit the LLP to carry on trading after insolvency becomes inevitable, but otherwise the capital regime for LLPs is very flexible, much more so than that of limited companies. Tax-wise, the LLP itself is not taxed as a separate entity. Instead, each member is taxed on their own share of profits (whether or not paid out). Individuals' shares of profit will generally be regarded as income generated on a self-employed basis, also meaning lower national insurance contributions than employment.

Joint and several liability avoided

As mentioned, the partners in a simple partnership are jointly and severally liable for its debts; LLP status means that only the assets of the LLP – and not those of its members – are at stake, provided the liability is only that of the LLP (and the LLP does not carry on trading when insolvent). LLP status does not necessarily prevent personal claims against its members or partners for negligence or breach of duty, even for work done in the name of the LLP, but a well-drafted set of terms of business should afford a good defence to any personal claim. The important issue is to make it clear that all business is done in the name of the firm, and any liability is that of the LLP and not its individual members.

No model constitution

There is no model or implied constitution for LLPs equivalent to the model constitution for private limited companies known as Table A. The LLP default position is limited and, akin to partnership default models, provides for each member to share profits/losses and capital equally, to participate in management, to approve new members or expulsions and to have no automatic right to remuneration. It is therefore highly advisable to have a written agreement between the members, setting out how these and other important issues are to be dealt with. It is even possible, by agreement of all founding members, to exclude the 'unfair prejudice' protections enshrined in company law, but which limited companies themselves cannot exclude. This may be a very useful concession when senior employees are awarded small stakes in the business.

NOT-FOR-PROFIT ORGANIZATIONS

From time to time, businesses will deal with other organizations such as charities, sports clubs, residents' companies or other associations that do not seek to make a profit. Official charities will also be registered with the Charity Commission, which requires their constitution to follow a model form or otherwise be approved. Where charities have a trading arm, this will usually be in the form of a private limited company which covenants its profits to the charity. The charity itself will often be a company limited by guarantee. This means that, instead of having members receiving shares in the company, each member undertakes to pay (that is, guarantee) a nominal sum (£1 or £10) towards the assets of the company if it is wound up. The charity trustees are often its effective board of directors, each of whom has the same responsibility as other company directors. As when dealing with any other form of business organization, it is important for those dealing with such organizations to be clear as to precisely what and whom they are dealing with, and to appreciate that there may be limited redress if the organization cannot pay its debts.

Companies and Contracts

COMPANY NAME AND NUMBER

Use of correct name

Companies should enter into contracts in their full and correct name as registered with the Registrar of Companies. If the name is incorrect, the company may not be bound by the contract. As with other signatories, the person signing for the company gives an implied warranty of their authority to commit the company to the contract, leaving the signatory personally liable on the contract if this is found not to be binding on the company. Similarly, a director who signs a cheque on behalf of a company where the company name is missing from the cheque can be obliged to honour it. This stems from the long-held concept that limited liability status is a privilege and is not to be implied.

Change of name

Provided they are not planning to use a prohibited name (see the Company and Business Names (Miscellaneous Provisions) Regulations 2009), companies can change their names very simply by a special resolution (75 per cent of the shareholders with due notice) and filing at Companies House. It cannot therefore be assumed that the company with which you have traded for many years under the same name is necessarily the same company that it has always been. The only thing that does not change is the company number, which remains constant throughout the company's life.

Company searches

What precautions should therefore be taken to check that you have the right name and to guard against name changes? The best course is:

1. Always check the name of any company you are dealing with against the formal records at Companies House (available on line at www.companieshouse.gov.uk).
2. Check that the name is correct and that there is no record of any recent change to the name.
3. Add reference to the company number to the details of the company on the contract.

   The *creditworthiness of a company* is also critical, whatever the apparent trappings of success – the flash cars may be on lease or just a sign of past profits not being invested in the business. Various searches and enquiries can be made. Credit reference agencies will normally have an up-to-date picture, as will trade debt insurers. Accounts for a private limited liability company or LLP should be filed at Companies House within nine months of the accounting year end (earlier for PLCs). The failure to file might alone give rise to questions. Although even filed accounts are often considerably out-of-date by the time they are filed, they do give an idea of the recent financial structure of the business, especially its underlying profitability, the level of reinvestment in capital, its current assets/liabilities ratio and the possible level of reliance on short-term funding. More recent management accounts can be requested.

CONTRACTS WITH GROUP COMPANIES

The principles

A company may form a subsidiary for various reasons, such as to carry on a different business, to acquire another company, or to give minority shareholders a small stake in a discrete part of the business. The first step is to check whether you are dealing with the top company or a subsidiary. In principle, the subsidiary, if duly incorporated as a separate company, will have its own limited liability. If the subsidiary incurs liabilities it cannot pay, its own limited liability could form an effective firewall to protect its holding company. Holding companies are not automatically liable for the debts of their subsidiaries, but they may undertake that liability if they expressly guarantee the subsidiary or act in such a controlling way over them as to be held to be a 'shadow director' of the subsidiary. Very often, as becomes all too apparent at times of crisis, there turn out to be cross-guarantees to the bank which might force the holding (or 'parent') company to pay the debts of the subsidiary or vice versa. This usually means that the bank comes first, but it could also bring down a healthy company if part of the same group gets into financial difficulties.

Practical steps

Here are some points to consider:

- Make certain that you know which company you are actually dealing with, especially if there is a late switch to what may be a newly formed subsidiary with no assets.
- Seek a parent company guarantee (it is rarely offered easily) or have a major contract taken in the name of the parent company, even if carried out through its subsidiary.
- Clarify intra-group trading liabilities or obligations – or even practices – where these might affect the ability of the trading subsidiary to fulfil its commitments.

Group company benefits from the contract may be important. For example, with a technology contract, such as a new software system, the acquiring company may want the system to be rolled out across the whole of its group. This needs to be expressly stated in the contract, as should the right to enforce the contract directly against the service provider via a suitable third-party rights clause. Groups also occasionally revise their structures for perfectly proper business reasons. Many contracts therefore permit a transfer or assignment of the contract to another company in the same group. In that case, however, it may be wise to insist that any transferee has at least equivalent financial strength to the company assigning the contract and to cover the change of control issue if that subsidiary later left the original group.

HOLDING AND SUBSIDIARY COMPANIES

'Holding company' and 'subsidiary' are both defined by s. 1159 of the Companies Act 2006, the main consolidating company law. There are three possible qualifications for the relationship: a) that the holding company holds a *majority of the votes* in the subsidiary; or b) that the holding company holds shares in and can appoint *a majority of the board* of directors of the subsidiary; or c) that the holding company holds shares in and is able, by virtue of an agreement with the other shareholders, to control a *majority of the voting rights* in the subsidiary. The subsidiary definition also covers a sub-subsidiary – that is, any company that is a subsidiary of an existing subsidiary. Section 1162 contains further definitions of 'parent and subsidiary undertakings', which go much further than holding company and subsidiary and need cross-references to schedules to the Act. Although 'group' and/or 'holding/subsidiary company' should be defined where those terms are used, for the most part the s.1162 'undertakings' terms are relevant only for accounting purposes and are best avoided in most business contracts.

TAKEOVERS – AND HOW THEY AFFECT CONTRACTS

A takeover is the purchase of enough shares in a company to give control, either directly through shareholder votes on major issues or indirectly by appointing more than half the board (and perhaps voting out any who dare to disagree). There are certain forms of legal protection for minority shareholders, but in practice there is little a minority can do against a powerful controlling shareholder who obeys company law, but steers the company in a new direction. That new direction may even involve a fundamental change in the business, or it may involve a closer working relationship with an entire new group of companies. A takeover may therefore take a company out of one group and into another group, whose agenda and business methods may be wholly different. That may, in turn, be offensive or threatening to another party to the contract, especially if, for example, the acquiring group is, or contains, a direct competitor. This change would arise automatically on the takeover and is not covered by a restriction on assignment. The other party to the contract will therefore have no redress unless there is a change of control clause which gives the 'innocent' party the right to terminate the contract if control of the other passes to a third party.

The definition of 'control' should ideally be flexible enough to reflect the different forms of control in the s.1159 definitions mentioned in the previous section, including a) shareholding control or b) control of the board. With quoted public companies, a 30 per cent – or even lower – shareholding can give effective control. The change of control clause used in several templates in this book is similar in scope but broader in language, partly to avoid reference back to statutory definitions.

Financial Guarantees and Alternatives

The general rule is that shareholders and directors do not have personal liability for the financial defaults of their companies. There are exceptions to this principle, such as certain cases where a director has acted entirely outside appropriate powers or has been personally negligent or whose company becomes insolvent (see below). But, in principle, if a third party wants a holding company or a director to back up a limited company's obligations, the third party needs a guarantee from the holding company or one or more directors, as appropriate.

Personal guarantees and holding company guarantees do, however, need to be treated very cautiously by those asked to give them. They expose the guarantor to potentially unlimited liability, thus effectively undoing the benefit of limited liability in respect of the specific third-party beneficiary of the guarantee. The argument may be that the guarantee 'concentrates the mind' of the guarantor, but it may also give the beneficiary a nuclear weapon that could blow away the guarantor's total assets. If given, therefore, guarantees should ideally be limited to a predetermined maximum amount that would make it painful for the guarantor, but would leave them still in business and with a roof over their heads. Mistaken optimism should not encourage businesspeople to prejudice their own, their company's or their family's future if there is any other viable way forward.

A sample side letter of guarantee might read along the following lines:

To: [relevant third party]

Subject as below, in return for your agreeing, at my request, to enter into an agreement (**Contract**) with my company, X Ltd, (**Company**) in relation to [broad summary of the products/services to be provided – or effective wording to forestall recovery or insolvency action for a current specific debt], I personally undertake and guarantee to you as follows:

1. the Company will strictly observe and perform all the terms of the Contract;
2. if the Company fails to do so, I will personally pay all sums due under the Contract and observe and perform all the terms of the Contract as if I had entered into the Contract in place of the Company.

This guarantee is payable on demand following failure by the Company to pay on time and you will have no obligation to take legal or other action first against the Company. I agree that any extra time or leniency you give me or the Company in insisting on performance of the obligations or other terms of the Contract, any delay in your enforcing any of the terms of the Contract or any variation of the terms of the Contract you agree with the Company will not release or affect any of my obligations under this guarantee.

[Finally, I confirm that my liability under this guarantee will not exceed whichever is the lesser of the liability of the Company under the Contract or [£…].]

Signed and delivered as a deed
by [guarantor]
in the presence of
[witness signature] ....
[witness full name and address]...….…

NOTES

1. A holding company would obviously vary the wording as appropriate.
2. The guarantee is best signed as a deed.
3. The second paragraph is advisable for two reasons. The first sentence avoids the (rather pointless in practice) need for the beneficiary of the guarantee to sue the

debtor company before pursuing the guarantor. The second sentence avoids the principle that guarantors should be responsible only for the deal they agreed to guarantee. In the absence of this wording, the guarantee would be wholly released if there was a variation of the contract or in the amount owed not countersigned by the guarantor.

4. The first part of the final paragraph may be necessary if the company's liability is limited in some way under the main contract, since, without this wording, the individual may be opening themselves up to a liability greater than their company has. The second part seeks to put an overall maximum on the amount of the guarantee, which aims, on this wording, to cap liability also for costs and interest.

5. There are major risks for guarantors, especially if they ever lose control of the debtor company. Ideally, the guarantor would want to include a term limiting the guarantee to the period when the guarantor controls the debtor, but the creditor is unlikely to accept this. An alternative approach is to seek the express right to release on providing a suitable substitute guarantor no less able to cover the amount of the debt. Either way, if the company is taken over, the guarantor should remember to insist that the purchaser takes on the liability and provides a substitute guarantee, although, unless there is a requirement to that effect in the guarantee, the creditor is not bound to accept a substitute.

6. The law on the subject can be complex. This section concentrates on some key aspects, but many guarantees have much lengthier provisions, and specialist advice should be taken.

7. *A letter of comfort* is a possible alternative. This is something less than a direct guarantee, but to avoid being a guarantee, it must be worded in a way that the party receiving it is not induced to rely on it as a binding obligation. To achieve that, it is advisable that the letter states expressly that it is not to be regarded as legally binding. It should therefore be carefully worded, geared to statements of broad intention at best, and legally vetted. If the letter does turn out to be binding and the terms are broken, the claim will be for damages for breach of contract, which, as a result of the calculation of damages rules, may be different from the amount 'guaranteed'.

A letter of intent is a variant where the letter is intended only to set out the outlines of a possible transaction. There will normally be an express statement that the letter is not binding except in relation to two or three provisions, being: a) an exclusivity or 'lock-out' period (the precise period of which must be specified) to enable negotiations to proceed between the two parties without other bids; b) confidentiality in relation to the negotiations and all data passing between the parties; and c) the costs incurred in any investigation of the project if the lock-out agreement is broken. These provisions will have legal effect but the rest of the terms will not, as they are intended to result in a full contract if all goes well.

Directors' Duties

Directors run the company on behalf of the shareholders/members and are taken to have general authority to make contracts on behalf of their companies. There are, however, some difficult areas where it pays third parties dealing with a director to act more cautiously. These areas are now considered in brief, concentrating on issues that may have an impact on the validity or enforceability of business contracts, rather than matters of pure company or securities law.

DIRECTORS' DUTIES – THE OUTLINES

Directors' primary responsibility is to the company they serve and, through the company itself, its shareholders. Even if a director is appointed to represent a particular section of shareholders, such as a financial investor or joint venture partner, the responsibility is owed first and foremost to the company itself. This inherent conflict is one which a company director must always recognize and deal with. Similar considerations apply if a director puts a personal interest ahead of the interest of the company.

The Companies Act 2006 consolidates the law, with over 1,000 sections and 16 schedules, and a new statutory code for directors. In essence, all directors have the duty to:

- act within their individual powers in accordance with the company's constitution
- act in good faith to promote the success of the company
- exercise independent judgement
- exercise reasonable care, skill and diligence
- avoid conflicts of interest
- not accept third-party benefits
- declare any personal interest in transactions with the company.

Members' approval is required, by way of formal resolution, to certain proposed transactions. This is because of directors' 'fiduciary' duty to act honestly and in good faith, which requires them to avoid, or deal fairly and openly with, any conflict which might arise between their own interests and those of the company (and to deal fairly between shareholders). Members' approval may be required where the director or a close associate (family or business) plans to enter into a 'substantial property transaction' with the company (buying or selling) or some other arrangement funded by or financially linked to the company or its assets. The broad test is whether the director has some personal involvement, which means that the company, its assets, other members or creditors, *could* be put at risk as a result.

All directors have these duties, whether executive or non-executive, as does a 'shadow' director, being anyone who is used to having a major influence on the activities and direction of the company. In technical terms, this is a person in 'accordance with whose directions or instructions the directors of the company are accustomed to act' (s. 251, Companies Act 2006), even if not formally appointed to the board. A major, but unseen backer or even a holding company might be held to be a shadow director and be as liable as the directors duly appointed to the board.

DIRECTORS' DEALINGS – THE EFFECT ON CONTRACTS

The principles

Why does this matter to other parties to a contract? A third party dealing in good faith with the company may generally assume that the directors are duly authorized to commit the company to the contract in question, but, occasionally, breach of the director's obligations can cause the transaction itself to be set aside. So it pays to be aware of anything that might be untoward.

Diverting business and secret profits

Difficulties can arise when directors use, for their own benefit, opportunities that first become available to them in their capacity as directors of their company. This may be 'inside' knowledge enabling them to make a 'secret profit' that is really due to the company. Assume that a trader has habitually dealt with company A. If the director with whom the trader normally deals suddenly switches the deal to company B, it pays to question why. If company B is not in the same group of companies as A or has a different ownership structure to company A, this may be an improper diversion for personal gain. If the trader goes ahead, the law is unlikely to rescue the trader from a bad bargain. The director may be liable for any loss caused, but that could be cold comfort.

Anticipating insolvency

This can be another problem area if a company is potentially insolvent at the time of a transaction or becomes insolvent shortly afterwards. Where a company sells an asset for materially less than its market value at the time, even in return for some other less tangible benefit, the transaction can, in some circumstances, be set aside if the company goes into insolvent liquidation shortly afterwards. Third parties should therefore be on heightened alert where there is evidence that the company may be in financial difficulty. A deal that looks too good to be true may be too bad to be enforced. In all these cases specialist professional advice should be taken in good time.

Good faith dealings

The law tries to protect third parties dealing honestly with the company, so that they are not prejudiced by the misbehaviour of the directors they deal with. If, for example, the transaction is one for which shareholders' approval should have been, but was not, obtained, the company's ability to have the transaction set aside may be defeated by a contractual third party able to prove that they acted in good faith, for value and without notice of the director's breach of duty. But if you become aware of something underhand, this could make you complicit and defeat the entitlement to protection if things go wrong. Third parties dealing with a company director therefore need to take care that they are selling or acquiring something for value and in good faith and without notice of any wrongdoing. Either way, the defaulting director (and any person 'connected' with the director) may have to both account to the company for any benefit received and indemnify the company against any loss resulting from the transaction. The message is therefore clear. If you acquire something of value from a company without paying a reasonable price, or are aware of any bad faith or failure to obtain shareholders' approval when necessary, you risk having the arrangement set aside and perhaps of having to indemnify the company for its loss.

Abuse of powers

In a similar vein, if directors enter into a transaction which is not for the benefit of their company – for example, if the assets or financial strength of one company are used to support another company or individual without material benefit to the first company – they may be acting outside their powers such that the transaction could be set aside. Failure of directors to satisfy themselves that a planned action is in the company's interests risks their incurring personal liability for breach of fiduciary duty. Again, third parties are generally protected unless they knew, or ought to have known, that the transaction was beyond the company's powers.

Directors' negligence

Directors may occasionally incur personal liability if they go beyond proper legal bounds in their actions. Such cases are rare, and the courts are reluctant to make directors personally liable in negligence where their actions are carried out in the normal course of their work for a company. The House of Lords decision in *Williams* v. *Natural Life Health Foods* (1998), for example, re-emphasized that directors will generally only be held liable for the negligence of their company if they expressly and personally accept responsibility and the other party relies on them personally. This decision was considered by the Court of Appeal in *MCA Records* v. *Charly Records (No. 5)* in 2001 concerning a director who had acted outside the proper company processes by deliberately permitting copyright infringements. On this occasion a claim against the director responsible in deceit, rather than negligence, did succeed because the director's action was wilful and not just careless.

Lifting the 'corporate veil'

There are also some, very rare, occasions when the law will step in to save an innocent party from exploitation where a wrongdoer deliberately uses a company with no assets to carry out a wrongful act, leaving the innocent party with a claim against a worthless company. In these rare cases the courts have the power – rather fancifully named 'lifting the corporate veil' – to look at the person behind the scenes who is really creating the problems. This will generally only apply if there is evidence of fraudulent intent from the outset. For example, in *Trustor AB* v. *Smallbone and others (No. 1)* (2001), a director was found jointly and severally liable with his sham company because there was a fraudulent intent and the transfers were a façade to conceal the true facts. Another example arose in the employment appeal tribunal case of *Millam* v. *The Print Factory* (2007) where a share transfer to a limited company was used as a device to try to defeat the legal rights of employees under the TUPE Regulations. These cases have, however, also emphasized that, in order to protect the fundamental principle that a company is separate from its members, the corporate veil will only be lifted in exceptional circumstances.

DIRECTORS' AND COMPANIES' CRIMINAL LIABILITY

Criminal liability may arise in several areas that affect contracts. First are areas such as health and safety at work, weights and measures, data protection, consumer protection, trade description, financial services and environmental health, where there may be absolute liability irrespective of awareness of the circumstances. These will be breaches of statutory duty on the part of the director, which will also give those affected by the breach potential personal claims against the delinquent director as a result. Second, some circumstances might amount to direct criminal negligence by the directors. This issue came to prominence in the inquiry into the 1987 Zeebrugge ferry disaster and then in the Lyme Bay canoeing disaster in 1993, where the company and its managing director were held criminally liable for the loss of life. Subsequent rail disaster cases highlighted the issue, but the law at that time needed evidence of a 'controlling mind' to find the company guilty. Eventually the Corporate Manslaughter and Corporate Homicide Act 2007 came into force in 2008 making an organization guilty of a criminal offence if the way in which 'senior managers' manage or organize its activities causes a person's death or there is gross breach of the organization's duty of care to that person. A senior manager is someone responsible for managing or making decisions about an organization's activities, and the organization must fall 'far below' expected standards. Juries will be asked to consider health and safety issues and any culture of non-compliance within the organization. Unlimited fines can be levied and could run into millions of pounds. The courts also have the weapon of ordering publicity on the issue – a direct threat to the company's reputation. Third, and the list is certainly not exhaustive, it looks likely that, following the publication of the Bribery Bill in 2009, there will be a new bribery law that will involve an corporate offence where companies or LLPs are negligent in failing to take adequate steps to prevent bribery by an employee or agent. This will effectively require proper awareness training in the same way as effectively now required by competition law (see Chapter 8). It seems likely that the new law will also hold directors and managers personally liable for bribery, and we might expect many more future business contracts to include clauses requiring that contractors have such policies in place.

The relevance of all this to contracts is that, where there is any element of personal risk, contracts should be clear as to who is responsible for what, especially where there may be joint responsibilities. Companies will need to train their staff to observe, and continue to reinforce, a proper safety culture. Two or more companies cannot easily share culture in this way, and it is suggested that health and safety responsibilities are unequivocally allocated and set out in any appropriate contract. These should be supported by an ongoing training commitment. It should also be noted that liability for death or personal injury cannot be excluded by contract, and indemnities against liability for death or personal injury are unenforceable. So the buck will stop with those who have, or should have had, the responsibility for the way in which the organization conducts its activities.

Insolvency

Failure to pay on time may be the first sign that a company is in trouble. The cheque may indeed be in the post, but if it consistently fails to arrive, further questions need to be asked. Some companies, of course, practise delayed payment as a form of profit enhancement, but in other cases either the rot will start more slowly or insolvency may occur suddenly as a domino effect when trading partners fail. This section looks at the different types of insolvency and how these may impact on contractual dealings. In most cases, insolvency will mean that the running of the company is ceded to an insolvency practitioner (IP), normally a qualified accountant specializing in insolvency work. The

IP will need to observe all appropriate insolvency rules and will be zealous about legal observance, since an IP licence is a valuable commodity.

TYPES OF CORPORATE INSOLVENCY

The main types of corporate insolvency are described below.

Receivership

Receiverships have become less common in recent years as the administration procedure (see below) has become more flexible and more widely used. An IP is appointed as 'receiver', typically under a bank charge. The receiver's job is to try to recover the debt due to the bank. If this can be achieved, the company is then handed back to the directors, who can continue to trade if they are able to. More often than not, once the receiver's job is done (and fees paid), the company is a shadow of its former self and goes straight into liquidation. Similar regimes can apply to LLPs but not to unincorporated partnerships, which do not have the ability to enter into fixed and floating charges over their assets – the forms of legal charge under which the right to appoint a receiver is normally granted. The equivalent for an individual is having a receiver appointed to specific assets, such as property rents, to ensure that these are paid to the holder of the relevant charge in priority to other creditors.

Administration

Administration is a halfway house, designed to give a company the chance of a rescue or, if this is not possible, a better and more controlled realization of its assets. An administrator can be appointed by the court, but in most cases will now be appointed on a resolution of the company itself. The directors, working with an insolvency practitioner, will need to show that its creditors are likely to be better off following an administration, which holds the creditors at bay to some extent while the administrator acts for the company to seek to achieve the approved administration plan for the benefit of all creditors, subject to overall supervision approved by the court. This may lead to a 'pre-pack' or other sale of the business or to its liquidation or, just occasionally, to a viable future.

Liquidation

Liquidation is the end of the road for a company. The business must cease immediately, and the liquidator has the job of collecting in the assets and paying creditors what may be left over. There are strict rules as to priority of payment, and most trading debts are within the general category of ordinary unsecured debts, typically receiving a payment of so many pence in the pound, if anything. There is a similar regime for LLPs and, in the case of an individual, the equivalent is bankruptcy.

Company voluntary arrangement (CVA)

As its name suggests, a CVA is a voluntary arrangement on the part of the company and its creditors. It is similar to an administration, except that the company needs to get support for a stated plan from (broadly) its secured creditors and at least 75 per cent (by value) of its unsecured creditors. If it can do so, the resulting 'arrangement' binds the other creditors. There is no formal transfer of powers by the directors here. The individual equivalent is the individual voluntary arrangement (IVA).

Voluntary liquidation

Voluntary liquidation may occur for entirely different reasons, and may be solvent or insolvent. A solvent liquidation may be used to reconstruct one or more companies, carrying across the assets and liabilities of the old business to the new company or companies. One procedure is, bizarrely, in accordance with the Insolvency Act, mainly to ensure that the interests of the company's creditors are not prejudiced by the reconstruction. This is why many clauses that provide for termination on liquidation, as opposed to insolvency, exclude (and should exclude) voluntary liquidation for the purposes of amalgamation or reconstruction.

INSOLVENCY CLAIMS

Very often when companies go down, creditors are left powerless and heavily out of pocket, vowing to look to the directors of the insolvent company instead. The most likely areas of claim, which are thus the areas that directors should take care to avoid, can be summarized as follows (the section numbers refer to the Insolvency Act 1986 as amended):

- *Wrongful trading* – trading and incurring or continuing liabilities past the point at which the company had no reasonable prospect of recovery and the directors then failed to take every step possible to protect creditors (s. 214).
- *Fraudulent trading* – deliberately trading with an intent to defraud creditors (very difficult to prove) (s. 213).
- *Preferences* – making payment or giving an advantage to one creditor at the expense of others and without clear commercial need (s. 239).
- *Sale of assets at an undervalue* – enabling the transaction to be set aside where the sale was on terms materially below market value, especially if the transaction was with another company or a person closely associated with the insolvent company or any of its directors (s. 238).

Aggrieved creditors should understand, however, that most of the claims that may be brought under the insolvency legislation are only available to a liquidator or other insolvency practitioner, and then only for the benefit of the company, so any proceeds are likely to be swallowed up by other creditors with larger or preferential claims. The fact that the defaulter may have to pay and/or be pursued by disqualification from acting as a director or manager of a company, for a period ranging from two to 15 years, may again be cold comfort.

THE EFFECT OF INSOLVENCY

Corporate revival

Although generally there is no coming back from liquidation, it is sometimes possible to restore a company to the register if assets or liabilities are only discovered later.

Dealing with the company after insolvency

This needs care. It's important to remember that the powers of the directors and managers with whom you are used to dealing may suddenly be removed. You should not to continue to deal with them once formal insolvency action takes place, at least not without the agreement of the receiver or administrator. Although liquidators do have the power to disclaim onerous contracts, which enables them to ignore the contract completely, they will try to turn to advantage any contract that has a clear value to the company in liquidation. The solvent party could therefore find itself with the liquidator taking the benefits of whatever was due at the date of insolvency and being left as an unsecured creditor for payments due to it. Alternatively, the liquidator might try to sell the benefit of the contract.

INSOLVENCY PROVISIONS IN CONTRACTS

Drafting considerations

For all these reasons, a suitable insolvency clause is often best expressed to operate immediately insolvency occurs (and some clauses actually seek to anticipate insolvency). This will not avoid the risk of bad debts but it will avoid your being forced to continue trading with an insolvent company – and the risk of the contract being sold on if there is no clause preventing assignment. A short-form clause might be:

> 3 *Either party may terminate this agreement at any time by serving written notice on the other party if the other party:*
> 3.1 *[breach provision; or]*
> 3.2 *becomes insolvent or unable to pay its debts as [and when] they fall due.*

Termination or the right to terminate?

This example gives the innocent party the right to terminate; other precedents provide for immediate termination. In practice, news of insolvency travels fast and you would probably want to exit any contract straight away. Occasionally, you might wish not to – for example, if you had made payment and were about to take delivery. In that case it would be far worse to terminate the contract, not get what you had paid for and hope to receive a few pence in the pound as unsecured creditor. Better to wait a little while and try to obtain what you had contracted to receive. An even worse outcome would be what you had paid for being sold to someone else because your contract had been terminated! Similar arguments might apply if you were the solvent supplier and your customer became insolvent, but you could not resell the goods to anyone else.

Defining insolvency

The above example does not define 'insolvent'. In practice, it will normally be very clear when there is insolvency. Inability to pay debts is a ground for winding up and is actually defined by s. 123 of the Insolvency Act 1986 (as amended). There are two commonly used tests, both of which are trickier than they look:

- Can the company pay its debts *as they fall due*? This is the test under s. 123(1)(e), but even the words 'as they fall due' bring problems, as the 2007 case of *Re Cheyne Finance plc* held. In that case, although the company had sufficient funds to pay its *current* debts as they fell due, there were known future obligations which, on its current cash flow projections, it would not be able to meet. It was therefore held to be insolvent under that sub-section. The addition of the words 'and when' (as in the example) may help, but equally it may need fuller provision if the issue could be in doubt.
- Another common test, under s. 123(2), is that a company is deemed unable to pay its debts if its assets are less than its liabilities, 'taking into account its contingent and prospective liabilities'. This does mean that a company may be deemed to be insolvent if its balance sheet is negative, even if only because it has made prudent reserves for liabilities or is being supported by its parent company, and even if it can easily pay its debts as they fall due.

The wording 'unable to pay its debts as they fall due' used in the sample clause above should be distinguished from the statutory 'inability to pay its debts', and in a longer insolvency clause it would be sensible expressly to exclude the ambit of s. 123(2) of the Act. Many contracts have much fuller provisions, some of which even try to treat some acts prior to formal insolvency or any form of unsatisfied judgment debt as evidence of insolvency. These clauses can be used oppressively in the hands of a party determined to bring pressure to bear.

An alternative short contract provision for UK contracts (s. 123 also covers Scotland and Northern Ireland) might be to use 'Insolvent' as a term separately defined as follows and refer only to s. 123(1) (thus avoiding the need to exclude s. 123(2) – but not the risks of s. 123(1)(e)), as follows:

'Insolvent *means unable to pay its debts within the terms of s. 123(1) Insolvency Act 1986.'*

RETENTION OF TITLE

The principle

The principle of retention of title (or ROT) is that, even when goods are sold and delivered, the legal title to those goods can be retained by the seller until the seller is paid by the buyer. A series of cases from the 1980s (*Clough Mill* v. *Martin*) through to the early 1990s established that such a clause in a contract for the sale of goods can be valid and effective since the Sale of Goods Act states that the parties can agree when title passes.

Types of ROT clause

There are two broad types of valid retention of title clause. The basic form states that title to the goods being sold under that contract is retained until those goods have been paid for in full. An extension of this clause was approved by the House of Lords decision in *Armour* v. *Thyssen* in 1991. This is known as an 'all monies' or 'current account' clause and provides that title is retained on the specific goods sold until payment of all amounts ('all monies') due from the debtor to the creditor have been paid in full. This type of clause has the great advantage that, in an ongoing trading relationship, the creditor does not have to identify each outstanding invoice to the specific goods covered by it. The creditor's ability to show what amounts are due and unpaid and which goods have been delivered is enough to start the claim.

The effect of resales

Of course, that is not the end of the matter. ROT clauses acknowledge that those buying goods on a trading account often resell them. Indeed, the resale is sometimes needed to pay for the purchase itself. Such clauses should therefore permit, or not seek to prevent, a resale of the goods by the buyer in the ordinary course of the buyer's business. All being well, the sub-purchaser who pays for the goods in good faith and would then take free from the original seller's retention of title claim. But attempts to latch the retention on to the proceeds of the sub-sale prove ineffective, unless, exceptionally, such an arrangement is documented as a legal charge and is registered against the debtor company. Since that will disturb any priority the debtor's bank might have, such arrangements, even if properly documented, prove impractical because the banks will then call in the company's credit and precipitate the crisis. However, there may be circumstances where the original seller's claim to retention will still apply even after resale, notably where the resale contains a further ROT clause (which means that the resale remains in law only an agreement for sale and not a concluded sale) or possibly a sale permitting the goods to be returned if unsold, for the same reason.

Drafting considerations

Three other points are worth making on ROT clauses:

- *Incorporation* – Basic contract law rules apply, so the ROT clause must be incorporated as a term before the contract is formed.
- *Speed* – Insolvency practitioners will need to be approached quickly and firmly with clear evidence of the ROT clause and how it was made a contract term. Even then, they will resist the claim if they can, but it will help creditors if the claim is clearly set out and their goods are still in their original packaging, clearly marked so as to be identifiable to the creditor claiming them.
- *Administration orders* – Prevent creditors from repossessing goods without the prior leave of the court, since the intent of the process is to have a form of moratorium.

Summary and Checklist

Think carefully through any corporate structures and related parties. In general, is it is safe to deal with a company acting through one or more of its directors, but care should be taken if there are any unusual circumstances, especially anything potentially to the company's detriment. For their part, directors should take care to ensure that they are acting lawfully, in accordance with company law and their company's constitution (and any shareholders' agreement), within their authority and in good faith.

- Take sensible steps to check the company you are dealing with by making a company search, checking the correct full name and company number.
- Before signing up, check again and also check that there are no insolvency notices registered.
- Use the company number if the contract is of any substance. Company names can be easily changed, but the company number remains constant.
- Consider the implications of the company being part of a group, what benefits should flow and what limitations should apply as a result.
- Consider the need for a third-party rights clause and a change of control clause (see Chapter 4).
- Check with your search that the person acting as a director has been registered as such.
- Where the transaction is at all unusual, not in the company's ordinary way of business or long-term, ask for evidence of its approval by the company's full board of directors. The board minutes, or an extract containing the relevant section signed by the chairman, should suffice.
- Take more care if there is anything unusual or suspicious about the transaction. It is generally better to risk an upset in diplomatic relations than to get caught out. Look out for cases where a director has a personal involvement or there is an obvious underpayment or a suggestion of hoodwinking or bypassing the board of directors.
- Double care is required if the company is having trouble paying its debts – you don't want to be forced to hand back property and be left with a worthless claim.
- Take specialist professional advice if in any doubt.
- If all seems fine, apart from making the basic checks, it's probably best to leave well alone. As the law stands, it may be better not to investigate further if there is nothing suspicious.
- If you are a company director, check that you do have authority to negotiate and sign the deal in question. Be sure that the board and, if necessary the shareholders, know exactly what is proposed, approves it and, if appropriate, that it is duly minuted, signed by the chairman and you have a copy.
- If you are the director negotiating a transaction in which you or a member of your family or a close business associate have, or may be likely to have, a personal interest or stand to gain, go to the board and disclose your position fully. If necessary, get the shareholders to approve it too. And have it all properly minuted.

CHAPTER 7

Risk, Exemption Clauses and Insurance

Introduction and outline – damages and recoverable losses – unfair contract terms – related contract clauses – insurance in relation to contract terms – negotiating exemption clauses – entire agreement clauses – some selected cases – summary and checklist

Introduction and Outline

Although everyone presumably enters into a contract hoping for the best, it has been estimated that 70 per cent of business contracts fail in some way, so the prospect of fall-out seems far greater than that of a harmonious conclusion. This chapter is about managing the financial fall-out.

The first question is to consider what contract terms cover the areas most likely to go wrong; the second is how the *risks* should be allocated, if indeed things do go wrong. The first issue is helped by a careful analysis of risk and the second by well-drafted obligations, setting out specifically who does what, when, how and for how much. The allocation of risk is then refined by provisions such as warranty, indemnity, limitation and exclusion and similar clauses. All these should be viewed as part of risk management.

Limitation and exclusion clauses are different types of exemption clause designed to avoid or limit liability for breach of contract. An exclusion clause, as implied, seeks to exclude liability, either generally or for specific risks, whereas an exemption clause accepts some liability, but limits that liability in some way. Some contracts may contain both, and, for convenience, references in this chapter to 'exemption' clauses include both unless otherwise indicated. Because such clauses can affect the primary obligations of the parties in the contract, a strong body of law has built up concerning them. To this has been added a series of regulations, mainly driven by the European 'fairness' concept. The courts can also look at linked clauses, such as indemnities and entire agreement clauses, which affect the contractual balance of risk on the basis that these may themselves operate as exemption clauses.

Insurance is part of managing risk. It may not always be available or at reasonable cost, and its impact on contractual obligations can be complex. For example, under the principle of *subrogation,* if one party accepts the obligation to compensate another for a loss and the party entitled to that compensation claims first against its insurers, the insurers will have the right to 'stand in the shoes' of its insured and claim direct against the party responsible. Subrogation gives the insurers similar rights to claim off the third party, either in contract or negligence, as the insured had.

It is often better to specify *obligations* more precisely than to leave these broad but with later limitations, because specific obligations are easier to define and there is always uncertainty as to how enforceable an exemption clause will be. To appreciate how damages for breach of contract are calculated and how exemption clauses may play out in court, some relevant case summaries are set out at the end of the chapter.

Damages and Recoverable Loss

Damages for breach of contract (see Chapter 19) are based on the cost of putting innocent parties in the position in which they would have been if the contract had been properly performed. In most contracts, damages are therefore likely to be the difference between the value of what the claimant *should have received* under the contract and what the claimant *actually received*, plus any extra costs incurred in the remedy process. This is putting the parties where they should have been, assuming all had gone to plan, and not back to where they were *before* the contract was created. Common law damages for breach of contract thus cover actual loss and expectation of loss or loss of the bargain contracted for. In contrast, damages for negligence are the amount necessary to compensate the innocent party for the loss suffered as a result of the negligence.

THE PRINCIPLES – HADLEY V. BAXENDALE (1854)

Hadley v. *Baxendale* dates from industrial England of 150 years ago, and the principles laid down the ground rules for the calculation of damages for breach of contract, which still hold good today. The contract was for the carriage of goods. The claimants were millers who contracted with carriers to deliver the millers' broken crankshaft to London for repair. The carriers delayed a few days, and the issue was whether the carriers were liable for the loss of profits suffered by the millers as a result. The millers had not stated, and the carriers did not know, that the millers had no replacement crankshaft ready and therefore were unable to continue milling until the broken shaft had been repaired and returned. In those circumstances, should the carriers be liable to the millers for the loss of profits that ensued from the carriers' delay?

The judgment is the basis of English law, and perhaps many other laws derived from it, that damages for breach of contract:

> *… should be such as may fairly and reasonably be considered either arising naturally i.e. according to the usual course of things, from such a breach itself, or such as may reasonably be supposed to have been in the contemplation of both parties, at the time they made the contract, as the probable result of the breach of it …. (Baron Alderson, Hadley at 354)*

Recoverable losses

There are thus two kinds of recoverable loss:

- losses that flows naturally from the breach, *and*
- losses that the parties to the contract might reasonably have expected to arise from breach, judged at the time the contract is made (and not with the benefit of hindsight).

Special circumstances

So what happens where the loss arises as a result of special circumstances, known to one but not the other party? Should the carriers in Hadley be liable for the loss arising from delay if they did not know that the millers could not operate without the repaired crankshaft? The judge decided on the evidence that the carriers did not know, and could not reasonably have anticipated, the millers' special circumstances and decided:

> It follows, therefore, that the loss of profits here cannot reasonably be considered such a consequence of the breach of contract as could have been fairly and reasonably contemplated by both the parties when they made this contract. (Baron Alderson, Hadley at 356)

This means that the party in breach must have actual or implied knowledge of those special circumstances if they are to be liable for the effects.

Variations to the test

The tests of directness and foreseeability have been expressed in slightly different words over the years, such as what a reasonable man should know to be the 'ordinary course of things' (*Victoria Laundry (Windsor)* v. *Newman Industries* (1949)) and 'what is within the reasonable contemplation of the parties' (Lord Morris, *Koufos (The Heron II)* (1969) at 425).

Loss of profits can be recovered, but only to the extent that the loss is *foreseeable* within the legal tests. Inevitably, each case has to be looked at on its own facts, both as to the circumstances at the time and the wording of the contract.

THE IMPLICATIONS OF HADLEY V. BAXENDALE FOR EXEMPTION CLAUSES

Hadley decided that damages are limited to losses which are;

a) *direct* – the natural result of the breach *or*
b) *foreseeable* – judged either objectively or subjectively.

Developing and applying those principles to the contract language:

* *Direct losses* are logically those arising or flowing directly and naturally from the breach without any intervening cause, within the first test of *Hadley*.
* *Indirect losses* do not flow directly and naturally from the breach. So, to be recoverable they must be *foreseeable*, either objectively or within the subjective test of special circumstances which were *actually known* or *should have been known* to the parties. So an exclusion of indirect loss, if it achieves its objective, should serve to exclude loss which does not flow directly from the breach. Self-evidently, indirect loss does not cover direct loss flowing naturally from the breach, and that is precisely where many exemption clauses fail.
* *Consequential losses* cause greater problems. Despite their name, they have been regarded by successive court decisions as *indirect* losses, unless clearly indicated

otherwise in the contract. This follows that part of the judgment in *Hadley* referring to losses that:

> ... *cannot reasonably be considered such a consequence of the breach of contract as could have been fairly and reasonably contemplated by both the parties when they made this contract. (Baron Alderson, Hadley, at 356)*

- *Special losses* suggest losses which were not direct but which might or might not have been in the minds of the parties at the time the contract was made, depending on whether they were aware of them. The millers' losses in *Hadley* were special losses, not known to, or reasonably foreseeable by, the carriers in that case and could not be recovered for that reason.
- *Irrecoverable losses* are those which the law will not enforce because they are deemed to be too remote or uncertain. They would fall outside the *Hadley* v. *Baxendale* test altogether.

Loss of profits therefore may be direct and/or indirect and objectively and/or subjectively foreseeable. Imagine a wholesaler unable to sell pre-ordered goods to a retailer because the manufacturer had failed to supply those goods to the wholesaler when agreed. The loss of the wholesaler's resale would probably be a *direct loss* (of the gross profit that the wholesaler would have made on that resale), because the wholesaler would be buying the goods for resale at a profit. The wholesaler would have to try to buy the goods elsewhere to reduce its loss which it is obliged to do (see 'Mitigation of loss', p. 356 in Chapter 19), in which case the damages would be the extra amount paid to secure those goods above the original manufacturer/wholesaler contract price.

Future loss of profits is a convenient name for the gross profits (normally after cost of goods and sale but before overheads that the trader would be incurring anyway) which the innocent party *might* have made from *future* dealings with another contract party. So, in the example above, if the wholesaler had told the manufacturer that he had a two-year exclusive agreement with the retailer to supply all the retailer's goods of that type, the manufacturer would be on notice of the potential effect of failure. Even then it is not automatic that a single failure by the wholesaler would be sufficient for the distributor's customer to want to end the agreement. So the wholesaler might have to show both that the manufacturer's breach was the real and the likely cause of the retailer's cancellation of its supply contract with the wholesaler's supply contract *and* how much business it lost with the retailer over the contract period (and at what levels of gross profit) as a result.

Economic loss is a term sometimes used as an alternative to future loss of profits or possibly loss of anticipated savings. The phrase is probably more relevant to damages for negligence, but the danger is that it is not clear what it might cover in relation to breach of contract. It is better therefore to refer to 'loss of profits' or similar wording.

Unfair Contract Terms

Because of the impact of these damages rules, many contracts seek to exclude or limit the loss that the innocent party can recover if things go wrong. In turn, the more extreme use of such exclusion and limitation clauses, leading to unfair results, has been curtailed by legislation.

UNFAIR TERMS LEGISLATION

The two main areas of legislation are the Unfair Contract Terms Act 1977 (UCTA), which is of general application, and the Unfair Terms in Consumer Contract Regulations 1999 (UTCCR), which are specifically for consumer transactions. UCTA is covered below.

The UTCCR go further than UCTA but only in the consumer field, reflecting European directives and in turn being extended by other consumer protection legislation. The main principle of the UTCCR is that a *consumer* is not bound by a *'standard term'* in a contract with a *supplier* if that term is *unfair*. The subject of consumer sales is dealt with in more detail in Chapter 10.

Future legislation may involve a review of UCTA and the UTCCR and their replacement by a single Act or to the UTCCR being consolidated with other consumer protection laws.

NON-EXCLUDABLE RISKS

Under UCTA the following cannot be excluded or limited in a contract:

- *liability for death or personal injury* resulting from that party's negligence – any attempt to exclude or limit this will be void, and may well be a criminal offence
- *implied warranty of title* – any exclusion will be ineffective in either a business or a consumer sale
- *implied warranty* as to compliance with description, quality, fitness and sample in consumer contracts
- *defective goods* in a consumer transaction by virtue of liability for defective goods in a consumer transaction by anything purporting to be a guarantee of those goods.

LIMITED EXEMPTIONS

Certain exclusions or limitations will only be valid *so far as regarded as reasonable* within the tests set out in UCTA. These are:

- terms implied by statute as to description, quality, fitness and sample in a business contract (wholly non-excludable in a consumer sale)
- liability for breach of contract (by the business supplier) where dealing with a consumer or dealing on the supplier's 'written standard terms of business'
- liability for negligence or failure to take reasonable care or exercise reasonable skill in the performance of the contract.

LIABILITY FOR FRAUD

It is now normal not to seek to exclude or limit liability for fraud or fraudulent action on the part of the breaching party or its employees.

THE UNFAIR CONTRACT TERMS ACT 1977 (UCTA)

UCTA was designed to counter excessive exemption clauses in sale of goods contracts. One guiding principle of the Act (in the cases of limited exemptions as mentioned above) is that, except so far as contract terms satisfy the standard of *reasonableness*, they *may not exclude or limit liability for one party's own breach* or permit a major departure from the obligations under the contract. This goes to the heart of what an exemption clause seeks to do. In fact, despite its name, UCTA is more concerned with the reasonableness of a term than its fairness. Even more confusingly, it is not limited to contract terms, but also covers negligence.

Sellers and unfair terms

In most cases, it is sellers who seek to rely on exemption clauses, although increasingly large buyers now 'call the shots' in insisting on their own (often one-sided) standard terms of business. UCTA can equally apply to them.

Standard terms

Where one party trades under its 'written standard terms of business', and those terms seek to limit or exclude liability for breach of contract or failure to perform its obligations, those terms will be subject to the reasonableness test below. The same principle also applies to consumer sales (irrespective of whether the terms are standard), but, with consumer transactions, the UTCCR tests will normally be tighter.

Reasonableness of exemption

What is reasonable is judged according to what the parties knew or ought to have known when they made the contract, each situation depending on its facts, but 'reasonableness' will have regard to:

- the alternatives open to the other party;
- the relative bargaining strength of the parties;
- whether the buyer received an 'inducement' to enter into the contract (such as a special price for a lower standard of liability); and
- the availability (or otherwise) of insurance for either party.

Exclusions

UCTA does not apply to contracts relating to:

- most international supply contracts
- insurance (being actual contracts of insurance)
- the transfer of land
- the creation or transfer or termination of certain intellectual property rights
- the formation or dissolution of companies
- the creation or transfer of any right or interest in securities.

Related Contract Clauses

Warranty and indemnity clauses affect responsibilities in contracts by creating liability where a party makes a false statement or a specified type of claim arises. Although not exemption clauses as such, these clauses may be subject to similar constraints to the extent that they shift the liability between the parties to the contract, especially in consumer contracts. Section 4 of UCTA specifically covers indemnity clauses in consumer transactions, applying the reasonableness test mentioned earlier to such provisions.

Entire agreement clauses are considered below.

Sole remedy clauses provide for a specific remedy, such as the return of the price or part of it, on the basis that this is the sole remedy of the relevant party against the other. This is effectively another form of exemption clause.

Force majeure clauses can also be exemption clauses, but should be reasonable and fair to the extent that they avoid a party being liable for breach of contract simply because they are unable to perform for reasons beyond their control. Force majeure should cover possible but unpredictable contingencies, but should not excuse the effects of mismanagement or predictable risks that could have been reasonably anticipated and prevented.

Insurance in Relation to Contract Terms

Insurance contracts are a specialist form of indemnity, as they compensate the party taking out the insurance (the *insured*) for all or part of the loss the insured may suffer if certain things happen (an *insured event*). This is a specialist legal area, so this section covers only some general points. In general, if an insured event occurs, and provided the insured has acted in good faith and strictly observed the policy terms, the insurer will pay for the loss suffered, subject to minimum and maximum levels of payment as below.

SOME POLICY TERMS

Excess/deductible

Policies almost inevitably require the insured to bear the first part of any loss, known as the self-insured excess or the deductible, meaning the amount insurers will deduct when paying out any claim. Likewise there will be a maximum that insurers will pay out for any one claim or perhaps over any one insurance period, specified in the policy terms, so there is no certainty that a huge claim will be fully covered by insurance. Insurance may also be on a 'claims arising' basis, being claims from events that occur in the policy year, or a 'claims notified' basis, being claims first notified during the policy year. It is vital to know which kind of policy you are dealing with and to notify insurers in sufficient detail immediately on becoming aware of a claim or events that might give rise to a claim.

Event

The policy wording as to what will trigger a claim will also vary. In one celebrated instance, the critical term was 'event'. The insurance in this case covered the twin towers of the World Trade Center in New York, infamously destroyed by terrorist-controlled planes.

The legal question was whether this was one event or two. The interpretation of that single word had a multi-billion-dollar price-tag attached to it.

Utmost good faith

Insurance is a relationship 'of the utmost good faith' (*uberrimae fidei* in Latin), which means not only that the proposal form must be faithfully completed, but also that any later material change in the position must be disclosed to insurers, failing which they may be able to disclaim liability. All these complexities do therefore mean that recovering losses from insurers is far from a foregone conclusion – a further factor to be borne in mind when negotiating the contract!

THE IMPACT OF INSURANCE ON CONTRACTS

Insurance review

It is clearly wise for every business to conduct periodic reviews of the business risks it is running and how far these are covered by insurance. Does the policy actually cover you for your own breach of contract? If not, you should try to limit the risk in the contract if the other party can more readily insure. If your policy does cover the risk, have you factored in the amount of the excess and how this relates to the levels in any exemption clause? How might the same principles apply to the other party?

Subrogation

This is the legal principle that the insurer can stand in the shoes of its insured and take legal action against a defaulting contract party in the insured's name. This is in fact why many cases come to court, since an innocent party may choose to claim against its insurance for the loss, rather than sue the other party. However, if it does so, the insurer may then claim that loss from the defaulting party. In such cases, insurers have little regard for future business relationships and will have funds and specialist advice to pursue a valid claim. So an exemption clause, if valid, may help against insurers too (see the *Ferryways* decision below).

Indemnities and insurance

What happens if the contract contains an express indemnity for certain events and the innocent party had insured against the event anyway? *Caledonia North Sea Ltd* v. *London Bridge Engineering* (2002) was a case arising out of the disaster on the Piper Alpha North Sea oil platform in 1988. The House of Lords decided that although the operator of the platform had recovered compensation from its insurers for the loss of its own staff, this did not release the contractor from the indemnity clause in the contract (enforceable by the insurers under subrogation principles). The contractor was bound to pay under the indemnity even though it would not have been liable at common law and even though the insurers had paid out to the deceased's estate. This decision is a reminder of why care should be taken with indemnity clauses, especially if there is no primary liability and the other party's risk may be adequately covered by insurance.

UNDERTAKING TO INSURE

Covenants to insure

Some contracts require a contracting party to take out and maintain suitable insurance to cover any contractual liability (and may even require the interest of the indemnified party to be noted on the policy). These requirements can be more onerous than they appear. Insurance is a market like any other; policies are normally negotiated on an annual basis, and there can be no certainty as to whether, or on what terms, renewal may be available. Insurers may also decline to note individual interests of contract parties on the policy. In addition,, insurance policies are normally confidential to the parties, so that the insurers' consent will be required for the policy terms to be disclosed. Whilst there are occasions when it is sensible to see that the other party is insured for the risks they are undertaking, it is difficult to see that failure to insure would cause any greater loss than the breach of contract which the insurance is designed to cover. Perhaps the better option is to have the right to see the policy cover and premium renewal receipt with an option to terminate the contract if this is not forthcoming or unsatisfactory.

Negotiating Exemption Clauses

Given these complexities and the number of failed attempts at exemption clauses, it would be rash to suggest any infallible wording on the subject. Nevertheless, and with suitable notes of caution, there are some suggested principles to improve the chances of success, and the clause that most closely observes the right principles is more likely to be accepted without litigation. When something does go wrong and the parties take legal advice, the commercial result often hangs on the strength or otherwise of the drafting.

Games players may liken the contractual allocation of risk to a game with several levels where one level has to be completed successfully in order to move on to the next. Failure at any level ends the game. And the game can, of course, be played both ways – by those seeking to enforce exemptions and by those seeking to overthrow them. This section seeks to apply the principles above to the game scenarios, followed by a piquant look at a few selected case summaries at the end of the chapter, which show the principles in operation and the complexity and unpredictability of playing the litigation game. And it is worth getting it right if you can. In one salutary case where exemption clauses were rejected under UCTA, damages of some £2.6 million were awarded (*Horace Holman Group Ltd* v. *Sherwood International Group Ltd* (2000))

LESSONS FROM THE COMMON LAW APPROACH TO RISK AND EXEMPTION CLAUSES

Is the exemption properly incorporated in the contract?

As explained in earlier chapters, a contract term applies only if it is properly incorporated in the contract in the first place. You cannot limit liability after the contract has been entered into.

Strict interpretation

An exclusion or exemption clause will be interpreted by the courts very strictly. This means that the clause must deal with the specific loss that arises. An exclusion of liability regarding, for example, defective design would not be regarded as covering defective workmanship.

Clauses construed against those seeking to rely on them

The courts will also tend to interpret exemption clauses against the party seeking to invoke them. This will often be the party who drafted the exemption in question (a principle known by the Latin maxim, *contra proferentem*).

Severance

If the contract so permits, the courts may cut out parts of a clause (under the 'blue-pencil' test) but will not rewrite it, and will regard the whole clause as void if it is too broad.

Blanket exemption clauses

These are more difficult to enforce, even in commercial contracts.

SUGGESTED GENERAL APPROACH

- *Speak up!* Don't be shy about discussing exemption and exclusion issues. They are likely to come up and significantly affect risk.
- *Be flexible.* Remember that dealings on unreasonable and unalterable standard terms are less likely to be upheld than negotiated terms.
- *Consider respective bargaining powers.* The more equal the bargaining power between the parties, the more the courts are likely to uphold the exemption. This includes whether the other party has a real choice, especially as to an alternative source of supply for an equivalent product or service. Can you offer a different level of risk at an alternative cost?
- *Be reasonable.* Trying to exclude all risks may cast doubt on your ability to perform and will be harder to enforce under UCTA. It is also more likely to create an adversarial position if something does go wrong. Be reasonable, too, on the level of any exemption.

TACTICS IN ALLOCATING RISK

Identify main risks

Consider the likely extent of loss you might suffer if the other party defaults (see Chapter 3 on risk in contract planning). For example, typical initial questions on risk in a technology contract might cover what loss might be caused by the following:

- a temporary breakdown or similar; or
- a complete failure of the system; or

- a complete failure of the system; or
- a loss of some data; or
- a systemic corruption of all or most data.

Risk management

If the situations listed above occurred, what would you do? What would you expect the other party to do? What reasonable immediate and foreseeable risks would the other party run if you fail to carry out your obligations with reasonable skill and care?

Special cases

If you have special circumstances, consider pointing them out in writing so that the other party is aware of them. You may be faced with an attempted exclusion or limitation clause, but at least you can focus on, and perhaps cover, the risk in some other way.

Allocating risks

Then decide who you think should bear which risks, and to what extent. Consider a reasonable limitation in respect of specific risks and an exclusion of others. Then discuss these and try to flush out what degree of risk each party should accept – often a matter for considerable negotiation! The conclusion should then be reflected in the contract.

Agreed damages

Consider a liquidated damages provision if the possible loss to you would be difficult to quantify. This might produce extra negotiation at the time, but it will make your claim less likely to falter if the worst happened.

The impact of insurance

The availability of insurance, the extent of, and limitations on, the cover and who bears the premium are all relevant to the existence or extent of any limitation on liability, as well as to the costs of the exercise.

DRAFTING CONSIDERATIONS

Define the obligations first

In the operative causes, set out clearly what you are going to do (or even what you will try to do, but are not committed to do) and what you are not going to do.

Obligations versus endeavours

If you can't be sure of your ability to do something, try to agree a 'best/reasonable endeavours' clause (see Chapter 4). But don't accept an endeavours clause if there should be an absolute obligation. Remember that it is much more difficult to show breach of an endeavours obligation than an absolute one, so build in some margin. For example, in a contract to build in accordance with agreed plans or specification, compliance with the plans or specifications is what matters, but the plans themselves must be right. If they aren't, whose responsibility will that be? Suppliers need to be cautious about commitments to achieve specific objectives, as ICL found to its cost in the *St Albans* case discussed in Chapter 3.

Precision

Be as precise as possible. For example, be precise about the nature of the risk limited.

Types of loss

There is no definitive list, but some issues to consider covering in your exemption clause are:

- *injury to people* (which can't be limited or excluded to the extent that the liability arises from the negligence of the party seeking the exemption)
- *damage to property*, such as:
  - buildings
  - plant and equipment
  - necessary rebuilding costs as a result (including legal and surveyor's fees)
  - disaster recovery costs
  - relocation costs in the event of serious damage
  - replacement systems and data recovery
  - staff costs
  - temporary staff hire
  - the cost of inability to reduce staff if redundancy had been planned.
- *wasted management time* (not always recoverable but there are precedents):
  - loss of profits
  - loss of immediate profits on current contracts
  - loss of revenue opportunities/future profits
  - loss of anticipated savings.

Consider which of these possible losses should be excluded and which limited, and how such a clause might satisfy the UCTA test of reasonableness.

Be careful about using words like 'including' and 'other'

In *Simkins Partnership* v. *Reeves Lund* (2003) the exclusion of 'any business or profits or any other consequential loss whatsoever or however arising' were held to exclude only indirect loss of profits because the words 'other consequential loss' indicated that only indirect loss of profits was to be excluded. Likewise, *in University of Keele* v. *Price Waterhouse* (2004), Price Waterhouse accepted liability for 'direct loss', but excluded all 'other liability, in particular consequential loss and failure to realise savings'. The reference to 'other' liability meant loss which was not direct, which Price Waterhouse accepted liability for. The court held on the facts here that the failure to realize the savings anticipated was a direct loss, for which Price Waterhouse accepted liability, even though loss of savings was specifically mentioned within the exclusions. These cases show just how hard courts will sometimes work to limit an exemption! The better approach in these cases would seem to have been to specify by name the risks accepted and those excluded, possibly in each case stated to be 'whether direct or indirect'.

Don't go too wide

It is better to include a severance clause and break the clause into more specific parts so that the court could delete (blue-pencil) just the void part and leave the rest standing.

Consequential loss does not mean losses arising in consequence of a breach, but is taken to mean indirect losses, which are recoverable only if known about. Exclusion of consequential loss thus excludes liability for indirect losses even if the supplier is aware of the risk! Reference to 'consequential loss' must now be suspect in consumer transactions as legalese, which the average consumer is unlikely to understand. For example, in 2008 the Financial Services Authority (FSA) in a statement opposing 'consequential loss' (and 'time of the essence') in FSA-regulated consumer contracts, suggested clear everyday terms (for example, in insurance contracts) such as:

- 'We will only pay costs which are incurred as a direct consequence of the event which led to the claim you are making under this policy' *or*
- 'We will not pay for any indirect losses, which result from the incident that caused you to claim. For example, replacing locks if you lose your keys.'

Limiting direct loss

A fair limitation on direct loss will depend on all the circumstances. Some suggestions are as follows:

- *Expertise* – If there is high expertise claimed and pricing to match, the buyer might reasonably insist that this is not diminished by excessive limitations of liability.
- *Value* – If the contract limits liability, for example by reference to the price being paid. Although lower levels are sometimes proposed, the contract value may be a reasonable starting-point, but each case should be looked at on its merits.
- *The availability and cost of insurance* is also relevant.

POSSIBLE OUTLINE OF A SUITABLE BASIC EXEMPTION CLAUSE

1. Exclude loss or damage, direct or indirect, related to peripheral aspects, such as failure to act in accordance with notified instructions or to take due care of the products supplied and so on.
2. Exclude indirect, consequential or special loss however arising.
3. Limit direct (and foreseeable?) loss to, for example, the total or annual contract value or a stated higher multiple of this.
4. Entire agreement clause to apply (see below).
5. No exclusion or exemption to apply in relation to any death or personal injury of any person or any loss or damage caused by fraud or fraudulent misrepresentation by [relevant party] supplier or its employees.

Pause and reflect

And finally, when negotiations begin to fall apart on what may seem like the peripheral aspect of the exemption clause, it may pay to step back to reflect. This may really be the first time that one of the most fundamental issues in the contract is negotiated, which is why it is sensible to address the question at an early stage.

Entire Agreement Clauses

An entire agreement clause (see the example below) states that the contract is the 'entire agreement' between the parties and includes all terms agreed by them to the exclusion of any other agreements. The aim is to try to give business certainty to the contract by excluding implied terms or the terms of a previous contract. Even so, such clauses can be subject to scrutiny under UCTA – for example, to the extent that they seek to exclude implied terms or informal, but understood, variations to the contract.

Non-reliance and release clauses are useful 'extras' – see below. Over recent years such clauses have been tested in the courts with varying degrees of success, and it is now clear that, whilst the courts accept entire agreement clauses as a valid risk allocation tool, they may also treat them as exclusion or exemption clauses and thus subject to scrutiny under UCTA.

DRAFTING TIPS FOR ENTIRE AGREEMENT CLAUSES

- It is generally worth including an entire agreement clause in your contract, but care should be taken to consider the circumstances and ensure precise drafting in each case.
- Check that there are no outstanding obligations to be carried through into the new agreement.
- If possible, add a release and/or covenant not to sue.
- Remember expressly to state that the clause does not exclude liability for fraud or fraudulent misrepresentation and is as reasonably balanced as it can be.

Common general short-form entire agreement clause

Many short-form business contracts contain wording such as:

12 Entire agreement: This agreement and the documents referred to in it constitute the entire agreement between the parties, and supersede all other agreements or arrangements between the parties (whether written or oral, express or implied), relating to the subject matter of this agreement.

Suggested extended form

12   Entire agreement:
12.1   This agreement and the documents referred to in it together constitute the entire agreement between the parties, to the exclusion of and superseding all other

negotiations, agreements, understandings, arrangements, terms, usage or course of dealing between the parties (whether written or oral, express or implied), relating to the subject matter of this agreement.

12.2   *Each party absolutely waives any claim and releases the other[s] from any liability arising or based on any of the matters excluded or superseded by clause 12.1.*

12.3   *Nothing in this clause [12] will operate so as to exclude or release any party from liability for fraud or fraudulent misrepresentation.*

Some Selected Cases

Many of the concepts mentioned in this chapter are quite complex. They also cross-relate and sometimes overlap. Reported cases can therefore be helpful for seeing potentially abstract principles in operation. The classic case of *Hadley* v. *Baxendale* was looked at in some detail earlier. Others show not only the legal principles, but also the unpredictability of court decisions.

ST ALBANS CITY AND DISTRICT COUNCIL V. INTERNATIONAL COMPUTERS LTD (1996) – LIMITATION CLAUSE HELD UNREASONABLE UNDER UCTA

Case

ICL agreed to supply St Albans Council with a computer system to collect the (much-hated) community charge. The software was defective, and, as a result, the council overestimated the population, set the charge too low and failed to recover the money it needed. There were many aspects to the judgment, but what is notable here is that the Court of Appeal upheld the trial judge's decision as follows:

a)   Even though the ITT set out St Albans' requirements, the contract incorporated ICL's standard terms of supply, which had not been materially changed in the negotiations. ICL was therefore treated as contracting on its 'written standard terms of business' within the scope of s. 3(1) of UCTA.

b)   ICL had failed to show that its limitation clause (the restriction of liability to the lesser of the cost of the supply or £100,000) satisfied the requirement of reasonableness under s. 3 and therefore could not rely on the limitation clause. The particular limitation to an amount which was a fraction of the contract price was unreasonable and thus ineffective.

Comment

The moral appears to be: first, you can never be certain of passing the UCTA reasonableness test; second, the stricter the clause, the less likely it is to be reasonable; and, third, if liability is capped, this should not normally be at less than the contract price.

WATFORD ELECTRONICS V. SANDERSON CFL LTD (2001) – EXEMPTION CLAUSE HELD REASONABLE AS RELATIVE EQUALITY OF BARGAINING POWER

This was another computer case for the supply of an accounts system, but here the exemption clause and an entire agreement clause were upheld. The contract: a) excluded indirect and consequential loss; and b) limited liability for direct loss to the contract price. Although some changes had been made to the supplier's terms, this was a contract on standard terms so that the UCTA test of reasonableness applied. Applying the guidelines in schedule 2 of UCTA, the Court of Appeal held that the parties in this case were both experienced and of similar bargaining power, and there were alternatives and insurance available. Moreover, the exclusion of indirect and consequential loss was a principle both parties understood, and limiting liability to the contract price was reasonable, since this was what the customer had committed to pay in the first place. Even though the system finally had to be scrapped and replaced, the limitation clause was reasonable. That principle was followed in other cases, including ones where the maximum liability for breach was expressed in terms of a money-back guarantee (*Sam Business Systems* v. *Hedley* (2002)).

REGUS V. EPCOT SOLUTIONS (2008) – EXEMPTION CLAUSE HELD REASONABLE

Case

Regus provided serviced offices to Epcot. The air-conditioning failed, leading Epcot to withhold payments to Regus, who sued. The serviced office agreement, on the Regus standard terms, included an exclusion and limitation clause, part of which excluded liability for any loss of profits or consequential loss. The Court of Appeal decided that: a) the clause did not exclude all remedies for defective air-conditioning, but merely loss of profits and similar losses, so Epcot was not precluded from claiming for reduction in value by reason of the defective air-conditioning; b) there was no inequality of bargaining power in this case; c) it was reasonable of Regus to exclude liability for loss of profits and consequential loss from the categories of loss for which it would be liable, especially as Epcot could more easily insure against these risks than Regus (since Epcot knew its own business); and d) the financial limitation to a specific amount of loss (the higher of £50,000 or 125 per cent of the annual fees) was in a separate sub-clause and was not unreasonable.

The Regus exemption clause

> *We are not liable for any loss as a result of our failure to provide a service as a result of mechanical breakdown, strike, delay, failure of staff, termination of our interest in the building containing the business centre or otherwise unless we do so deliberately or are negligent ... We will not in any circumstances have any liability for loss of business, loss of profits, loss of anticipated savings, loss of or damage to data, third-party claims or any consequential loss. We strongly advise you to insure against all such potential losses.*

Comment

This decision was greeted with some relief both by Regus and by those seeking clarity in the law. Regus had much at stake when its normal terms were challenged, whereas Epcot chose to challenge the exemption clause rather than (as the court suggested it could have done) seek compensation for the loss that was recoverable, which was the difference between the value of the premises with air-conditioning and without air-conditioning – a perfectly normal valuation assessment.

JACKSON V. RBS (2005) – REMOTENESS OF LOSS

This decision was mentioned in Chapter 5 on the subject of confidentiality. In short, RBS failed in its duty to its customer, Jackson, by revealing confidential information to its customer, another RBS client, who ceased business with Jackson as a result. The House of Lords held that there was a duty of confidentiality owed by RBS to Jackson, even without a written contract, and that:

a) the loss of repeat customer orders was foreseeable by the bank and not too remote – Jackson could recover damages on basis of continuing, though declining, orders;
b) once a type of loss is foreseeable, in the absence of any effective exemption clause, damages will reflect whatever loss resulted from that foreseeable area;
c) RBS could have included an exemption clause – even for breaches of confidentiality – but had not done so.

Comment

Here the risk was regarded as one which the bank should have been aware of, so Jackson's claim for loss of future profits succeeded, even with profits on a declining basis. If you are relying on the decision, it may be as well to check your bank's latest terms and conditions!

HOTEL SERVICES V. HILTON INT. HOTELS (2000) – THE MEANING OF 'CONSEQUENTIAL' LOSS

This is another picturesque case, this time concerning a defective minibar installed in hotels under long-term rental contracts. Hilton alleged repudiatory breach by the minibar supplier of the implied term of merchantable quality. The Court of Appeal upheld the judge's award of damages for a) rental overpaid, b) costs of removal and storage of chiller units, and c) loss of profits. The supplier claimed that these were all 'consequential' loss, which was excluded by the contract. The court disagreed and said that the losses in this case – even loss of profits, during the relevant period – were direct and outside the exclusion of consequential loss.

FERRYWAYS V. ASSOCIATED BRITISH PORTS (2008) – INDIRECT LOSS/ REASONABLENESS OF EXEMPTION

Case

This case – one of a series between the same parties – concerned a fatal accident to the chief officer of a Ferryways vessel apparently caused by a tugmaster vehicle operated by an employee of a subcontractor of Associated British Ports (ABP). ABP had an exemption clause in its stevedoring contract with Ferryways, excluding liability for any loss suffered by Ferryways across a range of issues, including losses of an 'indirect or consequential nature including without limitation … liabilities of [Ferryways] to any other party'. The court held that the chief officer's death was a direct and natural result of the breach of duty to exercise reasonable care and skill and was not indirect or consequential and not therefore excluded. The judge emphasized that 'very clear words indeed' are required to exclude losses falling outside the well-established meaning of indirect or consequential loss from *Hadley* v. *Baxendale* onwards.

Comment

This case concerned liability to third parties in respect of the death, rather than direct liability to the deceased's estate which was specifically not excluded. There was also a requirement that all claims were to be advised by Ferryways to ABP within 14 days of the relevant event. Ferryways complained that this restriction, under APB's standard terms, was unreasonable under UCTA. The judge disagreed. Taking into account the surrounding circumstances and bargaining position of the parties, he decided that Ferryways had full opportunity to consider APB's standard terms and suggest amendments to them (though in the event chose not to do so) and had every opportunity to insure against losses in respect of which ABP did not accept liability.

THOMAS WITTER V. TBP INDUSTRIES (1996) – ENTIRE AGREEMENT CLAUSE PRINCIPLES

The judge here took the practical view that whether one party relied on a representation by the other was a matter of fact, to be decided on the evidence of the case. If the evidence showed that one party had in fact relied on a statement by the other, but had just missed the 'small print' of the entire agreement clause, the courts should be prepared to acknowledge the reality of the position and disregard the entire agreement clause to the extent that it contradicted what had actually happened.

INNTREPRENEUR PUB CO. LTD V. EAST CROWN LTD (2000) – ENTIRE AGREEMENT CLAUSE

This case is worth noting on account of Mr Justice Lightman's celebrated statement when he upheld the principle of an entire agreement clause as legitimately designed to prevent one of the parties 'threshing through the undergrowth and finding, in the course of negotiations, some chance remark or statement upon which to found a claim' (*Inntrepreneur*, at 1). He nevertheless went on to decide that the exclusion of prior representations *can* be an exemption clause subject to the test of reasonableness under UCTA, with the onus on the party seeking to rely on the exemption to prove its reasonableness.

QUEST 4 FINANCE V. MAXFIELD (2007) – ENTIRE AGREEMENT CLAUSE INEFFECTIVE

This came after a number of other cases which broadly followed the *Thomas Witter* principles. Quest's financial product was specifically promoted on one basis, but its legal agreements, under a misleading clause heading, contained a personal guarantee – contrary to the promotional details. There was also a non-reliance clause. The court decided in the circumstances that Mr Maxfield could rely on the prior representation by Quest and was not 'estopped' from claiming his reliance on the Quest brochure; Quest could not show that they believed Maxfield's statement of non-reliance was true, so the non-reliance clause was ineffective.

PEEKAY INTERMARK LTD V. AUSTRALIA AND NEW ZEALAND BANKING GROUP LTD (2006) – ENTIRE AGREEMENT CLAUSE UPHELD

By contrast, in this case the Court of Appeal concluded that it should be possible for parties to an agreement to give up any rights to assert that they were induced into it by any representation or the like. This is not as incompatible with *Quest* as might at first appear. Even in *Witter* it was held that parties *could* give up their rights regarding pre-contract representations, but the evidence could show that they had not actually chosen to do so.

SIX CONTINENTS HOTELS V. EVENT HOTELS (2006) – GENERAL RELEASE AND COVENANT NOT TO SUE

A general release and covenant not to sue was held to be a valid contractual bar to prevent Event Hotels from suing for misrepresentation prior to the contract. It seemed to be accepted in this case, however, that an entire agreement clause *on its own* would *not* preclude or exclude liability for misrepresentation. The judge also considered whether the relevant clause satisfied the test of reasonableness under s. 3 of the Misrepresentation Act 1967. As the parties were substantial and the agreements sophisticated with no inequality of bargaining power, he held that the clause passed the reasonableness test.

INTERNET BROADCASTING CORPORATION (T/A NETTV) V. MARR LLC (T/A MARHEDGE) (2009) – EXCLUSION CLAUSES AND DELIBERATE BREACHES OF CONTRACT

In this case, NetTV had a contract to provide interactive Internet TV services to a hedge-fund company. The hedge-fund company terminated the agreement after one year without any right to do so under the contract and then relied on the exclusion and limitation clause in the contract to avoid or limit liability to the TV company. Although MARHedge's action was regarded as a deliberate breach that was severe enough to amount to repudiation of the contract (see Chapter 20), the court held that an exclusion clause *could* still apply to such cases. However, very clear language would be needed to show that this was the agreed intention of the parties and, in this case, the language did not justify that conclusion. The court put particular stress on the insurance aspect, holding that the proper function of an exemption clause is to allocate insurable risk between the parties. The deliberate breach by one party of its clear obligations under the contract is not normally insurable, and, in the absence of very clear intent, the exemption clause would not be extended to cover such an event.

Summary and Checklist

A simple approach would be to look at the practical and likely risks first, and then decide who should do what, when and how, and what might happen if they don't. This means checking the risks you will agree to take on and those you think the other party should bear. Consider what insurance is available and who should best take it out (and what the costs of that may be). Then try to plug the gaps by sensible warranty/indemnity provisions and appropriate liability exclusions and caps. In the process, consider all the circumstances, including the price paid and the level of expertise claimed, and suggest that the contract reflects these factors. And be clear on the use of terms like 'consequential' and 'indirect' loss.

CHECKLIST

* Estimates suggest that most business contracts go wrong in some respect.
* Exclusion and limitation clauses should be seen as part of risk planning.
* To handle these clauses correctly you need to understand how damages are calculated, including:
  - the principle of putting the claimant in the position they would have been in if the contract had been properly performed;
  - the losses that are deemed to flow naturally from the breach of contract;
  - the losses that might reasonably be expected to arise from the breach;
  - the difference between direct, indirect and consequential losses;
  - what are special losses;
  - how loss of profits may be direct or indirect or partly both.
* Unfair Contract Terms Act:
  - the principles – and the differences from the UTCCR;
  - what risks cannot be excluded;
  - what exclusions are subject to the test of reasonableness;
  - what are standard terms and how is the reasonableness test judged;
  - which contracts are not covered.
* Warranty and indemnity clauses – these may be affected by exclusion clauses.
* Insurance:
  - excess or deductible levels;
  - subrogation – and its effects;
  - undertakings to insure.
* Negotiating limitation clauses:
  - incorporating the clause in the contract;
  - *contra proferentem* and severance;

- – the benefits of being open, flexible and reasonable;
- – following through the risk management assessment and allocation;
- – agreed damages;
- – distinguishing obligations from aspirations;
- – analysing difference types of potential loss;
- – being clear with the language;
- – limiting liability for direct loss;
- – suitable clause outlines.
- • Entire agreement clauses – reflect on the real position before adding them.
- • Cases show the complexity and uncertainty of result.

8 *Restrictions and Competition Law*

Introduction – restrictions and restrictive covenants: the common law position – competition law – anti-competitive behavior (article 81/UK Chapter I) – vertical agreements – horizontal agreements (dealings with competitors) – abuse of dominant position (article 82/UK Chapter II) – practical issues relating to potential anti-competitive arrangements – competition law checklist

Introduction

Many business agreements contain restrictions of one kind or another, whether direct (such as a non-compete clause) or indirect (such as an exclusivity arrangement) and, whether in formal contracts or informal understandings, such arrangements need to tread a careful legal course. All will need to take account of the principles of English common law and some may engage the heavy forces of UK or European competition law. This chapter looks first at the common law issues and then turns to competition law, identifying the main issues and distinctions and seeking a path through the complexity. The rules of competition law are indeed complex, but the principles are in some ways deceptively simple. What increasingly matters is whether the arrangements do appreciably affect competition within a distinct market. Because of their size, smaller businesses are likely to be exempt from competition law provided they are not dominant in their market and they keep clear of so-called 'hardcore' restrictions, as considered below, but there is a need for constant vigilance as circumstances change and negotiations take place.

Restrictions and Restrictive Covenants: The Common Law Position

RESTRICTIONS IN AGREEMENTS

Is there a restriction?

Many contracts contain some form of restriction on one or both the parties to it. Take the case of a commission agent, who may not want to expend huge efforts in building customer bases or negotiating with third parties if their principal were able to come in and take the benefits by dealing directly with the customers brought in by the agent. Naturally, the agent will want to prevent this happening. One approach would be to agree that the principal will stay out of the agent's market, leaving the agent to introduce and negotiate the customer deals. This would mean excluding the principal from the agent's agreed marketplace during the agency period. An alternative approach would entitle the agent to commission if the deal takes place in the agreed market as the result of the agent's introduction, even if the principal later deals directly with the customer. This would be typical of the situation with an agent such as an estate agent, where the introduction of the buyer to the seller is everything (and why some unlucky sellers finish up owing two agents commission, because both have introduced the same buyer at different times). The first option – excluding the principal from the agent's market – imposes a clear restriction on the principal, but the second option does not, as it leaves both agent and principal to act in the market but with the agent receiving commission from any sale in the agreed territory, however that sale was agreed.

Mutual restrictions

The principal may in turn wish to limit the agent's activities, first by limiting the agent to a designated territory and, second, by other limitations, such as not to act for a competing supplier, or not to seek business of the same kind outside the designated territory. Such agreements where there are bilateral limitations are inherently more restrictive than unilateral ones, since they work on the principle that 'if you don't do this, I won't do that'. It would be an easy step from this kind of approach to carving up a territory or limiting effective price competition.

EXCLUSIVITY

Sole and exclusive rights

The sort of arrangements referred to above may lead to one party having sole or exclusive rights for a limited period in relation to an area and/or a product. Sole rights exclude third parties, whereas exclusive rights exclude the grantor of the rights also, so that a principal granting sole agency could sell into the same territory as the agent (subject to good faith considerations) but, by granting exclusive rights, a principal would be debarred from competing with the agent in the same territory. To do so would be in direct breach of the exclusivity granted.

Defining the terms

Whenever words like 'sole' and 'exclusive' are used, it is wise, in order to avoid later arguments, to set out precisely what the effect is, especially as regards whose activities they limit. For example, a distributor appointed as 'exclusive distributor' for a product and territory may think that no one else, including the supplier making the appointment, may supply anyone else with that product in that territory; however, the supplier may think the converse, that the distributor may not act for any other supplier of competing products in that area for the term of agreement. It could even be that both principles are intended. So, as ever, clarity in expression is important. Exclusivity almost certainly means that one or more of the parties to a contract will be restricted from competing in some way with the same or similar products in the defined area for a period of time. In other words, there is a legal restriction, and that restriction needs to be considered in the light of both common law and competition law principles.

Informal arrangements

Although this book is about contracts, it should be stressed that the long arm of competition law reaches out to arrangements or 'concerned practices' that may not be enshrined in any formal contract, but are evidenced by a tacit understanding of the way in which parties conduct their businesses. The answer is not just to keep restrictive arrangements legal, but to understand what is prohibited and why.

THE COMMON LAW APPROACH

Legal principles

If there are restrictions, even indirect ones, three important legal principles are likely to come into play, as follows:

1. *The restrictions must be clear.* This really follows from the comments in earlier chapters about clarity of drafting, but in this case any uncertainty about the extent of a restriction is likely to be interpreted against the party seeking to enforce it.
2. *The restrictions must be reasonable and appropriate.* This means that restrictions may not go further than is reasonably necessary to protect the legitimate business interests of the person seeking to enforce them. The test is to look at the specific business involved and decide what would be a fair level of protection for that business in the circumstances, and not to exceed that level.
3. *The restrictions must not be illegal*, and in particular must not breach competition law.

The effect of failure, whether in terms of clarity or the extent of restrictions, is likely to cause those restrictions to be unenforceable. In extreme cases, where the restrictions 'taint' the entire contract by being fundamentally unreasonable, the whole contract may be unenforceable. Illegality, especially under competition law, may be both more complex and more disastrous, since in addition to unenforceability, one or all of the parties may be faced with criminal charges, substantial fines and the risk of claims from third parties affected by their illegal behaviour.

Planning

As suggested above, it is always worth thinking about whether the parties' commercial objectives may be achieved another way, such as with the agent receiving commission on any deal in the agreed territory, so avoiding the need for the principal to be restricted in the market.

Key tests

With any restriction you should consider the following main elements:

- *where* the geographical limitation reaches;
- *what* products or services are covered by it; and
- *how long* the restriction will apply – while the agreement continues and afterwards.

Reasonableness of restrictions

To be enforceable, all these limitations must be reasonable in extent and no more than properly required to protect the business of the party seeking to enforce them. The principles are akin to the tests that apply to restrictive covenants on ex-employees, but the courts will give independent parties much more scope. The assumption is that, except where there is manifest unfairness, businesses contracting with one another have equal bargaining powers. There are a variety of conflicting cases on the points, so hard and fast rules are difficult to discern, but some guidance can be given.

Geographical extent   This should be equivalent to the likely area of operation of the business in question. To take an extreme, a worldwide ban on competition would be unreasonable where the contract granted rights to sell only in one part of England. But it may be reasonable, at least at common law, to limit the activities of the representative, agent or distributor to that one area and to exclude them from canvassing business in neighbouring areas in conflict with equivalent rights granted to another business there. In big cities, geographical restrictions are hard to enforce at all, but where they exist they should be very tightly limited to a narrow area.

Type of goods or services   Any restrictions should be limited to the goods or services being dealt with, or anything that would be directly competitive with them. A limitation simply preventing a sales agent from selling other types of goods is unlikely to be enforceable.

Time period   Anything continuing beyond the life of the relevant agreement will attract special scrutiny, but it will often be possible (outside employment relationships) to have something in place for up to a year after the end of the term of the agreement. Anything longer than a year may well cause problems. Even this extent can fall foul of competition law if not fully justified or in line with a relevant exemption.

'True' agency arrangements

These are often viewed as being outside the principles of common law and competition law control to the extent that the agent is really only an extension of the principal. This is looked at in more detail later in this chapter in relation to applicable competition law tests.

DEALING WITH UNREASONABLE RESTRICTIONS

Deleting offending words

As explained in Chapter 4, the courts may delete offending words in certain circumstances, but cannot add words where they are missing. Classic instances of unreasonable restraints occur when a restriction is without time or geographical limit. An extreme would be something such as: 'The Agent will not at any time seek to sell goods equivalent to the [defined] Products.' Irrespective of the definition of 'Products', the whole restriction would fail because there is no time or area limitation, and the courts will not imply one. It is no good the principal saying that the restriction was only meant to last for the agency term or one year after termination; such things have to be stated clearly.

Undertakings may be preferable to injunctions

If you find you are probably in breach of a restriction, consider whether to offer a form of undertaking to the other party. As there is always uncertainty on these issues, there may be scope to negotiate a deal that gives you sufficient flexibility but also affords the other party sufficient protection. This might also sit well with any court, in a borderline case, if the undertaking you have offered seems to give adequate protection. Whichever side you are on, you should act immediately the real circumstances become known to you; otherwise you may lose your rights through delay. On the other hand, where there is little legal doubt, failure to offer an undertaking to perform the contract terms may, coupled with some evidence of a possible intent to breach, be enough for the other party to seek and obtain an injunction, even before any breach occurs.

Injunctions and competition law

Injunctions are dealt with more fully in Chapter 19, and breach of a restrictive covenant is not something to be undertaken lightly, but there can be a risk for a party benefiting from a restriction if the covenant in question itself infringes competition law. The effect could be serious, and it may be too late to recant if the other party's response to a threatening letter is an immediate complaint to the Office of Fair Trading (OFT). The investigation that follows may prove far more draconian, and could involve fines and even criminal proceedings against the company and its officers responsible. In these situations, the fact that the complainant actually adhered to the restrictive practices for some time is no defence. Even if they were partly complicit to begin with, by complaining first they may be able to obtain complete immunity by applying for leniency from prosecution. The final blow may then be that any third party claiming to have been damaged by the restrictive arrangements can seek a compensation order for the damage caused. So, even though the main risk in such cases is that the restriction is unenforceable, competition law needs to be taken seriously!

Competition Law

Competition law has an entirely different approach from English common law, and this section looks at the principles in operation.

THE PRINCIPLES OF COMPETITION LAW

Form versus effect

The English common law approach concentrates on form rather than effect, whereas competition law starts from the opposite viewpoint. For example, in one early European case (*Brasserie De Hecht* v. *Wilkin* (1967)), a relatively modest restriction imposed by a brewery on all the bars it supplied in a single country was held to have an overall effect on the beer supply market in that country, because the accumulation of restrictions by the brewer reduced choice for customers of a large number of bars in a recognizable territorial area. This was no doubt what the brewer intended, so both the object of the restriction and its effect were to restrict supply or prices in a defined market.

The objective of competition law

A founding principle of the European Union, dating back to the Treaty of Rome in 1957, was as an economic community where there was substantially a 'level economic playing field' across all member states. To address this, European law, binding on all member countries (including the UK), outlaws, with limited exceptions, both anti-competitive practices that distort the relevant product market (covered by what is now article 81 of the European Treaty) and oppressive market behaviour by businesses that are dominant within their market (covered by what is now article 82). These laws were delegated back to member states to introduce into their own laws, so that the same concepts also apply to a relevant market within the boundaries of each individual EU member country where anti-competitive behaviour has an effect on that market. In the UK, articles 81 and 82 are reflected in Chapters I and II of the UK Competition Act 1998 as amended. These laws now need to be examined in some detail.

THE DANGER OF INFORMAL ANTI-COMPETITIVE PRACTICES

Although this is a book about contract law, the operational practices outside the formal agreement are likely to put businesses most at risk of infringing competition law, especially where there is evidence of price-fixing, market partitioning or cartel arrangements. As mentioned earlier, the immunity rules mean that those who report first may escape, so even the good business friend with whom you had a 'confidential' chat at the 19th hole of the golf club could land you in jail (and your group of companies with a massive fine), even if they were also complicit in, or had even proposed, the illegal plans from the outset. This may be counter to all principles of business integrity, but, as far as competition authorities are concerned, the gloves are now off. A little knowledge may be a dangerous thing, but complete ignorance of the law in this area can be far more dangerous.

THE OLD LAW

It is worth mentioning that two prior English laws have now been superseded. The Restrictive Trade Practices Act 1976 (RTPA) used to regulate the position under English law, but is relevant now only to old agreements entered into before 1 March 2000 and can otherwise be ignored. The Resale Prices Act 1976 (RPA) contained the old prohibition against suppliers imposing minimum resale prices for goods, repealed by the UK Competition Act with effect from 1 March 2000, although any attempt to control resale prices is now likely to be unlawful as a hardcore restriction under competition law.

EUROPEAN UNION AND UK COMPETITION LAW

The two main competition law prohibitions – anti-competitive practices and abuse of a dominant position – are therefore now covered respectively in articles 81 and

82 of the EC Treaty (or European Treaty). This is the cornerstone of the European Community, starting life as the Treaty of Rome in 1957 and being amended by various subsequent treaties including the Treaty on European Union signed in Maastricht, the Treaty of Amsterdam in 1997 and prospectively by the Treaty of Lisbon in 2007 once fully ratified. Articles 81 and 82 are in turn reflected in Chapters I and II of the UK Competition Act, with the European principles lending themselves to the UK legislation. The UK Act, though dating from 1998, came into full force from 1 March 2000 and was itself extended and supplemented by the Enterprise Act 2002, which dramatically increased the powers of the UK competition authorities. As UK competition law is modelled on the European law, it is sensible to deal with the two together. The following is outline guidance, as the rules are highly complex and up-to-date specialist professional advice is essential. Above all, it is important for businesses to recognize that these laws may affect what otherwise appear to be ordinary commercial dealings. Note that references to the European Union (EU) will, for the purposes of geographical market and similar tests, include the additional few member countries of the European Economic Area (EEA), and references here to the EU include the other EEA countries for convenience.

EXAMPLES OF POTENTIAL ANTI-COMPETITIVE PRACTICES

At this point, it helps to look at the principal examples of what the law is trying to prevent (the list is not, of course, exhaustive):

- fixing resale prices or other significant trading conditions
- limiting production, technical development or investment
- sharing (or partitioning) markets – or sources of supply between a few key players
- using unfair market power to force some parties to trade on worse terms than others
- linking essential supply arrangements to unrelated obligations.

THE INFORMATION YOU WILL NEED

More detailed definitions and applications are considered later, but, broadly, if you wish to understand or to receive specialist advice on your position under competition law, the following information, concerning the business of the parties, the nature of the arrangements proposed, the relevant market and the effect on it, will be most relevant (though never easy to obtain).

Your business

- What is your company's turnover within the EU and the UK?
- What is the turnover of any other part of your group of companies that deals in the same market within the EU or the UK? (This may need to be added to your turnover.)
- How many employees do you have?

The business of the other parties to the planned contracts

- What is their turnover (as above)?
- What is the turnover of any other part of their group in the same market (as above)?

The proposed contracts/arrangements

(For a further explanation of 'horizontal' and 'vertical' see below.)

- Are they horizontal (between parties at different levels in the supply chain)?
- Are they vertical (between competitors)?
- If horizontal, is one of the parties nevertheless a competitor of another party?

The relevant market

This is a key test in aspects of competition law. Consider:

- What is being provided – products or services?
- What are the broadest and the narrowest plausible definitions of your market?
- What products might be substitutable? (See 'The relevant market' below.)
- What is the share of the relevant market held by:
  - your business, and
  - the other parties with whom you are contracting?

The effect on the relevant market of the contract restrictions proposed

- Is it likely to affect the way in which your suppliers, customers or competitors behave?
- Is it likely to prevent new competitors joining your market or competing effectively?
- Where will the effect be and how might it be measured?
- Will there be real benefits to your customers that might justify the restrictions?

Anti-Competitive Behaviour (Article 81/UK Chapter I)

Article 81 of the European Treaty outlaws anti-competitive behaviour that may have an appreciable effect on trade, and the same principles apply in the UK under Chapter I. In looking at article 81, there is the need to distinguish between so-called 'vertical' agreements and the potentially more serious 'horizontal' agreements, which may involve competitors working together. There are potential exemptions from the application of these laws, such as for smaller companies or smaller market shares, but there is also the need to avoid 'hardcore' terms which are automatically illegal on their own and which will vitiate any exemption.

AGREEMENTS AND ARRANGEMENTS

The first step, is therefore to understand if and when competition law might apply and then to see if your arrangement or agreement fits within one of the general or specific exemptions. Bear in mind the need to be rigorous and that the law here does apply to both goods and services. The principles are as follows:

- *There must be two or more independent businesses involved in an agreement, arrangement or 'concerted practice'.* Arrangements made between parent companies and subsidiaries are (except in very rare cases) not regarded as being between separate businesses and are therefore not caught. Similarly, the prohibition does not generally apply to an agreement between principal and agent (provided the arrangement is a genuine agency for competition law purposes – see below). But the parties do not have to be based in the EU. If the arrangement has its effect in part of the EU, that is sufficient.
- *The practices involved must actually or potentially restrict or distort competition within the market.* An effect on trade within the EU may occur even if the arrangements apparently involve only one member state, if the practical effect is to restrict other businesses from competing. This effect (on trade) must be 'appreciable' – or perceptible – judged by:
  - whether *any of the participants* are prevented from competing in the market as fully as they might otherwise have done, or
  - whether *any third parties* are restricted from competing as effectively in that market.

If the agreement or practice in question makes no difference to the way in which other businesses behave or compete in the relevant market, it is less likely that any restrictions would be regarded as having an appreciable affect on trade.

THE EUROPEAN 'APPRECIABLE EFFECT' TEST

European guidelines suggest a combined test. There is a rebuttable presumption that there will be *no effect* on trade at certain levels of business if:

a) the aggregate market share of the parties in any relevant market is 5 per cent or less (of the relevant market) *and*
b) the annual turnover is €40 million or less.

This turnover figure needs close attention. For vertical agreements it is the annual EU turnover of the *supplier only*, but with horizontal agreements, the €40 million is the aggregate EU turnover of the products in question of *all the parties* concerned in the arrangement. This immediately flags the vital distinction between vertical and horizontal agreements, considered below.

'TRUE' AGENCY AGREEMENTS EXCLUDED

True agency

Although earlier examples in this chapter referred to agency agreements, the EU recognizes that the agent is effectively an extension of the principal rather than a fully independent party, such that true agency agreements are excluded from the rigours of competition law. Competition law does, however, fully apply to the relationship between a supplier and distributor, and care needs to be taken that the right names are used.

Risk

Fundamental to the distinction is that the agent does not take any material commercial or financial risk regarding the principal's transaction with the customer, apart from the potential loss of commission if the deal falls through. The following all indicate arrangements likely to fall outside the European Commission's guidelines on the issue and which may therefore need some other exemption, namely where 'agents':

- take title to goods;
- contribute at their own expense to the costs of sale or promotion;
- are obliged to provide after-sales services which the principal does not repay in full;
- bear more than the normal agency share of risk in a commercial transaction (such as material risk of non-payment if the buyer defaults); or
- have other arrangements in the relevant market which collectively mean that inter-brand competition is materially reduced.

VERTICAL AND HORIZONTAL AGREEMENTS

As suggested earlier, a clear understanding of the difference between vertical and horizontal arrangements is necessary to follow the impact of article 81/Chapter I.

Vertical relationships are those between parties at different levels in the supply chain, such as those between manufacturer/supplier/distributor/wholesaler, characterized by each relying on others in the overall progress of goods or services to the ultimate consumer.

Horizontal relationships are between parties at the same level in the supply chain, such as two or more manufacturers, who are thus more likely to be direct or indirect competitors of one another. Here, any collusion or restrictive arrangement could result in prices being kept artificially high or competing products being kept off the market, with the end-consumer being disadvantaged in either case.

Consumer benefits

The essence of competition law is to protect the consumer from unfair practices across or in the supply chain that lead to the consumer getting a worse deal than if there had been fair competition all the way down. Restrictions in horizontal agreements are thus regarded as more likely to be damaging than those in vertical agreements, such that a greater degree of latitude should be shown to the latter.

Tacit agreement

Although the principle is that, to infringe article 81, there is agreement or a concerted practice between two or more independent players, a single main party acting unilaterally (such as a trade association making decisions or recommendations for its members) can be sufficient if the other players expressly or tacitly accept, or go along with, the main player's apparent rules. If the competition authorities find evidence of coordinated behaviour, this may be enough to shift the burden of proof on to those involved to prove that they were not colluding.

AGREEMENTS OF MINOR IMPORTANCE

The essence of the Commission notice (NAOMI), discussed below, is that agreements between smaller businesses are unlikely to fall under article 81 because they are rarely capable of restricting competition (the *de minimis* principle). As always, there is more detail to think about if we are to understand how this may operate. The first step is consider what are known as SMEs.

Small and medium-sized businesses (SMEs)

If there is a vertical agreement and the parties are SMEs, the chances are that the agreement will fall outside article 81 altogether. There is never complete certainty on this, and it would be as well to beware any hardcore restrictions in any event (see below). An SME is defined for this purpose as having:

- fewer than 250 employees, *and*
- a turnover of €50 million or less, *or*
- assets of €43 million or less.

NAOMI (the *de minimis* notice)

In 2001 the European Commission issued a revised formal Notice on Agreements [which it deems as] of Minor Importance (NAOMI). This provides two alternative tests – one based on the size of the businesses involved and the other on their combined share of the relevant market. Although the notice is not expressly binding on national courts of member states, the fact that an arrangement would be exempt as *de minimis* is likely to be taken into account by national courts also.

The size of the business test

NAOMI will apply if the agreement is between SMEs.

The market share test

Even if the deal is not between SMEs, NAOMI provides an alternative safe harbour if you can get through certain market share tests. The level of the market share depends on whether the arrangement is vertical or horizontal (see above).

- If vertical, the combined share must not exceed 15 per cent.
- If horizontal (typically between competitors), the figure is lower, at 10 per cent.
- If the arrangement is mixed – vertical and horizontal – the 10 per cent threshold applies.
- If there may be more than two parties, such as similar agreements with a number of suppliers and customers in the same market, the threshold – for either horizontal or vertical agreements – falls to 5 per cent.

Provisos

There are three important provisos to these *de minimis* tests:

1. NAOMI recognizes that market shares may have a short surge and then drop back, so it provides that the relevant thresholds can be exceeded by up to two percentage points (up to 12 per cent for verticals and 17 per cent for horizontals) for up to two successive years without the minor importance exemption being lost.
2. The relevant market share test must take into account the share of that particular market held by other members of the same group to which the companies in question belong.
3. In any event, the concept of 'minor importance' does not apply to agreements containing *hardcore restrictions* or clauses blacklisted in nearly all contexts, considered further below.

Reviews

The fact that a proposed agreement does not fit within the minor importance thresholds does not mean that it will necessarily have an appreciable effect on trade within the relevant market, or that it may not benefit from one of the other exemptions (although it would greatly improve its defensibility if it should do so). In any event, both the turnover of the parties and the impact of the venture need to be kept under review by the parties involved since, if a venture becomes highly successful, it may come to affect trade in a way that did not exist at the outset (for example, by exceeding market-share thresholds) and thus cause the agreement to fall outside the general exemptions, possibly at a critical time.

THE RELEVANT MARKET

In looking at the effect of a restriction or arrangement (or the question of dominance under article 82), it is necessary to consider what the relevant market is, and this is one of the most difficult issues in competition law. To a large extent, the issue has become one for the economists rather than the lawyers, because, to use the analogy of a river, it may take some detailed study to see the ultimate upstream (back up the supply chain towards the producer) and/or downstream (down the supply chain towards the consumer) impact of a blockage or diversion in the normal water flow. The following is very much an overview. It may be of some limited practical comfort to believe that the European Commission is likely to want to concentrate its resources on investigating major misuse of market power rather than borderline cases.

Substitutability

The main consideration is how the market may be defined in relation to: a) products and b) geography. It is common to start with the narrowest possible definition of the market and consider the price, quality and intended use of the product. A widely used test is to consider how far could and would consumers accept another product or service in place of the one they first wanted or were used to.

The *product market* issue raises so-called 'demand-side' and 'supply-side' questions.

- On the *demand side*, the aim is to find whether customers consider there would be an effective substitute for the relevant product. In *United Brands Co. v. Commission* (1978), one leading case on dominance (see 'Anti-competitive law' below), the court decided that the relevant market was bananas (literally) rather than fruit as a whole. What would happen if a monopoly supplier in a narrow market (such as bananas) increased prices in the long term by 5–10 per cent? Would customers switch to the closest alternative fruit? If they continued to buy bananas anyway, the relevant product market would be bananas. Other factors that may be relevant include where and how the products are purchased, the extent of branding and promotion and the history of competitor responses and innovation in the past.
- The *supply-side* question looks at the same issue from the supplier's perspective. If the price of bananas did rise 5–10 per cent, would other suppliers previously not strong in bananas switch their supply into that fruit? That would involve considering how easy it would be for them to make that switch and what barriers to entry to that product market existed. This might also depend on questions of branding and the availability of brand licences to enable effective competition. A strong brand may increase the chances of a business being held to be dominant, since customers may be thought less likely to switch on grounds of price alone.

The geographic market will also be important. Similar tests apply by taking the smallest likely area and considering whether, if there were a price rise of 5–10 per cent in that area, customers would be likely to buy outside the area. Relevant factors in the decision could include the cost of transport, language differences and tax. A local bus company could easily be seen to be dominant in its local market if those without their own cars had no real viable alternatives to using it. (That does not make it automatically in breach of the law, but it does change the level of scrutiny of its own market behaviour, as will be seen, because it can act effectively without regard to how its competitors will react, since there is little effective competition.)

INDIVIDUAL EXEMPTION UNDER ARTICLE 81(3) OR THE COMPETITION ACT

Individual exemption

Whereas article 81(1) of the European Treaty sets out the prohibitions, article 81(3) sets out a possible gateway in the form of an exemption from article 81(1). Since 2004 the European Commission, national competition authorities and national courts have had concurrent jurisdiction to grant individual exemptions under article 81(3). UK courts again have to follow European rules and precedents in this respect. Exemption under article 81(3) or under a specific exemption (covered below) represents, in effect, a 'get out of jail free' card if you have landed within the broad prohibitions of article 81(1). To obtain and play the article 81(3) card is not easy, and you would have to demonstrate all four of the benefits set out below, whereas the specific exemptions are both clearer and more certain, such that it pays to fit within them if at all possible. The article 81(3) requirements are to show the following:

- The *arrangements contribute to improved production or distribution* or promote technical or economic progress (such as an improved technical or production process).
- *Consumers* (somewhat confusingly here not limited to end-users) *receive a fair share of the resulting benefits* (for example, better or cheaper goods or services).
- The *restrictions imposed on the parties* to the arrangement *are indispensable to achieving those objectives* (for example, limited – but not full – territorial protection may be sufficient for the purpose).
- The *arrangements do not altogether exclude effective competition* over a substantial part of the products in question.

Vertical Agreements

THE PRINCIPLES

As suggested above, vertical agreements (or 'arrangements' where they are informal) are those between parties at different levels in the supply chain, such as between manufacturer, supplier, distributor and/or wholesaler. Such vertical agreements are regarded as intrinsically less anti-competitive than 'horizontal agreements', such as those between two manufacturers. To support this, and assist certainty, competition law has provided certain safe harbours in the form of specific exemptions on the basis that arrangements falling within these exemptions will not be deemed to restrict competition. So if article 81(1) might apply, and especially if the agreement is not within the *de minimis* thresholds already mentioned, it is wise to try to bring the arrangements within a relevant specific exemption rather than rely on article 81(3). These exemptions will not apply, however, if there is any 'hardcore' term in the arrangement, and the exemptions provide their own definition of what is hardcore in this context. Note, however, that, provided there is no hardcore term, the fact that an arrangement falls outside a specific exemption (and outside the *de minimis* thresholds) does not mean that the arrangement is necessarily illegal; each case has to be considered individually.

In addition to the main specific exemption affecting vertical agreements there have also been specific exemptions relating to 'technology transfer', (including research and development), 'specialization' and specific industry sectors, such as insurance and car distribution. Many of these may lapse and not be renewed as the European Commission looks to consolidate most specific exemptions within the broad vertical agreements regime.

Staying within an exemption

If the contract falls within a specific exemption and has no hardcore elements, then all should be fine so long as it continues fully to do so. Many commercial contracts for major trading relationships are now drafted from the outset on this basis, but if this is not possible, it is worth reconsidering the arrangements or perhaps whether the restrictions are really needed at all. The position also needs to be monitored regularly, and, indeed, the change from the VRBE to the VAR, summarized below, may impact on some existing arrangements. The effect of future growth over the life of an agreement should be considered at the outset and reviewed regularly against the tolerances that the exemption may afford. If the venture is really successful, the arrangements might, in time, come to have an appreciable affect on trade, be such that the *de minimis* thresholds are exceeded or no longer satisfy the market tests. If this is at all likely, try to redraft the terms to fit within the exemption or consider the risk of market-share tests being exceeded in the future. Once again, the message is to keep commercial agreements under regular review.

THE VERTICAL RESTRAINTS BLOCK EXEMPTION (VRBE)

Applicability

The VBRE, applicable up to 2010, has been most relevant for distribution, supply and similar agreements without a strong technology aspect to them The VRBE is distinguished from other block exemptions, most notably the Technology Transfer Block Exemption (TTBE) where the licensing of intellectual property rights or know-how is the main theme of the agreement and different rules apply.

THE VERTICAL AGREEMENTS REGULATION (VAR)

As from 2010 a new exemption applies in the form of a regulation, thus having direct application in EU states. For convenience this is referred to as the Vertical Agreements Regulation or the VAR. A draft of the VAR was published as this chapter was being finalized, and the following comments assume that the new rules will come into force substantially as set out in the draft. Some details of the new rules are still a matter of debate as this text is being finalized and, where applicable, reference should be made to their final form. The VAR is to apply from 1 June 2010 to 31 May 2020.

What is covered by the VAR

Subject to various provisos as summarized below, the thrust of the VAR is that the prohibitions of article 81(1) will not apply to certain agreements or concerted practices between two or more undertakings, each of which operates at a different level of the production or distribution chain, and relating to the conditions under which the parties may purchase, sell or resell certain goods or services ('vertical agreements'). In other words, qualifying vertical agreements will be exempt from being deemed anti-competitive. Paragraph 4 of article 2 of the VAR also contains some provisions concerning what might otherwise be vertical agreements where one of the parties is operating at more than one level, such as manufacture and distribution or wholesale and retail.

Connected parties

In looking at parties that may be exempt under the VAR it is necessary to consider what the Regulation calls 'connected undertakings'. When calculating the applicable market share and the turnover test relating to associations, both the actual company concerned and its connected undertakings must be taken into account. In effect, therefore, it is the broader size, turnover or market share of the group that the relevant parties belong to that will matter, not just that of the party concerned. For this purpose a connected undertaking is broadly a member of the same group, being one under common control with other companies, although the exact VAR definition (which does not necessarily tally with other definitions of control) may need to be considered, especially if there are any relevant joint-venture arrangements which may extend its ambit.

Market-share tests

The Notice on Agreements of Minor Importance (NAOMI), mentioned earlier, already exempts pure vertical agreements where the combined share of the relevant market held by the parties involved does not exceed 15 per cent, provided there are no general hardcore restrictions, such as minimum resale prices. The VRBE went a stage further in extending exemption to vertical agreements from the NAOMI 15 per cent level to 30 per cent in relation to the turnover of the supplier or suppliers alone, or to the turnover of the buyer alone where the arrangement was an exclusive purchasing one. The VAR now requires that the market share of *each* of the parties involved in the arrangement must not exceed 30 per cent. Article 8 usefully adds some detail on how the market share threshold is to be calculated, and provides some tolerance levels where market share starts below and then rises above the threshold 30 per cent level. If your arrangements are likely to be at or near the maximum 30 per cent level, reference should be made to the detail of the Regulation, as the periods of tolerance are limited.

Turnover test

If the market share test is met there is no overall turnover limitation in either the VRBE or VAR. Article 2 of the VAR, however, covers associations of retailers. Where there is such an association, the VAR may apply to a vertical agreement between the *association* and its members or between the association and its suppliers, but only where a) all the association members are retailers of goods and b) no one member of the organization and its connected undertakings has an annual turnover exceeding €50 million. This test does not exclude liability for any horizontal arrangements affecting associations under article 81(1). Article 9 of the VAR goes into further detail as to the turnover calculation (which relates to all goods and services of the relevant groups), and provides for a 10 per cent threshold tolerance for up to two years.

Intellectual property rights in vertical agreements

Article 2, para. 3 of the VAR expressly permits the assignment to, or use by, the buyer of IP rights as part of the exempt vertical agreement provided that the IPR provisions are not the primary purpose of the agreement and are directly related to the use, sale or resale of the goods or services by the buyer or its customers, and provided that restrictions on use of the IPR do not, in effect, amount to a non-exempt vertical restraint. This suggests that use of the supplier's IPR must be strictly ancillary to the main supply of goods or services permitted under the agreement.

Removal of exemption

In Article 6 of the VAR the European Commission expressly reserves the right to withdraw the benefit of the VAR in any case where it finds that an arrangement, although technically compliant, is nevertheless seriously anti-competitive in its effect. This may be most likely to arise where there appears to be a series of parallel networks or similar restrictions imposed by competing suppliers or buyers. Article 7 of the VAR extends this by giving the Commission power to exclude the application of the VAR to vertical agreements where there are parallel networks of similar restraints which *overall* cover more than 50 per cent of a relevant market.

UK application

the VAR is of direct application and will therefore apply automatically to UK agreements or arrangements. The OFT will no doubt keep the guidelines on its website updated accordingly. There is a similar power for each national competition authority, faced with national anti-competitive effects, to withdraw the application of the VAR in specific cases in the same way as the powers of the Commission mentioned in the previous paragraph.

HARDCORE AND SEVERABLE RESTRICTIONS IN VERTICAL AGREEMENTS

Hardcore restrictions

Once again, exemption given by both the VRBE and the VAR is lost if there are any hardcore restrictions, which have their own definitions in regulations. If a single hardcore restriction is included in a vertical agreement, the whole agreement will fall outside the vertical agreement exemptions. There are two main hardcore areas to avoid:

- *Resale price maintenance (RPM)* – This covers specifying or fixing or agreeing the resale (not necessarily just retail) prices charged by the other party or third parties. This does not debar a *maximum* (as opposed to minimum) sale price nor a *recommended* sale price provided that these do not amount to a fixed or minimum sale price as a result of pressure from, or incentives offered by, any of the parties. Thus, any element of indirect RPM, such as fixing margins or making rebates or contract terms subject to specified price levels being observed, are likely to be hardcore.
- *Territorial restrictions for resales* – A party must not be limited, directly or indirectly, as to where they can sell (such as exclusive territories or customers), but there may be limitations as to:
  - *active* sales into the exclusive territory or to the exclusive customers of another where (a new slight concession under the VAR) the restriction does not limit sales by the buyer's own customers.

- any sales *by a wholesaler* to end-users.
- sales to an *unauthorized distributor* where there is a selective distribution system in place.
- sales of *components* (intended for the supplier's products) to a competitive manufacturer.

Hardcore terms in selective distribution systems

There are particular problems with what are called 'selective distribution systems', which is where a select group of distributors of similar products have a defined set of territories and quality standards to be met, subject to a set of specialized rules. Such selective distribution systems are a specialist subject outside the broad scope of this chapter, and the competition law position, including the detailed provisions of the VAR, will need to be scrutinized carefully by any business involved in such situations, especially restrictions, such as limitations on resales or on the sale of components to be used as spare parts or on selling competing brands.

Specifically excluded restrictions

There are some other restrictions expressly included by the VAR, meaning that the VAR would not exempt them and they would need to be judged anew under article 81(1). There are two types:

- *Non-compete obligations* (NCOs) (whether direct or indirect, and not limited to the terms of the agreement) are outside the VAR exemption if they are indefinite in duration or exceed five years, except that the five years may be extended in certain circumstances where the supplier owns or leases the premises from which the buyer has been trading. Note also that if the restriction is without time limit or is tacitly renewable after five years, the exemption is lost.
- *Post-termination obligations* (PTOs) – those limiting the buyer's ability to manufacture, buy, sell or resell goods or services *after termination* of the agreement – are not permitted unless they are limited to:
  - to goods or services competing with the contract goods or services; *and*
  - sales from the same premises as occupied by the buyer during the contract period; *and*
  - obligations which are indispensable to protect the know-how transferred by the supplier to the buyer; *and*
  - one year after termination of the agreement (except for possible limitations on the use and disclosure of know-how which has remained confidential and not become public knowledge in which case restrictions might be unlimited so long as the confidentiality is maintained

ACTIVE AND PASSIVE SALES AND THE INTERNET

The distinction that arises in several places between active and passive sales is difficult to apply in respect of Internet sales, where the seller's website is accessible from other jurisdictions. The European Commission's guidelines state that *the Internet is not generally to be regarded as a means of active selling.* This means that it should be assumed that every distributor must be free to use the Internet to advertise and sell products throughout EEA member states. In most cases a prohibition on website sales outside a distributor's permitted territory would take the agreement outside the VRBE, even if the language used in the territories is different, so particular care needs to be taken here. Alternatively there would need to be clear evidence that all or part of the website was specifically targeted at the other territory, which would be regarded as active selling. This area is likely to be reviewed as the pattern and effect of consumer use of the Internet becomes more apparent, and UK businesses should be extremely wary of any differentiation in terms of offer or supply to customers based in non-UK member states. Even regular delays or out-of-stock situations for continental deliveries could be seen as discrimination where the same products are readily available in the UK from the same supplier.

THE TECHNOLOGY TRANSFER BLOCK EXEMPTION (TTBE)

Protection for monopoly rights

This type of protection is even more complex, but deserves mention. The TTBE is mainly concerned with intellectual property rights (IPR) (see Chapter 14) and how these interrelate with competition law. There is, as can immediately be seen, a tension here because IPRs, by their nature, seek to give a form of monopoly right for a defined period, and monopolies are basically contrary to the principles of competition law. The broad intention behind the TTBE is to give a gateway for licences of IPR that permit its exploitation in return for a royalty, but do not impose excessive controls or restrictions on the licensee. Issues that typically arise are the usual suspects – exclusive territories, export bans, pricing restrictions and non-compete obligations.

Limited application

The TTBE, operative since 2004, applies to the licensing of EU patents or know-how, software copyright and a combination of the three. It applies only to agreements between two parties in relation to their EU dimension, and only where the licensee: a) manufactures the product; or b) provides the service licensed; or c) arranges the manufacture or service for its own account. It therefore does not cover agreements concerning copyright or trademarks which are not related to software or which are solely for the purpose of sale. In these cases the VRBE/VAR should be considered. With the TTBE, relevant agreements are protected so long as the underlying rights (such as the patent) are in force or, in the case of know-how, are kept secret.

Market-share test

As elsewhere, arrangements between competitors are more likely to be viewed as anti-competitive, and market share and hardcore provision tests apply. In this case, the market-share threshold for agreements between competitors is 20 per cent and, between non-competitors, 30 per cent – in each case double the level for general vertical agreements under NAOMI.

THE EFFECT ON COMPETITION

Benefits to consumers

Not all restrictive arrangements are necessarily bad or anti-competitive, and competition law recognizes that some restrictions may be acceptable or even essential to ensure that benefits ultimately flow to consumers – one of the litmus tests of the law. To reinvoke the river analogy, a dam would certainly be restrictive of the water flow, but might also enable both the water and the power of the water to be better controlled and harnessed for the benefit of many more people. Dams need huge investment, and that investment may need to be protected so that the investors in the technology, risk and finance can derive a fair return for the benefit they are creating.

Length of restrictions

However, unlike a dam, which one would not expect to be built for a limited period, restrictive arrangements will be expected to have a limited life, even where they are considered of benefit to ultimate consumers. The principle here, as with English common law, is that restrictions should last no longer than necessary for their purpose. So if supplier and distributor agree a degree of exclusivity during their relationship, that exclusivity should not last much longer than the relationship itself. It cannot be used as a means to restrict the relevant market in the longer term. The principles are followed with individual and specific exemptions, such as those referred to under 'Permitted restrictions' above.

Horizontal Agreements (Dealings with Competitors)

In 1776 Adam Smith wrote in *The Wealth of Nations*:

> *'People of the same trade seldom meet together, even for merriment and diversion, but the conversation ends in a conspiracy against the public, or in some contrivance to raise prices.'*

That comment reflects the view of competition authorities even today!

CONSUMER HARM

A key focus in relation to horizontal agreements is whether there is the prospect of consumer harm. This may be the result of arrangements that ultimately limit consumer choice or mean higher consumer prices than would be appropriate in a fully effective competitive market.

OBJECT OR EFFECT?

An important further distinction at this level is to consider whether the arrangements are:

- restrictive in their *objective* – in which case they are liable to be anti-competitive regardless of whether or not they are seen to have any actual effect on competition, or

- potentially restrictive in their *effect* (but not in their objective) – in which case it is necessary to consider their actual effect and whether this restricts competition, especially if this causes, or may cause, consumer detriment.

Cartels are a classic example of the former category by being restrictive in their objective, and are thus regarded as one of the most serious breaches of competition law, such that authorities can impose a fine whether or not there is any actual effect on competition or consumer harm. Cartels are most likely to come about through unwritten understandings, arrangements or concerted commercial behaviour between parties operating in very similar markets. Examples might include a dinner discussion, which might only be of a few minutes' duration, between senior executives of competing auction houses about commission levels or new commission structures, or a high-street retailer encouraging its supplier of replica football shirts to maintain artificially high prices and/or to limit supplies elsewhere, or loyalty rebates paid to suppliers in return for tacit exclusivity of supply.

The restrictive effect of an agreement (the second category above) can be judged in various ways, one being how possible or easy it would be for a new entrant to the market to come in and compete effectively. As soon as supply is restricted in an existing market, it can become difficult for new entrants to gain a foothold in that market. Accordingly, businesses need to look not just at their current competitors, but also at their potential future competitors, to consider whether either group is liable to be excluded from the market with the ultimate effect of causing consumer harm.

SHARING COMMERCIAL INFORMATION

It is highly dangerous in terms of competition law for independent companies to share or discuss information which may be commercially sensitive as such actions suggest an increased ability to coordinate competitive behaviour. Any business would need a very good reason to share commercially confidential information with anyone who is, or is likely to be, a competitor. The basic position is that no commercially or strategically sensitive information should be exchanged. If market-share data is communicated, directly or indirectly, this should be aggregated over the whole market (not just over particular companies) and be historic (rather than being current information or future projections).

Some possible practical measures for any business entering into an arrangement that may be capable of being regarded as anti-competitive are as follows:

- Create *sound paper trails* – for example, by analysing in writing the commercial rationale and benefits to the market (both those directly involved and third parties) of the proposed arrangement before taking matters further. If there are no advantages to others, think again.
- Have clear *minutes of meetings* showing what did (legitimately) take place at trade meetings (including why the meeting was necessary, remembering Adam Smith as above). If the minutes cannot be made available to all, consider why not and what this suggests.

- *Use 'Chinese walls'* and people not involved with 'the other side' of the business – for example, another group or company in a more competitive position with those with whom you are dealing.
- *Use a reputable third party* to obtain and process, on a strictly confidential basis, any commercially sensitive information from others – for example, to obtain an overall market picture.
- *Beware of the market narrowing further* or a reduction in the competition to only a few key players.
- *Beware of collective dealings or boycotts* or anything encouraging them or having the same effect (although joint purchasing may be pro-competitive in certain cases).
- *Try to fit within NAOMI* or the relevant *specific exemptions*.
- Refer to the latest *competition law guidelines* published by the European Commission or OFT.

Abuse of a Dominant Position (Article 82/UK Chapter II)

Article 82, reflected in Chapter II of the UK Competition Act, regulates abuse of a dominant position where this has an impact on a relevant market.

DOMINANCE

Dominance in a market can be judged by whether or not the relevant business has the power to behave, to an appreciable extent, independently of its competitors or customers. In short, does it have the market power to dominate those around it? Dominance is also considered by reference to market share. In general, a market share of below 40 per cent is unlikely to be viewed as dominant, but a market share of 50 per cent or more suggests dominance. These are not absolute figures and there could still be dominance with a market share of 25 per cent if, for example, this is the largest share by far and most of the other players in that market have only very small shares. Dominance of itself is not an offence, but abuse of that dominance is. If a company is dominant, and is unable to show that such actions can be objectively justified, it might abuse that dominant position by the following types of behaviour:

- levying excessive, unfair or discriminatory prices,
- being selective, other than on objective grounds, as to which resellers or others it will supply its products or services,
- granting discriminatory fidelity rebates, or
- 'bundling' arrangements, by making the sale of one product or service conditional on other purchases of goods or services.

No exemptions

Specific or individual exemptions cannot assist if there is an abuse of a dominant position. By definition, any company that holds a dominant position in its market will have a market share outside the permitted maximum share to qualify under a block exemption (as set out above), and that market share is also likely to be high enough that any restrictions the company places on others will tend ultimately to exclude those others from effective competition in the relevant market. The practical effect of this is that dominant companies will have little, if any, scope to enter into exclusivity arrangements.

Breach of article 82 and the dominant position rules carry the same sanctions as breach of article 81, but fines and penalties are likely to be even harsher. As mentioned, a similar regime operates under English law as chapter II of the Competition Act.

KEEPING CONTROL

Companies who are, or may be, dominant in their market are likely to have a battery of competition lawyers readily to hand to keep them on the right path. For that reason, the issue is not dealt with here in any detail. But it pays to remember that even a smaller company could be dominant in a narrow market (such as the local bus service), and even large companies do sometimes go astray. Here again, whilst they may have the right written agreements and policies in place, the competitive pressure that made them so successful may encourage members of their teams to forget their training and go further than the law allows. But if you are planning to suggest that a big business has abused its dominant position, the allegation is unlikely to be welcomed and your evidence needs to be very persuasive!

Practical Issues Relating to Potential Anti-competitive Arrangements

Key points for drafting and understanding commercial agreements depend on whether the agreement is between competitors or not. The following are likely issues:

- *Price fixing*, as might be expected, is hardcore and to be avoided in any form.
- *Limitations on output* of a licensed product or service may be hardcore and need careful planning.
- *Certain market-sharing restrictions* are hardcore, although, again, this needs to be looked at in detail.
- *Restrictions on both active and passive sales* may be hardcore, but there maybe some flexibility in the detail in relation to active sales (see the VAR).
- *Component part contracts* need to be carefully checked against the relevant exemption.
- *Non-compete restrictions* need to be limited in scope or product and market and time.
- *Provisions prohibiting any challenge* to the licensor's IPR.

NO-CHALLENGE CLAUSES

A no-challenge clause is one which prohibits a licensee from challenging its licensor's ownership to an intellectual property right – typically, a trademark. As an absolute prohibition is anti-competitive, a licensor will often protect itself in practice by reserving power to terminate the agreement if the licensee does challenge ownership of the IP right. This problem needs to be borne carefully in mind when there is settlement of a dispute between competitive trademark uses, and the draft settlement agreement contains mutual no-challenge clauses.

THE PENALTIES FOR BREACH OF COMPETITION LAW

Non-compliance with competition law may have serious effects. The restrictions themselves are likely to be unenforceable, and the competition authorities may levy substantial fines of up to 10 per cent of the total turnover of the offender's group of companies, making those involved doubly unpopular. In addition, third parties affected by the restrictions may have the right to seek injunctions, and possibly damages, against those involved in the agreement. If the parties fall out, and one threatens to sue the other for breach of contract, the potential defendant's lawyer may look at the terms of the agreement and also what is happening in practice. A potential breach of competition law, either in drafting or in the way in which the agreement is operated, is a doubly effective stick with which to beat the potential claimant. Not only may the relevant restrictions be unenforceable and give the restricted party a cause of action in turn, but the very claim of a competition law defence may also alert the competition authorities to investigate, and that is likely to be the most serious threat of all.

Criminal penalties

The UK competition authorities are clear in their opposition to cartels in particular. In additional to swingeing fines, prison sentences can be, and have been, handed out to those directors and senior managers involved. Moreover, any non-compliance with the investigation, let alone a furtive shredding of key documents, is likely to increase punishments substantially. Those 'blowing the whistle' first on anti-competitive behaviour will be likely to benefit from leniency. Typically, quite complex rules have already built up round this area, but speed is vital if a business is to take advantage. Although only one party can hope to gain 100 per cent leniency, there are still worthwhile prizes for also-rans, such as reductions in fines for subsequent applicants who add value to the investigative process (50 per cent for the second applicant and lesser amounts for those that follow). So those involved in something that they realize may be illegal should take urgent advice and be prepared to sacrifice their principles of honour to trade colleagues if they wish to take advantage of leniency. Whether or not this is a desirable social objective is a separate matter of debate.

Competition Law Checklist

ANTI-COMPETITIVE BEHAVIOUR

Drafting Contracts

When drafting contracts beware of sensitive issues, notably:

- **prices** – trying directly or indirectly to fix the buying or selling prices or margins of other parties.
- **discounts** – seeking common discounts, rebates or collusive bids.
- **promotional terms**/special promotions – where these may limit fair competition from others.

- **boycotts** – or refusal to deal with customers or suppliers.
- **limitations** – on supply, production, technology or advertising.
- **trading terms and conditions** – which might have possible anti-competitive effects.
- **market allocation** – geographical areas, products or customers.

Business dealings

When discussing or meeting others in the same market, don't:

- **discuss** or recommend or agree 'sensitive issues' with competitors.
- **meet** or stay in meetings with competitors where 'sensitive issues' are discussed.
- **exchange** or receive price lists unless the list is publicly available.

Avoidance techniques

- **Maintain secrecy** – keep your pricing and other 'sensitive issues' plans secret until you announce them to all.
- **Leave** any meeting where there is discussion of sensitive issues.
- **Record** your departure from the meeting by note or similar.

DOMINANCE

To avoid suggesting or abusing a dominant position, don't:

- use the **language of dominance**.
- **set predatory prices** – that is, price so low as to cut out competition from your market.
- **tie loyalty** by rebates or other deals to tie suppliers or customers to you.
- **promote or act** in such as way as to exclude effective competition.
- **link** one deal to another.

Avoidance techniques

- **Watch** the relevant market/your market share (especially if you achieve more than 30 per cent).
- **Check** that you are maintaining profit margins on price cuts.
- **Look out for** potential complainants and deal scrupulously with them.

COMPETITION LAW TESTS

General questions

Does your agreement contain any explicit or implicit restrictions limiting any of the parties to act with complete competitive freedom in all respects? If so:

- What is the broadest 'relevant market' that might apply to the products or services involved, applying the product and geographical tests?

- What share of that market do you hold (with other group companies if relevant)?
- What market share is held by the other parties to the contract?
- Is the agreement vertical, horizontal or 'collective'?

Agreements of minor importance (NAOMI)

Do the combined market shares of all parties to the contract exceed any of the following:

- 15 per cent (vertical)?
- 10 per cent (horizontal)? or
- 5 per cent (collective)?

If the answer is 'no' to all, and if the agreement does not contain any hardcore restrictions (for example, resale price maintenance) NAOMI should apply, but it pays to keep the position under review.

Vertical agreements exemption

You need to answer 'yes' to all the following questions. Does your agreement:

- have only parties at different levels within the supply chain?
- not include any effective competitor at the same level in the supply chain?
- involve parties, each of whom have less than 30 per cent of the relevant market?
- relate to products or services falling within the following market share thresholds:
    - supplier's share 30 per cent or less?
    - if an exclusive purchase agreement, buyer's share 30 per cent or less?
- not constitute a selective distribution system?
- contain no hardcore provisions applicable during its term?
- contain no hardcore provisions applicable after its term?

If you cannot answer 'yes' to any of these vertical agreement questions, consider amending the draft agreement so as to comply.

Dominant position

Are you a potential monopoly or do you have a potentially dominant position?

- *Market position* – Do you have disgruntled business partners or competitors who might consider reporting you to the European Commission or the OFT?
- *Market power* – might you be using your position in an abusive way?

No exemptions

If you are involved in something potentially anti-competitive, are not dominant and do not appear to fit within any other exemptions, have you worked out the basis on which you can be reasonably confident that you could obtain an individual article 83(1) exemption?

PART

III
CONTRACTS FOR SALES AND SERVICES

9 Sales of Goods – Implied Terms and Standard Terms of Business

Introduction – the legal framework – terms and conditions of business – detailed review of sample terms of business – some other sale of goods issues – joint supply of goods and services – summary and checklist

Introduction

In selling their goods, many companies rely on an order form or process coupled with their own standard terms of business (TOB). Buyers of goods, faced with the seller's TOB, have to decide whether just to accept those terms or to try to negotiate them. Increasingly, when larger corporations such as supermarkets are purchasers, it is they as buyer who will insist on their own TOB, often leaving the seller little scope for renegotiation. Businesses need to know what such terms actually mean, which of them may be important and how they might be negotiated. This chapter covers the sale and purchase of goods, either alone or when part of a joint supply of goods and services. Services on their own, covered in Chapter 12, may have different laws and issues. Exclusion and limitation clauses, which affect contracts for both goods and services, have been broadly covered in Chapter 7, the implications of which need to be kept in mind throughout this and all subsequent chapters.

The Legal Framework

Some names of relevant statutes and regulations are repeated occasionally, but the following abbreviations are also used (all Acts and Regulations referred to here are to be treated as amended by subsequent legislation):

> SGA Sale of Goods Act 1979
> SGSA Supply of Goods and Services Act 1982
> UCTA Unfair Contract Terms Act 1977
> UTCCR Unfair Terms in Consumer Contracts Regulations 1999

COMMON LAW AND LEGISLATION

No UK commercial code

In contrast to the position in some continental European countries, English law does not have a statutory commercial code, so there is no single point of easy reference. In any event, regulations always spawn uncertainties and unfairness; when something is unclear or falls on the perceived wrong side of the line, the courts may be called in to decide the uncertainty or redress the unfairness, so there is a continuous interplay between regulations and court judgments.

Regulating unfairness

In theory, our judges do not make new law, but interpret and clarify what the law is, even if, in the process, the law sometimes appears to alter! When social change requires faster action, parliament brings in legislation aiming to cure the problem or fill the gap, prompted possibly by a decided case, by the Law Commission or by political considerations. These new rules are in turn tested by practice, honed (or confused in some cases) by court decisions and then further amended or consolidated in new legislation. And so the process continues. As Lord Hope said at the start of his judgment in *Chartbrook Ltd* v. *Persimmon Homes Ltd* in 2009, 'One of the strengths of the common law is that it can take a fresh look at itself so that it can keep pace with changing circumstances' (at para. 2).

EUROPEAN LAW

Our laws are also driven by the European Union. The European Treaty (formerly the Treaty of Rome) is not just the bedrock of the European Union, but effectively also part of the UK constitution. The Treaty is the basis of European law and the source of the authority of the European Commission which, together with the European Parliament, and in consultation with member states and the other bodies of the Union, develops the law primarily through regulations and directives. Regulations have direct effect in member states from the date that they come into force; directives are obligations on member states to introduce the necessary legislation in their own countries within a given time. In the UK that legislation is usually in the form of statutory instruments, which have the same effect as a formal statute. Alongside this process the ever-increasing international nature of trade gives added impetus to the harmonization of cross-border terms and practices of trading, inside and outside the strict framework of legislation (see Chapter 17).

TERMS IMPLIED BY STATUTE OR REGULATION

Implied terms are terms which common law or, more usually, legislation implies into certain contracts, especially in contracts for the sale of goods under laws such as the Sale of Goods Act 1979 (SGA). As already seen, some of those implied terms are regarded as sacrosanct and cannot be excluded or varied by the contract. The main implied terms in sale of goods contracts, looked at in more detail below, are that:

- the goods must be of satisfactory quality
- the seller must legally own the goods at the time they are sold to the buyer
- the goods must comply with any description or sample
- the advertising or marketing of the goods must not be misleading
- any exclusion or limitation of liability terms must be reasonable.

REGULATORY AUTHORITIES

The main custodian of consumer protection in UK is the Office of Fair Trading (OFT), which has a role in the overall enforcement of fair trading and competition law. It has considerable power to challenge traders in many areas, including issuing stop notices in respect of unfair practices and generally intervening even where the effect on consumers is indirect (such as seen in relation to competition law – see Chapter 8). The website of the UK Department for Business, Innovation and Skills (BIS, formerly BERR, the Department of Enterprise and Regulatory Reform) is an especially good point of first reference for many of the regulations covered here.

WHAT ARE GOODS?

Goods defined

Goods are things which have (or will, when they are produced, have) a physical character, apart from money itself, which is governed by a separate set of laws. The definition specifically excludes intangible rights such as copyrights and trademarks. This distinction can be significant, since the sale of goods legislation requires that goods must be of satisfactory quality and fit for their intended purpose. However, as will be seen in later chapters, the previously clear distinction between goods and services is becoming more blurred, especially in the digital arena.

Consumer sales

If the sale is to a personal consumer (or end-user in technology terms), more stringent regulations apply, and modern consumer protection laws increasingly concentrate on 'products', which may be a mix of goods and services or, indeed, pure services. This highlights the critical distinction between business and consumer transactions, Chapter 10 being devoted specifically to the latter.

Terms and Conditions of Business

The common tendency in *preparing standard terms of business* is to plagiarize another company's terms! However, apart from the risk of potential breach of copyright (even terms of business have copyright), the other company's terms may be oversimplistic, out-of-date, inappropriate or plain unlawful. The other extreme – extracting every possible clause from anywhere and everywhere to produce the kitchen sink of extensive terms – is equally to be avoided. The best way forward, in most cases, may be for the business itself to consider and record its own policy and practice and then to incorporate those principles within a draft or, if you are less experienced, an outline brief from which your lawyer can prepare a draft.

Matching the terms to the business is important in several respects. First, if the terms and conditions of a business do not match the organization's philosophy, there tends to be inconsistency between the theory of the standard terms and the practice actually followed. This easily creates confusion and mixed messages, and could ultimately also suggest that the standard terms have been waived or overridden by agreement. Second, business terms should reflect attitude to risk, which will vary from business to business. The tolerance factor (see Chapter 3) is also relevant here. If the standard terms give no margin or impose unreasonable deadlines, conflict will be created because unreasonable terms are made or not enforced. An extreme view in written terms but leniency in practice may only confuse and alienate customers and create uncertainty in the minds of the employees who have to operate the policy. For this reason, the directors responsible for sales fulfilment should be fully involved in, and supportive of, the process of creating an appropriate set of 'standard' terms. Third, the terms of business must obviously comply with the law and achieve legally what they are expected to achieve.

A sample set of terms for the sale of products by a seller to a customer is set out below. This is followed by a closer look at some of the issues that arise and how these are dealt with by law. It should be stressed that these are short-form and sample terms only and not a recommended precedent, for all the reasons set out in this book! They may be a useful starting-point for the process suggested in previous paragraphs, but legal advice should be taken on specific circumstances and any changes that may have occurred in law or practice.

The following points should be noted:

- The terms are reasonably – but not entirely – neutral.
- It is assumed that they will be set out on the back of an order form which, if practical, both seller and customer will sign or, if transmitted electronically, indicate that they accept. They may be in table form so that fairly detailed terms can fit on to one side of an A4 sheet, but the print size must be adequate, as terms that are barely legible are likely to be unfair.
- Definitions are in bold type.
- Wording shown in square brackets will depend on the specific circumstances, and also highlight some areas which a buyer may seek to amend.

A SHORT-FORM SET OF TERMS OF BUSINESS (FOR BUSINESS TO BUSINESS SALES)

TERMS AND CONDITIONS OF SALE/BUSINESS

1. **Applicability of terms**. The terms and conditions below (**these terms**) apply to and are deemed incorporated into each contract (**Contract**) for the sale of **Products** by **Seller** to **Buyer**, each as described on the order form overleaf/attached (**Order Form**).

2. **Delivery**. Seller will [use its reasonable endeavours to] deliver Products to Buyers at the address shown in the Order Form (**Delivery**) by the [est*imated*] delivery date shown on the Order Form and for this purpose:
    a) Delivery is deemed to take place when the Products are actually delivered to Buyer's premises;
    b) [Seller does not guarantee the date and will have no liability to Buyer for any delay in delivery beyond the estimated date;]

c)   If Seller is unable to complete Delivery within 14 days after the estimated delivery date Buyer may by written notice to Seller cancel the Contract;

d)   Products are sold on a firm sale basis without right of return or refund except for damaged Products as set out below.

3.   **Price and payment**. The price payable for Products (**Price**) is shown on the Order Form, exclusive of VAT which is payable at the applicable rate. [*Delivery provisions and costs?*] Buyer will pay Seller in full in cleared funds by no later than [date *or* the number of days shown on the order form counting from the date of Delivery (*or invoice?*) *or*, if no period is stated, payment will be made in full in cleared funds on and as a condition of delivery and release of the Products to Buyer]. If Seller terminates as permitted by these terms because of Buyer's insolvency all sums due and payable by Buyer to Seller on any account will be immediately due and payable.

4.   **Risk in Products**. Risk in the Products will pass to Buyer immediately on Delivery.

5.   **Title to Products**. Title to the Products will remain with Seller until all amounts due to Seller from Buyer for the Products and on any other account between Seller and Buyer have been paid in full. Until title passes Buyer will hold the Products as bailee for Seller and will keep them secure, separate and intact in their original packaging and will permit Seller to enter Buyer's premises to retrieve the Products if Buyer becomes insolvent or fails to pay any sum to Seller when due, at which point any right of Buyer to resell any Products will immediately cease.

6.   **Defects**. Buyer must [inspect the Products and] notify Seller in writing within 14 days of Delivery if Delivery appears inconsistent with the Order Form or as soon as practicable, and in any event within [14 days], of the date on which Buyer became or should reasonably first have become aware of any apparent defect in or damage to the Products.

7.   **Remedies**. Provided Buyer has complied with 6 above Seller at its sole option and as Buyer's sole remedy will arrange to replace any defective Products [*or* to give Buyer credit for any defective Products at the unit price per Unit specified on the Order Form].

8.   **Liability**. Seller will not be liable to Buyer for any failure on the part of Seller caused by circumstances beyond its reasonable control.

9.   **Insolvency**. Without limiting either party's other rights under the Contract:

a)   Seller or Buyer may serve written notice on the other terminating the Contract with immediate effect if the other becomes [or proposes or indicates an intention to become] insolvent;

b)   Insolvent in these terms includes entering into bankruptcy or liquidation, or having an administrator or administrative receiver appointed or any general composition or voluntary arrangement with creditors or that the party is unable to pay its debts as [and when] they fall due.

10. **General**

a)   *Notices*: Any notice or other communication given under these terms must be in writing delivered personally, or sent by first-class post, or sent by e-mail with a delivery receipt, to the relevant party's address specified in the Order Form or to such other address and e-mail address as either party may have last notified to the other. Any notice is deemed duly given on the day it is delivered personally, or on the second day following the date it was sent by post, or on the next normal working day following e-mail delivery receipt.

b) *Entire agreement*: The Order Form and these terms constitute the entire agreement between the parties, and supersede all other agreements or arrangements between Seller and Buyer (whether written or oral, express or implied), relating to the Products.

c) *Assignment*: Buyer [*or* neither party] may [not] assign or transfer its rights or obligations without the prior written consent of Seller [other].

d) *Severability*: Any provision in these terms which is held by any competent court or tribunal to be illegal or unenforceable will to the extent necessary be regarded as omitted from these terms and the enforceability of the remainder will not be affected.

e) *Waivers*: Neither party will be affected by any delay or failure in exercising or any partial exercising of its rights under this agreement unless it has signed an express written waiver or release.

f) *Variations*: No variations of this agreement are effective unless made in writing signed by Seller and Buyer or their authorized agents.

g) *Right of third parties*: The parties intend that no term of this agreement may be enforced by any person who is not a party to it.

h) *Law and jurisdiction*: This agreement will be governed and construed in accordance with the laws of England and Wales and the parties submit to the jurisdiction of the English courts.

Detailed Review of Sample Terms of Business

These comments follow the same numbering as the sample.

1 APPLICABILITY OF TERMS AND IDENTIFYING THE PRODUCTS

Incorporation into the contract

These terms must be 'incorporated' into the contract before the contract is finalized and should therefore be introduced at the first opportunity and referred to clearly in all relevant correspondence. In this case having the terms set out on the back of the order form, which both parties need to sign or agree to before the contract comes into existence, will help to ensure this incorporation, provided the right process is followed. The standard terms should also be referred to on the front of the order form and again on invoices. (See also the example of negotiating this issue, p. 20 onwards in Chapter 2.)

Unfair terms

The terms may be subject to scrutiny if the buyer challenges them under UCTA (or, in the case of a consumer sale, the UTCCR). In a consumer sale especially (for which the terms above would need to be adapted as per Chapter 10), the seller should draw the buyer's attention to the terms (for which there will often be a reminder or even a tick box on the front of the order form), and the terms should comply with the principles of both UCTA and the UTCCR (see Chapters 7 and 10 respectively). If there is any other linked deal, this may need to be referred to.

1 PRODUCTS – IDENTIFYING THE GOODS AND COMPLIANCE WITH DESCRIPTION

Checking the description is the first thing the buyer should do, as it goes to the root of the deal.

Special requirements

If there are extras or special functions, these should be clearly stated. The buyer also needs to think about such things as whether the product ordered is the latest model or the technical specification is clear and whether the packaging and labelling need to be specified. Most disputes, other than those arising from the buyer's failure to pay on time, are likely to arise from an unfulfilled expectation of the buyer, so the more clearly the buyer's requirements have been stated, the less likelihood there is of an escalating dispute.

Sale by description

Under SGA s. 13, goods must comply with their description where the buyer has relied on the description without seeing the actual goods; it may also apply where the goods have been seen, but non-compliance with description was not readily apparent. Reference to description includes the quantity or weight of goods, their measurements and their overall get-up and packaging. Minor discrepancies may be overlooked.

2 DELIVERY AND ACCEPTANCE

Time and place of delivery

These may be critical terms. The general delivery and acceptance provisions in the SGA are subject to any different intentions expressed by the parties in the sale contract. The place of delivery should be clearly stated but, subject to some rare exceptions, there is no implication in the SGA as to particular delivery date, other than that this should be within a 'reasonable time', which is inevitably a question of fact in each case. Unless otherwise agreed, the buyer is not obliged to accept partial delivery, but may accept some parts and reject others which are defective or delayed. The SGA does set out detailed rules as to acceptance; these rules should be consulted if the parties have not expressly agreed on the issue.

Delivery dates

These can be a major problem, especially if goods are made to order, and failure by the seller to supply on time might create major problems. The seller will want to state that delivery is not guaranteed by any particular date, but the buyer needs to consider this carefully. With food products, for example, it is likely that the time of delivery, the freshness of the product and its freedom from harmful bacteria are critical. Delivery of an out-of-date, even if not unsafe, product may be rejected by the retailer, ultimate supplier or consumer. Other cases may have different issues, and the buyer should be explicit with the seller if timing is important. If, for example, a new till system is required for a shop opening, the potential losses in delaying the shop opening could be substantial, and far higher than the value of the goods, if the system is not installed and properly functioning in time. This also relates to the level of risk allocated between the parties. If the buyer has insisted on a heavy discount, it may have to accept a greater risk. The seller might want to avoid giving way on both price and risk. Both parties will need to consider corresponding terms in any contracts with their own suppliers and sub-purchasers. In this case, the buyer is given a right to cancel after a relatively short period of time, which may help to overcome the lack of delivery date certainty.

Time of the essence

If the delivery date is critical, the buyer should stipulate that the time of delivery 'is of the essence', meaning that failure to deliver on time will amount to the breach of a fundamental term such that the buyer could terminate the whole contract and/or claim damages if the delivery date is missed, even by a single day. Obviously a seller should agree such a clause only if certain of performing on time and should look out for this in a buyer's standard terms of purchase. Even a liquidated damages clause might be preferable. Such provisions need to be reserved for special cases.

Post-delivery inspection

The buyer may be required to inspect, within a reasonable time, what has been delivered and report back to the seller any apparent deficiencies. What is a reasonable time will depend on the circumstances. Sometimes the buyer will need time and ability to inspect and detect whether the goods supplied differ from the earlier sample or from the quality identified in an order. With bulk goods, a tolerance of plus or minus 5–10 per cent from the volume or weight originally ordered may be agreed, but the implications for onward supplies should then be considered. If the goods are intended for resale in their existing packaging, the buyer may be unable to discover whether they are defective until the goods are finally delivered to, and used by, the ultimate consumer. If they are defective, the business which sold to that consumer will doubtless have to repair or replace them, and a claim for redress is likely to be carried back up the supply chain.

Rejecting goods

Any rejection of goods must be communicated to the seller quickly and unequivocally to be effective since any delay may kill off any possibility of the right to reject in law. In such cases, excess tolerance may work against a buyer, but buyers should take care that their action is reasonable in the overall context, since, otherwise, the seller may claim full payment anyway.

3 PRICE AND PAYMENT

Price is normally the one thing that parties agree on in a sale of goods, and it is unlikely that the terms of the bargain would have sufficient certainty to constitute a legal contract if the price were not agreed. But sometimes this happens, or the price is subject to (unspecified) variation. Where no price is specified, the courts may – somewhat reluctantly – imply a reasonable price by reference to trade custom, clearly known market price or even previous dealings between the same parties. For all goods, the cost of delivery and, where applicable, customs duties, other taxes, packaging costs and insurance should also be considered and specified where appropriate.

Price increases

In inflationary times, sellers like to have the right to increase the price in certain circumstances. Unilateral price increases are likely to be unfair on the buyer, probably invalid in consumer sales and potentially ineffective in business sales. If there is a provision for a price increase, this should provide for notice to be given to the buyer plus a reasonable opportunity for the buyer to terminate the contract and have any deposit returned, either for any price increase or for an increase above a certain amount or percentage. Buyers should take care that any such notices are carefully monitored and acted on where necessary.

Price decreases

Especially in times of financial uncertainty, buyers may remember that costs – and thus prices – may go down as well as up. Even in better times there are areas where overseas production and heavy competition have tended to drive prices down over the years. In times of negative growth and even falls in the cost of living there may be many challenges to established ideas of price.

Time of payment

The SGA default position is that payment is due on delivery. Let buyers beware: there is no implication of any credit period at all, which means that delayed payment should be specifically agreed in each case. The date for payment is a vital part of any well-drafted conditions of sale and should also be brought clearly to the attention of the parties on the face of the contract document. In consumer sales, however, payment is likely to be due on or before delivery. If a buyer defaults in making payment, the seller will ultimately have the right to terminate the contract. If the seller still has the goods, it may need to seek to mitigate its loss by reselling them, on the best reasonably available market terms at that time, and then claim from the buyer the difference between the overall contract price and the resale price, less any direct costs incurred in the process.

Commercial payment terms

Different industries tend to have different norms, ranging from on delivery to 90 days or, in some cases, even longer. The terms should clearly state the date from which time periods run plus where and how payment should be made. If payment is calculated as a number of days from invoice, sellers should ensure that the invoice is delivered at the same time as the goods. The buyer, on the other hand, will want to ensure that the invoice is not dated prior to delivery and, particularly in overseas transactions, that a copy of the invoice is sent by fax or PDF e-mail immediately it is issued. Payment may be specified as a number of days from end of month, being the end of the month in which the invoice is sent (or received), and this can, on average, increase the payment days by a further 15. If appropriate, the terms should specify currency, and may require payment direct to the seller's bank, net of all bank charges. If other currencies may be used, the seller will usually want to stipulate the exchange-rate mechanism. Care also needs to be taken with contracts stipulating delivery of goods by instalments or where payments are required on account. In such cases, the seller may wish to ensure that date for payment of the instalments or on account is of the essence of the contract or at least to provide that the goods do not have to be delivered if there is any subsisting instalment payment failure.

4 THE PASSING OF RISK

Risk in the goods will normally pass at the same time as ownership of the goods, unless the contract specifies otherwise. Many conditions of sale specify that risk passes on delivery, which may be earlier than when ownership passes. The practical effect of this is that the buyer takes the risk of loss or damage to the goods after delivery and should insure them as from the point of delivery. The contract should therefore make clear when delivery is deemed to occur, as this is a classic area for dispute. This may be deemed to be at any time from the moment of departure from the seller's premises to the point of safe receipt in the buyer's premises, with a range of options in between, especially in international sales. Both parties should also check how this impacts on their insurance, just in case the goods are actually destroyed.

5 TITLE (OWNERSHIP IN THE GOODS)

Warranty of title

The SGA (ss 12 and 18) implies a term in the contract that the seller has title to the goods (also known as ownership of or property in them) and a warranty that the seller can pass good title to the buyer free from any third-party claims. UCTA reinforces this by making void any attempt to exclude this implied warranty.

Retention of title

In the example, retention of title is covered by delaying transfer of ownership of the products until, in this case, all amounts due from the buyer to the seller are paid. The subject of retention of title and the drafting issues arising are dealt with more fully under 'Insolvency' (p. 105) in Chapter 6.

6 DEFECTS (QUALITY AND FITNESS FOR PURPOSE)

Satisfactory quality

SGA s. 14 implies in sale of goods contracts that the goods must be both of 'satisfactory quality' (replacing the former 'merchantable quality') and fit for their actual purpose. Satisfactory quality is a broad concept, judged by whether the goods are of an objective standard which a reasonable person would regard as satisfactory in all the circumstances, including the price charged for them. Appearance, finish, safety, durability and freedom from minor defects may all be relevant.

Fitness for purpose

This is associated with the question of quality, and buyers will want sellers to be aware of the purpose for which the buyer intends to use the goods, especially if this is not immediately obvious. The implied term will not apply to cases where the buyer is an expert, or where the seller declares he has no expertise in relation to the products, or the buyer expressly agrees to take the goods as they are. 'Sold as seen' is, however, not a reliable disclaimer if the seller has not specifically drawn the buyer's attention to any defects or the buyer has not expressly taken time to examine the goods or agreed to accept the goods with any inadequacies they may have.

7/8 REMEDIES AND LIABILITY

Exclusion and limitation clauses are dealt with in detail in Chapter 7. A seller cannot simply disclaim all liability for the quality or suitability of goods, but there is nevertheless scope for carefully drafted exclusion or limitation clauses, tailored to the particular circumstances. In commercial agreements it may be worth the parties specifically negotiating and agreeing terms to reduce the chances of these being held 'standard' terms and thus more likely to be unenforceable under UCTA. Buyers, for their part, should take special care with limitation clauses, which are obviously unlikely to appear in any buyer's standard conditions of purchase. In the above example, the limitation applies only to force majeure issues, well short of a general exclusion clause, but the 'sole remedy' wording in paragraph 7 is effectively a limitation clause.

9 INSOLVENCY

The issues surrounding insolvency are dealt with in more detail in Chapter 6.

10 GENERAL

These are typical 'boilerplate' clauses, dealt with in more detail in Chapter 4 and in some specialist sections of this book.

Some Other Sale of Goods Issues

This chapter concentrates on typical terms for the sale of goods. Chapter 10 considers the issues arising in consumer (including website) sales, and typical distribution terms are dealt with in Chapter 11. This section now looks at some other relevant or related express or implied terms in sale of goods transactions.

SPECIFIC AND UNASCERTAINED GOODS

Selecting goods

The precise point when risk in goods passes to a buyer is important in deciding who bears any loss. This is usually clear, but becomes complex with what the SGA calls 'specific, ascertained and unascertained goods'. This is best illustrated through the heady world of wine. If I go to my local off-licence or supermarket and select a bottle, it will be specific. If, on the other hand, I join one of the wine clubs which selects the wine within a pre-agreed price bracket, the wine will be 'unascertained' (at least by me) until I am notified what it is or it is actually delivered. Under the SGA, the title to unascertained goods cannot pass until they have become ascertained. However, the SGA rules only apply if the intention of the parties is unclear. So, if the parties to the contract agree when title passes, they can override the implied terms of the SGA. The detailed rules in SGA s. 18 are complex, but the following are worth noting:

- If I order a case of specific wine from the off-licence or my wine club and they agree to deliver it, the wine is technically mine already. If payment is expressed to be a precondition of handing over, however, such as cash on delivery, the wine does not become mine until the condition is satisfied by payment being made.
- If the goods are not in a state to be delivered, the title does not pass until they are ready and I, as the buyer, have been told this.
- If the seller has to carry out a step, such as weighing the goods in order to fix the price, title does not pass until the weighing has been done and the buyer informed.
- Where the buyer needs to approve the goods or there is sale or return, title only passes when the buyer accepts the goods or retains them for an unreasonable length of time. Consumption of the wine (without complaint), for example, might be safely regarded as acceptance, as would giving it away to friends.

Theft of goods

So, if I order my mystery case of wine, it becomes specific when the bottles are selected and the case is picked up by the carrier for delivery to the waiting tipplers. What if I am out, the case is left in my front porch and stolen from there? It depends on whether the legal risk in the wine has passed to me. In the circumstances mentioned, assuming that I had already paid the bill or that I was a trusted customer who paid later on receipt of the wine company's account, the SGA rules would say that the property in the goods had passed to me. Since risk will pass at the latest when title passes (and often before, as seen in the terms of business above), the risk and, accordingly, the loss would therefore be mine.

SALE BY SAMPLE (SGA S. 15)

Where a buyer sees sample goods and agrees to buy by reference to that sample, the remainder of the goods must conform to the sample. SGA s. 15 confirms this and gives a reasonable opportunity for inspection before the goods are deemed to have been accepted by the buyer.

BAILMENT

Bailment is another ancient legal concept which arises where one of the parties has obligations to store or look after the goods in some way, and there may be special obligations on the party with the storage obligation (the bailee). Whilst not covered by the SGA, in general the law will imply a duty of reasonable care on the bailee where payment is made for the storage services or where this forms part of the overall contract. The standard of care will be much less where no payment is made and the storage is provided on a voluntary basis.

BRINGING/INCORPORATING THE TERMS INTO THE CONTRACT

Keeping adequate records of how and when the relevant terms were incorporated into the contract is important, not just the fact that this has happened. If there is a dispute as to whose terms apply or if the buyer becomes insolvent and the seller claims retention of title, the parties will need to show *how* and *when* the relevant terms were incorporated into the sale contract. The seller (or the buyer if the buyer is trying to enforce its own conditions) will therefore need very clear records as to what conditions were in force at any one time and how these conditions were notified to the buyer before the contract was made. For this reason, when sellers first adopt or later change their conditions of sale, they would do well to submit copies to all their normal business customers and further copies with all estimates and quotations, ideally with a date on them. With written quotations, standard conditions may be printed on the reverse or sent in full at the same time as the estimate/quotation. If, however, orders are generally taken by telephone and are legally effective on order, the terms and conditions must have been notified to potential buyers beforehand. Simply printing standard conditions on sales order confirmation notes or invoices will not of itself suffice, since the contract will already have come into being before the invoice is submitted.

COURSE OF DEALINGS

There is one important exception to the general principle that failure to incorporate terms of business before the contract is concluded will be fatal to relying on those terms. Where there is a regular course of dealings between the same parties they may be regarded as having accepted, expressly or by implication, that these dealings should be governed by the same terms and conditions as used previously between them. Those terms may then be regarded as incorporated in the contract. Whilst it is unwise for sellers to rely on this, buyers should take note that, in this instance, if sellers do, for example, include conditions of sale on the reverse of their invoices and also refer to the existence of standard terms and conditions on paperwork circulated before the contract is made, those conditions may well be regarded as incorporated into the contract when the next deal is made.

THE BATTLE OF THE FORMS

What, then, if the seller sends off a set of conditions of sale and the buyer responds with its standard conditions of purchase? As seen in Chapters 1 and 2, acceptance on different terms destroys the original offer and creates a counter-offer. If the buyer's acceptance introduces, or is subject to, new terms, this destroys the seller's previous offer and creates a counter-offer by the buyer, which it is up to the seller to accept or reject. If there is no further correspondence and the seller delivers the goods, delivery will be deemed acceptance by the seller of the buyer's counter-offer, and the buyer's terms will then apply. If the seller replies, noting the buyer's offer but sending a new quotation form for the buyer to countersign, incorporating the seller's terms, this will be a further counter-offer which the buyer could accept by signature. If the buyer signs, the seller's terms would then apply. As a last resort in the absence of agreement as to terms before delivery, the TOB could be attached to the packaging of the goods themselves when they are delivered, stating that the terms are a condition of acceptance of the goods. If the buyer then accepts the goods and signs for them on the seller's delivery note, the seller's TOB should be deemed accepted. Simply stating that your terms will prevail will be ineffective. What matters, in the battle of the forms, is 'who fired the last shot' before acceptance, so be vigilant and determined not to be outflanked!

Joint Supply of Goods and Services

The Sale of Goods Act (SGA) applies to goods which are actually sold; it does not deal with the supply of services or with hiring and leasing agreements or other agreements for the supply of goods short of outright sale where the statutory protection is set out in the Supply of Goods and Services Act 1982 as amended (SGSA). Hire purchase and credit sale are not covered by this Act and are regulated separately.

SUPPLY OF GOODS ELEMENT

Part I of the SGSA sets out a set of implied terms which are largely parallel to the implied terms in the SGA for circumstances where there is a supply, but less than a full or outright sale, of goods. These terms also apply where there is a mixed supply of goods and services, such as under a building contract where the builder supplies the materials as well as the labour. The materials that are supplied under the contract are effectively sold as goods and must comply with implied terms as to quality and fitness for purpose, equivalent to those set out in the SGA.

SUPPLY OF SERVICES ELEMENT

Part II of the SGSA deals with services supplied in the course of a business. The provider of those services has an implied obligation to provide them with reasonable care and skill. The level of care and skill depends on the level of care and skill that an ordinary competent supplier of those services would be expected to have. Contracts for pure services are explored further in Chapter 12.

AN EXAMPLE OF A MIXED SALE OF GOODS AND SERVICE CONTRACT

Cruncher & Co., chartered accountants, are refurbishing their offices and planning a new file storage system. They engage Stargazers, space planners, to design and install the new layout. Stargazers, after measuring up the site and discussing Cruncher's requirements with their facilities manager, design a system which consists of a number of standard units linked to purpose-made partitions and shelving.

Terms are agreed and client approval is given, but there is no written contract. Stargazers order the standard cabinets from Morris Furniture Supplies and engage Chippy Brothers to carry out the partitioning and shelving work. Everything is installed, and Crunchers move back into the space. To their dismay, they find that several of the cabinets have been put in different places from the agreed plan (limiting their office layout) and some cabinets are of the wrong size for their files. Some of the shelves are loose and unable to support heavy files and, overall, the space is substantially short of the firm's planned new filing requirements.

Contract Analysis

1. The main contract is between Crunchers, the accountants, and Stargazers, the space planners. As Stargazers have undertaken the overall project, this is a supply of goods and services contract governed by the SGSA.
2. Stargazers have entered into a subcontract with Morris for the purchase of cabinets. This is a straight sale of goods contract governed by the SGA.
3. Stargazers have also entered into a subcontract with Chippy Brothers for the fit-out work. This is a supply of goods and services contract governed by the SGSA.

Duties of care follow, according to the nature of each contract.

1. *The services element* – Stargazers, as space planning specialists, have, under the SGSA, an *implied duty to exercise reasonable skill and care* at a level which would be expected of competent space planners. This is a higher duty on the planning side than would be expected of a general builder or carpenter. Crunchers are entitled to assume that Stargazers would measure the space and the cabinets correctly and will have relied on their expertise to do so. Moreover, Stargazers supplied all the materials to Crunchers. The shelves should have been expected to bear the weight of papers; the *shelves were therefore unfit for their purpose* as well as probably being of *unsatisfactory quality*. The poor fitting is also Stargazers' responsibility to Crunchers under the SGSA, as is the fact that the cabinets have been put in the wrong positions. Stargazers may have their own claims against Chippy Brothers for the work, but their claims will depend on how far Stargazers could show that they had relayed to Chippy exactly what was actually required.
2. *Adequate filing space* may be more a more difficult issue. There will be no term implied by the SGSA that Stargazers, as suppliers, have guaranteed to produce any specific minimum amount of filing space, but there may well be an express or implied term

in the contract arising from discussions between Crunchers and Stargazers. Stargazers may accept liability for the defective work, but resist a claim for the 'lost' filing space and the misplaced cabinets. It will then be a question of going through the papers and taking statements from the parties to decide whether those issues were actually agreed as part of the contract. If Stargazers had used their own form of contract with Crunchers, they might have considered excluding or limiting their liability on these issues.

3. *Sale of goods* – In supplying cabinets to Stargazers, Morris will be bound by the provisions of the SGA, notably whether the cabinets supplied were of *satisfactory quality* and *complied with any description or sample* given by Morris to Stargazers. The main question would be whether Stargazers had drawn up the correct plans and specifications or whether Morris had failed to supply cabinets as specified. In either event, it is likely that Stargazers would be liable to Crunchers, and would have to consider its contract with Morris as to whether Stargazers themselves had any remedy against Morris. If there was a breach of the implied terms as to quality and compliance with description or sample, Morris might be liable to Stargazers for the direct and foreseeable loss arising to Stargazers as a result. If Morris had supplied on its own terms of business, any exclusion or limitation of liability on its part would have to be reasonable.

4. *Installation work* – Similar considerations apply to the contract between Stargazers and Chippy, but here judged according to the SGSA rather than the SGA in relation to the workmanship and the SGA in relation to the materials. Chippy would be expected to fit out the offices according to reasonable standards of specialists in that kind of work. Chippy would also be entitled to assume that Stargazers would get the measurements of the space and the cabinets right, unless, of course, Chippy had participated in preparing the planning and specifications in the first place.

Summary and Checklist

Probably more business contracts are entered into on standard forms than on any other basis, yet they are frequently regarded as the Cinderella of the business. Time taken in the preparation – and regular review – of the terms and conditions and their relevance to the particular business and its methods will be repaid many times over in avoiding disputes or being able to solve them rapidly and effectively. At the same time, your sales and purchasing teams need to understand the process and act consistently with your own terms of business, and to know how to ensure that these are properly incorporated as part of the contract.

In terms of legalities there are some terms that will be automatically implied into the sale or purchase of your goods unless you exclude or modify them. These are mainly concerned with ownership of, or title to, the goods, when title passes to the buyer, whether the goods are satisfactory, whether they comply with description or sample and whether they are fit for their intended purpose. It is important to understand the implied terms in order to ensure that your own terms are compliant and to enforce such terms against other parties if need be. Remember that different rules apply to services and rental situations and to consumer sales, covered in other chapters.

OUTLINE SELLER'S CHECKLIST

- Are you dealing with goods or services – or a mix of the two?
- Are you planning to use standard terms and, if so, has their existence been clearly indicated to the other party and are they are incorporated into the contract?
- Do they tie in with the sale or order details on the front of the form or contained in other documents?
- Do your order, invoice and delivery processes ensure that your terms are fully incorporated into the sale contract?
- When drafting sale terms, are the goods and delivery sufficiently clear for you to be able to establish that the contract has been properly performed?
- If drafting purchase conditions, are these tied in with a clear description of the specification of the goods and the performance criteria in terms which can be tested in practice? If necessary, link payment obligations into acceptance tests.
- Are there clear provisions as to delivery, inspection, price, payment, risk and title?
- Has the intended purpose of the goods has been made known and are they are fit for that purpose?
- Do the goods need to comply with description and/or sample?
- Are the goods free from all defects or has the buyer expressly agreed to accept specific faults?
- Do you have a warranty policy or other term dealing with alleged defects? If so, check that this does not exclude non-excludable statutory rights.
- Do you have unascertained goods that need to be dealt with separately?
- Is there an effective retention of title clause?
- Have you briefed people not to override your carefully drafted standard terms of business by even oral misrepresentations of your products or services?
- Are there any customs and practices of the particular industry, or of the buying or selling power of the businesses concerned, which might affect the issue?
- If there is an unusual term, have you drawn it specifically to the attention of the other party, particularly in consumer sales? Specifically negotiate terms for non-standard situations or potential high-risk or high-liability areas.
- Do you have good delivery and proof of delivery (POD) procedures? Cover the position which would arise if the buyer fails to collect or accept delivery (or tries to impose its terms at the last minute).
- Have you fully differentiated and covered off the services element? If appropriate, clear your terms and conditions and your procedures with your insurers to ensure they are in line with your cover.
- Look out for a course of dealings and its possible effects.
- Make sure that you fire the last shot in the battle of the forms.

10 *Sales to Consumers and Website Sales*

Introduction – consumer protection: main principles and objectives – the Unfair Terms in Consumer Contracts Regulations 1999 (UTCCR) – Consumer Protection Regulations 2008 (CPRs) – defective products and the Consumer Protection Act 1987 (CPA) – other sales, advertising and marketing regulations – website terms and conditions: an outline – summary and checklist

Introduction: Consumer Protection, the Web Revolution and Some Related Issues

The most fundamental change in the world of contracts over recent years has been the shift to contracting electronically, by e-mail and via websites. The technology has, in turn, encouraged many more businesses than before to sell 'business to consumer' (B2C) (increasingly 'direct to consumer' – D2C). Electronic contracting has, in turn, challenged and already changed many aspects of contract law, including consumer sales.

New routes to market mean that there is now much less personal contact between buyer and seller, so that the traditional commercial principle of *caveat emptor* or 'let the buyer beware' has been turned on its head. The consumer will expect to be fully informed and not misled before making a purchase decision and is now likely to have effective sanctions available if this is not the case.

Chapter 2 showed that, for most practical purposes, *e-mails* are written documents with the full chain of negotiations visible from the electronic exchanges, which can then be examined if there is uncertainty as to what was said. So e-mails are a very effective, but also challenging, tool for business.

Websites take electronic contracting to another level and raise more basic questions. For example, are goods or services marketed via a website offers for sale or 'mere invitations to treat', like goods on display in a shop? If the latter, how does purchasing from a website work legally? How does the law deal with the impersonal nature of electronic contracting and handing over of personal and financial details online? The website is the effective shop window in the online shopping mall, and the new rules affect how goods and services are put on display and how the digital till mechanism works. As the consumer cannot see or touch (or usually even ask about) the products (goods *or* services) online, the law regards the consumer as needing extra protection – in knowing exactly what is on offer, what is or is not claimed for it, what it costs, when the contract is created, when it has to be paid for, when it is likely to be received and what happens if things go wrong.

New laws have been spawned as a result, many driven by the single-market consistency and consumer protection principles of the EU. In the process, legal regulation has had to play catch-up with technological change, and there is the danger of piling new laws on old. These changes will continue, so this chapter looks first at some broader principles and intentions behind the new regulations, so that changes can be seen in perspective. It then examines some of the current detail.

Privacy and data protection comes to the fore with consumer purchasing via the Web, together with issues of distance-selling. And behind the consumer relationship is a further network of contractual arrangements with those who design, build and operate the websites, advertise and market the products and fulfil the Web orders. Around all these relationships is the position of the Internet service providers (ISPs), whose powers and responsibilities also have to be considered. All these, considered in some detail in Chapter 16, are the backdrop to what can be offered to consumers and how, which is why the shop-front of consumer protection needs to be considered before the back office operating the website.

Product in this chapter should generally be taken to include reference to goods and/or services, as indeed is now the trend with recent consumer legislation.

Consumer finance is a specialist area with substantial regulation, but is outside the scope of this book, as are weights and measures issues and dealings with specific products such as food, agriculture, medicines and financial products.

NEGLIGENCE

Quite outside the statutory framework, the laws of negligence may apply where a) there is a duty of care to the user of products, b) a breach of that duty arises and c) damage or loss results. This overriding legal duty exists outside contract, but its potential implications need to be considered as part of many overall contracts, often leading to indemnity clauses to cover the cost of third-party claims.

Consumer Protection: Main Principles and Objectives

BIS is the acronym for the Department for Business, Innovation and Skills (formerly BERR, the Department for Enterprise and Regulatory Reform), which is leading the consumer protection reform process in the UK, but readily acknowledges that, to a large extent, it is implementing the overall requirements of successive European directives. Nevertheless, BERR (as it then was) in its 'Consultation Paper on EU Proposals for a Consumer Rights Directive' (2008) referred to the objective of 'expanding the choice and boosting the confidence of consumers, as well as reducing burdens on business' (p. 3). With new technologies and global markets offering more choice, sped on by e-commerce, old rules quickly become outdated. This challenges government to afford consumers adequate protection within a regime that is coherent and consistent overall, but without overburdening business. For the latest or more detailed position, reference may be made to the most recent updates of the BIS website (www.bis.gov.uk) or the very useful Trading Standards websites (www.direct.gov.org or www.tradingstandards.gov.uk).

The main areas of regulation are those needed to balance commercial practices against contract fairness and to deal with issues of product and service quality, accurate quantity measurement and product safety. We can expect to see a number of disparate Acts and regulations, some dating from the 1970s, repealed in favour of new rules, hopefully coordinated and following consistent principles. Whether the result will indeed be shorter and simpler is another matter, but the main thrust seems likely to cover the following four main subject areas:

- *Unfair contract terms/commercial practices* – building on the unfair consumer terms (UTCCR) framework covered later in this chapter
- *Supply of goods and services* – being regulated together as the distinction becomes more difficult in practice (examples of mixed supply of goods and services being mobile phones with ring tones or goods with linked maintenance agreements)
- *Cancellation rights* – such as those already given by the Distance Selling Regulations
- *Product safety* – rules which may affect all those handling goods before the ultimate sale to the consumer.

Consolidation

These changes seem likely to result in the consolidation of many different consumer-protection areas (such as doorstep selling, distance selling, unfair contract terms and sale of goods) into a single consumer rights directive and corresponding national regulations.

Vulnerable consumers are likely to be given special protection within each of these areas. We have already seen the WC3 Web Content Accessibility Guidelines lay down objectives for the visually and other impaired in accessing websites, and disability protection seems likely to extend further to those who are potentially vulnerable as a result of social factors (such as poverty and low educational attainment) as well. In all these areas the government recognizes the inherent tension between certainty and flexibility that is the hallmark of democratically-made law. The more prescriptive the rules, potentially the more certain they are, but the more unfair the borderline cases can be.

SAFETY

Where goods, rather than services, are concerned (and, in some cases, with services too), awareness of the various safety obligations is important for all businesses that deal, at any stage in the chain, with consumer goods, since the potential liabilities arising may be relevant to any sale, purchase, agency or distribution contract made between any of those parties.

SELF-HELP

In addition to its stated wish to avoid burdens on business, the government does not wish to burden itself and will increasingly leave enforcement to those consumers capable of direct enforcement. The new regime is therefore likely to lean towards education, information and correct pre-purchase policies and effective redress afterwards, including dispute resolution and ultimate legal rights. Behind this will be the enforcement authorities of Trading Standards and, behind them, the OFT, which is likely to become more focused on consistency in prevention and enforcement proportionate to risk to the consumer. The trend in consumer protection can already be seen in the ground-breaking Unfair Trading Regulations, covered below, and we can expect to see similar concepts repeated and developed in later regulations. In addition, consumer groups, such as the Consumers' Association, are being given powers to take collective action.

ELECTRONIC OFFER AND ACCEPTANCE

Terms of business

One immediate benefit for online suppliers is the ability to set out their terms of business on their website, insisting that the customer accepts these before the order stage. This helps ensure that the terms and conditions are incorporated into the sale contract, but equally reduces customer negotiation, so new rules arise to fill the void. And companies still have to be commercially sensible since, as some companies have found out to their cost, making 'irresistible' website offers may lead to far more takers than you bargained for. The *Carbolic Smoke Ball* case principles, discussed in Chapter 1, can apply on the Web, and the consequences have to be honoured!

Offer and acceptance

Rules of offer and acceptance apply on the Web too, even if acceptance is often limited to a tick box or 'submit' button. For acceptance, the principle is that electronic communications are effective only when received (the EU Electronic Commerce Directive 2000 – commonly known as the E-Commerce Directive and the UK Electronic Commerce (EC Directive) Regulations 2002). The process can, however, be more complex when it involves servers in different legal jurisdictions. The law now requires an electronic offer to a consumer to set out precisely how it can be accepted; this is most likely to be when payment is taken and charged to the customer's account or when the seller is able to specify a delivery date. Since the offer terms will have specified the acceptance process, the contract is formed when the requirements of the offer are complied with. So, in most D2C cases, the issue of acceptance is now academic because it is pre-specified, although it can still raise uncertainty in email exchanges and in B2B transactions which are not made on fixed order terms.

Consideration

Consideration will normally be payment, typically by credit card, but it is worth noting that providing personal information to a potential supplier may of itself be valuable consideration and sufficient to ground a breach of contract claim if the supplier were to claim that there was no contract because no money changed hands.

BUYING ON THE WEB – THE E-COMMERCE REGULATIONS

The E-Commerce Directive refers to 'information society services', which are essentially services provided for remuneration, at a distance, by electronic equipment, at the individual request of a receiver of the service. (Note that this can include B2B (business to business) as well as B2C services.) Where information society services are being provided, the UK Electronic Commerce Regulations 2002 require the provider in general (not all the rules strictly apply to e-mails) to make known to the receiver the following details:

- the name, details and VAT number of the service provider with their geographic and e-mail address;

- details of any trade registrations, codes or practice and any supervisory authority (for example, the FSA);
- details of any promotional offers, competitions or games;
- how to access the contract terms and exactly how to enter into a contract;
- how and when it is deemed concluded;
- what will happen if the supplier is out of stock;
- how any input errors will be rectified;
- any alternative languages available.

The contract terms are typically included in a compulsory section of the Web order form which the buyer needs to click (or 'check') to indicate acceptance. The only variation that may be offered is whether the customer agrees to personal details being used by the supplier for future product and marketing information. This 'click-wrap' process needs to be carefully planned and clear on-screen. The terms of business may be displayed on the website itself or be accessible by means of a hyperlink to another website. Then, when an order is placed by the customer, the seller must acknowledge receipt promptly and show how any incorrect information will be corrected before the order is finalized. These provisions should now be reasonably familiar to Web users, although on some sites the necessary details are hard to find, if available at all. Often, too, the fulfilment of the order, including order and payment processing and delivery, will be contracted out to a specialist company, sometimes apparent when the order process engages a third-party website.

Standard terms of business will need to be substantially rewritten for website use, especially if the company is shifting from B2B to predominantly B2C dealings, as much of the regulation falls on consumer sales. So this is an area for early and specialist guidance.

The Unfair Terms in Consumer Contracts Regulations 1999 (UTCCR)

The UTCCR result from EU initiatives and are designed to protect consumers against *unfair standard contract terms in the sale of products generally*. This focus on the consumer and the wider scope of the rules distinguishes the UTCCR from the Unfair Contract Terms Act 1977 (UCTA), reviewed in relation to limitation clauses in Chapter 7. It is necessary to look at the detail to assess the impact of the UTCCR and to bear in mind that similar regimes apply in other EU member states.

THE UTCCR – THE FRAMEWORK

Consumers

The definition of 'consumer' under the UTCCR s. 3(1) is 'any natural person who, in contracts covered by these Regulations, is acting for purposes which are outside his trade, business or profession'. This can therefore include businesspeople buying outside their normal business activities.

Standard terms

These are terms pre-set by the business and not individually negotiated with the consumer, such as found in the 'small print' at the foot or on the back of a sales order form. A standard term will be unfair if, contrary to good faith, it creates a 'significant imbalance in the parties' rights and obligations arising under the contract, to the detriment of the consumer' (s. 5(1)). The broad test is to see what would be the position, especially for the consumer, if the potentially offending term did not appear in the contract.

Products

As mentioned, the UTCCR cover products, meaning the services as well as goods, except as specifically excluded by the Regulations.

Excluded contracts

The following are the main types of contract *excluded* from the UTCCR:

- employment (which is separately regulated);
- inheritance and family law rights (where there are major national differences);
- the formation and constitution of companies and partnerships (which are already heavily regulated); and
- the transfer of property rights in land (which have their own national characteristics).

  Included within the rules are the relevant provisions of:

- financial services contracts;
- insurance policies, other than the risk and liability definitions which affect premium levels;
- provisions relating to the supply of services in a building, such as serviced accommodation.

UNFAIRNESS – THE KEY UTCCR TESTS

Overall balance

Taking into account the relative bargaining strengths of the parties and the existence of any inducements, do any of the contract terms create a significant imbalance in the relationship between business and consumer contrary to the requirement of good faith?

Language and small print

Are the written terms in plain, intelligible language and clearly phrased and printed? Did the consumer have time to read them? If not, the consumer is to have the benefit of the doubt, which is contrary to normal contract interpretation rules and could mean that an unclear term might result in that term being held unfair, regardless of its actual meaning. The principle is that consumers should have the chance to discuss and amend the terms so that they are individually negotiated (although perhaps a discussion on the finer points of contract law with the average sales assistant may be regarded more as a theoretical than a real prospect).

Good faith

Has the supplier followed principles of 'fair and open dealing', recognizing the legitimate interest of customers?

THE SCHEDULE 2 LIST –TERMS LIKELY TO BE UNFAIR

Presumed unfair terms are set out in schedule 2 to the UTCCR and are effectively presumed unfair unless they can be justified by the supplier. Schedule 2 is an indicative and non-exhaustive list of terms which may be held to be unfair. They are not automatically unfair, but there will need to be a very good reason for a court to uphold them. They are fairly carefully worded, but the main provisions held to be unfair can be summarized as those which:

- *limit liability for death or personal injury* of a customer resulting from an act or omission of the seller or supplier – this is potentially wider than the UCTA provision;
- *'inappropriately' limit the rights of the consumer* where the supplier has not fully performed;
- *permit the supplier to retain the customer's deposit* if the customer decides not to go ahead with the deal, unless the customer is given a similar right against the supplier;
- *require compensation* for non-fulfilment of the contract if the compensation is 'disproportionately' high;
- *permit opt-out by the supplier* but not the customer, or permit the supplier to retain amounts paid by the customer where the supplier has terminated the contract;
- *entitle the supplier, but not the customer, to terminate the contract on short or no notice* (unless there are serious grounds for doing so);
- *extend the contract* – entitle the supplier unilaterally to extend a fixed-term contract unreasonably early;
- *bind the customer* to contract terms which the customer has had no real chance to study;
- *enable the supplier to vary the terms* without good reason;
- *give the supplier the sole right* to decide whether the goods or services have been properly supplied or if there has been a breach of contract;
- *permit the seller to raise the price* to any material extent without giving the customer the right to cancel; or
- *restrict the buyer's rights* to take immediate legal action for breach; or
- *force consumers to defend legal action* in a country where they don't normally live.

EXCLUSIONS, EXCEPTIONS AND OTHER ISSUES

Exclusions

The Regulations do not cover terms setting the prices of the goods or services or terms defining the product (known as core terms).

Exceptions

There are some exceptions – for example, in relation to certain aspects of financial services and international treaties limiting compensation, such as for airline passengers.

Enforceability

If a term is unfair under the UTCCR, that term will be unenforceable by the supplier, but the rest of the contract will stand unless it is unworkable without the offending term.

OFT

The Office of Fair Trading (OFT) has considerable power to intervene and encourage a supplier to mend its ways and improve the fairness of its contracts. It may take action against the supplier concerned by seeking undertakings or a court injunction if persuasion does not succeed, but only authorized bodies may make a complaint direct to the OFT.

Consumer Direct

Individual consumers are able to use the Regulations as a defence in any relevant court action. They may also complain to local trading standards officers or directly to Consumer Direct at www.consumerdirect.gov.uk (a website worth checking for businesses that may want to see what consumers are being told).

The Consumer Protection from Unfair Trading Regulations 2008 (CPRs)

OUTLINE

Major change

The CPRs, implementing the EU Unfair Commercial Practices Directive of 11 May 2005, represented the biggest shake-up for many years in the consumer trading area. The aim is to harmonize unfair trading laws across EU member states by prohibiting businesses from treating their customers unfairly during any stage of a commercial transaction. The CPRs effectively ban commercial practices that are 'misleading' to consumers. Inevitably, to do so they have to define what a commercial practice is and when this is deemed to be misleading. Note here the emphasis on the concept of 'misleading', being something liable to induce a purchase on a misapprehension. Although they go wider, the CPRs really focus on the pre-contract 'trading' period rather than on the interpretation of the (often standard) terms of the contract as with the unfair terms laws. Existing terms of sale that may pass the tests under the unfair terms laws may nevertheless fall foul of the provisions of the CPRs, especially if they are not explicit or might mislead, so those selling to consumers need to check across both areas. Hiding a critical term in small print, for example, is likely to breach both unfair terms and unfair trading regulations.

Consolidation

In keeping with the principle of consolidation of consumer law, the CPRs repeal and replace some of the old law (notably much of the Trade Descriptions Act 1968, Part III of the Consumer Protection Act 1977 and the Control of Misleading Advertisements Regulations 1988). However, the last of these, in relation to B2B sales, is in turn replaced by the Business Protection from Misleading Marketing Regulations 2008 (see below), which is the B2B marketing equivalent of the CPRs in relation to consumer marketing. One can again see the increasing differentiation of the levels of protection made available to consumers, as opposed to businesses purchasing in the course of trade.

OBJECTIVE AND DEFINITIONS

Informed decision-making by the consumer as to the product or service intended to be purchased is the objective of the CPRs. Anything the trader says or does that might impair that decision, or cause the consumer to buy something they would not otherwise buy, risks 'materially distorting' the consumer's economic behaviour. The description need not be on the label of the product but could be within an advert, used as an illustration or as part of a sales pitch. It could cover the size or quantity, what the product was made of, where it was made or its suitability for a given purpose. It could relate to any endorsement or support for the product. Both the CPRs and the business protection rules even cover rights and obligations and, notably, land and property. To understand how widely these provisions range, we need to look at some of the definitions in more detail.

Commercial practice

This is widely defined in the CPRs, and it is easiest to break the definition into constituent parts:

- 'any act, omission, course of conduct, representation or commercial communication (including advertising and marketing) by a trader,
- which is directly connected with the promotion, sale or supply of a product [goods or services],
- to or from consumers,
- whether occurring before, during or after a commercial transaction ... in relation to a product' (Regulation 2.1).

Unfair commercial practice

This is defined as a practice which breaches 'professional diligence', or materially distorts (or is likely to distort) the economic behaviour of the average consumer with regard to a product, or it is a misleading action, a misleading omission, it is aggressive, or it is specifically listed in Schedule 1. A wide definition indeed!

CPRs IN MORE DETAIL

New concepts

It can already be seen that this is wide-ranging language, bringing further into English law concepts such as 'professional diligence' and 'economic behaviour', which initially seem to have more in common with contracts for professional services and competition law. Some of the rules are drafted very tightly to catch specific practices and some very generally to set out an expected standard. There are also useful guidelines available from the OFT Consumer Protection website (www.oft.gov.uk/oft or www.consumer/direct.gov. uk) giving examples of behaviour that would or might be caught.

The 'professional diligence' definition in many ways begs more questions than it answers. It requires a standard of 'special' skill and care that a trader might reasonably be expected to exercise towards its customers in line with either honest market practice or general principles of good faith, in either case in that trader's field of activity. So market practice is relevant, but only at the honest and fair end.

Average consumer

All this applies to an 'average consumer', who is defined as someone who is reasonably well informed, reasonably observant and circumspect. The average consumer will be an average member of any particular group of consumers,

Vulnerable consumers

Where a group is regarded as vulnerable to the practice or the product because of age or physical or mental infirmity, higher standards are required. The trader need not necessarily make enquiries of individual customers, but needs to think about which groups are likely to be interested in the product or attracted by the marketing. Is the average member of that group likely to be regarded as vulnerable? Special thought is also required if children or disadvantaged groups may be the likely buyers

MISLEADING PRACTICES UNDER THE CPRs

Misleading commercial practice

This is broadly a practice that contains false information, or creates confusion with a competitor's product, or fails to comply with an advertised code of conduct applicable to that trader, where any of those factors induces a false buying decision by the consumer.

Interestingly, the provision about creating confusion with a competitor's product may now create a statutory, as well as a civil law, offence of 'passing-off' (see Chapter 14).

False information

This includes information which, even if technically correct, is misleading. In summary, false information may relate to the fact that a product exists, its nature or main characteristics (including availability, fitness for purpose and specification), what the trader commits to provide, how the sale is conducted, any sponsorship or product endorsement, pricing or price advantages, servicing or repair arrangements and/or consumer rights and risks.

Misleading omission

A misleading omission will arise when what the consumer is told omits or conceals material information of the kind the consumer would want to know, or provides it in a way that is unclear or ambiguous or has some hidden intent. As before, there is the second test that the information (or lack of it) is material enough, such that the consumer is misled into making a purchasing decision that would not otherwise have been made. Limitations on the way in which the information is presented or lack of clarity about delivery or taxes could both be misleading omissions.

Examples

Schedule 1 to the CPRs lists no fewer than 31 practices that would be regarded as unfair. Here is an illustrative sample:

- offering products at a specified price without disclosing that supplies may be limited or unavailable on those terms, or falsely suggesting that supplies are limited in order to encourage a rushed decision;
- offering products and then failing to take orders or encouraging consumers to take a different product;
- promoting a product as if it was made by a different manufacturer;
- failing to distinguish pure advertising from paid-for editorial (or 'advertorial') comment;
- 'pyramid' selling;
- claiming something is free if it is not;
- offering a competition prize without awarding one;
- over-eager follow-up to solicit an order;
- exhorting children to buy – or aiming the exhortation at parents via children (as opposed to a straight advertisement).

THE EFFECTS OF BREACHING THE CONSUMER PROTECTION REGULATIONS

Defences

The Regulations do not quite create an absolute offence, like speeding in a car. Traders have a 'due diligence' defence, which requires them to show a high standard of care on the part of all staff. Advertisers have an 'innocent dissemination' defence for those independently in the advertising business, not as a second-tier defence for traders who themselves advertise.

Complaints

Whilst the Regulations are overseen by the OFT, it will be open to any person, even a competitor, to lodge a complaint that may lead to an investigation, which may in turn lead to prosecution. So the Regulations are an additional weapon for trade rivals, as evidenced by an interim judgment in *Tiscali UK Ltd* v. *British Telecommunications Plc* (2008), where Tiscali was allowed to add to its complaint that BT had misled customers to switch to BT a claim under the CPRs (and also under the Business Protection Regulations (BPRs) – see below).

Sanctions

As is increasingly common with consumer laws, breach of the CPRs is a criminal offence, in this case with exposure to fines and/or up to two years' imprisonment. There is also the potential stigma of adverse publicity.

Summary

These are broad principles with tight sanctions, which businesses supplying customers direct will have to master. The idea is that those who are straight with their customers have nothing to fear, but, however laudable the objective, experience suggests that this degree of detail is rarely without its problems.

Defective Products and the Consumer Protection Act 1987 (CPA)

Product safety is at the heart of the Consumer Protection Act 1987 (CPA), which has been substantially amended over the years.

PART I CPA – DEFECTIVE PRODUCTS

Right to compensation

Part 1 of the CPA gives a victim of a defective product the right to claim compensation against any producer (widely defined, as seen below) of the product for any damage which the victim can show that the product has caused. A victim in these circumstances does not need first to show that the producer was negligent. For this purpose:

- *Damage* covers personal injury, death and damage to private property, loss of or damage to the goods themselves or pure financial loss.
- *Defective* means that the safety of something is not at the level that people are entitled to expect. There is an objective test, covering how the product is marketed, what is expected to be done with it and any instructions or warnings given with it.

- *Producer* can include the manufacturer and any others in the production chain who produced the raw materials or processed, packaged, imported or branded any part of the product.
- *Product* is widely defined and includes ingredients in another product. It may also include labelling and product information which might make the product unsafe.
- *Suppliers* who are not producers may suffer a claim but are generally not liable *provided* they identify the producer when requested to do so by an affected customer.

The burden of proof effectively falls on the producer once the consumer victim can show that a product has caused damage which the victim could not reasonably have expected. To escape liability, the producer will have to establish one of a number of defences. These require the producer to *disprove* his involvement in the chain or the cause of the defect *or* prove that the defect resulted from compliance with relevant legislation or regulations *or* that the defect was not known as a risk in the light of scientific and technical knowledge at the time of supply. The producer may not disclaim or contract out of liability under the Act, but the victim must bring the claim to court within three years of discovering the damage or the link with the product or the identity of the producer. There is a ten-year, long-stop cut-off date.

PART II CPA – PRODUCT SAFETY

This part, dealing with product safety as opposed to other defects, has been effectively replaced by the General Product Safety Regulations 2005 which aim to set up standards for safe consumer products. Breach is a criminal offence. There is a limited 'due diligence' defence. Relevant authorities may make safety regulations including safety standards and information and warning requirements. Local trading standards officers are responsible for enforcement and have wide-ranging powers. The fact that something has been sold without complaint for some time is no protection against the view of a trading standards officer that the product is unsafe. Kitchen equipment, children's toys – and products which might be mistaken for children's toys – are particular examples of products where great care needs to be taken. The enforcement authorities' powers include ordering suspension of the production or sale of products which they consider unsafe, even without a court judgment, coupled with power to apply for offending products to be forfeited and destroyed.

PART III CPA – TRADING RULES

This part has been repealed and updated by the CPRs, the unfair trading regulations mentioned above.

PRACTICAL PRODUCT SAFETY LIABILITY MEASURES

Here are some suggestions as to how businesses might protect themselves:

- *Suppliers* should keep adequate records of the businesses from which they obtain particular products or batches in the hope that they can trace the product back to its source.

- *Retailers* should try to include, as a written term of their contracts with suppliers, a requirement that the supplier give full credit for any products alleged to be defective.
- *Retailers* might seek an indemnity from suppliers against any claims in relation to products supplied (although suppliers might well resist this for the reasons explained in the 'Warranties and indemnities' section on p. 64 in Chapter 4).
- *Importers* need to take special care that they are not likely to be regarded as 'producers' under the Regulations and have greater difficulty in enforcing redress against their own suppliers.
- *Insurance* – Producers, suppliers and retailers down the supply chain should, in any event, check that their product liability insurance is in good order.

Other Sales, Advertising and Marketing Regulations

This is a complex area, with no single consolidating Act but a mix of laws and codes of practice that have gradually been replaced and consolidated as part of an overall updating process. For example, the Trade Descriptions Act 1968 (summarized below) was a base on which much else in the field was subsequently built, but which now needs overhaul of its own. Technology – and its uses – blurs traditional distinctions, not just between goods and services, but also between areas such as printed media, Internet services and broadcasting. What follows is therefore an outline only.

DISTANCE AND HOME SELLING REGULATIONS

The Consumer Protection (Distance Selling) Regulations 2000

Generally known as the Distance Selling Regulations, these are derived from the EU Distance Selling Directive of 1997 and need to be taken into account in website sales to consumers. They apply not just to Internet sales, but also to any B2C transaction (to a consumer not acting in the course of a business) where the supplier and consumer do not meet face-to-face.

Withdrawal The main feature of the Regulations is to give consumers the right to withdraw from the contract within seven working days after delivery of the goods or conclusion of a contract for services ordered online (provided that, in the case of services, the work has not already started or been delivered). If the right to terminate is exercised, the customer may return the goods at the supplier's expense and require repayment of the purchase price and delivery costs within 30 days of the rejection. This refund must technically be made even if the goods have not been returned by that date.

30-day rule There is also a general requirement that the contract must be fulfilled by the supplier within 30 days unless a later date is agreed.

Exceptions There are some excepted contracts, such as those for accommodation, transport and catering services, and some contracts which are non-cancellable, such as for software that has been unsealed (unwrapped), magazines and personalized goods.

Betting and gaming contracts are, not unreasonably, also non-cancellable. There is also a separate set of distance marketing regulations relating to consumer financial products.

The Cancellation of Contracts Made in a Consumer's Home or Place of Work etc Regulations 2008

This snappy title is a fair summary of what the Regulations do, revoking earlier 1987 rules and giving appropriate rights of cancellation in relation to goods or services purchased during a visit to a consumer's home or office.

BUSINESS PROTECTION FROM MISLEADING MARKETING REGULATIONS 2008 (BPRS)

The Business Protection from Misleading Marketing Regulations 2008 (BPRs) are the CPRs equivalent for businesses, with the principle that any advertising which is misleading is prohibited. They go on to make it an offence to mislead other businesses about goods and services, including immoveable property, rights and obligations. Notably BPRs protect not just trade buyers of the product, but also competitors who may be injured by the advertising.

Comparative advertising is covered by BPR s. 4 which specifically outlaws such matters as:

- *misleading comparisons* of products or services designed for different uses;
- *confusing comparisons* with competitors' products;
- suggestions that the products bear *trademarks or brands* which they do not;
- other advertising that *misleads traders or consumers.*

Enforcement is by Trading Standards with notice to the OFT. Breach may be a criminal offence involving a potentially unlimited fine and up to two years' imprisonment, and sanctions may extend to officers (broadly defined to include directors, managers and partners) of a company that has consented to, or connived in the commission of the offence. Trading Standards and the OFT have considerable investigatory powers and options of injunctions or seeking enforceable undertakings from the defaulting business.

Defences are limited to *due diligence* (relying on honest mistake, another's default, accident or other cause beyond the control of the business concerned) and *innocent publication*, to protect the advertiser publishing the advertisement in the ordinary course of business with no reason to disbelieve its accuracy.

PRICE STATEMENTS AND CODES OF PRACTICE

Prices indicators on marketing and advertising, including website references, have separate rules, partly derived from the new laws and partly set out in regularly updated codes of practice, such as the British Code of Advertising Practice (CAP) and the Advertising Standards Authority (ASA) regarding sales promotions. There is also the DTI Code of Practice for Traders on Price Indications, updated to reflect changes in the law. Those working in the relevant areas will need to have good working knowledge of these codes, which may be readily accessed from appropriate websites.

The consumer price should, of course, include VAT, but for the retailer or wholesaler this is another aspect that may give further complications. VAT and tax are outside the scope of this book in general, but it is worth highlighting here that goods and services may attract different VAT rates. One such case is books, which are regarded as socially desirable such that they are zero-rated in physical form, whether printed or in the form of audio cassette or CD. Digital books, however, currently attract the standard rate of VAT, so that e-books downloaded or transmitted over the Internet or wirelessly are subject to VAT. Moreover, that VAT rate may vary between countries, even within the European Union. Digital deliveries from other countries outside the EU with a VAT or equivalent regime are expected to have to conform to the regime at the point of delivery to the consumer, but there is much work still to do in this whole arena.

The overriding principle is that adverts must be decent, honest, truthful and not misleading, and that – perhaps most importantly – any claims for products must be capable of being proved. Typical problem areas are claims that something is 'free' when in fact there is payment to be made in one form or another, comparative prices (which should not be misleading) and references to guide price, normal retail price and the like (which need to comply with strict guidelines). All these should be carefully vetted. There are other rules relating to the need not to cause widespread offence (largely related to the target audience) and not to hide qualifications or conditions. There are also special provisions regarding children that require special attention.

TRADING DISCLOSURES OF COMPANY DETAILS

Business communications from limited companies and limited liability partnerships (LLPs) must refer to the company registration number, place of registration and the registered office address of the business. This applies to websites and e-mails too, where reference in the e-mail footer will suffice (Companies Act 2006 and the Companies (Trading Disclosures) Regulations of 2008).

PRIVACY AND ELECTRONIC COMMUNICATIONS REGULATIONS 2003

These regulations are an extension of the protection of personal data regime, designed to prevent unwanted 'spam' e-mails. The rules generally require an 'opt-in' from a consumer before direct marketing e-mails can be sent. Even then, the consumer must be given an opt-out option with each subsequent communication. The sender of the e-mail must be made clear, and the consumer must be fully informed about any 'cookies' on the website.

Website Terms and Conditions: An Outline

Having looked at the (many) main legal elements to be considered when offering products by website, it is appropriate to consider some of the things a set of website terms and conditions may cover. Such terms vary enormously, so that what follows are notes on what might be expected to be included, rather than a draft set of actual terms. For the sake of completeness, these notes cover possible comments or other content, such as feedback, posted by users on the website, where many other issues may arise. These notes are not exhaustive; some will be especially relevant and others less so. Some may need to be bolstered for sites which children might be expected to access. The terms might be preceded by a general introduction to the site and followed by a suitable privacy policy.

GENERAL CONDITIONS OF USE

- *Access and use* constitutes acceptance of the terms – the 'click-wrap licence'.
- *Interpretation* – Use either a formal approach, with definitions such as 'company' and 'user', or informal 'you' and 'we' language.
- *Brands* – The user will have no right to use any trade names or brands featured on the site.
- *Content ownership* – This will set out who owns and can use a) the original website content and b) any user-generated content (UGC) added by those accessing the website. The original content is normally the copyright of the site owner, with an absolute bar on further copying, adaptation or use of that content in any form. The UGC, which may have been created by the content provider (user- created content) or 'borrowed' from another source, is usually subject to a royalty-free worldwide licence for the website owner to use, edit and adapt it for the website, but issues can arise as to what other uses may be made of it. Some social network sites have been forced hurriedly to retract overstated terms in this area.
- *Content liability* is a tricky area for website terms, and there may be several provisions. First, the user providing content should expressly agree not to post any prohibited content. This would typically be content that is: a) false, libellous, obscene, pornographic, threatening, harassing, ethnically offensive or conducive to breach of law or contract (or otherwise inappropriate); or b) an infringement of third-party copyright, moral rights, privacy, confidentiality, data protection or the like. (These terms may have to explain what is covered by such prohibitions!) There may be further restrictions against content that advertises or solicits business or personal information from anyone else. Second, there will be a large measure of freedom for the website owner to edit, remove or amend any prohibited or potentially prohibited material, since they may well be legally responsible for that content (see Chapter 16).
- *Indemnity* – The terms may well include an indemnity from the customer in favour of the website operator/supplier in respect of any liability caused by the customer posting any content on, or other improper use of, the website. This will need very straightforward language to be effective, with the meaning of 'indemnity' preferably explained.
- *The right to remove content/terminate access* by the website owner is often included, either because of breach of the content rules or even generally (although unjustified termination of access might raise other issues).
- *Hypertext links* are a difficult area. The website owner may want to reserve the right to include links to other websites, but this could raise issues of endorsement of the content of those other sites and even potential liability for that other content. If there may be links, the terms should include a suitable disclaimer for anything on the linked site (which may, of course, change at any time) or anything accessed or done on that linked site.

- *Bulletin boards* may have their own rules.
- *Downtime/security* terms might include a statement as to reasonable care, but no guarantee of continuous service or complete security online. This may be reinforced in relation to payment arrangements, which should be encrypted, but should make it clear that the risk of mis-processing between customer and website lies with the customer.
- *Limitation of liability*, especially in US website terms, is likely to be extensive, may be in oppressive capitals (making it more like a harangue!) and may seek to exclude all liability that can be excluded by law (see Chapter 7). Much specific consumer protection cannot in fact be excluded, and generalized exclusions have been criticized as misleading (and possibly unenforceable under the UTCCR). Other exclusions seem to be aimed at preventing extreme claims by those users who are assumed to have limited mental faculties and need to be expressly told what not to do.
- *Contact details* – Because of the frustration that can be caused by remote website selling, including some real glitches in the website system itself, there should be some contact point given, and a supported helpline.
- *General provisions* – Normal boilerplate terms will usually be provided.
- *Feedback* – An e-mail address should be provided for comments on the operation of the site and suggestions for improvement.
- *Marketing details* – Although the general rule is that express consent must be obtained from consumers for further use of their personal details supplied on order forms, and there must be the chance to opt out completely, many order forms include what is known as a 'soft opt-in', which may extend the use of personal details more widely.

ORDERING FROM A WEBSITE

- *Registration* – Where this is a prelude to ordering, including how to register, the need for accuracy of the data and protection of any password should be stressed. Registration does not amount to an order or an agreement to accept an order.
- Submitting an order will normally be regarded as acceptance of the terms.
- Contract creation will need to be specified, normally with a confirmatory e-mail.

PRODUCT INSTRUCTIONS AND WARNINGS

Price and payment

Prices need to indicate that they are inclusive of VAT (unless exempt from that requirement) and whether they include delivery or, if not, how delivery is charged. Unless the price is completely fixed, the possibility of prices changing before the contract creation date should be covered, as should the possibility of stock shortages or other delays. Generally e-mail contact can be used for any enquiries or confirmation, and the terms should confirm this process. Payment will normally be in £ sterling by specified debit or credit card, subject to suitable credit checks.

Delivery

Different rules for delivery outside the UK (and any import or other duties arising) and any other variations need to be stated clearly. Issues such as those in the short-form terms of business at p. 166 in Chapter 9 will apply, suitably adapted for consumer sales.

Risk and title

These have similar provisions to those for trade sales, as above. Title is unlikely to pass until full payment is made and cleared; risk will probably pass on delivery.

Cancellation and returns

This is a critical area on which terms must be clear. For most website sales, the Distance Selling Regulations give the customer a period in which to cancel the transaction for any reason, and the seven-day period may be extended (but not shortened) by the website terms. There is also the issue of damaged or defective goods, where the timescale for return would reasonably be longer than seven days. Adequate details or reference to the return address should be given, and the original packaging is likely to be required. The cost of return, as well as the cost of the goods, should be refunded by the supplier once the goods have been checked and found defective or if the goods have been returned under the Distance Selling Regulations. This is normally done through credit card and *not* cash.

PRIVACY POLICY (SEE ALSO CHAPTER 5)

Data protection

A close adjunct to the website terms and conditions will be the website privacy policy, designed to highlight and ensure compliance with the Data Protection Act 1998 (DPA) and principles and their application to website sales. The policy will typically start with a statement that the customer's rights under the DPA legislation are taken seriously, with perhaps a summary of the main approach to dealings with the customer's details. The policy should or might usefully include the following:

- *Collection and use of data* – This will cover:
    - what data will be collected (such as feedback and suggestions or contact regarding competitions)
    - how it will be used
    - who will have access to the data inside and outside the organization and for what purpose – in enough detail to ensure that there is informed consent to its storage and use.

    There may also be reference to disclosure to official bodies where required by law.
- *Bulletin board and similar use* – Where some information is to be made public, registration of personal details with the company will usually be required (at least to have some redress for inappropriate statements as in the terms and conditions

above), but the policy should be clear as to whether the subject will be named or otherwise identified in what is made public.

- *Security of information* – As the Internet is not wholly secure there will be no guarantee that information given is necessarily secure.
- *How long the information is held* is often stated fairly generally but will be subject to the DPA tests in any event.
- *Unsubscribing* – Consumers must have the right to have their e-mail details removed from e-mail lists at any time on notice to the website.
- *Web links* may be provided, and it is sensible to mention that the linked site's privacy terms may be different.
- *Cookies and tracking* – Where appropriate there should be some explanation and policy as to how and when cookies and tracking are used – in simple enough terms for the non-technically-minded. It may be important to give assurances that this information does not track the customer's use of other websites.
- *A message for parents and guardians* – This is a fraught area where more regulation may be expected. The most important thing is probably making children who do use the Internet aware not only that it is not fully secure, but also that disclosure of names and addresses or ages or photographs can attract entirely the wrong sort of interest. Major steps are being taken by business to protect children and by the police to tackle Internet pornography and misuse, but the basic lessons need to begin at home.

Summary and Checklist

More and more businesses are now likely to be selling direct to consumers through their websites. Especially for those with little experience of previous direct to consumer selling, this gives rise to a series of challenges, both in approach and detail. Businesses involved in this area need an understanding of the more protective nature of consumer laws, data protection and electronic contracting, all of which are fast-changing areas with constant new regulation, recommendations and codes of conduct, with consumer protest able to be supported by consumer bodies and the direct threat of officially sanctioned adverse publicity. Points to remember include the following:

- Take a clear and responsible approach to e-commerce and consumer contracts.
- Comply with the E-Commerce Regulations.
- Be aware of the Unfair Terms in Consumer Contracts Regulations in terms of:
  - overall balance in the fairness of the terms
  - clear print and accessible language
  - no inappropriate exclusions or limitations
  - no one-sided provisions.
- Be aware of and comply with the Unfair Trading Regulations with regard to:
  - avoiding unfair commercial practices
  - carrying on business with professional diligence
  - suitable protection of vulnerable customers
  - ensuring that information supplied is not misleading
  - responding quickly and appropriately to complaints.
- Take best-practice steps to avoid liability for defective products.

- Comply with distance selling regulations.
- Ensure that business advertising is not misleading (including comparative advertising).
- Ensure that price indicators are not misleading.
- Avoid unlawful spam e-mails.
- Set up legally compliant and responsible website terms, paying special attention to:
  - ownership of content supplied by users
  - a realistic approach to liability for that content
  - clear and understandable language
  - care regarding web links
  - providing contact and feedback details
  - a clear ordering procedure with suitable cancellation and returns provisions
  - proper protection of personal data
  - the right to unsubscribe.
  - suitable awareness of, and protection for, children likely to be using the site.

CHAPTER 1

11 *Agency and Distribution Contracts*

Introduction – representatives – agency and distribution: the main distinctions – the Commercial Agents Regulations – agency and distribution contracts: the main terms – competition law issues – summary: distributor or agent? – summary and checklist

Introduction

Products rarely go straight from manufacturer to customer, or even straight to the shop. There are usually several intermediaries involved, linked by separate contracts with one another, but with a potential 'knock-on' effect up or down the chain if things go wrong. Further, the links in the chain may have very different legal standing with potentially different legal implications, so it is as well to be clear on the nature of each party's role. There are, for example, material differences in law between the typical roles of representative, agent and distributor, and the roles of wholesaler and retailer may have different legal effects too. Whereas Chapter 10 concentrated on consumer and Internet sales, which carry additional rules and implications, this chapter concentrates on the physical world of selling.

Representatives

A representative, by the nature of the word, 'represents' someone (the 'principal') by showcasing the wares of their principal and clarifying what they have for sale. Representatives may not have the power or authority to negotiate or conclude all aspects of the sale. In some cases they may be able to sign up a customer on standard terms, but, in many cases, the deal has to be ratified by those further up the corporate structure. This has a number of implications in law. First, the representatives may or may not be employees. Second, whether or not they are employees, they may or may not have authority to negotiate and agree the terms of a contract – or any different terms. It is therefore worth checking what their authority is. This is particularly important if they make a representation about the goods on which a buyer actually relies, because the buyer will want to be confident that the seller will be bound by the representation. Otherwise, the buyer may be forced to take goods that don't match the statements made about them and be left with a claim against a possibly impecunious independent representative.

Vicarious liability

If the representative is an employee, irrespective of the representative's ability to negotiate and agree a deal, their employer will have vicarious responsibility for anything they do in the course of their employment. So an employer will be legally liable for damage resulting from the negligence of an employed representative acting *in the course of* their employment. This is a different test from whether they were acting in accordance *with the terms of* their employment. For example, companies have been held responsible for employees who collude in breach of competition laws if they do so in the normal course of their employment, even if it breaches their employment terms. To avoid liability, the employer may have to show a high level of positive training and reinforcement of the principles and laws involved. At the other end of the equation, an innocent party dealing with representatives of another should be able to rely on the fact that those representatives do indeed 'represent' their company without having to enquire as to what their terms of employment are, provided that the representatives appear to be acting within the scope and course of their job. If they go off 'on a frolic of their own', to use the picaresque judicial phrase applied in these cases, it should be clear to the sensible businessperson that they are no longer representing their company. However, in practice this can be a fine distinction.

Authority

In some cases, the term 'representative' may indicate a limitation on the powers of the person concerned, distinguishing them from executive or manager. This may be important in determining whether the representative has actual authority or 'ostensible' authority to enter into the contract in question. This is considered further in Chapters 6 and 19 in relation to companies and problem contracts respectively. A similar distinction may also be important in relation to whether the person is a 'mere' representative or a commercial agent within the meaning of the Commercial Agents Regulations considered below.

Agency and Distribution: The Main Distinctions

In this section it is convenient to refer to a business which appoints an agent as the 'principal' and a business which appoints a distributor as a 'supplier'.

CUSTOMERS

An agent may introduce and negotiate a deal, but the actual sale is from principal to customer. This has several important implications. The first of these is that the customer, even if introduced by the agent, becomes a customer of the principal, and the legal parties to the sales contract are principal and customer. The principal will therefore have all the customer's details, which can be significant. Contrast the position with a distributor, where there are two contracts – one between supplier and distributor and one between distributor and customer. The supplier knows that the goods that have been ordered, but may not know where and for whom they are ultimately intended. The distributor, rather than the supplier, will have the current and ongoing relationship with the customer. This distinction can be important in several respects, both during the contract period, when the issue of exclusivity may be significant, and also when the main agreement terminates and the goodwill of the business of agent or distributor may be heavily dependent on their continuing relationships with the customers.

TITLE TO GOODS

In an agency, the principal appoints the agent to sell the principal's goods. The goods remain in the ownership of the principal until they are sold to a customer. The agent never takes title to them, but is paid a fee by the principal, normally by way of commission. By contrast, in a distribution arrangement, the supplier sells the goods to the distributor who then resells them to the customer. In the process, the distributor takes title to the goods and is paid by reference to the difference between the price at which he buys from the supplier and sells to the customer. The use of the term 'distributor' needs to be distinguished from what might be called a 'logistical distributor', one only concerned with transporting goods from one place to another. Clearly there are many arrangements under which transport and other companies store and distribute products for others without title in the products ever passing.

RESALE PRICING AND PAYMENT

Resale prices

There are significant differences in terms of control and risk between agency and distribution. An agent can be given precise terms on which the goods can be sold, including price. Competition law prevents suppliers from specifying the price or range at which distributors or ultimate retailers may resell those goods. These restrictions do not apply to true agents (see below and Chapter 8 as to the distinction), and, as a result, a supplier will have much closer control over customer sales through an agent than through a distributor. For that reason businesses wishing to control resale prices should consider appointing an agent rather than a distributor, but must accept that they still will not be able to control the price at which the goods are sold by the ultimate retailer.

Customer creditworthiness and risk

Since the agent never takes title, the goods will remain the property of the principal until title passes to the customer (and if the principal passes that risk on to the agent this could change the competition law position – see Chapter 8). The principal will therefore be directly affected by the customer's creditworthiness and will want to know that the agent carries out adequate credit reference and other checks. A supplier, on the other hand, will not be directly concerned with the creditworthiness of the ultimate customer, since the distributor is obliged to pay its supplier whether or not the distributor is itself paid on time or at all. But if a big customer fails to pay the distributor, that failure is liable to impact on the distributor's ability to pay the supplier in turn. If the customer does not pay, and the distributor is caught in cash-flow problems, the supplier may be faced with the difficult decision of cutting off supplies to its own distributor or hoping that the distributor can trade out of the problem. So the supplier does have a concern as to the quality of the distributor's own receivables, and the failure of a contracting party down the sales chain can have a knock-on effect all the way back to the top of that chain.

DIFFERENT KINDS OF AGENT

'Agency' covers a multitude of situations, such as estate agents, insurance agents, agents on commodity markets and implied agency situations where one party is given authority by another to act on that other's behalf. There are also more specific legal designations. The term 'special agent', for example, applies not only to the James Bonds of this world, but also to those appointed to act for a specific transaction outside their ordinary course of business. As such, they are distinguished from a general agent. There are brokers who are normally expected to deal as agents and not as principals; there are 'factors' who may deal as both, although the term is now more commonly used in relation to debt finance. A specific type of agent, known as a *del credere* agent, is unusual in that the appointment is a guarantee to the principal that the third-party customer will perform the contract, leaving the *del credere* agent at risk if the customer does not pay. This chapter concentrates on the commercial agent who acts generally in seeking product sales for one or more principals, but does not take personal risk on the principal's transactions.

AUTHORITY AND OBLIGATIONS OF AN AGENT

Actual authority will involve an express authority by the principal to permit the agent to enter into contracts on behalf of the principal. Those contracts will then be binding upon the principal if made in the principal's name or if made in the agent's name expressly on behalf of the principal. By contracting or signing on behalf of a principal, the agent gives an implied warranty of authority to act on behalf of the principal and will be liable to a third party who relies on that warranty and suffers loss because the principal fails to confirm or honour the order.

Usual authority may arise where the third party does not check the position and relies on the apparent authority which the agent has, being the authority expected of a person holding that position in the ordinary course of their work. In cases of doubt, some form of actual or implied representation will need to be shown that the principal did in fact authorize or 'hold out' the agent to carry out the transaction. When dealing with agents, therefore, even if the act appears within the agent's authority, it is much safer to have the principal expressly sign the contract since, if the agent was acting outside their actual and apparent authority, the principal will not be bound by the transaction unless they accept or ratify it in some clear way.

There are certain obligations on an agent implied by law – notably, obligations to act in good faith and with reasonable skill and care in performing the agency duties, and to act within the lawful and reasonable instructions and authority given by the principal. The agent's overriding duty of good faith to the principal covers not only the duty to act in a financially responsible manner and maintain proper accounts, but also an absolute need to act transparently and to avoid conflicts of interest. The Court of Appeal judgment in *Imageview Management* v. *Jack* (2009) shows what can happen when agents secretly seek commission from two parties and how robust the courts tend to be about such issues.

Even so, it is worth spelling out these obligations in the contract, as not all agents have read the law reports.

Commission

Over the years, English common law has protected the agent in the basic right to earn commission, but has done little more. If the principal terminates the agency agreement, the only remedy given to the agent under common law is to be paid what was properly due during the contract period, including a proper period of notice. The fact that the agent may have spent years building up the principal's business interests, only to be deprived of all further benefit from the connections, was not something the law recognized until such rights were ultimately codified in an EEC Council Directive of December 1986 on the protection of commercial agents, which is now considered in some detail.

PROTECTION FOR THE COMMERCIAL AGENT

New regulations were finally introduced in Britain by the Commercial Agents (Council Directive) Regulations 1993. Known as the Commercial Agents Regulations, they aim to harmonize treatment of agents in the UK with those in other European member states. The same rules therefore broadly apply in each state of the European Union, with some minor modifications applicable to the agency activities normally carried on in that country.

The Commercial Agents Regulations

This section gives an overview and then looks at some of the specific areas in more detail. It is important to appreciate at the outset that these Regulations are not 'toothless'. It is not possible to exclude (or 'derogate from') most of the Regulations, especially those as to the duty of good faith, the provisions as to termination and (for the most part) the goodwill payment obligations. Most agents are well aware of their entitlements.

WHO IS A COMMERCIAL AGENT FOR THE PURPOSES OF THE REGULATIONS?

- The agent may be an individual or a company, but must be *independent* from the principal.
- Only agents who *sell (or buy) goods* (not services) are included; 'goods', for this purpose, excludes land, so estate agency is excluded.
- The agent's authority needs to have some form of *continuity*. A single agency commission will not suffice.
- The agency *does not need to be in writing* for the Regulations to apply.
- A commercial agent must have *authority* either *to negotiate* or *to negotiate and conclude* sales on behalf of the principal. This generally excludes a representative, unless that person does have actual authority to negotiate the deal or to sign up a customer.
- Agency must be the *main business*, so those whose agency is secondary to another main activity, such as distribution, are unlikely to be covered.

WHAT MAIN DUTIES ARISE?

- *A formal duty of good faith* is established both ways between principal and agent. This carries quite a strong obligation in law, especially European law, which is the main touchstone for the legal obligation under the Regulations.
- There are specific obligations regarding *commission and payment* on termination.

WHAT ABOUT COMMISSION PAYMENTS?

- At a minimum the principal must *account* to the agent at least quarterly, showing the sales made through the agency and the commission generated as a result, and must pay the agent within one month after that.
- In the absence of other provision, *commission payment* is strictly due when the goods are delivered and invoiced, not when they are paid for. For this reason some principals will provide that the timing flows from customer payment, rather than delivery.

WHAT HAPPENS ON TERMINATION OF A COMMERCIAL AGENCY?

- The principal may terminate the agency only by *written notice* of at least one month and up to three months, depending how long the agency has lasted. Notice must expire at the end of a month unless the contract states otherwise.
- The agent is entitled to *commission* not only on orders secured before the agency terminated and delivered afterwards, but also on orders secured afterwards which were 'derived from the agent's efforts' before termination. The contract may provide for commission to be shared between old and new agents where it is equitable to do so (and principals should take care in their contracts to avoid liability for double commission).
- Unless the agent terminates voluntarily, with no fault on the part of the principal, or the principal terminates on the grounds of such a serious breach by the agent as would justify summary termination, the principal must pay the agent *compensation* or an indemnity. This will broadly represent payment for the goodwill which the agent has built up for the principal, and is considered in more detail below.
- *Restrictive covenants*, which may be enforced by the principal against the agent, are limited.

GOODWILL OR TERMINATION PAYMENTS

The choice

The termination payment is intended either to compensate the agent for the goodwill the principal acquires in taking over the agents' customers and business ('compensation') or to indemnify the agent for the loss of the agency ('indemnity'). A choice may be made between the two in the agency agreement but, if the agreement does not specify otherwise, compensation will be payable. Moreover, compensation is potentially unlimited. If, however, the written agency agreement specifies an indemnity payment, this can be limited to an amount equivalent to one year's commission averaged over the last few years of the agency. If the contract specifies an indemnity and the principal can establish that the agent has not generated any new customers or increased business with existing customers, it is unlikely any indemnity payment will be justified.

The calculation

As these were new concepts to English law there has been considerable confusion as to how to calculate compensation in particular, with cases swinging one way and then the other. Many settlements were made for payments equivalent to three or six months' average annual commission, but then came a series of cases – one of them quite exceptional in the case of an individual agent approaching retirement – where an award equivalent to several years' commission was made.

The debate then tended towards whether French or the German precedents should apply, the one suggesting two years' average annual commission and the other one year's average annual commission as the benchmark. Then in 2007 came the House of Lords decision in *Lonsdale* v. *Howard & Hallam,* in which the court reviewed the whole position and concluded that the real basis of compensation was indeed to pay the agent for the value of the goodwill effectively built up by the agent and acquired by the principal at the time the agency is terminated. If the business was in terminal decline at the point of termination, the agent should be paid for the value of that business at that time, based on an independent market valuation and not on some artificial multiplier based on past earnings. Conversely, where an agent had built up a successful operation from scratch and then has it absorbed by the principal once the market and customer base have been established, the agent may receive proper recompense for the value created. On the same principles, a goodwill payment is due even on the retirement, illness, infirmity or death of the agent, so as to reflect the value 'inherited' by the principal.

Compensation or indemnity

A principal preparing a draft agency agreement can decide whether to mention the compensation or indemnity subject or not. If there is no mention, compensation will apply, and may be unlimited. If the principal wants to limit the claim, an indemnity must be specified. This flags the termination payment issue to the agent (who will probably be aware of the issue in any case), but an indemnity payment may well be a cheaper outcome for the principal – especially if the business has progressed and is valuable by that time – than compensation which may both be more expensive and involve the expense and uncertainty of an valuation of the business.

Timing

It will pay both parties to consider when to terminate. For principals granting or renewing agency agreements of any lengthy period, an express indemnity clause may help limit the maximum amount payable. Agents, on the other hand, might try to negotiate for a long enough agency period to build up real goodwill in the business, insist on compensation and keep funds in hand for a battle if need be!

THE COMMERCIAL AGENTS REGULATIONS – THE INTERNATIONAL ASPECT

These Regulations apply to the activities of commercial agents that are carried out in Great Britain, and there are equivalent regulations for those operating in Northern Ireland. It is the place where the agent mainly operates, not where the principal is located, which decides the issue. It is possible to make agency agreements subject to the law of another EU member state, where equivalent protection should be available, although there may be some differences, especially in the choice and rate of compensation or indemnity, but it is not possible to contract out of the Regulations when the agent is active in an EU member state.

Agency and Distribution Contracts: The Main Terms

Although the legal structure of agency and distribution agreements is significantly different, the contractual framework involves considering many of the same issues. In this section 'supplier' is used to cover both the principal of an agent and the supplier to a distributor. The comments that follow are, however, all subject to competition law considerations, in the case of distributors generally and for agents who bear any element of financial or commercial risk. See the competition law section later in this chapter and the fuller treatment in Chapter 8.

- *Territory*. It is usual for the appointment to apply and be limited to a particular territory, ranging from an entire country to a small, clearly defined geographical area. Parallel arrangements may then be set up with other agents or distributors for other territories.
- *Exclusivity*. 'Sole' agent or distributor means that the supplier will not appoint another agent/distributor in the same territory for the same purpose. It does not mean that the supplier will not itself sell the same products direct into the same area. The word 'exclusive', however, operates to exclude the supplier also. It is unnecessary to refer to 'sole and exclusive', as the latter automatically includes the former, but not vice versa. Exclusivity flags competition law implications; it may also raise questions of possible breach of the implied 'good faith' obligations in agency contracts covered by the Regulations if either principal or agent has not been fully open with the other.

  The *principal's freedom to sell direct* is an associated point. Both types of agreement may see suppliers reserving the right to sell direct into the territory. This right may be limited to *international accounts* – for example, where there is a customer with headquarters or at least a base in another territory – or *national or major accounts* – particularly where there may be suppliers for a number of depots – or *house accounts* – customers who are traditionally serviced direct. These exclusions need to be very clearly defined to avoid abuse or disputes.
- *Post-termination restrictions*. With both agent and distributor, non-compete provisions after termination of the agency are subject to the normal rules of enforceability of restrictive covenants (see Chapters 5 and 8). The Commercial Agents Regulations also state that a post-termination restraint clause will be invalid against a commercial agent if it goes beyond the agent's geographical area, customer base, relevant goods or two years' duration.

- *Terms of the agreement.* In this complex area there are several points to consider:
    - *Compensation*: Whereas an agent will be entitled to compensation on the agency coming to an end, there is no such entitlement for distributors, who may find that their business is suddenly lost without compensation. Both agent and distributor will often therefore wish to negotiate a longer, rather than a shorter, term for their agreement, and this can work well if they are conscientious and successful. But the principal or supplier needs to guard against poor or only average performance by restricting the term or setting out performance targets, especially where the agreement is an exclusive one.
    - *Exclusivity*: A key feature here may be whether the agent/distributor deals in competitors' products or is restricted solely to the one supplier's products in that market. If this is the main or only business, the agent/distributor is likely to be fully focused on making the operation successful. Correspondingly, they are much more vulnerable to changes by their supplier.
    - *Management changes:* – Changes, such as new supplier management or reporting structures, can be more insidious and begin to damage the business relationship, possibly fatally. This is more likely to happen in large corporations than in owner-run businesses, although in the latter case the issue of change of control still needs to be considered.
    - *Performance*: The supplier may want to keep the term short to see how the arrangement works, but may be prepared to extend the term in return for some form of performance target, such as minimum sales, considered below.
    - *Investment:* Another factor will be the capital expenditure that the agent or distributor may need to lay out, which will need a sufficient term of operation to amortize the upfront costs incurred. The same applies to renewal, and, as many long-term agents or distributors have found to their cost, past loyalty, like profits, is no guide to future performance.
- *Minimum purchase or sales targets.* Such clauses need to be carefully thought out and drafted. They are likely to be looked at in great detail when expectations are not fulfilled and can result in litigation. Distributors should beware of absolute commitment to targets which may cost them substantial damages if not met. For a supplier, a clear minimum obligation on the part of the distributor is to be preferred to reliance on more general obligations to market and sell. These clauses – also known in some cases as 'take or pay' clauses – should be drafted as obligations of the relevant party, rather than as damages for breach, which might more readily be treated as an irrecoverable penalty. Where competition law might be engaged, especially where the groups or their market share are substantial, it may be best to draft any solus-type arrangements to come within an appropriate specific exemption (see 'Vertical agreements exemptions' below). Termination may, in any case, be a last-ditch remedy, as it may cause the distributor to rush into the arms of the supplier's main competitor. Suppliers should therefore consider including suitable post-termination restrictions, but carefully drafted within competition law rules; distributors should be equally wary of losing the distributorship and being out of the market for a period.
- *Commission or margin.* Commission rates for agents are normally agreed, but, if not, market rates can be fixed by the courts under the Commercial Agents Regulations. With distributors, profit depends on buying and selling prices. This customer price is

very much dictated by the market, and suppliers probably reference export or similar list prices as the basis to negotiate discounts. Here again, exclusive distributors will have some protection against being undersold by their suppliers in their own market, but, correspondingly, this may raise issues of differential pricing between or within member states if suppliers try to partition the market. The points raised in Chapter 9 on price changes will also be relevant here.

- *Exchange rates and payment terms*. Payment terms for commission or, with distributors, payment for the products should be set out clearly. These terms will include proper accounting arrangements.
- *International*. Where there are international aspects to the sale, the contract should stipulate the currency and place of payment (see also Chapter 17 on the international dimension). Distributors need to be cautious about currency fluctuations when buying from a supplier based overseas and when buying and selling in different currencies. With an agency, many of these questions are avoided.
- *Allocation of responsibilities*. Careful arrangements need to be made about packaging, labelling, delivery, risk/insurance, title in the goods and delivery notes to ensure that both parties are kept fully up-to-date with the position. This will also affect the pricing structure.
- *Service elements*. Many distribution agreements contain service obligations on the distributor in relation to the physical handling of goods, covering such aspects as timeliness and accuracy of the handling and despatch process. The relevant contract provisions should have regard to the comments in Chapters 12 and 13 on agreements for services and outsourcing, especially in relation to service levels and key performance indicators.

TERMINATION AND EFFECTS OF TERMINATION

Termination is inevitable at some point, and should be thought about and planned for from the outset, both as to how and when it is likely to happen and what the effects will be. So far as the agent is concerned, the break may be sweetened by continuing commission and the possibility of a compensation or indemnity payment. Where there is a distribution agreement, the supplier will not want the distributor to unload the remaining stock on to the market at a low price when the agreement expires. Accordingly, many distribution agreements will include a provision enabling the supplier to repurchase stock from the distributor at cost (or similar) on termination. This needs to be done in a way that does not breach competition law or the terms of any vertical agreement exemption relied on. If the agreement may fall foul of article 81(1) and the *de minimis* thresholds or other exemptions do not apply, it may be best for the agreement merely to give the distributor the right to require the supplier to buy the stock back. Either way, the period of notice (and minimum periods if the Commercial Agents Regulations apply) and the sell-off period need some thought. The sell-off period should be long enough to preserve continuity for customers and give the agent or distributor a fair chance of finalizing sales. but not so long as to give the opportunity for any damage to be caused, especially where termination causes (or is caused by) bad blood between the parties.

EMPLOYEE TRANSFER REGULATIONS

Will TUPE apply?

The grant or termination of either an agency or distribution agreement may affect the employees engaged in the business affected by the change. Typical areas include sales, servicing and technical functions, which may be transferred by operation of law under the Transfer of Undertakings (Protection of Employment) Regulations (TUPE), updated in 2006. The broad effect of these Regulations is to safeguard the jobs of employees of the business (or part of the business) that is transferred, whether directly or indirectly, to a new service provider.

Planning ahead

These questions really need to be considered at the outset by both parties. If the TUPE Regulations apply, the employees affected will automatically transfer to the agent/ distributor in the first place and then on to the supplier when the agreements ends, and possibly then on to any new distributor. It is the transferee – the business to which the employees are deemed transferred – which will inherit most of the problems, so it should be considered how the Regulations may affect the deal and who should bear the risks and costs involved. As it is not possible to contract out of TUPE, it may be appropriate to include in the original agreement an indemnity in respect of any employee claims resulting from operation of the Regulations. The TUPE Regulations are considered in more detail in Chapter 13 on outsourcing.

Competition Law Issues

The issue of restrictions and competition law is always potentially relevant to agency and especially distribution agreements. Competition law is discussed in more detail in Chapter 8, but some reminders are appropriate here.

AGENCY AGREEMENTS AND COMPETITION LAW

As mentioned earlier, an agency agreement only falls outside the competition rules on restrictive agreements (that is, article 81(1)/Chapter I prohibition) if it is a 'true' agency. The main test is whether the agent bears any material commercial or financial risk in relation to contracts concluded or negotiated on behalf of the principal. Things that might indicate that an agent is bearing material commercial or financial risks, and is thus not a true agent and therefore subject to competition law, include the following obligations on the part of the agent:

- to purchase goods and/or pay for their transportation costs (which means that actual distribution agreements will rarely satisfy the 'true agency' test because the distributor normally buys and resells the goods);
- to keep any material level of stock of the goods at the agent's own property or at its own risk;

- to provide substantial after-sales service (unless fully reimbursed by the principal);
- to invest in, or contribute to the cost of, sales promotions;
- to invest in equipment, premises or the training of personnel; or
- to accept responsibility towards third parties for damage caused by the products sold (unless the agent is at fault as agent).

Further issues

If there is a risk that the agreement does not constitute genuine agency, provisions to avoid would include: a) any bans on the agent accepting unsolicited orders from outside its permitted territory (that is, passive sales restrictions); or b) provisions enabling the principal to determine the resale price. Even where there is a genuine agency, the scope and duration of any post-term restrictions need to follow the normal rules covered elsewhere in this chapter, as such provisions only take effect once the agency has come to an end. As a general rule, restrictions which limit or prevent the agent from competing with its former principal or soliciting the principal's customers should be limited to a maximum of one year after termination of the agency.

Dominance

Even if the agreement creates a genuine agency relationship between principal and agent, and so falls outside the prohibition on restrictive agreements, the prohibition on the abuse of a dominant position (article 82/Chapter II prohibition) will still apply where the principal is dominant in the relevant product market.

Planning

If you are dealing with a distribution agreement or even an agency agreement where there is a risk that the agent may be independent (and thus outside the so-called 'safe harbour' for true agency agreements under competition law as mentioned above), it may pay to try to keep the agreement within the terms of the vertical agreements specific exemption as discussed in some detail in Chapter 8 and covered briefly below.

THE VERTICAL AGREEMENTS EXEMPTION

Territorial restrictions for resales

The terms of the Vertical Agreements Regulation (VAR), effective from June 2010 and replacing the old Vertical Agreements Block Exemption (VRBE), should nearly always be considered in relation to the drafting of distribution agreements. In general, competition law frowns on direct or indirect restrictions on where a distributor can resell a supplier's goods, but, provided there are no hardcore restrictions elsewhere, the VAR does not (in its draft form – see Chapter 8) exclude the following possible restrictions:

- *active* sales into the exclusive territory or exclusive customer group reserved to the supplier or allocated to another distributor where the restriction does not limit resales by the buyer's own customers

- any sales *by a wholesaler* to end-users
- any sales to an *unauthorized distributor* where there is a selective distribution system in place
- sales of *components* (intended for the supplier's products) to a competitive manufacturer.

Active sales and wholesales

These two issues are most relevant to a normal distribution agreement. In terms of active sales, the prohibition may extend either to the exclusive territory of another or to an exclusive customer group reserved to the supplier or allocated to another distributor, where onward sales are not limited. In contrast, passive sales (where a customer approaches the distributor) can be prohibited only in limited circumstances. The wholesale issue is clearly designed to encourage wholesalers to act as such and not to use cost advantages to undermine retailers in supplying consumers – a point worth considering in relation to Internet sales and follow-up. For both purposes, Internet sales will generally be regarded as passive sales unless they are specifically targeted.

Non-compete clauses

As set out in Chapter 8, non-compete obligations (NCOs) will, with limited exceptions, take a vertical agreement outside the VAR exemption if they exceed five years or are indefinite in duration. Post-termination obligations (PTOs), which limit the buyer's ability to manufacture, buy, sell or resell goods or services after termination of the agreement, are only permitted if they are limited to competing goods or services, sold from the same premises as before, and if the restrictions are essential to protect the supplier's know-how acquired by the buyer during the term of the agreement. If these conditions are satisfied, the restrictions must be limited to one year after termination of the agreement, although a longer period may be possible regarding the supplier's know-how where and so long as this remains fully out of the public domain.

Summary: Distributor or Agent?

So which should you appoint or be appointed as?

PRICES AND PAYMENT

An agent is more under the control of the principal than a distributor and, if resale prices are important, the agent may be the natural choice. The sale will be direct from principal to customer, meaning that the principal takes the direct risk of the customer failing to pay. It is therefore important to be clear with the agent as to whether principal or agent undertakes the necessary references and credit checks, and indeed whether the agent gets paid if the principal does not. The distributor, by contrast, has direct responsibility for securing payment from the customer and to pay the supplier in any event, but the supplier needs to know that the distributor's business is robust enough to take the occasional financial knock.

CUSTOMERS

With agency, the principal may have to deal directly with customer queries, product liability and contractual problems, which the agent may not be able to handle – or handle well. The distributor, on the other hand, is likely to have an organization geared not only to sales and delivery, but also to marketing and after-sales service. The distributor will deal directly with any customer problems in the first instance and will often be able to resolve installation and service issues and supply spare parts from stock, relieving the supplier of the problems of small orders and individual customer attention. Indeed, the distributor should be very experienced and knowledgeable in the market in question – a particularly valuable asset when dealing across international borders.

TERMINATION

Termination will engage two main issues. First, the agent will probably be entitled to a goodwill payment whereas a distributor will not (although there are some equivalent provisions for certain distributors in some European states, so care needs to be taken if the distributor is based abroad). Second, and perhaps more important in the long run, is the issue of knowing the customers and their details. A principal, even if working via an agent, will contract and deal directly with the customers, will know their requirements and details and can take active steps to retain them when the agreement ends. The supplier may not even know the end-destination of the distributor's sales and, even if it does know, is unlikely to have any significant relationship with the customers in many cases. In many ways, the retention or loss of the customer connection is the reason why the commercial agent is entitled to a goodwill payment whereas the distributor is not. The ultimate decision may therefore depend on how the parties see their relationships with the customers during and after the agreement period, so it pays to think ahead. In that context, the ability of the agent or distributor, having built up the market, simply to switch to an alternative supplier is something to be carefully considered.

COMPETITION LAW

A distributor is more likely to come within the ambit of competition law and special care will be needed with any form of tied (or solus) or exclusive arrangement, and even more so where there could be any appreciable effect on any relevant market. And hardcore restrictions (see Chapter 8) should be avoided in any event.

Summary and Checklist

There is a major difference in law between a commercial agent and a distributor, although the terms are sometimes used confusingly. A representative has more limited powers and authority. Considerations and the main terms to be negotiated include:

- *Liability* – If the person is your employee, you will have vicarious responsibility for their actions.

- *Authority* – What is the representative or agent authorized to agree? Are there clear terms agreed with them and will their authority – and any limits on it – be apparent to third parties?
- *Customers* – Are the customers to be yours, suggesting you appoint an agent, or the reseller's, suggesting a distributor?
- *Title to goods* – Do you retain control of and title to goods until they are sold to the final customer? If so, you should appoint an agent (or have a strong retention of title clause – see Chapter 9).
- *Resale pricing* – You cannot retain control of resale pricing once you appoint a distributor or otherwise sell the goods on.
- *Payment* – If you rely on the end-customer paying you, appoint an agent; otherwise, you will be dependent on the distributor or other reseller making payment.
- *Continuing authority* – Does your agent have continuing authority in relation to the sale or purchase of goods? If so, the agent is likely to be a commercial agent for the purposes of the Commercial Agents Regulations.
- *Primary activities* – If the agent's main business is something other than agency, the Regulations may not apply.
- *Commission* – Paying a commission suggests agency whereas a profit on resale suggests distributorship. Is the position clearly set out?
- *Minimum targets* – Are there any minimum targets and, if so, are they clear and do they risk breaching competition law?
- *Service elements* – Are any service levels carefully spelt out? (see Chapters 12 and 13.)
- *Term of the agreement* – Is this perfectly clear and are any preconditions for renewal carefully spelt out?
- *Agency termination payment* – Have you factored in the likely need to pay the agent when the agency terminates, even through no fault of yours? Are you clear how this amount is likely to be calculated?
- *Exclusivity* – Is there to be any exclusivity in the arrangement? If so, this needs to be carefully defined. If the other party is not a true agent, competition law implications may arise.
- *Competition law* – If there is a distribution agreement with restrictions, does the agreement (and the practice) comply with the Vertical Agreements Regulation (VAR)?
- *International* – Have you taken account of any different laws that may apply and any possible currency fluctuation risks?
- *TUPE* – Might TUPE apply either at the outset or on termination? (See also Chapter 13.)

12 *Contracts for Services*

Introduction – statutory protection for the supply of services – freelance and consultancy services – a sample letter-form consultancy agreement – corporate consultancies – terms of business for services – other issues in contracts for services – summary and checklist

Introduction

The distinction between goods and services can be important in many areas of the law relating to contracts. Chapters 9, 10 (to some extent) and 11 have dealt primarily with issues arising from the sale of goods, whereas this chapter concentrates on the general legal issues relating to contracts for 'pure' services, linking in turn with some later chapters looking at specialist areas, such as technology and outsourcing contracts. Services are often more difficult to define and evaluate than goods, so the scope for misunderstanding may be much greater.

The human element adds greatly to the mix with services, which are ultimately about the way in which people perform. At a personal level, you might be unhappy that your decorator has torn your new wallpaper in one corner of the room, but approaching the issue might open up your whole relationship with the decorator. Raising the issue at the wrong time, or in the wrong way, or possibly at all, might lead to the decorator walking off and the job never being finished. The temptation is therefore to leave the issue until the rest of the work is done and the bill has to be paid, but that can be the worst possible time to resolve it amicably, and it could easily spill over into a dispute about money. Emotions can then rapidly spiral out of control. The same thing can happen even in business contracts.

Contracts for individuals to provide occasional services to a business are typically in the form of consultancy or freelance commission arrangements. There is also, of course, actual employment, where the relationship is highly regulated and requires that employers do tackle employee problems at the earliest stage and progress them, if need be, by a formal procedure that aims to get to the root of the problem, to specify remedial action and give support and time for the improvement required. Traditionally, few contracts for services have had that kind of procedure built in because the freelance relationship is essentially different from the employment relationship in that the freelancer is expected to be capable of the job from day one, but general review and dispute resolution procedures are now increasingly common, especially in more major contracts.

Statutory Protection in Relation to the Supply of Services

REASONABLE CARE AND SKILL

Chapter 9 covers Part I of the SGSA (Supply of Goods and Services Act 1982) in relation to a mixed supply of goods and service. Part II of the SGSA deals with the supply of services alone, without goods, in the course of a business. The provider of those services has an implied obligation to provide them with reasonable care and skill. The level of care and skill depends on the level of care and skill that an ordinary competent supplier of those services would be expected to have. That level, in turn, will relate to the standards that the supplier of the services actually professes to have (either expressly or by implication) in relation to the nature of their calling. So if you ask an electrician to carry out wiring work, you are entitled to have the work carried out to the standard that a competent electrician would be expected to achieve. But if you ask a carpenter to carry out electrical work, you cannot expect the same standard unless the carpenter has represented that he is indeed a competent electrician. With services there is no obligation on the supplier to achieve a specific result unless the contract includes such a term.

REASONABLE CHARGE

In contracts covered by the SGSA there is also an implied term (in s. 15) that the buyer will pay a reasonable charge for what is supplied if the parties have not agreed a price. If therefore you ask a builder to carry out some work for you, and you do not fix clear terms of reference, the law will imply terms as to the quality of the work and materials and the price of the deal. That, of course, still leaves open the question of how much work the builder was asked to do in the first place and to what degree that original agreement was subsequently changed. This is an area in which disputes can easily arise and be difficult to resolve, making it even more important to have clear terms agreed from the outset in contracts for services.

UNFAIR TERMS RULES

As seen elsewhere, the unfair contract terms laws can apply to the supply of services. Whilst UCTA s. 6 applies only to goods, other sections of the same Act make any attempt to avoid the consequences of a party's negligence – even in relation to the provision of services – subject to the test of reasonableness (see Chapter 9).

Freelance and Consultancy Services

Whereas an employee works for, under the direction of and on behalf of an employer, a consultant or a service provider is an independent contractor providing agreed services to a client in much the same way as a producer of goods might provide those goods to a customer. Although many of the hallmarks of employment and even agency apply to the consultancy relationship, the legal independence of the consultant is one of the key features of the arrangement. Within this broad framework there are a full range of possibilities which are now considered further.

CONSULTANTS AND COMPANY DIRECTORS

Executive directors tend to have managerial roles and be company employees. Non-executive directors, on the other hand, may be self-employed if they do not hold an executive position in the company in question and their directorship is limited to matters of policy. They may also have consultancies with the company in specific professional or advisory areas. HMRC (the Inland Revenue) starts from the position that directors are employees of the companies on whose boards they sit, but do have fairly narrow exemptions which should be specifically considered if a director is not to be paid subject to PAYE (pay-as you-earn income tax).

CONSULTANCY DISTINGUISHED FROM EMPLOYMENT

Service contract – or contract for services?

'Service agreement' indicates employment whereas 'agreement for services' suggests – in law – freelance or consultancy services. This legal distinction is about as arcane as hearing employees referred to in contracts as 'servants'! This section seeks to set out some guidance.

Consultants are paid fees, rather than salary and benefits. Those fees will normally be at a market level that reflects the fact that the occupation is not full-time and does not include senior employment benefits, such as car expenses, pension contributions and insurances. To this might be added an allowance for the lack of employment protection and cover for holidays and sickness. Since an independent consultant takes the risk of void periods and enforced absences, it can readily be seen that an equivalent hourly rate of remuneration for a freelance may be substantially higher than the hourly rate of an equivalent employee. To provide any of the benefits mentioned above to a consultant separately on top of a fee rate would strongly indicate an employment relationship.

Tax implications

Employees are taxed under Schedule E, subject to deduction of PAYE and employees' national insurance contributions (NIC). Further, NIC is payable by the employer on each employee. A freelance or independent consultant, on the other hand, is taxed under Schedule D as a self-employed person and pays a reduced level of NIC, albeit with lesser benefits. It has long been a temptation to treat what might be an employment relationship as a consultancy in order to mitigate tax, but the tests are quite stringent and the penalty for getting it wrong can be high. If the relationship is, on Inland Revenue (HMRC) tests, one of employment, HMRC can claim direct from the effective employer the tax and NIC which has not been deducted, together with interest and penalties. Even if the freelance has paid their tax, 'employers' can be liable for the excess, but if the freelance has not paid at all, the bill could be considerable. That is why, in the Williams and Chambers agreement in the example set out below, Williams has included an indemnity on the tax issue even though the agreement has all the hallmarks of a genuine freelance relationship.

The agreement also implies the assumption that Williams could find and recover the tax from Chambers if the issue ever arises, so it is wise to make enquiries! HMRC can carry out spot-checks, and non-compliance can result in a fine and full audit. In extreme cases, the wrong choice may even be adjudged to be tax evasion and a criminal fraud on HMRC, so it pays to be very careful in this area.

TESTS OF EMPLOYMENT

Businesses engaging freelancers will naturally want some sort of assurance that they will not be 'bitten' by employee tax or employment protection at a later date, but unfortunately the tests used by HMRC for tax purposes and employment tribunals for employment relationships are different, and there is no certain route or 'safe harbour' for this purpose.

If there is one overall 'snapshot' test, it is probably to see whether there is any 'mutuality' of obligation between the parties. Typically, in an employment relationship mutuality will be expressed in the employer having the obligation to provide work for the employee and the employee having the obligation to do that work.

Indicators

Looking more specifically at the contractor, there are three useful indicators of freelance status, as follows:

1. *Ready equipped* – Does the 'freelance' come to the relationship complete with all skills and, if appropriate, all tools to do the job and accept the risk of providing the services with reasonable skill and care and of being accountable for failure to do so?
2. *Flexibility* – Does the freelance have a large measure of discretion as to how and when, within an agreed overall timescale, the services are performed? (This reduces the mutuality aspect.)
3. *Independence* – Can the freelance really be said to be working on his or her own account? Are they economically not dependent on the employer's business? Having other clients and freelance commissions tend to support freelance status.
   Any of the following indicators may suffice to indicate employment:
   - The worker has to do the work themselves.
   - The 'employer' has control over where and how the work is done.
   - There are disciplinary processes and policies on minimum/maximum working hours and holiday approval in place.
   - The 'employer' has the right to dismiss.
   - There is payment of a regular and consistent wage or salary, calculated by reference to hours, days or weeks worked.
   - The worker is 'integrated' with the business, such as receiving a staff handbook, attending the Christmas party, having regular use of the staff canteen.
   - A company car and/or other major equipment are provided.
   - The worker receives overtime or bonus payments, paid holidays, sick pay or other benefits.
   - There is eligibility to join a company pension scheme.
   - The worker may not, or does not, work for anyone else.

- The 'employer' has the obligation to provide regular work.

The following are indicators of a self-employment (although their absence of itself does not necessarily indicate employment):

- The worker may turn down work.
- The worker receives a fixed sum for the work, rather than an hourly rate.
- The worker can decide how, when and where the job is done (within a broad remit).
- The worker can work, and is regularly working, for others during the contract period.
- The worker may subcontract some or all of the work.
- The worker uses their own main equipment and/or risks their own money.
- The worker must correct any unsatisfactory work at their own expense.
- The worker has their own VAT registration (if they have turnover above minimum levels) and submits their own tax returns.

Other implications

The decision as to whether or not to employ someone providing services may have other significant consequences, such as employment protection rights and vicarious liability for employees' accidents and injuries.

A Sample Letter-form Consultancy Agreement

Let us assume that Williams, an office furniture wholesaler, decides to engage the business advisory services of consultant Cheryl Chambers. This is a two-part engagement, with the second part being dependent on the Williams' directors accepting the initial Chambers' report and recommendations. Chambers may write with a statement of her general terms and conditions, but this example assumes that Williams wants something more specific and writes to Chambers accordingly:

> Dear Cheryl,
>
> Further to our meetings I am pleased to write to confirm the terms we have agreed for you to provide consultancy services (**Services**) to Williams Limited (**Company**).
>
> 1. The first stage of the Services will be to investigate and report on the current markets in which the Company carries on business, to consider other suitable markets into which it might extend its operations, to advise on the advantages and disadvantages and potential returns from each of those markets and to provide detailed and reasoned recommendations, together with cost and profit implications, of a revised marketing strategy (overall the **Project**). You will then advise and assist us further in implementing the chosen strategy, which will be the second stage of the Services. We will be relying on your experience, skill and knowledge in considering your report and, in all probability, acting on it.

2. The first stage of the Project report is to be complete and in final form for presentation to my board by no later than 31 January next. In view of the need for the new plan to be in place before the international trade fair on 20 February, time for completion of the Project will be of the essence. The second stage will probably last six months after that, but must be complete by no later than end November in any event.

3. The second stage is entirely conditional upon the board approving your report and recommendations, in which case we do require you to be available throughout that second-stage period, as set out below. If the board do not agree to proceed to the second stage, neither we nor you have any obligation to take matters further. If the board does agree, it is essential that you are personally able to supervise and complete the second stage within the terms of this agreement.

4. You will be carrying out the work from your own office and will be responsible for all the research and collation work yourself. You will decide and let us have preferably two days' prior notice (by e-mail to my secretary) of the days when you would like to attend or use our offices and of any facilities you wish to use or any documents to which you require access. We will do our best to assist you without disrupting our normal activities. (As you know, our space is already somewhat cramped!) It is up to you how many hours you [and your team] put into the first stage. During the second stage it will be up to us to let you know when we need you, but each month we will require up to ten hours of your own time [and potentially up to ten hours of the time of one of your assistants].

5. Your fee for the services will be according to the two stages. For the first stage it will be the fixed sum of £10,000 plus VAT for the project. This is to be invoiced on presentation of your completed, final project report with payment 30 days after invoice. For the second stage it will be at the rate of £1,000 per day for yourself and between £500 and £600 per day plus VAT for an assistant, subject to our agreeing an overall budget. These second-stage fees are to be invoiced each month for work carried out at our request in the previous month, with payment again to be 30 days after invoice. In addition, we will reimburse you for invoiced travel and other direct third-party costs for the second-stage work (but not the first stage which is covered in your overall first-stage fee) reasonably incurred by you in accordance with our requests.

6. This agreement may be terminated by either of us on written notice to the other if the other [materially] breaches this agreement and the breach, if capable of remedy, is not remedied within 21 days of written notice identifying the breach and requiring its remedy. As indicated, a failure on your part to deliver the project report by the due date will be a [material] breach incapable of remedy. Either of us may also terminate this agreement on written notice to the other if the other becomes insolvent, including liquidation, receivership, administration, voluntary arrangement or bankruptcy.

7. You will treat [and take all practicable steps to ensure that all your staff treat] as confidential all information you [or they] receive in providing the Services regarding our company, its business, finances, suppliers, customers and actual and potential marketing plans. You and they must not at any time make use of any such information for any purpose or disclose it to any third party without our prior written agreement. This restriction will not apply to information which becomes public knowledge without breach of this agreement on your or their part. You will promptly return to us

on completion of the services all property belonging to us, including all documents and copy documents in your possession or under your control.

8.   You have confirmed that you are self-employed and are to be treated as an independent contractor and that you will be responsible for all taxation and similar liabilities arising in relation to the fees payable to you. You accordingly undertake to indemnify us in full against all claims or liabilities in relation to income tax, national insurance contributions, costs, penalties or other charges against us which arise from or relate to the services.

9.   This agreement is personal to you and is to be performed [or supervised] by you personally. It may not be subcontracted or assigned [except that you may assign it to your company, Chambers Consultants Limited, subject to our prior written consent which we will not unreasonably withhold provided that the company is and remains under your control and you continue personally to remain a party to this agreement].

I trust this letter is a fair reflection of our discussions. If so, please sign and return the duplicate to me to confirm your agreement. If not, please telephone me as soon as possible so that we may seek to resolve matters. The board is very excited about this project, and we look forward to working with you and seeing your report.

With kind regards

Yours sincerely

Walter Williams
for and on behalf of
Williams Limited

COMMENT ON THE EXAMPLE

Williams' view

This letter, in fact, covers a great deal of ground and gives Walter Williams the chance to set out clearly his own expectations. It might be sensible to have an interim approval point, even during the first stage, to highlight any misunderstanding early on. Williams might also like to consider some form of restriction prohibiting Chambers from doing similar work for a competitor for a period, which may depend on the nature of the work which Chambers normally does.

Chambers' view

There are rather more points for Cheryl Chambers. The following, among others, are worth considering:

• *Exclusions* – Chambers may want to consider any limitations on the work, for example specifically excluding certain types of specialist subjects and/or setting a maximum level of liability and specifically limiting certain claims (see Chapter 7).

- *Time of the essence* – Chambers may seek to vary this clause in view of the severe implications of missing the deadline; she might also add that the right information must be available on time from Williams to enable deadlines to be met.
- *Non-availability* – Chambers may want to negotiate provisions for absence on holiday or incapacity not exceeding stated periods. (Note that this would be an allowable period away from the job, not paid holiday or sick leave, which would be clear indicators of employment status.)
- *Chambers' own terms of business* – These might be added if she has them, and they might cover some of these other points.
- *Interest* – Provisions on late payment of invoices might be worth including.
- *The right to subcontract* – This might be added if appropriate and not expressly included.

The two-stage contract is problematic where the second stage is conditional on the client being satisfied with the first stage. Williams understandably wants to limit its commitment, but Chambers will want to have as much certainty as possible because she might have to turn down other work to be available for the second stage. She might even be left with a team she has to pay and for which she has no work. One approach might be for her to seek to specify a minimum time involvement or fee under stage 2 to ensure her ongoing availability. Another approach would be for her to require a minimum period either of going ahead with or cancelling stage 2, so that she has adequate time to make alternative arrangements. The problem with the cancellation approach is that it would be difficult for the parties to work out the second-stage contract until they have the report and recommendations from the first stage, so this probably works only if the shape and detail of the project are clear and the only likely question is whether or not to go ahead.

Covering the full value of the stage 1 work should also be thought about. Have the planning and design elements been fully included in the stage 1 fee so that, if Williams went ahead with someone else or in another way, Chambers would have received due reward for her work? If not, Chambers might want to negotiate a top-up fee for the planning and design if she is not retained for the stage 2 work. There is also the question of the stage 2 fee, even if stage 2 does go ahead, since Williams has built in the need for prior approval of any work. Here again, Chambers may want a minimum number of hours or a minimum monthly fee while the engagement continues to ensure that she does not get caught out by needing to be available but not earning in the meantime.

Intellectual property rights in the work produced, and the data behind it, are linked to this and should be specified in such a case. This is explored in more detail in Chapter 14, but it should be considered here how the IP rights arising should best be dealt with.

Corporate Consultancies

Limited companies

The advantages of contracting via a limited company are varied. Many authors and celebrities, for example, enter into contracts for tax-planning reasons through companies which they own and control. On the liability aspect, an engineer designing a project in which an error could have serious repercussions may feel better protected by operating through a limited company (although this might not avoid liability for the engineer's personal negligence).

The contractual position

If you agree with an independent contractor for their services to be provided by their company, the contract will be between you, as the client, and the contractor's limited company. If you left it at that, your redress under the contract would be limited to the assets of the company, without recourse to the individual behind it. Will this arrangement expose you to any material risk? If so, you might want to consider joining the individual as a guarantor of the company's obligations under the agreement, either by their becoming a party to the actual contract or by signing a side letter.

Personal involvement of the individual chosen may be an essential for the client. One approach is then to have the consultant's company ('service company') provide the services of a named individual ('consultant'), consistent with the principle that a contract for personal services is to be performed by the individual in question and is non-assignable. Further comment on this and a sample side letter are set out below.

Personal liability

Even if the contract is made through a service company, the consultant could still have personal liability in negligence (see p. 182 in Chapter 10 and elsewhere in this book). The point to note here is that liability in negligence arises outside the framework of a contract, so contracting through a service company will not necessarily protect the individual providing the services, especially if there is a professional responsibility, such as that of an engineer, which might extend to third parties (such as visitors to a building or passers-by) liable to be affected by breaches of professional standards of care. There are, however, steps that can be taken to seek to deflect personal liability – as seen in the client letter and in paragraph 11 of the terms of business below.

PERSONAL GUARANTEES OF A COMPANY'S SERVICE OBLIGATIONS

Important questions to consider when planning a contract under which an individual's services are to be provided by a company include:

- Should there be a personal commitment from the consultant to stand behind the service company financially and/or to commit personally to carrying out the work in question?
- If so, should this be in the contract itself or in a side letter?
- Either way, is there sufficient 'consideration' from the consultant?

The wording needs to satisfy the requirements of a valid guarantee as set out in Chapter 1, 'Contract Basics' and Chapter 6, 'Dealing with Companies' and should cover all or, as just stated, parts of the service company's obligations. The consultant needs to think quite hard as to whether to commit fully to personal responsibility. This will be harder to resist if the service company is of limited value. But there is no point in having terms excluding personal liability and then giving a personal guarantee! Insurance should also be considered. If the service company is covered, the policy should extend to the consultant personally. There may also be an advantage in having some form of life and/ or critical illness policy on the consultant in favour of the client to protect any material investment in the project.

Terms of Business for Services

Standard terms of business are a worthwhile investment for a service-based company. Indeed, many professional bodies insist that their member firms specify their terms and conditions with formal engagement letters containing the basis of the contract with their clients. This is partly because many, if not most, claims against professional firms arise from disputes about the *cost* of the services and/or what has been done or not done. The key is be clear at the outset both what services are and are not being offered, and how much that will cost. Financial services (see the latest terms and conditions received from your bank), mortgage lenders and credit card providers have similar approaches. They work within highly regulated environments, but their relationship with customers is based on contract law.

A SAMPLE CLIENT LETTER

Leaving aside highly regulated areas, the example below sets out a basic framework for a contract for services. The aim is to deal with the real issues in a fair and concise way. As with selling goods, the terms and conditions are suitable for an ongoing relationship and future orders or services between the same parties. They are therefore best accompanied by a cover letter or order form setting out details of the services in question and the main charging basis. Just as it is critical to describe the goods clearly and correctly in a sale of goods, so it pays to be as specific as to what the services are.

Dear [.........]

Further to our recent [meeting/discussion], this letter and the attached terms and conditions (**terms**) set out the basis on which we have agreed to provide our services to you. Where there is a conflict between this letter and the terms, this letter will prevail.

1. In this agreement our services means [...............]. [*Note the importance of being clear on this definition.*]
2. Our services will be supervised/ carried out by [..........]. [*It is a requirement for many professional firms to state who is responsible for the work, and it is good practice as part of managing client expectations and standards. Contact details are useful here too.*]
3. The cost of our services will be invoiced and paid in accordance with the terms and will be calculated as follows: [*set out some viable formula that can be understood and checked if any questions arise, possibly with some review mechanism*].

Please sign and return the enclosed duplicate of this letter to confirm your agreement [on behalf of XYZ Limited].

Yours sincerely

Partner/ Manager/ Director
For ABC [Limited/LLP etc]

Terms and Conditions

1. **Applicability of terms** – These terms and conditions apply to all services provided by ABC [Limited] (**we**, **us** or **our**) to the client to whom our services are provided (**client**, **you** or **your**).

2. **Reliance on information** – We rely on you to inform us of all facts or circumstances, or any change in them, which may be relevant to the way, time or place in which we carry out our services, and to check with reasonable care any confirmation or other non-technical details we forward to you relating to our services.

3. **Provision of services** – Subject to paragraph 2 above, we will carry out our services with reasonable skill and care in light of the circumstances at the time.

4. **Forms of communication** – Although you accept that electronic communication is not wholly secure, you consent to our communicating with you by any appropriate means, including e-mail unless you instruct us otherwise in writing. Our e-mails, incoming and outgoing, may be monitored for professional or management purposes.

5. **Expenses** – We may charge you expenses, additional to our fees, where these are necessarily incurred in performing our services. [*The client would probably want to negotiate the ability to give prior authorization of both the circumstances and the level of expense, for example for class of travel/hotel.*]

6. **Payment** – You will pay our fees and expenses (plus VAT at the appropriate rate at the time of invoice) by credit to our bank account within 30 days of our invoice. Where you pay by cheque, sufficient time should be allowed for the transfer of funds into our account by that time. Payment must be made gross and any charges from your bank are to your account. We may charge you interest, calculated on a daily basis, at three percentage points above [...] Bank base rate (or its then equivalent) for any amounts unpaid after the due 30 days.

7. **Regulatory provisions** – [*For example, Proceeds of Crime Act 2002 provisions – each firm will have a slightly different approach but will want to make the provision of services conditional on compliance with the statutory procedures, notably personal or corporate identification. The term may also build in contractual consent for the obligation to comply with the law and a disclaimer as to any loss so caused.*]

8. **Documents** – We may retain any of your files, papers or other property until we have been paid in full, but have no obligation to retain any documents or other property on your behalf after our services have been completed. [*Client may want to request that prior notice is given before any files are destroyed or removed.*]

9. **Intellectual property** – The copyright and other intellectual property rights in all and any materials or data in any written or electronic or other form produced or dealt with under our engagement for services will belong to the party producing the relevant materials or data, subject to our respective obligations as to confidentiality set out below. [*This retains the client's IPR in the materials given to the consultant and the consultant's rights in material produced for the client, which may be more a matter for negotiation depending on the circumstances and nature of the assignment. For example, this may leave the consultant in possession of highly confidential information. – See also Chapters 5 and 14.*]

10. **Confidentiality** – The detail of your instructions to us, all unpublished materials and data you give us and our services to you will be treated as confidential by us and by you, but the fact that we provide services to you as a client will not be deemed confidential unless otherwise agreed in writing. [*This issue is always worth thinking about, and some adjustment in the letter may be necessary.*]

11. **Responsibility** – Your agreement is with ABC [Limited] only and any of our services provided to you by an individual are carried out on our behalf. Such services are not carried out by that person individually and they accept no responsibility or liability to you in their personal capacity. [*Note: see earlier comments as to personal responsibility*].

12. **Liability** – We and any individual providing our services will not be liable to you for any loss caused by or resulting from your breach of these terms or any change in circumstances beyond our control or any indirect or consequential loss or damage caused by or attributable to us, except that we will be liable for any personal injury or death caused by the negligence of us or our employees or resulting from fraud or fraudulent misrepresentation or other liability which may not be excluded by law. [*This may need to be negotiated and may lead to a removal of the blanket exclusion in return for a cap on liability – see Chapter 7 regarding exclusion and limitation clauses generally*].

13. **Termination** – Without limiting any of our other rights, we may serve written notice on you terminating the engagement for our services with immediate effect if you become insolvent. **Insolvent** in these terms includes entering into bankruptcy, liquidation, the appointment of an administrator or administrative receiver or any general composition or voluntary arrangement with creditors.

14. **Entire agreement** – This agreement, comprising our letter and these terms, constitutes the entire agreement between us and you, and supersedes all other agreements or arrangements between us relating to our future services. No

variations of this agreement are effective unless made in writing signed by us and you or our respective authorized agents.

15. **Right of third parties** – No term of this agreement may be enforced by any person who is not a party to it, with the exception of an individual providing all or part of our services, who is intended to benefit from the agreement in paragraphs 11 and 12.

16. **Law and jurisdiction** – This agreement is governed by the laws of England and Wales and the parties submit to the jurisdiction of the English courts.

Other Issues in Contracts for Services

ASSIGNMENT AND SUBCONTRACTING

Imagine a contract between a manager and a singer or even a rock band. This is personal to the parties by its nature, since the choice of individual is key. Another example is a publishing agreement where it is that writer who is required and no one else. Where a contract is a personal contract, it may be personal to both parties. A writer will sign with a specific publisher or the singer with a particular manager or recording label because that is where they have the relationships and the confidence. So provisions regarding the assignment of contracts for service need close attention as they may be inappropriate on either or both sides. This issue, together with subcontracting and novation, is dealt with in more detail in Chapter 18.

TERM AND TERMINATION

Service quality is an issue that goes to the root of the term of an agreement for services. The need for the services may not be indefinite, and the client may not want to be tied to a provider who does not live up to expected standards. But even consultants like a degree of certainty. Those who are self-employed may have little steady income, having to plan to utilize their time to best effect, as in the Williams/Chambers example above. Even if Chambers does not have to invest much in the project apart from her time, she will have her own car, mobile phone, laptop and working facilities, all of which need to be paid for. Consider, further, a distribution network where the distributor will have to retain premises, equipment and staff to handle the business and will want a minimum contract period to pay for the investment in set-up time and cost.

Cost and quality variables may have a major influence on the length of an agreement. How certain will these be going forward? The less certainty there is on quality (for example, a new and untested working relationship), the shorter contract the period the client will want to seek, the tighter the controls and/or the more extensive the termination provisions. All these issues interrelate. Termination and advance planning for it is considered in other chapters and in more detail for services in Chapter 13 on outsourcing, where it is especially relevant.

RESTRICTIONS AFTER TERMINATION

Protecting the team

If there are several people in a consultancy team they may have very close contact with the client that engages them. Take the case of a specialist IT team sent in by an external consultancy to perform a three-year project which is a major part of a client's development plan. If the project finishes before the end of the three years, the parties may move on to something else. On the other hand, it may be that the relationship between the team and the client has developed to such an extent that the client would wish to take on the team – or members of the team – as direct consultants or even as employees, bypassing the original consultancy. Does the contract cover this possibility? The consultancy may have invested heavily in the recruitment, training and development of the team members.

The choices

A restrictive covenant is one possibility, but an introductory commission may be more appropriate and easier to enforce, especially where it is more common for employees to move to a client and vice versa. The commission would aim to compensate the old employer for its costs of training and development of the employees over a period and cover the potential costs of recruiting a replacement. As seen in Chapter 19, 'Damages' (p. 355), the commission would need to be genuine (perhaps reflecting employment agency terms) or, if it operated as liquidated damages for breach, an accurate pre-estimate of loss, since a penalty clause as such would be unenforceable.

Other scenarios

There are two variations on this scenario. First, the IT team may decide to become autonomous and pitch for the new contract itself, probably undercutting the consultancy in the process. Here the consultancy should be considering suitable non-competition provisions, which would need to be included in the team members' contracts before the venture starts. Second, the converse may apply and the consultancy may want to hire some of the client's staff. In practice, this is less common because it is likely to be the end of the relationship between consultant and company! But if there is to be a restriction protecting staff, it would be sensible to make it mutual.

Restrictions must be specific and limited in scope, extent and time, in accordance with the principles of restrictive covenants. For this reason, and also because restraining someone from moving jobs to further their career is emotive and tends to be self-defeating, a commission arrangement may be a better way of deterring the casual shift of allegiance.

Confidential information may shift the balance. A commission payment may not suffice if the employees in question possess material information which is confidential to, and might be used against, their (old) employer. A specific clause can protect this information, but unlawful disclosure is very hard to prove in court. For that reason, courts are often more prepared to grant injunctions where there is a restrictive covenant that is reasonable in its terms and the old employer is able to show a real risk of prejudice to its business if confidential information is almost inevitably liable to seep from the ex-employee into the knowledge of new employer who is competitor.

Summary and Checklist

Special care, particularly in relation to tax, is required if your freelance/consultant:

- is also a director of your company
- is or has been an employee of your company
- is obliged to do regular or ongoing work for you and you to provide work for them
- is paid on a regular ongoing basis
- does not come ready equipped with all the necessary skills and equipment for the work
- cannot be said to be working on their own account
- does not have some reasonable control over how and where the work is done
- is subject to company disciplinary or similar processes
- enjoys company benefits
- is paid overtime, sick pay or the like
- does not work for anyone else.

A clear letter or formal agreement setting out the terms on which services will be provided and payment made is advisable – see the examples provided, including possible terms and conditions. Check that:

- the task or project to be carried out is defined
- any milestones or targets are clearly expressed
- the fee structure is explicit.

Freelancers or consultants may operate through their own companies. Points to consider include:

- being clear on the right of redress – and the ability or otherwise to claim against the individual
- personal involvement of the known consultant
- personal liability aspects for the consultant and how to cover these
- possible guarantee requirements.

Other aspects to consider include:

- assignment and subcontracting
- term of the agreement and how it can be terminated
- how intellectual property rights created in the course of the agreement are to be dealt with
- possible restrictions after termination
- confidentiality of information.

PART IV

TECHNICAL CONTRACTS

13 *Outsourcing Agreements*

Introduction – some key features of outsourcing agreements – term and termination of the outsourcing agreement – selecting a service provider – the implementation process – service quality standards – intellectual property (IP) and information technology (IT) aspects of outsourcing – TUPE and other employment law aspects of outsourcing – some other outsourcing points to consider – summary and checklist

Introduction

Outsourcing is the contracting-out to third parties of a defined part or specified functions of a business. This may arise for various reasons, but normally because the service provider is a specialist in the functions to be outsourced and is able to manage the outsourced function more effectively than the client, both in terms of performance and cost. There may be a transfer of some assets, but outsourcing is essentially a contract for services. Some outsourced activities are now very specific, including sophisticated procedures with their own rules, and specialist professional help is highly advisable. This chapter sets out a general approach and some of the detail involved. Legal agreements may use different names for the parties, but the terms 'client' and 'provider' are used here for ease of reference.

Some Key Features of Outsourcing Agreements

THE FRAMEWORK

Although outsourcing is essentially an arrangement for services (see Chapter 12), there is normally a strong technology function involved (see Chapter 15), so that both of these areas overlap with the contents of this chapter to some degree. Outsourcing contracts are likely, however, to have the following main differences, discussed in greater detail in the following sections:

- There is often more at stake and more detail.
- The contract period is likely to be much longer.
- Set-up costs for implementation are likely to be higher, needing greater certainty as to the levels of work and fees involved to justify those costs.
- Quality control provisions are likely to be more stringent.
- Termination is more complex (and inevitable) and needs to be planned for from the outset.

- Some staff may transfer, which gives rise to some major employment law issues.

FLEXIBILITY

Changes in client requirements, circumstances and technology will mean that the contract has to be both specific enough to deal with what is known about at the outset and flexible enough to cope as changes occur. This is a factor to be taken into account in the provider selection and evaluation process, as well as in the contract terms.

RISK

Risk is a major factor in outsourcing. Costs, risks and benefits all interrelate with one another and need careful planning, possibly with a full risk analysis, risk rating and a risk register. Even then, the unthinkable may happen, as seen when overdependence on outsourced facilities has come home to roost during times of global economic crisis. Now, more than ever, it is worth asking: 'What would happen if it all went wrong?'

JUMPING THE GUN

Many of the issues that apply to technology contracts, covered in Chapter 15, also arise with regard to outsourcing contracts. The recommendations here and in that chapter, aimed at avoiding the pitfalls of a major handover without a signed agreement, apply to both situations. Jumping the gun will make reaching a balanced contract far more difficult, and in outsourcing both parties might have much to lose in different areas if there is no settled agreement.

Term and Termination of the Outsourcing Agreement

TERM

Assuming all goes well, the term – the planned length of the agreement – will need to be long enough for both parties to have obtained the essential benefits of the arrangement and to have amortized the potentially significant costs of the transfer of operations. The length of notice to terminate, on a no-fault basis, will need to be long enough to plan an orderly handover, either back to the client or to the new provider, but not so long as to cause all involved to become frustrated with the position and impending change.

TERMINATION AND ITS EFFECTS

Sooner or later, the arrangement will terminate. This means that the parties need to be planning the end of the outsourced process at the same time as planning the beginning. This is similar to the practice in most joint ventures and other commercial arrangements, such as agency or distribution, where the potential implications of termination are best planned at the outset. This is especially true where employees are involved and transferred by operation of law, whether the parties like it or not. Following unprecedented changes in the economic climate since the banking meltdown in 2008, assumptions as to future minimum service levels or costs will need to be challenged to avoid both client and provider potentially signing up to any agreement that could become a financial millstone if assumptions prove unfounded and things change greatly.

Termination points to consider include:

- smooth running of the services until actual termination – and any longer run-off period
- a cooperative handover and repatriation of essential assets
- suitable information and assistance for the client – or new provider – to pick up the service
- the treatment of software and technology
- the re-transfer of employees.

TERMINATION FOR BREACH

The normal termination issues will arise, but there may be much more at stake here, especially if breach is alleged as a possible alternative to early termination compensation (see below). With service levels, suitable mechanisms can be built in to give every chance of compensation or remedy. In other cases, the contract will probably stipulate that the breach needs to be material/fundamental or persistent, since persistent failure to get it right could undermine the relationship as much as major failure. The termination clause will include the normal obligation to give notice requiring any remedial breach to be remedied and may specify exactly what a persistent breach would be.

EARLY TERMINATION

There may be external changes or performance issues that cause problems, but fall short of the level triggering default. The client will not want to be stuck and unable to change if the outsourced processes threaten to have serious affects on its business. But the provider may not have yet made any profit from the arrangement, and might even not have recouped the costs of the migration and implementation itself. In the absence of any other provision, a client wanting to terminate early might be faced with a bill for the provider's fees for the rest of the contract period. To avoid this, but to ensure that the provider is guaranteed some profit from the arrangement, there may be a sliding scale of early termination compensation agreed at the outset, starting at quite high levels in the early years and decreasing to nil by the end of the planned contract term. This must be set out clearly and, as described elsewhere, be a genuine pre-estimate of the potential loss and not a penalty.

PARTIAL TERMINATION

If there are many strands to the outsourced service, it is possible that some may work better than others, so it's worth including partial termination provisions. This might also take the sting out of potential contention as to service levels for termination purposes and the effects of termination on both parties, as some parts of the service may be more peripheral and easier for each party to replace. Partial termination does require very careful drafting throughout the agreement to achieve its intended effect.

TRANSITIONING

Transition from one provider to another can be fraught with problems, especially if the client and provider have fallen out. The issue needs to be addressed in the agreement, but a realistic solution may be to provide some form of incentive payment to the outgoing provider to encourage full cooperation. Without this, the cost to the client might be much higher.

Selecting a Service Provider

DUE DILIGENCE

As with any other major project, selecting the right contract partner is critically important. Due diligence has already been mentioned in earlier chapters, and it pays for both parties to investigate thoroughly who they are dealing with and to be prepared to ask awkward questions if the need arises.

COMPETITIVE PROCUREMENT

This may be a way forward in bigger projects, with several parties submitting bids on the basis of a standard invitation to tender (ITT). If used, an ITT should contain all the information required to make an effective competitive bid. Where this involves a public body, the public procurement rules are likely to apply, as would potential future disclosure of the details under the Freedom of Information Act. These rules are a specialist area, but they can be a useful point of reference for any major outsourcing arrangement. In any event, competitive tendering will involve several very detailed stages, all of which are likely to require adequate time. ITTs may be accompanied by the client's desired form of contract, or at least key contract requirements, requiring headline comments on the draft to be submitted along with the response to the ITT.

INDIVIDUAL NEGOTIATION

Companies which have already identified a shortlist of potential providers are likely to prefer individual negotiations, possibly honing the choice down so as to seek to progress with a very few interested parties. The key issue here is likely to be getting all relevant factors on the table at the outset and keeping an open mind on the options before making the choice. If this is not done, the risk is that negotiations appear to go swimmingly until a specific point or relevant detail is encountered, and things then go rapidly downhill from there. Individual negotiation needs realism and a willingness on the part of those involved to explore areas of potential disagreement, as well as those of agreement. The process can be assisted by a 'request for proposals/information' (RFP or RFI), a kind of mini-ITT, encouraged to flush out the provider's attitude to a number of key issues such as those highlighted in this chapter.

TIMETABLE/IMPLEMENTATION PLAN

All this complexity will be reflected in the timetable, which should be drawn up and agreed in good time, be realistic and, if at all possible, be adhered to. Implementation issues should be checked so that each stage of the process can be seen to be achievable in the way and in the timescale anticipated.

The Implementation Process

CONFIDENTIALITY

The parties are likely to be providing each other with information which could be commercially sensitive. It is advisable therefore to have a confidentially agreement or non-disclosure agreement (NDA) signed at an early stage. As it is likely that the information flow will be both ways, this is best made mutual from the start.

PLANNING

Transferring a vital part or process of a business will need to be planned in considerable detail, and the managers who will be responsible for implementation and integration (not just the project team) should be involved from an early stage in providing detailed actions and requirements. These details can in turn be fed back into the ongoing negotiations. It is, for example, easy to forget that any financial formulae used may have to be operated and audited by accountants, so it's worth having the accountants check the formulae first. (This may sound obvious but it's just the kind of precaution so often overlooked.) In this way, any procedural issues can be highlighted and the action prepared in good time, so that the contract process runs alongside, and is fully compatible with, the implementation planning. Whilst this means that time and attention will need to be given to matters of detail before the deal itself becomes certain, it does ensure that practical issues are addressed and catered for from the outset, and reduces the risk of 'jumping the gun' before the contract is signed.

MILESTONES

One way of measuring progress in implementation is through 'milestones'. As no client wants to wait to find out at the end of the period that the service provider has completely failed to do what was agreed, 'milestones' may be useful to mark in advance predetermined stages of progress in a project. These help ensure that the project stays on time and on track. Once milestones are successfully passed, they might then trigger interim payments.

MIGRATION AND INTEGRATION

Migration and integration are especially relevant to IT systems, but could apply to any aspect of the processes that are due to transfer (migrate) from client to provider. In simple terms, the parties will need to know that the provider's system will be able to take on, and work with, the data and processes from the client's system – and, if not, what changes must be made. The reverse process must be possible if and when the agreement terminates. The cost of changes may be a very significant factor in any decision as to whether, how and with whom to go ahead.

HANDOVER

Another important stage is handover, which, again, is worth thinking about from the start. Handover is, after all, the first point where the practicality of the new arrangement is likely to be fully tested. Accordingly, a specific schedule may be planned and set out in the agreement, setting what is to be done, when and by whom.

Assets to be transferred will need to be free from third-party claims (such as loan, lease or hire purchase) and/or third-party contracts, such as maintenance and servicing agreements, which may need to be terminated or transferred, perhaps with appropriate third-party consents.

Service Quality Standards

Services are intrinsically more difficult to evaluate and measure than goods but, as the provider is entrusted with key parts of the client's business process, the right quality of service is essential. The client will want standards by which to judge performance and, if necessary, will want to enforce sanctions if those standards are not met. Ultimately, the client will want the right to terminate the contract if the standards dip below certain minimum levels. The provider, for its part, will only want to sign up to commitments which are reasonable for the situation. One approach, using concepts from personal performance reviews, might be to seek to agree standards which are:

>   **S**pecific – identifying specific services and specific levels to be achieved;
>   **M**easurable – as to whether the required level has been achieved or not;
>   **A**chievable – reasonably capable of being achieved;
>   **R**ealistic – for the service provided and the real needs of the client's business;
>   **T**ime-bounded – geared to specific dates or periods for achievement.

As mentioned above, achievability is critical to ensuring that there is neither unreasonable expectation from the client nor unfair penalty on the provider. One refinement would be to distinguish between three levels:

a) base – the minimum level required to avoid severe sanctions,
b) target – being the standard expected to be achieved, and
c) 'aspirational' – the sort of level that might attract an incentive payment.

These principles could then flow through into the SLA and KPIs discussed below.

The *service-level agreement (SLA)* is a basis for establishing and recording the service standards, which will vary greatly according to industry and process, striking a sensible balance between insufficient precision and overprescription. Draconian provisions designed to penalize a service provider at every stage are unlikely to be justified and even less likely to provide a good working relationship. The worst-case scenario may be if they are consistently ignored by both parties and then suddenly invoked when a dispute arises.

KPIs (key performance indicators) are detailed standards set out and attached as a schedule or appendix to the contract. Such KPIs tend to be detailed and industry-specific, geared to maintaining standards and identifying where improvements should be made. Examples in a distribution services agreement would be the speed and accuracy of tasks such as receipt, recording and storage of goods coming in, accuracy or record-keeping of stocks held, absence of stock losses and speed/accuracy of picking and dispatch of goods ordered.

Service credits may apply if the provider falls below target levels. These may be financial disincentives for the provider, to encourage it to hit target, rather than a mechanism for fully compensating the client. They can be much less emotive and easier to implement than liquidated damages, but should not be drafted so as to preclude other remedies in cases of material loss to the client.

A dispute escalation procedure may apply to any part of the contract but is most likely to be relevant to quality and performance issues, including suggestions of the client's own contribution to problems. The idea is that there should be an opportunity for performance review (such as benchmarking above), a proper opportunity for the parties to remedy any problems and then a process for escalating any remaining areas of dispute to agreed higher levels in the respective companies. The final step may be a partial withdrawal by the client of part of the appointment and the taking back of this part in-house, leaving the remainder in place.

Audit rights may help to ensure that the client has some means of verification of price changes and internal compliance by the provider with the terms of the agreement.

Intellectual Property (IP) and Information Technology (IT) Aspects of Outsourcing

Some specific points in relation to outsourcing may be emphasized in addition to the general comments in the following chapters and elsewhere in this book.

- *IP and IT rights* which are relevant to the outsourcing will need to be identified and warranted by the client as part of due diligence in the planning process and properly dealt with in the outsourcing contract. It will need to be established whether there are trademarks, patents, copyrights and/or database rights involved and, if they are, which of these may be subject to licence from third parties rights and, where applicable, under what contracts those rights arise.
- *Know-how* needs to be considered specifically. It may be a vital part of the mix in outsourcing and similar arrangements (think, for example, of the importance of process in most franchising arrangements). The parties need to consider who really has the know-how and the extent to which it needs to be recorded in writing or in some systematized way to ensure that it is properly passed on and protected.
- *Assignments or licences* of those rights will be necessary.
- *Third-party rights* to be transferred to the provider may require the consent of those third parties, and there will be the issue of re-transfer (to the client or new provider) when the outsourcing agreement ends.

- *Indemnities* may be required to protect each party against breach of third-party rights in the use of any of the IP or IT or in the outsourcing itself, with associated claims-handling provisions.
- *IP created during the outsourcing* will need careful attention. Some of this may logically accrue to the client as being unique or specific to its business; other IP will be more properly related to the provider as a development of the provider's technical expertise, and in that case the client will need to ensure that it is able to license the new technology or know-how during the term of the agreement and afterwards.
- *Upgrades and capacity issues* should be factored in as a part of the continuous improvement programme.
- *Back-up facilities and storage* also require pre-planning.
- *Hardware and software rights* will need to be clearly distinguished, especially where ownership may change later.
- *Support functions* of certain kinds may continue to be available on an arm's-length basis.
- *Source code* issues may be relevant.
- *International compliance* may require special levels of investment or support.
- *Data migration* may be sensitive, especially any transfer of data outside the EU.
- *Assignment and change of control clauses* will need to be considered in all associated contracts, as will entire agreement clauses, so that these do not exclude other parts of the overall deal.
- *Offshore outsourcing contracts* take all these issues to another management and risk level!

TUPE and Other Employment Law Implications of Outsourcing

It would be easy to overlook the impact of employment-related laws when considering a small outsourcing arrangement, but it is dangerous to do so. As with other aspects of outsourcing, it is important to consider the end as well as the beginning. Two main areas stand out:

- *Employee tax* – The importance of dealing correctly with the tax status of employees was touched on in Chapter 12 regarding contracts for services. With outsourcing, the need to check applies both to any staff of the new provider who might work so closely with the client as to be seen to be its employees and to those individuals previously engaged by the client who are now doing more or less the same job on their own account as part of the new provider team. In both cases, the client needs to be sure that there is genuine self-employed status, ideally recognized by both employment law and HMRC. Otherwise there is a risk that responsibilities under employment, tax and other laws will simply remain with the old employer, now the client.
- *TUPE* – More often, the provider will be an existing independent business specializing in the services in question, to which some of the clients' staff might transfer. Such arrangements are likely to fall within the ambit of the Transfer of Business (Protection of Employment) Regulations, known as TUPE or the Transfer Regulations and need special attention to ensure that the expectations of the parties are not derailed by the effects of complex employment protection laws. The principle of TUPE, derived from

the 1977 Acquired Rights Directive and formally updated in 2006, is to protect the rights of employees, enabling them to retain their jobs and job entitlements (their 'acquired rights') if and when the whole or part of the business for which they work is transferred to new owners. Despite their name, there does not need to be any formal 'transfer' of the ownership of the business for the Transfer Regulations to apply.

TUPE – AN OVERVIEW FOR OUTSOURCING PROJECTS

Suspend disbelief

Rather like health and safety and competition law, it is sometimes necessary to suspend disbelief when dealing with TUPE. The theory sounds fine, but the detail and the practice can seem like something from a Kafka novel.

Incoming and outgoing

It is also worth remembering at the outset that what comes around goes around – and so it is with TUPE. The principles applying when the outsourcing starts will (unless the law changes in a surprising way) also apply when the outsourcing ends. This tends to mean that the arguments as to who bears the liability on entry will be reversed when planning the exit.

The principles

Where TUPE applies, the contract of employment between the 'old owner' and the 'transferring' employee is treated as if it had been made between the employee and the new owner of the business or the new provider of the services in question. As a result, the new owner has all the obligations of the old owner/employer under the employment contract, except for criminal liabilities and certain rights attaching to occupational pension schemes.

Informing and consulting employees

This is another key feature of TUPE and its associated information and consultation regulations. Proper information must be given, and consultation may have to take place with the employees affected by the transfer (a wide-ranging definition) and/or their representatives. The combination of detailed regulations and the latest interpretation of how these are properly fulfilled mean that early specialist advice is essential for both parties on this aspect.

Redundancies

Redundancies can still arise when projects are outsourced and, in addition to having regard for the TUPE obligations, employers need to remember that if there is a potential redundancy situation, the normal redundancy consultation and selection rules will apply, together with the consultation and notification rules if 20 or more employees are to be made redundant within a 90-day period. Because of the wide-ranging impact of TUPE, it is always likely that any redundancies implemented around the same time as an outsourcing will be deemed connected to the TUPE transfer and may therefore be deemed to be automatically unfair, so the careful planning that TUPE transfers require should extend to any further material changes that may be planned by the new owner in the near future.

Pooling

It is not always clear which employees will actually transfer, and some may become redundant if their role effectively disappears before or after (but not as a result of) the transfer. The parties must therefore be prepared to go through correct pooling processes for those potentially affected by the change. This requires careful planning of the legal issues and regulations, and the parties must also be prepared for the disruption and the potential effect on morale which the process will cause.

TUPE – A SUMMARY OF THE MAIN IMPLICATIONS

- TUPE applies where the whole or part of a business passes from one owner (the 'old owner') to another (the 'new owner'), even if there is no formal contract between the old owner and the new owner.
- The effect of TUPE is that employees who worked mostly in or for that part of the business that passes over to the new owner are taken over by the new owner on the same terms and conditions of their employment with the old owner.
- Dismissal of the employees (by redundancy or otherwise) by the old owner to facilitate the transfer will, in most cases, be automatically unfair dismissal. This means that any 'slimming down' of the workforce preparatory to transfer creates a risk of unfair dismissal.
- Dismissal of the employees by the new owner for reasons connected with the transfer will be automatically unfair unless the new owner can show a specific economic, technical or organizational (ETO) justification requiring a change in the workforce generally.
- The employees will transfer automatically unless (as they are entitled to) they refuse to do so, but in that case (as their jobs have gone and they have declined to follow them) they are treated as resigning without any claims against the old owner or the new owner unless they have grounds for claiming constructive dismissal.
- Before the transfer, the old owner must provide information to any members of its workforce who may be affected by the transfer through recognized unions or through employee representatives elected for the purpose. The new owner may need to provide information to its existing workforce in advance of the transfer.
- Where either the old owner or new owner envisages taking 'measures' (for example, redundancies or changes to terms and conditions or working practices), it will be necessary for them to consult their respective workforces with a view to seeking their agreement to those intended measures.
- At least 14 days before the transfer, the old owner must provide the new owner with certain information about the transferring employees.
- The usual qualifying period (currently one year starting from the date that the employee was first employed by the transferring business) is still required for any

employee to claim unfair dismissal (subject to further case law or statutory change on the subject). Any changes in terms and conditions before or after, but connected with, the transfer which are detrimental to the employee are of themselves void and may give grounds for constructive unfair dismissal.

- TUPE 2006 increases the chances of an outsourcing arrangement being regarded as falling within the Transfer Regulations regime.
- A TUPE transfer is not something to be left to the last minute and rushed through!

WILL TUPE APPLY? A QUICK TEST

As a starter, it may be useful to consider the questions below. If the answer to each is *likely* to be 'yes', then it is best to assume that TUPE is likely to apply. If you decide not to consider the issues, you should be prepared to face the consequences in terms of staff relationships, possible disputes and tribunal claims and, of course, cost. Likewise, if your contract does not allocate the liabilities by way of indemnity, the TUPE rules will do so, which will mean that most (although not all) of the risk will fall on the new owner, be they the provider in the first instance or the client on taking the function back in-house or the second-generation provider if the function is outsourced again.

- Do the activities in question involve one or more individuals or groups of individuals who work together in a similar area (such as – but not limited to – catering, cleaning, design, marketing, IT, finance, production or sales)?
- Are those people assigned to the relevant activity, in the sense that they spend all, or a large part of, their time on the function in question?
- Are those people actually employees?
- Will the same activities effectively be carried on by the new owner?

WILL TUPE APPLY? THE FORMAL TUPE TESTS

General test

Is there is a business, an identifiable part of a business or an operation within a business, which ceases (or reduces) in one ownership and reappears elsewhere? This has been clarified over the years and is now codified in TUPE 2006, such that there are two types of transaction that can bring TUPE into play. The first of these is a clear transfer and the second an effective move of resources, such as outsourcing involves. Some circumstances may be clearly within one and some may be a mix of the two, but 'satisfying' either test means that TUPE will probably apply.

The 'business transfer' test

Is there a transfer of an 'economic entity' which 'retains its identity' following the transfer? An economic entity need not, and probably will not, be a separate business or division, but will involve some form of organized grouping of resources. If this grouping becomes dispersed on the transfer, it may be argued that the business transfer test is not satisfied, but it is normally best to err on the side of caution. It is not, however, necessary for the activity to be central to the economic objectives of the entity concerned, which means that the activity can be peripheral to the main business as long as the resources are sufficiently grouped to retain an identity as some form of economic entity.

The 'service provision change' test

Is there a transfer of service functions? TUPE 2006 makes it clear that the Transfer Regulations catch transfers of service functions, whether initial outsourcing, second-generation outsourcing (where the contract passes from one provider or service provider to another) or an exit or 'insourcing' (where it passes back in-house). There are subconditions for this to apply, which are essentially those set out earlier, but it is worth noting that TUPE will not apply where the activities in question consist wholly or mainly of the supply of goods for the client's use. An example would be where a client transfers an IT contract from one provider to another. In this situation the employees involved in supplying the system may not transfer (unless this is treated as services or the business transfer test applies), but those responsible for providing the client with support services under the contract, where there is a continuing role, may transfer under the service provision change test.

No escape

It is essential to plan for TUPE at the outset of any business transfer or service agreement. You cannot contract out of TUPE, so the key decisions are to decide whether TUPE might apply and, if so, how to get the process right and who should bear the costs and risks involved. And the interests of the parties may not be the same, as the old employer may well want TUPE to apply to avoid being responsible for any redundancy costs of the employees affected. Because the answer can rarely be certain, the only safe test is that, some years later, no claims have been made.

The rough and the smooth

Because TUPE constrains any reorganization (or the costs and risks of a reorganization), the benefits of the change may be more expensive or more delayed than the provider would have hoped. Care also needs to be taken with those staff who actually do transfer on the transfer date. For example, the provider may inherit some of the client's staff (or those of a previous provider) who may not be wanted, perhaps in circumstances where the old provider is being replaced because of poor performance. It is not unknown for some poorly performing employees to be 'dumped' into a TUPE transfer from other parts of the business of the transferor. Conversely, the provider will want to be sure of those key staff regarded as essential to the running of the business, and must beware those staff being redeployed by the client pre-transfer or deciding not to transfer – as no employee can be forced to transfer under TUPE. The due diligence plus the statutory information exchange and consultation process might be useful in clarifying some of these issues.

Takeovers and mergers carried out by sale or transfer of shares are not in themselves TUPE transfers, because the employees remain employed by the same entity on the same terms when the takeover occurs, even if ownership of the entity changes. Subsequent changes are dealt with by normal employment laws. There may, however, be a TUPE transfer prior to, or following, a takeover or merger where all or part of the activity acquired is then transferred to another part of the acquiring group.

TUPE – THE COST IMPLICATIONS

The cost implications need to be considered both on a business sale or transfer and, as mentioned earlier, on the termination of agency/distribution contracts and agreements for services. The following are the main cost headings – a potentially fearsome list:
Some costs that will arise in any event:

- notice periods payable in any event for any employees dismissed
- redundancy payments if there are true redundancies
- future remuneration on the employees' terms of employment prior to the transfer
- any liability of the old owner/client/previous provider for arrears of pay (including bonus or benefits), holiday pay claims, equal pay claims, discrimination, unlawful wages deduction and any other past liabilities in relation to periods before as well as after the transfer date.

Some costs that may arise if there are hidden liabilities or correct procedures are not followed:

- unfair dismissal or constructive dismissal compensation when dismissal is associated with the transfer (for example, if the new owner breaks the contract or changes it to the employee's detriment without their agreement)
- possible reinstatement/re-engagement orders and compensation for non-compliance
- statutory compensation for each employee affected where the relevant information and consultation requirements have not been properly complied with
- possible pension rights complications, especially related to issues such as early retirement benefits
- possible compensation order if the old owner fails to comply with the obligation to provide required employee information (usually at least £500 per affected employee).

These areas should be allocated and covered by appropriate indemnities in respect of liability for periods prior to and after the transfer date (and in relation to original outsourcing and re-transfer on termination).

ASSESSING THE RISK AND COST IMPLICATIONS

Assumptions

As suggested, if there is any doubt, the parties should assume that TUPE applies, and plan for the consequences. There will be direct and foreseeable costs of employing the relevant people, together with additional risk element costs. Claims can still arise a year or more later if things go wrong and there is an employment breach at some stage which is deemed to be connected with the transfer. Specialist employment law advice is absolutely essential here, as the subject is highly complex and continually changing. That advice should also be taken as early as possible in the transaction – ideally, right from the start – because TUPE considerations can affect the planning of a deal as much as tax or other key financial terms.

Checklist for the provider (or client/new provider on a re-transfer)

Having looked at the prospects of the transfer being subject to TUPE, the new provider should consider, among other things:

- Which people are employed by the old owner and 'assigned' to the relevant part of its business?
- How long have they been continuously employed? (Because unfair dismissal or redundancy payment calculations will take this into account.)
- What are their terms and conditions of employment? (Because the new provider will need to honour existing contractual terms.)
- Are all the transferring employees likely to be required after completion of the transfer? If not, there will be costs, and any termination costs may include unfair dismissal compensation as well as the cost of redundancy payments.
- Do the employees transferring include key people? If so, the provider or new owner will want to ensure that they do transfer, but the old owner may try to encourage them to remain with the old business in a different role. If so, how can they be secured, and what would be the value of the deal if they left or did/did not transfer?
- Does the new employer pay at least the same rates of pay, benefits and bonus as the old owner? If not, the new employer could be faced with a lengthy period of maintaining the old rates and a possible dispute with existing staff. if they realize that the transferring employees are on better terms.
- Will there be any problems for the new owner in having employees with two (or more) different sets of employment terms after completion of the deal?

TUPE PLANNING – WARRANTIES AND INDEMNITIES

Due diligence

The client must give the provider full details of employees who might be affected by the outsourcing, plus their terms of employment. The provider will need to consider these closely, since it will inherit the same terms for those who do transfer under TUPE. For this reason also, the provider will require a warranty of the accuracy of the information given and of the absence of employment claims or issues as at the transfer date.

Allocating the TUPE risk

Where TUPE might apply, the parties need to consider and negotiate who bears the risk and to what extent. Very clear contract provisions and indemnities will be needed to cover these points. The TUPE regulations mean that, with the very limited exceptions mentioned, the transferee (provider or client/new provider on a re-transfer) will acquire any liability for past breaches by the transferor (client or old provider on a re-transfer) and the same employment terms, however different those terms may be from the transferee's terms for its existing staff. The transferee will need to inform and consult with its own existing employees to the extent that they are affected by measures taken in connection with the transfer, but the transferee does not have to consult with the transferor's staff before the transfer. This may all have to be handled against the backdrop of highly confidential negotiations regarding the outsourcing deal itself, leading to many areas of possible tension and scope for misunderstanding.

Preparing the ground

There is always the risk of losing some good employees in this process, as some may decide to opt out of the transfer, even without compensation, or may see a better future with the old owner in some other part of the original business. Conversely, the provider, some time before the transfer and in anticipation of losing the outsourcing contract at renewal stage, may have quietly transferred some less effective employees into the business. These, and the problems associated with them, would then be inherited by the new owner. The parties need to be alive to all these issues. If the ITT does not include indemnities, the would-be provider needs to decide whether this is a key point or whether to take the chance and build in some margin for cost and delay in reorganizing the workforce. Ideally, however, the client will have thought about the issue when first outsourcing and will have included suitable TUPE provisions in the original contract.

The position on termination needs to be considered at the same time, as the same principles will apply when the staff involved with the project transfer back to the client or on to a replacement provider. If the client gives the provider an indemnity at the outset, the client will probably expect the benefit of an indemnity from the provider when the outsourcing contract terminates, and to have the benefit of that indemnity available for the replacement provider. There may also be provisions against changes of staff, especially in the last few months of the contract, unless it is with the consent of the client, and the client may also require, both for itself and any new provider, an express indemnity claim against the provider if the client inherits undisclosed liabilities when the contract terminates. These provisions need to be built into the outsourcing agreement from the start.

OTHER EMPLOYMENT ASPECTS OF OUTSOURCING

Changing and enforcing employment terms

As mentioned above, the transferee must be careful if changing the terms and conditions of any staff transferring by TUPE, lest this is seen as being in connection with the transfer and giving the employee the right of constructive unfair dismissal or subsequently grounds to claim that the variation was ineffective. Clients and replacement providers also need to watch out for the previous provider improving the terms of employees before transfer, such as giving lengthy notice periods or enhanced redundancy rights in a way that could hit the future transferee but not the provider giving the benefits. The outsourcing contract should therefore contain suitable warranties and restraints on material changes to employment terms without agreement. Likewise, as the client may inherit underperforming employees, the client would want to have the right to require the provider to take disciplinary action against relevant employees where the circumstances warranted it.

Restrictive covenants

Restrictive covenants should likewise be thought about in good time, and ideally before any relevant employees join the client's business in the first place, because it is very difficult to impose such covenants during employment. The transfer will not destroy the covenants, since the contract is treated as having been made between the employee and the new owner, but the covenants will be looked at cautiously by the courts. The covenants may, for example, relate only to the old business or the customers of the transferor and therefore be of no benefit to the transferee unless they are changed. But any changes will, in turn, require employee consent and will have to be carefully negotiated. This is a further part of the risk assessment for both parties. For example, one or more key members of the outsourced team may decide that the new arrangements are not ideal for them and leave. Worse still, they could join a competitor, either of the client or the provider. This would then diminish the outsourced service and lead to valuable former employees actively working in competition. Both parties to the outsourcing contract should therefore be concerned to include suitable and enforceable provisions in the relevant contracts. This is another aspect of due diligence supported by appropriate warranties.

Employees and service levels

Service and quality are hallmarks of successful outsourcing, but in turn depend on competent, trained and motivated staff. Concern for quality control may therefore mean that the client should have the right to require the provider to train and take any necessary disciplinary action against any of the staff, whether transferred or not.

Some Other Outsourcing Points to Consider

- *Group structures* – If appropriate, thought should be given to the involvement of group companies – see Chapter 6.
- *Assets* – If assets are to be transferred, their life expectancy, repair and replacement programmes should be brought into account.
- *Client obligations* – There are, at least to some extent, mutual dependencies between the parties. The provider may be dependent on the client in achieving the requirements of the contract, and especially agreed service levels, as much as the other way round. In theory there should be mutual benefit in spelling out the interdependent obligations, but it is worth these being specific enough without becoming overpowering and unrealistic. The agreement should therefore make allowance for any deficiencies in the provider's services caused by the client's defaults or delays.
- *Exclusivity* may be an issue. In practice the client is unlikely to want to go through a similar process with other parties, but needs to beware of being prevented from going elsewhere if there is good reason to do so. Likewise exclusivity might mean that the client would require tighter service obligations and stronger powers to terminate. The example of the bakery business in Chapter 3 applies equally here.
- *Change management* – There will be changes required, and many agreements build in a change management process so that this can be done – and recorded – in a timely and managed way. This can be a complex area in its own right, but it does uphold the

principle, mentioned regularly in this book, that contracts should be flexible enough to meet the changing demands of business and the times.

- *Continuous performance improvement* – It should be clear as to how this is to be managed. In general terms, the client will expect the contactor to be the specialist and to recommend and implement necessary or advisable improvements after suitable consultation. This could include obligations for the provider to maintain compatibility with industry standards that are likely to be demanded, in turn, by the client's own customers. The cost implications of this will need to be brought into the equation.
- *Benchmarking* against suitable competitors of the provider may be a way of measuring performance and cost levels, with appropriate provisions built into the agreement;

Summary and Checklist

Outsourcing has many benefits, but the parties concerned should be prepared to become involved in a complex and detailed process to maximize the prospects of success and minimize the risk. In terms of employees, the message for business is clear – look after your employee contracts and include TUPE considerations in your contract planning checklist from the outset. Failure to do so and failure to review carefully the cost and benefit implications of your actions could seriously damage both employee relations and your pocket.

THE SERVICE PROVIDER

- Have you taken care in selecting the right service provider in terms of their skills and experience and ability to perform the services better than you could?
- Have you checked their financial status?
- Have you benchmarked their price by some form of competitive tendering?
- If there specific personnel you want included, does the contract cover this?

IMPLEMENTATION

- Is a confidentiality undertaking (NDA) in place?
- Is there a clear timetable and milestones, if appropriate?
- Are the migration and integration mechanics established and recorded?
- How will satisfactory handover be judged?

SERVICE LEVELS

- Are there service standards/SLAs in place and have these been finalized?
- Are there KPIs?
- Is it clear what will happen if the SLAs are not met – for example, service credits, compensation up to termination?
- Are there suitable audit rights for compliance?

INTELLECTUAL PROPERTY

- Is the contract clear as to which rights are owned and are to be owned by which party?
- Have any appropriate assignments or third-party consents been obtained?
- Are updates and upgrades fully dealt with?
- What about back-up and storage?
- Has the source code been deposited, and are the terms of any escrow agreement suitable?

TUPE AND EMPLOYEE ISSUES

- Do or might the TUPE Regulations apply either at the start or the end of the outsourcing? (Consider both the business transfer and service provision tests.)
- Which individuals or jobs might be affected?
- Which are, or may be, the key people, and how much depends on their decision?
- Have the information and consultation regulations been properly dealt with?
- Have the pooling implications been considered?
- Have any relevant employment contracts been checked?
- Have the extra costs and risks been factored in?
- Will there be a resulting inconsistency in contract terms or rates of pay?
- Have appropriate indemnities been negotiated and included?
- Are there any restrictive covenant implications?

14 *Intellectual Property and IP Contracts*

Introduction – patents: an outline – trademarks (including passing-off and image management) – copyright – know-how – intellectual property contracts – franchises and franchise agreements – summary and checklist

Introduction

We live in a world of brands. However simple they may seem, these brands derive from a creative process just as much as writing, composing, painting or designing a new software program. This investment of mental or intellectual effort is characterized as 'intellectual property', with the derivative expression 'intellectual property rights' or IPRs covering patents, trademarks, copyright and similar rights in non-physical property. These are frequently of substantial value and a key part of commercial transactions. More recently, the European Commission's inclusion of IPRs within the remit of the 'knowledge economy' clearly indicates the commercial and financial value of knowledge and its application. But 'ideas', however original they are, are not protected as IPRs until and unless they are expressed in writing or otherwise recorded in some protectable form. Until that happens, they are either have limited protection under the law of confidentiality or none at all.

Design rights and registered designs are specialist areas outside the scope of this book, but important for anyone involved in issues where design, or its protection, is integral to the performance of a product or service.

Patents: An Outline

THE PRINCIPLE

In return for an inventor's investment of time, effort and money and disclosure of the invention to the public, a patent may be granted as an official state monopoly right in the key aspects of an invention. A patent thus is the exclusive right to use an invention, which may be a product or a process. Like most property rights, a patent may be bought, sold or licensed. To obtain patent protection, an invention must: a) be novel; b) contain an inventive step (one which is not obvious to a person skilled in the particular art); c) be capable of industrial use; and d) not be specifically excluded from patentability. Excluded from patent protection are matters such as literary works and most computer programs (as these are protected by copyright and possibly by database rights), scientific theories, immoral or offensive discoveries and some plant or biological processes, although these latter areas now have major political, social and environmental implications which will continue to be the subject of hot debate in the future. Patents last for 20 years, subject to certain renewal fees being paid and the patent not being declared invalid or revoked meanwhile. Patents may be registered in UK, through a general international application or through the European Patent office in Munich. Patent law and practice is a highly specialized field, only mentioned in passing here, and professional advice is recommended from the outset.

NOVELTY

The greatest problem comes with novelty, since the invention must not be something already generally known. Once published or made public, the novelty and thus patentability are likely to be lost. Full confidentiality should therefore be maintained up to the time that the patent application is made. The greatest mistake is to show a potential patent to someone without first protecting confidentiality by a formal non-disclosure agreement.

BUYING AND SELLING PATENTS

Specialist advice is recommended here, too. The owner of the patent may exploit it directly or may assign or license it to a third party in return for a lump sum or royalty or a combination of the two. There are many sad tales told by disappointed inventors, who sell their patent rights and forget that, once a patent has been sold outright, it is up to the buyer what – if anything – is done with it. Without clear obligations (and a good business case), the buyer may buy up the patent simply to squash it – for example, if it competes with one of their existing products. To prevent this, the inventor may want a substantial premium or to negotiate minimum annual royalties with a buy-back option if the patent is not developed. But if you are investing in a patent bought from an inventor, you will want to know that it was novel, the application valid and that the patent will not be revoked. This involves not only sensible checks before the agreement is made, but also appropriate warranties (possibly backed by a suitable retention and termination rights) against third-party claims or attempted revocation.

Trademarks

A trademark, such as a brand name, is a distinctive name, design or sign given to goods or services to help brand recognition and reputation which, as a result, may form a material part of the goodwill of a business. Trademarks exist in registered and unregistered form. Factors common to both are an identifying name, symbol or style, or even the get-up of a particular product, which is recognizable and distinctive, and not merely descriptive. Confusion can, however, easily arise in a marketplace if there is duplication or overlapping between brands, especially relating to the same product or service area, potentially misleading consumers (see Chapter 10) and causing potential loss to the original brand owners. This has, in turn, led to an increase in the number of rules governing comparative advertising.

REGISTERED TRADEMARKS

Greater protection is given to a trademark owner through registration, mainly because conflicting use by a third party may constitute breach without further evidence of confusion. The infringement rules, set out in s. 10 of the Trade Marks Act 1994, are complex. The way in which they apply varies according to whether the potentially infringing mark is *identical* or just similar, whether the *products it relates to are identical or similar* and, where the *mark or the products are similar but not identical*, the *level of confusion* that may be caused to the public or the degree of *unfair advantage* being taken or damage to the distinctive character or repute of the mark.

To be registrable, a mark must be capable of being represented graphically and of distinguishing the goods or services of the business in question from those of other businesses. It is possible to register a wide range of marks, including those relating to words, designs, letters, numbers, the shape of goods, their packaging and even smells, provided they can be clearly described in writing. Marks are now administered through the Intellectual Property Office (IPO) whose website (www.ipo.gov.uk) is a useful reference point for trademark and similar issues. The website is also useful for finding which of the 45 classes of registration may be relevant (classes 1 to 34 being for goods and 35 to 45 for services) and for a basic trademark search to see if there may be obvious conflicting registrations.

The first step to registration is to check that there is no similar mark registered already and that the proposed mark is indeed distinctive enough to be registered. This check will also disclose existing marks which might be infringed by the proposed use. The UK and CTM (European Community Trademark) offices now take a more relaxed view and will not necessarily block new applications because of prior conflicting registrations. Increasingly, where the matter is not clear-cut, they may leave the issue of potential conflict to those directly affected, although they may notify the proprietor of any existing mark to give them the chance of challenge once the new application is published. Trademark registration applies for a ten-year term which can be extended on payment of a renewal fee. The marks are registered in relation to certain classes of goods or services (with separate fees for each class) and may well straddle two or more registration classes.

CTM

Registration in several countries is time-consuming and expensive. An increasingly used alternative in Europe is the European Community Trademark (often known as a CTM), which will cover all EU countries, and there is the possibility of broader international registration via the World Intellectual Property Organization (WIPO).

™ and ®

For UK purposes, ® denotes a registered trademark, also covered by RTM (for registered trademark) and ™ is used to indicate a name or sign that is regarded as unique or special to that business or product. Despite popular belief, ™ does not, however, mean that the trademark is necessarily registered, and the owner of a ™ may therefore have a tougher task to protect that name. Because of its higher protection level, ® or RTM may only be used if the mark is registered, and it is a criminal offence to use the symbol without registration.

UNREGISTERED TRADEMARKS

Passing-off

Registration is normally advantageous but not essential to protect a trademark. Without it, the brand owner will have to establish a reputation in the brand and that people have been confused into believing that the allegedly infringing items were 'from the same stable'. If the same or a similar mark is used to confuse people, this could be 'passing-off' because the infringer would be passing off its products or services to look like those of the real owner. The courts treat this as a misrepresentation and will intervene to protect the rightful owner if confusion in the marketplace can be proved and the rightful owner stands to lose out as a result. The status of passing-off as a significant and wide-ranging legal remedy has been extended in the consumer field by the Consumer Protection from Unfair Trading Regulations 2008 (see Chapter 10).

Image management

The right to take action for passing-off may be claimed by celebrities or others with sufficient reputation to protect their own image for sponsorship or product endorsement. *Irvine* v. *Talksport*, which went to the Court of Appeal in 2003, reinforced that principle and the fact that there need be no similar 'field of activity' in the use of the image. Talksport used a photograph of Eddie Irvine, then a major media personality and main contender for the Formula 1 motor racing championship, without Irvine's permission, manipulating the picture so that the mobile phone Irvine was listening to became transposed as a portable radio, with a by-line suggesting that Irvine endorsed the Talksport radio programme. He was awarded damages at the level of the likely potential endorsement fee he might have charged had he consented to the endorsement. He did not need a reputation in radios or sports programmes or any registration of his name or image as a trademark to succeed in his claim; his reputation as a famous racing driver and personality was sufficient.

TRADEMARK CHECKS

It is obviously sensible (but not always done!) to carry out a search in the public registers before any new product or business name is chosen to see if the proposed name is already registered or the subject of appending registration. This is not as easy as it sounds, for several reasons. The first question is whether to keep to the name or to check similar names or phonetic equivalents. If there is a logo, this adds a further dimension. The second question is which of the trademark categories to search against, as each adds to the expense. The third main question is whether to search just in the UK and CTM or whether to extend the search abroad. Each extra adds to the costs, and the cost has to be weighed against the potential benefit. It is always a good idea also to check in any relevant trade catalogues and, in any event, to make a search against the name and any close variants in one or more of the main Web search engines. In appropriate cases it may be possible to obtain a licence from a trademark owner and to enter into a 'coexistence' agreement which allows each mark to be used in specific ways in specific territories at the same time.

DOMAIN NAMES

Domain names may be highly valuable in their own right (think lastminute.com), and it is wise for businesses to seek to register their domain names as soon as possible, before they become a target for the unscrupulous. Issues can still arise with 'cyber-squatters' who register a famous name or brand as a domain name and refuse to relinquish it without a substantial fee. This is the digital equivalent of unauthorized wheel-clamping. Greater difficulty can exist with those, in the UK or abroad, who have registered and actually use the same domain name. In the UK, Nominet provides a resolution service for UK domain names, and the Internet Corporation for Assigned Names and Numbers (ICANN) is the recognized body for regulating the main domain name structure and resolving disputes as to many of the main issues arising. Inevitably, because similar names have grown up legitimately in different territories, we now have to learn to live with the coexistence of some famous names in relation to more than one product or territory.

TRADEMARK ASSIGNMENTS AND LICENCES

Any assignments of a registered mark should be in writing and registered with the relevant trademark office. If a third party wishes to use the trademark, the trademark owner may grant them a licence, specifying permitted countries and types of goods or services. The licence terms may be strict, with the fees depending on the value of the mark and the owner's brand protection policy. A sample short-form trademark licence is set out in Appendix D in order to illustrate some likely terms.

TRADEMARK INFRINGEMENT

Infringing trademarks can be expensive. For example, if you buy in a large quantity of fashion merchandise, which has been pre-sold at a healthy profit, and then find that the labels infringe third-party trademarks, you may end up with the stock being not only unsaleable, but also impounded, and be on the receiving end of a claim from an irate buyer as well. You will then want to be able to claim against your supplier. This is a clear example of a material risk to be covered by an express warranty and indemnity in the original agreement for the purchase of the merchandise. With fashion goods, copyright infringement claims may also easily arise

Copyright

Copyright arises automatically when a work is produced. This is a monopoly right, whereby the copyright owner, normally the first creator of the work, is the only one able to copy or license copying of that work. Copyright does not require registration to be effective (and nor is this possible in the UK). The classic example is authorship of a book. The ideas in the author's head have no copyright until expressed and recorded in some available tangible form. It is this expression of ideas that is then protectable as a copyright work. Separate copyrights may exist in different forms of recording of an image or a performance. While copyright may not seem generally relevant to non-creative businesses, in fact its importance permeates businesses as diverse as clothing, luggage, furniture design and software.

COPYRIGHT OUTLINES

Copyright law is substantially codified in the Copyright, Designs and Patents Act 1988, as amended, mostly via European harmonization. The main points are summarized below.

- Copyright arises in literary, dramatic, musical and artistic works, as well as sound recordings, broadcast and cable programmes and typographical arrangement of published editions of work and can also exist in physical products from a pair of designer jeans or the design of a suitcase through to a book, video, film or CD.
- Provided the work qualifies for protection, copyright arises automatically as and when the work is generated. In the case of literary, dramatic and musical works, this requires that the work is recorded in some permanent or semi-permanent form.
- A work must be original. Obviously no one person has a monopoly on facts or ideas; copyright is the protection of the actual expression of the facts or ideas in some recordable form.
- There must be skill and labour involved, although this may be minimal (and may not be recognized as skill by everyone).
- Compilations such as computer databases or TV programme listings will also obtain copyright protection as original works if labour and skill have been used to produce the work. They may also have a separate database right.
- Adaptations may acquire their own copyright if skill and effort are used to produce the work, but the owner of the original work must consent to the adaptation.
- There may be several copyrights in the same work. In a musical recording, the composer will have copyright, together with the musicians and the artistes. Their rights will need to have been contractually established between them.
- If there has been joint input, either there will be joint copyright, if an individual's work cannot be distinguished, or individual copyright in separate parts, as with authors of individual chapters.
- In the case of literary, dramatic, musical and artistic work, the author or director is the first owner of the copyright. Special rules exist with regard to sound recordings, films, broadcasts and cable programmes.
- A literary, dramatic, musical or artistic work made by an employee *during the course of employment* is the copyright of the employer, unless agreed otherwise. If the work is made in the employee's spare time and not as part of their job, the employee will be the owner (and the employer would need it to be assigned if the employer wished to use it).
- Copyright is the main basis of protection of software and computer programs (see Chapter 15).
- Copyright in literary, dramatic, musical, film and artistic works now lasts for 70 years from the end of the year in which the author dies (or, in the case of a film, the last among the writer, producer, director or composer to die). With regard to sound recordings and broadcasts, the copyright period is 50 years from the end of

the calendar year when the sound recording or broadcast was made, rising under EU proposals to lengthen the period to 70 years in respect of sound recordings (not the 95 years previously suggested).

- There is a separate 25-year publication right for works which were created long ago but have never been published in the UK or another European Economic Area country.
- The copyright owner has the right to copy or adapt the work, to issue copies of the work to the public, perform, show or play the work in public, to broadcast the work or include it in a cable programme service.

COMMERCIAL EXPLOITATION OF COPYRIGHT WORKS

The original creator of a copyright work can assign ownership or license use of the copyright work to anyone else in return for a lump sum and/or royalty payments. This is covered in the section below on IP contracts. It is important to remember that exclusivity of use is not implied, except in very limited cases. For example, unless there is an assignment or exclusive licence, a designer engaged to produce a design on a commission basis for one client will not be prevented from producing the same or a substantially similar work for someone else (see the *Cala Homes* case in Chapter 3 – and below.)

INFRINGEMENT OF COPYRIGHT

Infringement of a literary, dramatic, artistic or musical work occurs when all or a substantial part of a copyright work is reproduced without the consent of the copyright holder. Wholly independent creation of the same work will not be infringement, but clearly there might be a heavy onus to prove the independence of the creation. Issuing copies of the work to the public or performing the work in public without consent are also infringements. Secondary infringement occurs when infringing copies of literary, dramatic or musical works – such as pirate copies or even copies legitimately produced abroad but not licensed for sale in UK – are imported into the UK.

Criminal, as well as a civil, liabilities may arise in certain circumstances, as counterfeiting can be big business. Infringement generally needs to be met with swift action, and injunctions are issued very speedily if there is clear evidence of breach and unequivocal undertakings are not given to cease infringement and hand over offending material. If you become involved in this area, be prepared to act fast.

Remedies for copyright infringement are not limited to an injunction or damages. An 'account of profits' may also be available. The potential value of this can best be demonstrated by the claim of Michael Baigent and Richard Leigh, two of the three authors of *The Holy Blood and the Holy Grail* – also reissued as *Holy Blood, Holy Grail* (*HBHG*) – against The Random House Group, the UK publisher, in respect of Dan Brown's runaway bestseller, *The Da Vinci Code* (*DVC*). The claim alleged that Brown had used in *DVC* key themes developed by Baigent and Leigh in their own, highly successful, *HBHG*. Random Houses's response was that these themes were no more than ideas and historical conjectures over which no one could have monopoly rights. Although an injunction was claimed at the outset (and briefly threatened the film), Baigent and Leigh had in fact benefited greatly from *DVC* which had driven increased sales of their own book, so their main threat was a claim for an account of profits. Had they succeeded they would have been entitled to a percentage of the sales revenue earned by Random House on every copy of *DVC* it sold. The claim (*Baigent* v. *The Random House Group Ltd*) was rejected at first instance in 2006 and again by the Court of Appeal in 2007, but not without causing some consternation in the literary world that such a case could have come to court at all.

ACTS NOT INFRINGING COPYRIGHT

Not all copying is infringement. Some acts are permitted, such as fair dealing – for instance, when a person wishes to carry out research or private study in relation to a work. If you wish to review, criticize or report a work, you should acknowledge the copyright owner and use only what is fairly needed for the purpose of criticism or review. In other cases, unless something less than a 'substantial part' is reproduced (which may be as little as a single line of a famous poem or song or a short paragraph of a famous book), commercial use of work will not be fair dealing and will probably amount to infringement. If in doubt it is best to seek permission (see below) or early specialist advice and also to remember that the UK fair-dealing rules are much tighter than US 'fair use' concepts.

JOINTLY OWNED COPYRIGHTS

In the *Cala Homes* case mentioned in Chapter 3, joint copyright gave Cala Homes an effective remedy in preventing use of house plans subject to joint copyright plans without its consent. The same issues can arise with other IPRs, but joint copyright can create especial problems, particularly in the music industry where there is often collaboration and many pieces have resonances of other music. This was seen in a case that caught the public interest in 2008. In *Fisher* v. *Brooker* Matthew Fisher, the former organist of the band Procol Harum, claimed to have composed the distinctive eight-bar melody of the introductory organ solo to the 1960s hit song 'Whiter Shade of Pale', the melody being derived from a classical (out of copyright) piece. He also claimed that this very distinctive part of the overall composition made such a creative contribution to the overall work as to entitle him to a joint share of the copyright in the song as a whole. The court agreed with this. But Fisher had waited and stood quietly by for no less than 38 years before making his claim. Although the Court of Appeal held Fisher guilty of excessive and inexcusable delay in making his claim to joint copyright, it was overruled by the House of Lords in late July 2009. Accordingly, Fisher was confirmed in his right to a 40 per cent share in the copyright of the music, and even his great delay did not preclude him from sharing the benefits. The Court of Appeal had ruled that the delay was so lengthy as to amount to what the law calls 'laches', but the Lords decided that laches was an equitable remedy which could not defeat Fisher's joint interest in the copyright and, in any event, the other relevant band members could not show that they had been prejudiced by the delay. So the case is authority for those seeking a share of copyright to emerge many years later, with little effective limitation on the time for such a claim to be brought.

THE COPYRIGHT SYMBOL

The UK is party to the Universal Copyright Convention and the Berne Convention, which states that, between the signatories, no legal formalities are required to protect copyright. Although this is not a requirement of protection under English law, the Universal Copyright Convention recognizes the use of the symbol © and the name of the copyright owner and date of first publication of the work as ingredients for the international recognition of the rights of the copyright owner. The use of the symbol is therefore advisable if the work is likely to be used abroad. It is also a sensible reminder to third parties that the work is protected by copyright and not to be copied without consent.

MORAL RIGHTS

Moral rights are essentially personal rights which can be waived in whole, but not assigned. There are four moral rights:

- the right to be identified as author of a work ('paternity right');
- the right to object to derogatory treatment of the work (for example, parody and burlesque);
- the right to not to be falsely attributed to a work; and
- the right to privacy in respect of certain photographs and films (separate from the general human right to privacy).

These rights last for the term of copyright, except the right not to be falsely attributed to a work, which applies for 20 years after death. They are generally specifically asserted by their owner.

DATABASE RIGHTS

Databases may have separate protection, partly to overcome the issue of potential lack of originality in the constituent parts as opposed to the collation or compilation of the material. This is a fairly technical area which will need separate study if appropriate, and very much depends on the specific facts in question.

Know-how

Although not separately protected, know-how is a significant intellectual property right. It extends to all manner of processes or ways of doing business. These rely not on patents, but on specialized ways of doing business, such as typically set out in manuals or computer programs but sometimes only residing in the heads of those with the relevant knowledge and expertise. Know-how thus becomes part of the 'intellectual capital' of an enterprise, mainly protected at law by the laws relating to confidentiality and non-competition, covering information that is unique to a business, ranging from secret formulae to profit margins. When the information forms part of the *general* learning and experience of an individual, as opposed to trade secrets, the law will be reluctant to prevent that person using that knowledge and expertise elsewhere. Where, however, the information is confidential to that business, it can generally be protected, so long as it remains confidential within the business, by a confidentiality undertaking or suitably targeted restrictive covenants. Where the information is written down, such as in a manual, copyright will apply; an employee who 'walks off' with the manual for use in a new job will probably breach both confidentiality and copyright. Know-how can therefore be *protected by contract*, but it also needs to be *protected by behaviour*, by being treated as confidential. Otherwise, whatever the contract may say, it will lose its confidential nature and the protection of the law.

Intellectual Property Contracts

This section looks at the main contracts likely to be encountered when dealing with IPRs, with the main business emphasis on trademarks and copyrights. One material difference between them, as seen above, is that the most valuable trademarks are usually registered, whereas copyright arises automatically. It is easiest to look at the points of similarity first.

IP LICENCES – A TYPICAL STRUCTURE

- Names and details of the parties.
- An introduction (if appropriate).
- A list of defined terms (if appropriate but often useful).
- Provisions as to the creation or registration process, be it a trademark application/ registration or the writing of an article or book or composition of a piece of music.
- The formal licence terms, describing the extent, ambit and duration of the grant.
- Any promotional obligations, such as on the part of a celebrity author or musician.
- Express provisions as to how the rights are and are not to be used.
- Requirements as to the range and level of consents required to use the rights.
- The payment structure, which might include fees and/or royalties dependent on sales or other volumes, a share of sub-licence income and an advance against those future earnings.
- Reporting and accounting provisions.
- Warranties and indemnities as to the IP rights granted.
- Claims-handling (between the parties and in relation to third parties).
- Non-compete provisions (if appropriate).
- Options for future work if appropriate (less likely with trademarks).
- Termination and consequences of termination.
- Assignment and sub-licensing.
- General and boilerplate provisions.
- Schedules (if applicable).

Differences

Where trademark and copyright agreements are likely to differ is in the creative and editorial aspects. A trademark needs to be reproduced in exactly the same form and colours as the registered mark, and there is no leeway for the licensee to adapt this; watering down of the mark could undermine its continued registration. With copyright there may be an editorial and adaptation process to produce a final polished piece suitable for publication or distribution.

Exclusivity

This will be a key issue. Exclusive copyright, for example, is often granted for the full term of copyright and is only likely to be lost by major breach of contract or a reversion of rights clause (see above). Exclusivity will bar the original creator of the copyright work from reproducing or exploiting it themselves without the consent of the exclusive licensee. Without exclusivity, however, the licensee will be competing with the creator and any third parties who have been granted similar rights, and will be thus much less inclined to invest heavily in exploitation.

Minimum targets

A trademark brand owner may impose a minimum level of target production or sales or may require the licensee to guarantee a minimum royalty payable, whether or not production or sales meet that level. The licensee failing to meet these minimum levels is likely to give the licensor the right to terminate the licence. In some cases, the agreement may be drafted so that the licensor is not obliged to terminate and can simply insist on the minimum royalty being paid year on year over a lengthy term. The licensee needs to be alert to this and should not let wild optimism cloud commercial judgement. The copyright equivalent is effectively the advance against royalties, which is payable whether or not sales ultimately justify the advance.

TRADEMARK LICENCES

Trademark licences will normally be limited to the scope and period of the trademark registration, possibly including a renewal, although registration is not a prerequisite and licences may, for example, cover some countries in which the trademark is not registered. For the brand owner, limiting use of the brand to a precise reproduction of the mark to retain its distinctiveness and maintaining the reputation of the mark – and its use on any of its licensed products – are crucial; this retains the ability to stop any licensee bringing the mark into disrepute. The licensee will want as free rein as possible, balanced against the level of trademark fees for the privilege, without too many restrictions or prior approvals, and also without too many 'tripwires' that trigger termination. After all, if the licensee uses the brand name for a significant part of its business's product range, a sudden loss of the rights to use the name could have drastic consequences. A basic template trademark licence embodying these and other drafting issues is set out in Appendix D, with a brief commentary on certain of the clauses.

ASSIGNMENT OF COPYRIGHT (SEE ALSO CHAPTER 18)

Where copyright is transferred, this will be by an assignment of the 'intangible' right – something that cannot be transferred manually, normally for a one-off fee, but occasionally for a royalty or a mix of fee and royalty. An assignment should always be in writing. Although copyright is not usually assigned for a full-length literary work, assignment may be appropriate for a piece specially commissioned for a particular purpose or for illustrations to, or specific sections of, a larger work. In the field of technology, it may be appropriate to assign copyrights, such as in a specific website design to a client's specification. Assignment of copyright will, however, mean that the creator may not use the same work in future without the consent of the new copyright owner, so it may not be appropriate where the work contains elements that its creator might wish to use elsewhere; in this case, a licence should be used instead.

Future works can be assigned, such as those commissioned for a particular purpose, provided this is made clear, after defining the 'Work', by a suitable recital clause and wording, as in the following example:

> *In consideration of £[...] (receipt of which the [Author/Creator/Designer] acknowledges) the [Author/Creator/Designer] assigns by way of present assignment all current and future copyright in the Work.*

Note that this is an actual assignment and not just an agreement to assign, avoiding the need for a further assignment once the work is created. Where payment is still to be made, the creator may wish to wait until full payment is made before assigning the copyright. The best sanction for non-payment is still that the copyright in the work remains with, or reverts back, to its creator.

Partial assignment is possible, but generally best avoided. If it proves necessary – for example, to split a work into two or more sections with each assigned to different parties – it pays to be ultra-clear in definitions, leaving no room for doubt, and for the assignment to deal specifically with any content or features appearing in more than one part. It would be better to deal with this as a novation (see Chapter 18.)

COPYRIGHT PERMISSIONS (CONSENT TO USE AN EXTRACT FROM A WORK)

Quotations or extracts from another person's work are permitted, without the consent of the copyright owner, within the rules of 'fair dealing'. These rules are much tighter than the US 'fair use' rules, so it is dangerous to assume that the same extent of a quotation in a US publication can be reproduced in a UK work. There is no fixed extent; in a long UK work, a couple of short paragraphs might be permissible, but anything beyond that might well be regarded as 'substantial' and infringement of copyright unless used with permission. In a short work, the extract length might be less, and possibly as short as one very well-known line of a well-known poem or song lyric. Such quotations should not be confused with the promotional extracts from a book available by way of link on many websites, and intended as the digital equivalent of bookshop browsing, with copy, paste and print functions normally disabled. Whether and on what terms to grant permission is up to the rights holder, but most major publishers will accede to a request for a modest payment and signature of a standard permissions form.

COPYRIGHT LICENCES

'Copyright licence' here suggests a licence for a full work, as opposed to the permission to use an extract' discussed above. An author, for example, will sign a publishing agreement giving a publisher exclusive licence to publish the author's specific work. The terms of the licence will depend somewhat on the publisher or agent involved, and will vary substantially between the general consumer book market and the educational/scientific, medical and technical (SMT) markets and even more between different formats such as literary, dramatic and musical compositions. Some main distinguishing features of a copyright licence are set out below; these are based on book publishing contracts by way of example, but similar issues are likely to apply, with appropriate adaptations, to ghost/co-writers, translators, illustrators, composers or other creative talent.

Form of publication

Many book-publishing contracts are still traditional in form, covering hardback publication which then extends into paperback rights, and adapted more recently to cater for electronic books (e-books). There may be a separate grant of audio rights in non-dramatized form, both for physical copies such as cassette and CD and for the digital audio market.

Territory and language

At their simplest, rights may be granted on a 'whole world/all languages' basis, with power to sub-license foreign-language versions if appropriate. The publisher can then decide when and where to sub-license, such as to specialist foreign publishing houses which will be better placed to market and sell in their own territories. In consumer book publishing, the English-language world has long been divided between the USA and the UK and their respective adherents. Philippines and US military bases (and recently sometimes Canada) tend to be exclusive territories granted to the US publisher, whereas British Commonwealth (including or excluding Canada) rights have normally been exclusive to the UK publisher. Several factors have intervened to challenge the old ways, with flashpoints now arising in relation to the EU countries, Australia, New Zealand and India especially. The issues here tend to relate, in the case of Europe, to the EU's copyright 'exhaustion' rules, to a growing drive to have an open market (that is, one not subject to exclusivity of either US and UK editions) in the case of Australia and New Zealand, and, in the case of India, to achieving proper regulation of a fast-growing market that has now started to tackle widespread copyright infringement.

Term

Consumer book-publishing licences are normally for full term of copyright, being 70 years from the end of the year of the author's death. Sub-licence contracts are often for shorter periods, perhaps even down to five or ten years. Where the term is lengthy, authors' agents will often require a suitable 'reversion' clause, originally to provide that, if the work goes out of print, the author can require the publisher to decide whether to print and publish a new edition or permit the rights to 'revert' to the author. The author could then start again with another publisher. As the need to retain stocks in a warehouse became environmentally unsound and print-on-demand capability increased, authors have moved more towards a minimum sales requirement for the publisher to achieve in order to retain the copyright licence. The level of this sales requirement remains a matter of negotiation to achieve a fair balance between publishers' (often substantial) investment in the author's advance and publishing costs, and their ability to recover this over 'long-tail' sales, and authors' wish not have their work 'locked up' for many years.

Delivery and timing

As most publishing agreements cover works still to be written, there is a great need for clarity, by reference to an extract, synopsis and possibly word-count, to indicate the content, style and length of the work. When delivered by the author to the publisher, the work will need editing (and possibly a legal read to check for legal risks – see below) before being set in final form, printed, distributed and finally published to the wider world. The contract will normally give suitable timescales for this and, occasionally – say, if publication is a tied in to a TV series or specific event – the date of delivery of the work to the publisher will be 'of the essence'.

Consents

An author basically grants the publisher the right to publish the work in the form the author submits it to the publisher, but even good books need some editing. Many authors or their agents will insist on agreeing to any changes to their work, or any extracts from or abridgements of the work. In any case, most authors want to see and approve the book jacket. However, many levels of consent add to the administrative process, and, again, a sensible balance needs to be struck.

Financial terms

The author may be paid an 'advance', being a prepayment against the royalties and sub-rights income which they hope to earn under the contract. Traditionally, this was the author's 'wages' while the book was being written. These days the advance is largely a function of market forces, leading to a sharp polarization between the expected mega-sellers, where rights are literally auctioned off to the highest publisher bidder by the author's agents, and the large number of smaller sellers where advances are likely to be modest. The advance then has to be 'earned-out' by royalties and sub-rights income accruing to the author's account. Only when the publisher has recouped the full amount of the advance will the author receive further payment. Royalties can be complex, but a critical distinction is whether royalties are calculated on the recommended retail price (RRP) of the book sold or on the publisher's price received (PR), which will reflect the level of discount the publisher has to give the retailer or wholesaler. Also there tends to be distinct differences between different markets such that educational books and consumer books for export are frequently PR-based.

Warranties and indemnities

Warranties and indemnities can be significant in author contracts and should be fully understood by authors. The author will typically be asked to warrant a series of things that are designed to give the publisher confidence that it is unlikely to be sued as a result of publishing the book. Warranties typically cover the following:

- *Originality* – The work is the original work of the author and previously unpublished.

- *Confidentiality* – The contents do not breach an obligation of confidentiality owed to someone else either specifically by contract (such as a settlement agreement) or by implication of law (see Chapter 5).
- *Trademark/copyright/moral right* – The work does not breach such rights of any third party.
- *Libel/malicious falsehood* – This is possibly the principal risk; even if the publisher has the work read for libel, the author needs to take great care and be certain that any statement or allegation that could lower someone in the eyes of others is true and provable. If not, the defences to libel need to be carefully considered or the words changed. It is sometimes just too easy for an author intent on adding a bit of spice to a story to 'heighten' the language and tip a balanced comment over the edge into a libel.
- *Privacy* – This is the new and fast-growing kid on the legal risks block, looked at in more detail in a broader perspective in Chapter 5.
- *Truth* – The line between fiction and non-fiction is becoming ever more blurred but a written work needs to be clear whether it is fact or fiction. Even fictional work can be libellous, deliberately or by mistake in using the name of a real person, or breach copyright or privacy if a 'fictional' character can be identified as a living person. A non-fiction work can also come to grief if a material part of it is made up, as the entire book may have to be withdrawn, and in extreme cases, such an act could lead to claims if people have acted in reliance on its being true.

Franchises and Franchise Agreements

FRANCHISING AND PYRAMID SELLING

Franchising is a commercial arrangement under which one trader buys the right to use the branding and know-how developed by another, often well-known, consumer brand. To the outside world, the business looks just like a branch of the brand owner, but in fact the business is independently owned and staffed by employees of the independent business. Sometimes, however, the term 'franchising' is used for schemes which are actually something else – multi-level marketing or even pyramid selling. These activities usually involve a number of levels of distributors of products, or even money, where distributors are encouraged to recruit more distributors and are given financial incentives to do so. The incentive for participants is to recruit more of their number, rather than to sell more products, and such schemes tend therefore to abuse the rights of the lower levels of participants and to do nothing to improve competition in the marketplace. One relevant official website, which can also be accessed from the new BIS website, is at http://www.berr.gov.uk/whatwedo/consumers/buying-selling/Trading-Schemes/index.html. This summarizes the position as at 29 August 2009 as follows:

> *Trading schemes may be called direct selling, network marketing, pyramid selling, multi-level marketing or other names. Whatever it is called, it is a way of selling goods or services through a trading scheme which operates on more than one level.*

People who join such schemes are self-employed and earn money by selling the schemes' goods or services. In some schemes participants may increase their earnings from the sales made by their recruits.

Such schemes are not illegal in the UK but they must comply with the provisions in Part XI of the Fair Trading Act as amended by the Trading Scheme Act 1996 and the Trading Scheme Regulations 1997.

A related link to the relevant factsheet (http://www.berr.gov.uk/whatwedo/consumers/fact-sheets/page38561.html) also covers chain letters as trading schemes as follows:

There is precedent for schemes operating as chain letters being subject to the Lotteries and Amusement Act 1976. However, under the Gambling Act 2005 (when commenced) it will be an offence for a person to invite someone to join a chain-gift scheme or for them to knowingly participate in the promotion, administration of management of a chain-gift scheme. The Department for Culture, Media and Sport (DCMS) have [sic] policy responsibility for the Gambling Act 2005.

So it can readily be seen that the position is not simple and that involvement in a trading scheme of any kind needs to be approached with considerable caution.

FRANCHISING – AN OUTLINE

We think of franchises for products such as printing services, health foods and fast food, typical of 'business format franchising' where, to the outside eye, there is little or no difference between the directly owned outlet and the franchise shop. So what goes on behind the scenes? A typical franchise relationship has most, if not all, of the features mentioned below:

- The franchisor has a *distinctive name*, associated with a trademark, experience and reputation in a particular area of business *and an established procedure for conducting that business*, all of which are suitable for 'packaging' and applying to suitable, strongly branded premises, and/or types of services.
- The *franchisee is an independent business*, which buys the right to use the trade name and the know-how for the period of the franchise.
- There is a *detailed procedure for operating the business* set out in manuals and a bespoke software system. This will contain highly confidential information, updated regularly.
- The franchisee will *pay a capital sum* at the start of the franchise term, *followed by regular payments*, generally based on the turnover of the franchised business.
- The *franchisor will be able to review the accounts*, books and records of the franchisee.
- The franchisee may be required to *buy certain materials through approved suppliers* to maintain product and service quality.
- The franchisee must keep the *franchised business separate and distinct from any other business*, to use the trademark and trade names and know-how exactly as prescribed by the franchisor and to *maintain the confidentiality* of all the know-how.

- The *franchisor will retain sufficient control* over the business to ensure that the franchisee complies with its obligations and maximizes the potential of the franchise.
- There will be *appropriate training* for the key employees of the franchisee.
- The franchisor provides national *advertising* and probably assists with, and retains close control over, local marketing.
- The franchise will be limited to a *stated area/range of products/services*, with no right to establish a base outside the agreed territory or range of products or services.
- The franchisee's *ability to assign or transfer the business will be limited* to enable the franchisor to maintain control over the choice of any incoming franchisee.
- The franchisor will have strong termination rights on serious franchisee default.

THE BENEFITS AND CHALLENGES OF FRANCHISING

Franchising offers franchisors the chance to build up business and turnover at a faster rate than might otherwise be possible and to tap into the extra energy of entrepreneurial franchisees. Franchisees have the opportunity to run their own businesses and be self-employed without the need to be specialists or total innovators. Financially there should be a reduced risk of failure in following a precedent with an established success record and, correspondingly, less difficulty in raising start-up finance. But franchisees must pay for the privilege and accept tight control by their franchisors. Successful franchisees may also become potential competitors of their franchisors, which is where the strength of the franchisor's brand and reputation and levels of cost and service may be critical.

Trademark registration is normally an important ingredient of franchising, but brand awareness also requires strong visibility on the high street and of products or advertising, since products without a strong brand image are extremely difficult to protect. Franchising may also be successful on a national or international basis, but significant further issues arise here, including technical competition law considerations, which are beyond the general scope of this chapter. A good starting-point for more information on the subject is the British Franchise Association, whose website (www.thebfa.org) contains useful links and background.

Summary and Checklist

Intellectual property rights are increasingly important and valuable in business life, and are liable to be relevant to a broad range of contracts. Listed below are some issues to consider.

IP RIGHTS

- Is there a patentable element involved and, if so, is full confidentiality being maintained?
- Have you done a trademark search to check for identical or similar marks to your own (or proposed) mark? (Many trademark agents will provide a 'watching' service to advise you of any similar applications in the future.)

- Is your name or logo distinctive enough for registration, and do the costs and procedures justify it? In what classes and in how many countries would you need to be registered?
- Have you checked any new name in good time by an internet search, in relevant trade journals and directories?
- Is your know-how as well protected as it can be?
- Have you registered your domain name?

IP CONTRACTS

- What is the extent of the rights being licensed?
- How are improvements and derivations dealt with?
- To what extent is the licence to be exclusive or non-exclusive?
- What is the period (term) of the agreement and what provisions for termination exist?
- How much is payable as licence fee, advance and royalties?
- Are there requirements for minimum sales/payments and/or penalties for not reaching them?
- Are there obligations as to record-keeping, reporting and auditing the records?
- Are there provisions as to quality control and observance of agreed procedures?
- Are there warranties on ownership of the rights, registration and non-infringement of third-party rights?
- Are there indemnities for breach of warranty and third-party claims?
- Are there provisions for dealing with claims?
- Are there limitations on liability and insurance requirements?
- Are there confidentiality and non-competition clauses?
- Have you checked that nothing infringes competition law?
- Have you included rights of assignment, subcontracting and sub-licensing?
- Have you included boilerplate clauses?

15 *Technology Contracts*

Introduction – type of technology contract – headline issues in technology contracts – jumping the gun – IT development agreements: more detailed issues – software – drafting or reviewing IT agreements – maintenance agreements – summary

Introduction

Technology supply and development contracts, the focus of this chapter, offer great opportunities for a mismatch between the technical specification offered by a supplier and the functionality sought by a client. This can be compounded by technical language, incomplete specifications, narrow definitions and supposed industry norms. Such contracts face many of the challenges encountered by other agreements, such as service (Chapter 12), outsourcing (Chapter 13) or Internet-related elements (Chapter 16), but also have a range of issues of their own. The key issues for technology contracts include clarity in what is to be achieved, how the process is to be performed and measured in terms of acceptability and, thereafter, ongoing support. And behind all this is the inevitable question of risk and its allocation between the parties.

Types of Technology Contract

Standard agreements abound in IT, but should not deter an informed challenge when appropriate. Indeed, not all IT providers are well served by their current contracts. Some are very one-sided agreements imposed on the client word-for-word; others show signs of having grown like Topsy, with a multiplicity of amendments and cross-references by different people at different times in the light of (often bad) experience, resulting in an amalgam of inconsistencies. This difference may match the distinction between a prepackaged proprietary system and a highly bespoke system. The proprietary system will almost certainly come with standard terms and conditions. The buyer will have little scope to amend these terms and will need to concentrate on understanding the implications, particularly what is stated within the contract and what is not covered at all. Although it covers many key proprietary system issues, this chapter puts more emphasis on bespoke solutions in which the contract negotiations will be more open, aiming to achieve an agreement with the right mix of cost, benefit and risk for all parties. This takes time, so the discussion on essential terms should start in good time and ideally blend into discussion on the contract terms as soon as the parties start thinking seriously about working together.

Headline Issues in Technology Contracts

Some headline issues are taken first and explored in more detail below.

CONCEPT, DESIGN AND IP IN TECHNOLOGY

Ideas

As noted in Chapter 14, ideas are not protected by copyright law, so care is required as to what is disclosed, when and to whom. At the start of a project, a non-disclosure agreement (NDA – see Chapter 5) is therefore advisable.

Designs

Designs can attract copyright and other IP protection. Are there design rights in the system being planned? If so, how are they distinguished between the overall design (what the system or software does) and the detailed code (the technological mechanism to achieve that result)? Which of developer (or its subcontractor) and client have rights in which element, and how are these rights to be captured and dealt with?

Intellectual property ownership

The contract should make it clear who owns each part of the design, the technology, the system and the manuals. The developer will not want to lose its previous or general IP; the client will not want to compromise its own integral business IP, and any third-party proprietary rights element will have to be separated but continue to be usable. And both developer and client should seek to avoid the pitfall of shared copyright, requiring both to consent to exploitation and therefore each being able to stymie the other's use in the future.

Exclusivity is a linked issue. For most practical purposes, an exclusive licence will carry the same benefits as an assignment of the relevant IP, so a battle over assignment (or outright ownership) may be unnecessary. But non-exclusive IP rights are another matter; they are inevitable with most common platforms, but not necessarily appropriate with heavily bespoke systems.

Assignments of IP have to be in writing to be effective, so that if the IP is to be owned by the client, the transfers of design and copyrights produced by independent contractors should be for value (consideration), put in writing and signed off at the time.

DEFINING WHAT IS TO BE DELIVERED, WHEN AND HOW IT IS MEASURED

Specifications

The distinction between the technical specification (what the service provider will want to provide) and the functional specification (what the client will want) also has implications for acceptance testing, service levels and future liability. Be prepared to put in the effort at the outset to define exactly what the system is expected to achieve – more specifically:

a) what exactly will be provided;

b) by whom (what is their level of experience; and are they the people you know/expect/
   have dealt with before?); and
c) how – what will be the end-result?

Schedules

The technical specification is often set out in a schedule to the development agreement,
but there is no reason why the functional specification should not also be set out,
provided the two are suitably compatible. The project plan may also usefully be added as
a schedule to establish the agreed methodology and planned timescale.

Acceptance

Acceptance or non-acceptance is the trigger point for other actions under the agreement,
so tests must be specific and measurable; each test to be carried out should be itemized
and should be capable of giving a clear answer as to whether the system does indeed
achieve what is expected and whether this is to a required standard. If problems are not
dealt with then, it will often be very difficult to tackle them successfully later. Providers
will, for their part, be concerned that they are not caught out by network vagaries or lack
of adequate client preparedness.

When

Timing is often critical with IT projects because of the need to coordinate various plans.
What happens if a key member of the service provider's team is absent or there are
unexpected delays elsewhere? How fixed or flexible is the arrangement to be? Is time
to be of the essence? What is the risk – and the compensation – if the project runs over
time?

Use of the services

Is the client limited in the use of the services paid for and, if so, how? Are the services also
to be used by subsidiary or other associated companies and can group companies enforce
any remedies directly against the service provider?

FINANCIAL CONSIDERATIONS

Cost

To what extent is the cost fixed? Is this capped by the overall budget or calculated on
daily rates for a specified (minimum/maximum) number of days? Is there a rate card or
schedule of day rates for relevant team members? Are there RPI indexation provisions
and, if so, do they allow for falls as well as rises in RPI? If not, how is the cost regulated?
Are the expenses specified and clear and do they, for example, include travel from the
individual's home to the client's premises or only the travel between the client's sites?
Is the type of travel specified or can an overall figure be agreed? Is the wording about

additional charges specific enough and should the client first approve the cost as part of the project? Are there any penalties for late payment?

Invoicing and payment

Is it clear how and when the service provider will invoice? The development fee is likely to be payable in stages, dependent on achieving milestones, and the client will want to make the final payment some weeks after go-live to ensure that the system stands the test of normal operation. Sometimes the payments are pre-specified and the contract will effectively act as the invoice, but the client's accounts department won't pay without an invoice. A payment may then not be made, and the parties can fall out as a result. The contract should strike a sensible balance between encouraging prompt payment and giving no tolerance for unintended error.

Jumping the Gun

There is a real risk that actual work on an IT development process will start before the contract is agreed. The parties will often claim that the reason for this is that the legal process is taking too long, but often it is because the legal process has not started early enough or key issues have not been tackled in good time. Indeed, delay is often caused by lack of early agreement on the final specification of the system. If this happens, and neither party has made suitable preparations, both parties may finish up severely disappointed and potentially out of pocket, with valuable development time lost.

A case in point

In the case of *CWS* v. *ICL* (2003) ICL started detailed work on the new system for CWS (the former Co-Operative Wholesale Society) before the development contract was agreed and signed. After some six months of negotiation, CWS sought to terminate the alleged contract and sued ICL for repudiatory breach of that contract because of alleged errors and delay by ICL. ICL denied that a contract had been made and counter-claimed over £1 million for extensive work that it had already carried out. The trial judge held that the parties were so far apart, especially on the question of liquidated damages, that there was little prospect that they would have reached agreement anyway. The case went to the Court of Appeal which, whilst not necessarily disagreeing with many of the judge's findings on fact, was so critical of his judgment and the award made to ICL that (most unusually for a civil case) it ordered a retrial, causing even greater cost and uncertainty.

Planning ahead

To avoid this situation some possible practical approaches might be as follows:

• Agree all the key commercial terms before detailed drafting or run the two negotiations in parallel, and do allow sufficient time for the contract process.

- Do not regard key terms, such as an exemption clause and agreement to pay liquidated damages, as just part of the 'legal stuff'. They are a vital part of the risk/reward equation and are directly linked to price.
- Don't start work before the contract is agreed and signed, but if starting is essential, agree in writing:
  - that it is an interim arrangement;
  - as to exactly how much work is to be carried out (setting a maximum); and
  - how and when this work is to be paid for.

IT Development Agreements: More Detailed Issues

SYSTEM DETAILS

Bespoke systems tend to have several facets. The key parts are likely to be:

- the *development process* under which the software is designed and configured;
- the *acceptance process* of testing and proving it does what is claimed;
- *payment arrangements* – how much and when;
- the *licence period* and terms for use of the commissioned software; and
- *maintenance*/support arrangements.

Consistency

If there is more than one agreement, it is important that they are consistent, preferably with the same defined and general terms and a proper interlinking. However, the development and support agreements should be able to operate independently, so that the client does not lose its software rights simply because it wants to change support arrangements.

Interfaces and integration

How are the technology bridges between the developer's and client's systems to be created? Is it clear as to who is responsible for each part of this stage (which involves both parties), who pays for it and who owns it? How does this relate to any third-party software?

Software

LEGAL PROTECTION

As seen in previous chapters, software is protected in law by a mix of copyright, database rights and confidentiality (know-how); there may also be some aspects of patent protection. Several different types of software rights may be involved, of which the most likely are set out below – distinctions that should be sorted out at the outset.

CHANGES

Software normally goes through several stages of development, starting with the testing process. The first may be bug-fixes and the like, characterized as troubleshooting and resolution. The second will be updates or even new versions, with relatively minor changes and improvements to the previous issue. The third stage may be upgrades with potentially improved functionality. Upgrades and updates are sometimes characterized numerically, starting from 1.0, with 2.0, for example, being the first new version of the first upgrade and 3.2 being the second revision of the second upgrade. The fourth stage might be a complete new program, albeit one that develops concepts from the previous one. Revisions and upgrades should in turn be distinguished from maintenance obligations in relation to the smooth running of the existing software, dealt with later in this chapter.

PROPRIETARY SOFTWARE

'Common platform' software may be provided by large software corporations under a standard-form non-exclusive third-party licence, enabling the client or developer to use it for limited purposes. There will be usually be little scope for the IT provider or the client to negotiate or amend the terms of this sub-licence, but the developer should ensure that this extends to the proposed system. If proprietary software is included in the new system, what will happen if the third-party software itself changes? The first sign may be a new automatically downloaded proprietary upgrade which the client's bespoke software simply cannot handle, because it was built on the framework of the software. How will the developer support this and at whose cost?

BESPOKE SOFTWARE

The developer will write the program and grant the client a licence to use it and take back-up copies. If the program has been created for the client alone, as the 'bespoke' tailoring analogy suggests, the client may expect it not to be used by anyone else. This kind of restriction is not implied and would require an outright assignment of the program, which is highly unlikely, or an exclusive licence from the developer to the client. This needs to be addressed up-front. The developer needs to be sure that any exclusivity does not compromise planned use of parts of the software for its other clients or other purposes.

OPEN-SOURCE SOFTWARE

Open-source software has the underlying programming code made available on a standard form of licence in such a way that developers and users can utilize it non-exclusively and free of charge. Typically, any derivation or modification of open-source software must itself be made open-source, so that any exclusivity or financial benefits must be limited to the enhanced applications developed and maintained by the service provider.

A COMBINED SYSTEM

The developer may build a bespoke application on to a more generic operating structure, the result being a 'shared platform'. The contract should entitle the client to the benefit of both, but any discussions as to exclusive rights would naturally be limited to the bespoke element, and the client will need to be careful not to risk any breach of the proprietary software terms, which could lose it the ability to use the bespoke system by the back door.

INDUSTRY SOFTWARE

There may be a combination of proprietary basics with already developed applications for a particular industry, which can present particular challenges if the client has contributed know-how or disclosed confidential information, even as to its prices or margins. The same program could then enable competitors to access and exploit that information if the software were licensed to them. On the other hand, the developer may want to use its work and design to roll out the same sort of model to others in the same area of business. It may be prepared to work with the first client to develop a generic basis for the industry while agreeing to offer the client a limited exclusivity period (say 6–12 months) or the prototype at a lower cost. Such issues will require careful thought and clarity in the contract.

IDENTIFYING THE SYSTEM AND WHAT IT DOES – SOME KEY QUESTIONS

- *Standard terms* – Is the system standard or bespoke? Terms for bespoke contracts are likely to be more negotiable, but even standard terms or small print should not be assumed to be inviolate, and clients should not feel intimidated by being presented with a version of the supplier's contract in PDF form!
- *Third-party systems* – Does the system use existing third-party proprietary software (TPPS)? If it does, the supplier will probably not be prepared to offer any more rights (or remedies) than it has vis-à-vis the third party. What is important here is, first, knowing that the supplier is authorized to use (and sub-license) the TPPS as part of the new system and, second, having adequate rights and remedies in respect of the TPPS, either direct against the third party (for example, under their standard terms and conditions for third-party licensees) or through the system supplier itself.
- *Acceptance testing* – If bespoke, how are the performance criteria expressed and how will they be tested as part of acceptance testing before 'go-live'. Effective testing according to pre-agreed criteria is key to establishing that the system does what is claimed for it. It is the testing, and the criteria laid down in relation to this, that should help translate between the technical specification and the customer's business requirements (see below).
- *System compatibility* – The client needs to be sure from the outset that the new program will be compatible with, and work on, its existing software (and hardware) network. The parties need to be clear whether this is the supplier's or the client's responsibility and what the implications are if there is incompatibility. This is something for the earliest stages of negotiation and should be reflected in the contract itself. If future development is expected, which the client would hope to benefit from, it needs to be checked that this will be fully compatible with the client's existing facilities.
- *Change of underlying third-party software* – What effect would such a change have? It could mean that the new bespoke system built onto the TPPS would cease to work – or be incapable of effective maintenance or upgrade. There may no easy answer to this.

Drafting or Reviewing IT Agreements

Although technology contracts (especially regarding software development) come in a huge range of shapes and sizes, there are several key aspects that are likely to arise in almost any contract of this type. Lack of agreement on some of these fundamental aspects can be as damaging to negotiations as failure to agree on price, so they are best considered before the stage of detailed drafting or negotiation of the contract.

THE PARTIES

Typically, the contract will be between two parties only – the software developer/service provider (developer/provider) and the customer (client). Either or both may be part of a larger group, and the implications of that need to be considered. Both, of course, should be legal entities in their own right, and, as with any contract of some material financial commitment, each party should carry out suitable due diligence on the other. If you are, or are dealing with, a group company, look especially at the section in Chapter 6 on 'Contracts with group companies' (p. 98) and 'Takeovers' (p. 99).

DEFINING THE DEVELOPMENT AND THE SYSTEM

The program details are often best set out in sufficient detail in a schedule to the agreement, but there can be confusion between such terms as: 'System', typically the whole of an operating program including third-party software; 'Software', which is likely to be the bespoke software being designed and installed by the developer under the contract; and 'Documentation', which will be the supporting manuals. The three elements should be clearly distinguished from the outset. There can be a term to cover the software and the documentation together, as both will be subject to the overall licence. The client's equipment may also be defined, which will highlight the importance of ensuring that the equipment is not only compatible, but is also free of defects and of adequate capacity to enable the new software to work.

SCHEDULE/APPENDIX – THE SYSTEM/SOFTWARE SPECIFICATION

If a tender was prepared, the description there may be sufficient cross-reference, updated for any agreed changes, but otherwise there should be a clear technical and/or functional specification linked to the contractual testing and acceptance criteria. To check that it is complete and clear, it is no bad idea to test it out on a colleague unrelated to the deal in question to see what, if any, questions they need to ask.

DELIVERY, INSTALLATION AND TESTING

Installation

The software will typically be installed by disk, file transfer or download. Whichever the method, it needs to be clearly specified how and when delivery is to be made.

Acceptance process

Specifying the acceptance testing and commissioning process, together with an appropriate chronology for the process, is obviously crucial to a smooth handover, as is ensuring that associated definitions, such as 'Acceptance Date' and 'Delivery Date' tie in consistently. These not only mark the end of the development phase, but also trigger payment obligations and the start of any warranty and maintenance commitments. In the same way, care should be taken with any 'deemed acceptance' clauses that set out unreasonable time periods for the client.

Testing and commissioning

This process can be complex, and the contractual arrangements should be explicit, geared to the functionality required and not left to assumptions. Some software has three levels of testing, alpha testing by the development team at the developer's premises, beta testing via a limited range of contacts outside the development team and final acceptance testing of the software once installed in, and operating as part of, the client's system. The client will expect the software to have been at least alpha tested before delivery. Whether there is beta testing may depend on to what extent the software is an early prototype or exclusive to the client. It is essential that the client's technical team is well informed in this area and that there is full communication between them and those preparing or reviewing the development contract. If the client does take a product at the beta-testing stage, it may gain the advantage of its being an early release and perhaps discounted in price, but it is unlikely to receive normal guarantees from the provider – and this means that the client would have no recourse if the product malfunctions, possibly even disabling the new system. The client should consider whether it has the skills to test at this level; if not, this is expertise that can be acquired, and the cost of doing so may be a sound investment against the risk and cost of accepting a substandard system.

What if testing proves unsuccessful?

The contract should provide, in clear terms, what happens if the system fails the acceptance tests – for example:

* What further chances or periods of time does the provider have to get the system right?
* What rights does the client have at the end of this period?
* What happens if the system is 95 per cent effective but there remain material gaps between contracted and actual performance?
* What effect does this have on price and payment?
* How does the failure affect guarantees and guarantee periods and support arrangements?

TRAINING

* Is training to be included in the services to be provided and, if so, to what extent, level and cost?

- What if the training is poor or some staff need further training – is there something built in to cover this?
- Will that also cover possible future changes in the developed or even third-party software?

THE RIGHTS AND TERM GRANTED

The client will want to have rights that are as broad as possible and the supplier will seek the reverse. Typical issues are as follows.

Territory and purpose

This is normally limited to specified circumstances and is unlikely to be a problem unless the client intends wide-ranging uses or has significant remote access requirements.

Exclusivity

The relevance of exclusivity was referred to above in terms of IP rights, and the agreed concepts will flow through to the software licence terms. It is vital area for the parties to get right as exclusivity will determine what use can be made of the system by other parties, including the provider. Where there is a mix of third-party and bespoke software, there may need to be a distinction as to which part of the software is exclusive, assuming that this is technically possible.

Licensed users

The first question to address is which company is to be the main user and whether the use is to extend to other members of the same group of companies (and possibly to sub-licensees associated with those businesses). This then raises issues of change of control if any of those parties change ownership. If, for example, a subsidiary has rights to use the system (but is not party to the agreement itself), the licence might be limited to its period as part of the group. There may also be a limitation on the number of permitted users or client sites to be served. All these extensions or limitations on use are likely to affect both the software development fee and the maintenance charge, and will also affect the transferability of the rights (see below).

Copies/back-ups and adaptations

The client will want the right to keep appropriate back-ups of the software to guard against any degradation of the original program. Because this is a form of copying, it should be expressly authorized. Amendment or modification of the software is normally prohibited because the intellectual property rights in the software could be affected and the lines of responsibility for any failure would be blurred as a result.

New releases and upgrades

The client needs to think about and provide in the contract for future versions, new releases and substantial upgrades at the outset. New versions may be covered, but the contract will often not cover upgrades on the basis that these will have a materially different specification. This could mean that the client may have to pay all over again just to secure a 5 per cent enhancement. It may therefore be wise to negotiate a beneficial option as to upgrades at the time of the first deal. Updated documentation/guidance for such upgrades should also be required as and when they are issued.

Intellectual property

As mentioned at the start of this chapter, the ownership of and rights to use the IP relating to the technology need to be clearly set out.

PAYMENT ARRANGEMENTS

Acceptance process

Payment by the client for the new software is likely to be in stages, with the final payments tied into delivery and acceptance. This is a potential area for dispute, as the client will wish to ensure that the system is operating as it was expected to operate and will want to retain sufficient sums until this is accomplished, but the developer will not want to hand over the system in full working order without certainty of payment. Clear and workable testing and acceptance processes are again key here.

The costs of *updates and upgrades* need to be considered, in terms of the extent to which these are part of the package of rights on sale, when they are included in the price and when they will incur extra costs. These may well be on common platform standard terms delivered via the Web.

TRANSFERABILITY

Client transfers

If the client, having bought the rights, decides to sell its business, it will want to be able to transfer the system too. If the sale is by takeover (a share sale), no assignment is necessary, but the client would not want to be hamstrung by a change of control clause. With a sale of business and assets as a going concern, the client's ability to assign the software development and maintenance contracts is likely to be a key factor, so the original technology contract needs to cover this. Third-party or proprietary software may require new licences, but there should be a ready market for them. Sometimes the position may be more complex with bespoke software, especially if this is ground-breaking and not generally available. The developer may then not want the licence to be assigned to certain parties, and especially not to its trade competitors or one of their associated group companies. A balance therefore needs to be found between this and the client's needs to be able to assign in most cases.

Developer transfers

The converse may also apply, with the developer wanting to have the flexibility to sell its business and the benefit of the licence agreements (and the benefit/burden of the maintenance obligations) to a third party. The client then needs to consider if that might be a problem. Usually it will not be, but the position might be different in the rare case when the software contains significant content that is unique to the client and could be a material advantage to its competitors. The client would also want to restrict assignment during the development period, when success may be especially reliant on the key developer team.

Transfer within groups is normally non-objectionable, but may be subject to suitable change of control mechanism if the company in question is later sold off to an organization outside its group.

TERMINATION

Once the new software has been developed and installed there should be little desire for the client and very limited rights for the developer to terminate the licence to use it. However, there are some exceptions, examples of which are outlined below.

Misuse

Where the client misuses the software in a way that is outside the licence but not seriously prejudicial, such as exceeding stated limits of use, there should be every chance to remedy or pay a market rate for the additional usage. Termination should be a last resort.

Serious breach

Examples of serious breach likely to be prejudicial to the provider would include unauthorized copying or an attempt to decompile or reverse engineer the software – functions expressly prohibited by most licences – or a significant modification to the software that has major effects on its general operability, which would be likely to impact on any warranty and certainly on the overall maintenance and support aspect of the contract. These breaches may be regarded as irremediable.

Payment failure

Failure to pay the right amounts on time is most likely to be remediable, but severe delay in agreed payment during the development and commissioning phase may give the developer rights to suspend work and/or ultimately terminate the agreement (but only after due warnings). These rights need to be balanced against the client's right to withhold appropriate payment if there has been material default by the developer. This is a fertile area for dispute, and, here again, sensible contract terms and strict observance of these generally offer the best prospects for success.

What is terminated

The client should not accept (unless there is very good reason) that the developer has the right to terminate the software licence itself on the grounds of breach (or termination for other reasons) of the maintenance agreement.

Sub-licences

If there is termination, what effect this will have on any sub-licences that have been granted by the client? Provided any sub-licences were granted in accordance with the terms of the main contract, the contract can provide that they should continue in force even if the head licence is terminated. The sub-licensee would then become a direct licensee of the developer/provider. Otherwise, a sub-licensee is at risk of losing its rights without having been responsible for the original breach by the main client. This might, however, make the developer more cautious about accepting sub-licences, especially if these could become an administrative burden that is not adequately reflected in the fee structure.

Escrow arrangements

The development contract should provide for the source code (the human-readable programming language for the software) to be deposited with an independent escrow agent (such as the NCC Group (www.nccgroup.com)) which would hold it and only release it to the client on the developer's insolvency or established breach of the main agreement. A separate three-party escrow agreement will be entered into to reflect this. Most such agreements, however, provide for the source code to be delivered up by the escrow agent only if the developer becomes insolvent, or possibly because of termination following the developer's breach. But this leaves the client at risk if the contract is terminated for some other good reason, such as no-fault notice. Standard escrow agreements should therefore be looked at carefully and adapted as necessary to protect both parties from logical outcomes.

WARRANTIES AND INDEMNITIES

The principles

The provider warranties will depend on the circumstances, the type of system and the software. Warranties in this sense should be distinguished from the limited guarantee that may be given (and often called 'warranty') as to the performance of the system/software, which is more properly covered in the performance section of the agreement. It may in effect be no more than an initial free maintenance period and may indeed operate as an effective exemption clause if it precludes other redress (in which case UCTA might apply).

Mutual warranties

As with most commercial contracts, each party will usually be expected to warrant that it is entitled to enter the agreement and able to perform it on the terms set out.

Copyright warranty

The provider should warrant either that it owns the copyright in the software or that it is entitled by the copyright owner to grant the rights set out, that there are no third-party claims against the software and that it does not itself infringe third-party rights. This should extend to subcontractor work. With proprietary (off-the-shelf) software, the provider will at best pass on such warranties as it may have under its own purchase/ licence contract. As with trademarks, warranties may be limited to the territories in which the software is permitted to be used.

Software defects

The client will wish to know that there are no material problems and to have effective redress if there are defects or bugs, ultimately with the right to cancel (and seek the return of its money) if the defects materially detract from the working of the system or its intended use. This may be separate from acceptance testing.

Viruses may be different. Even if great care is taken, there can be no absolute guarantee against infection. Indemnities might reasonably therefore be limited to the effects of failure to comply with industry-standard virus-checkers and, even then, liability may be limited.

Indemnities and claims handling

Indemnities (dealt with elsewhere in this book) need to be carefully drafted and limited. The client will expect to receive an indemnity from the provider in respect of third-party IP claims, and this might be mutual to the extent of any IP contributed by the client, if this is used elsewhere by the provider. If a claim arises, each party should be obliged to inform and consult with the other as to how it is best handled and to take any practical steps reasonably available to secure any necessary licence or to resolve the issue. If matters go further, the party giving the indemnity may want either conduct of the claim or the need to approve its handling and any settlement, with consent not to be unreasonably withheld to avoid a sensible settlement being blocked.

LIMITATION OF LIABILITY (SEE ALSO CHAPTER 7)

To counter the express and implied terms of the contract, the developer will usually wish to restrict claims for its own breach. This is a complex area, and the legal treatment of exclusion and limitations clauses is set out in some detail in Chapter 7, together with some case summaries very relevant to technology contracts. Suppliers should note that insistence on their own written standard terms of business will bring in the unfair contract terms tests of UCTA, which require the limitations to be examined for 'reasonableness'. An extreme clause, a material disparity in the relative bargaining position of the parties and/or a blanket refusal of the supplier to change terms will all increase the risk that an exemption clause will fail in its intended effect. For the better management of risk between the parties, it may be worth breaking down any exemption clauses into separate parts, according to the nature and extent of risk. Some key steps to take are as follows:

- Try to narrow the obligations first, rather than have broad obligations and restrict liability.
- Specify where and how far liability will be accepted (such as through specific positive warranty obligations), rather than exclude liability entirely.
- Don't try to exclude non-excludable statutory and implied warranties.
- Don't limit liability for personal injury or death caused by negligence.
- Do state that limitations do not exclude or limit liability for fraudulent action.
- Watch the wording carefully and avoid phrases such as 'consequential loss' unless you are clear what they mean.
- Consider different levels of limitation for different types of loss. For example, loss of client's data (which might involve both costs of restoring the data as well as consequential issues arising from the data becoming publicly available) or damage by viruses might need different approaches.
- It may help a supplier's case for having its exemption clause accepted to offer express warranties relating to services and deliverables, possibly supported by an agreement to seek to rectify any problem issues, to limit liability to those warranties and to specify a fixed maximum liability.
- Consider also:
  - negotiating fair compensation (liquidated damages) for delays or other specific loss; and
  - whether liquidated damages should be the client's sole remedy.
    If so, ensure that the claim is in the alternative (that is, not additional to the liquidated amount) and limited to the specific breaches, so that the exemption clause does not operate as a general exclusion for fundamental breach, which a court is unlikely to uphold.
- With group companies or sub-licensees, consider the third-party rights and change of control clause.
- Consider who can insure against what risks, for what amounts and at what cost. This affects how courts view the exemption clause. If the provider could have managed the risk and the client would be unable to obtain insurance at all or at reasonable cost for the issue in question, an exclusion or exemption clause may be more likely to be struck down.
- If possible, make any exemption clause flexible enough for possible severance (see Chapter 4) so that, even if some parts of it failed, others could remain effective.

FORCE MAJEURE (SEE ALSO CHAPTERS 4 ('COMMON CONTRACT TERMS') AND 7 ('NEGOTIATING EXEMPTION CLAUSES'))

In technology contracts, if force majeure does apply, there will come a time when both developer and client would prefer to be released from the contract. The client may want a shorter period, especially where time is critical and other factors mean that the new system has to be fully operational by a specified date. Maintenance contract charges will normally not be levied during any suspension period, but the position is not so simple where there is a development contract. Many force majeure clauses do not deal with the question of payment on termination because of force majeure. The system may be almost complete, capable of being finalized with modest adjustment. On the other hand, the work done by the provider may be completely wasted; in this case, the client will lose vital time and have to start all over again, but the provider will have incurred cost and may expect to be paid pro rata. There is no easy answer. One approach is to have provision for an independent person to be appointed to decide a fair value based on the value of the work done or its value to the client. In the absence of any other provision, the client would probably be obliged to pay and the provider entitled to receive what was due and payable under the contract to that date, but no more, which may suit both – or neither – of the parties.

CONFIDENTIALITY (SEE ALSO CHAPTER 5)

Know-how is best covered expressly in the development contract, and the information marked and kept confidential. Her are some other points to consider:

- Is there a non-disclosure agreement (NDA)? If so, check its terms as it may be limited in time or fall away when the development agreement is signed.
- Are there aspects of the system or functionality itself which are not to be revealed to third parties for any reason?
- Are the terms of the agreement themselves confidential and not to be disclosed – for example, because of preferential financial terms or other aspects unique to the parties?
- Is the existence of the agreement to be disclosed? If so, the parties may want to pre-agree any press release of other details.

BOILERPLATE CLAUSES (SEE ALSO CHAPTERS 4 AND 17)

Third-party rights – consider group companies and possible sub-licensees, so that they have direct recourse if things go wrong. Watch also the linkage with exemption clauses if the exemption is limited to the client alone and not its fellow group companies, if they are entitled to benefit.

Entire agreement clauses should be checked – are there any prior representations that the client (or the provider) is still really relying on but which are not in the written contract?

Choice of law and jurisdiction clauses

Many IT contracts provide for US state law and courts to apply to any disputes, even where the installation is being carried out in the UK. This sort of clause would probably be ineffective in consumer sales, but also might impose an unreasonable burden on business clients based in the UK, which would be especially significant where the client is using the new system or software to provide services to UK-based third parties.

Maintenance Agreements (see also Chapters 12 and 13)

Maintenance (or support) terms may be set out either as a schedule to the main development agreement or as an agreed form of document to be entered into at go-live. The advantage of the former is that cross-reference can be made to all the defined terms and many of the general provisions of the main agreement, but the latter gives a self-contained agreement that does not need to cross-refer to the main agreement.

Term and renewal of agreement

The provider will want a long enough period to justify setting up the maintenance arrangements, whereas the client will want sufficient flexibility in the support agreement to be able to change provider, or subcontract elsewhere for a limited purpose or period, if the support is inadequate. Typically, the support contract will be renewable annually unless terminated on a stated period of notice before the anniversary/renewal date. In practice, much will depend on the alternatives available. The more bespoke the system and the more difficult it would be to find alternative support services at reasonable cost, the more the client needs to consider both the ability to renew on reasonable terms and the potential effects of failure to receive the required level of support in the future.

Service levels

These are key to maintenance agreements, as they set out the speed of response and resolution times expected or required of the provider. The provider will, however, generally be prepared to commit to *action*, rather than commit to a *solution*, and there will be different times and charging structures for remote or on-site attendance. There is also the identity and experience of the support team. The client may expect those involved with the design and development of new software to be available for support, but the provider's business may require them to be concentrating on development and not maintenance issues. If the provider wants to delegate support to a third party, this will raise issues of competence, training, product knowledge and, possibly, confidentiality.

Termination

Apart from termination for insolvency and un-remedied material breach, persistent breach can create problems, either from the client in late payment or from the provider in late or poor support. The latter may be covered by specific provisions in the SLA, leading to the eventual right to terminate for persistent support failure. In any case, termination of the maintenance agreement should not automatically terminate the software licence.

The source code

This remains a vital part of the mix. The same issues as raised under escrow agreements above will be relevant here.

Summary

An example technology agreement checklist, picking up many of the issues raised in this chapter, is set out in Appendix E.

16 *Internet-related Contracts*

Introduction – use and misuse of the Internet: the battle lines – the E-Commerce Directive and safe harbours – liability for Internet content – common features in Internet-related contracts – web links – content licensing, hosting and reseller agreements – summary and checklist

Introduction

A MOVING TARGET

This area of law is moving even faster than perhaps any other area covered in this book – so fast in fact that there will be many new developments by the time this book is printed. At the same time there is a need to keep some sense of overall bearings and, whilst, therefore, the detail of future laws will take some time to emerge and will continue to develop, many of the underlying legal principles and areas of debate can now be discerned.

WEBSITES

This chapter follows up Chapter 10 on consumer and website sales and Chapter 15 on technology agreements with a behind-the-scenes view of some legal aspects of Internet and Web operations, including how the law relates to the many new technological and social issues raised by the Internet. Behind the World Wide Web is another complex web of contractual relationships, and the analogy illustrates the point that, in this realm, the connections may not be direct, because the structure of a web depends not just on the main strands (radials) spun out from the centre, but also on their connections with the cross-links (spirals).

ISPS

The practical centre of the Web is occupied by the cluster of Internet service providers (ISPs), which are the main interface between the World Wide Web and the user. Through Web 2.0 technologies parties have direct contact with one another, which helps drive the growth of social and business networks. The structure depends on the ISP at the centre; customers ('subscribers') contract with ISPs radially to provide an Internet connection. The subscribers and third parties communicate with one another via both radials and spirals, creating business contracts in the process by direct e-mails or a website, facilitated through the ISP, but the third party may have no direct contract with the ISP.

TERMS USED IN THIS CHAPTER

Cache/caching: [providing] a temporary storage area for rapid access to frequently accessed data.

Consumer: a buyer of a product (or service) for their own [non-business] use.

Domain name: the name of a specific website.

DRM: digital rights management.

End–user: a consumer using a digital product.

EULA: end-user licence agreement.

Hosting: providing facilities for storing data on an Internet-connected server.

ISP: Internet service provider.

P2P: peer to peer (such as personal user to personal user).

Subscriber: a business or consumer using the Internet via a contract with an ISP.

URL: Uniform Resource Locator – unique locator for a website.

WWW: World Wide Web.

Use and Misuse of the Internet: The Battle Lines

THE LIABILITY ISSUE

The 'pure' ISP has no immediate control over what a third party does with its Internet connection, but what if the subscriber uses it in ways that are illegal? This might be anything from copyright infringement through defamation to promoting terrorism. Look at this another way. If the subscriber uses an Internet connection to run a business which puts third parties in touch with one another, should the subscriber have any responsibility for what those parties then get up to? Consider a dating website. One would probably not expect the operator of the site, be they ISP or subscriber, to have any liability for what the dating parties do when they meet, perhaps beyond a duty of care on the operator to give sensible guidelines for personal safety. But if a website deliberately sets up or devotes a site to illegal activities, one might take a different view. Where, in this mix, would be the position of a marketplace or auction site, such as eBay, or a site encouraging P2P file-sharing? Both auction and P2P activities can be used for entirely proper and lawful means, but they can also be misused by those wishing to breach trademark or copyright laws. When does facilitation amount to encouragement such as to justify legal responsibility? And if ISPs have a responsibility, how far should that go? ISPs' view is that their role is no more or less than that of a conduit, like the post office or a telecoms company, and to expect them to act as censors is unfair and unrealistic. Providers of content and others affected by intellectual property infringement take a different view when the 'mere conduit' element seems designed to assist unlawful copying or similar activity.

THE E-COMMERCE DIRECTIVE AND THE 'SAFE HARBOUR' PROVISIONS

The E-Commerce Regulations applying the E-Commerce Directive in the UK give an ISP the 'safe harbour' of immunity (both civil and criminal) as a 'service provider', which means a provider of information society services (also mentioned in Chapter 10) with the characteristics of:

- providing services for the processing and storage of data,
- normally for remuneration (although this might just mean 'in the course of a business' even if not specifically charged for),
- at a distance,
- by means of electronic equipment,
- at the request of a recipient of that service.

The safe harbour can be achieved by: a) acting as a '*mere conduit*' in transmitting content; b) '*caching*' content; and c) '*hosting*' content (see definitions above). This is subject to the proviso (in the case of hosting) that the ISP has no actual knowledge of unlawful activity or, where and when it does have such knowledge, it acts 'expeditiously' to remove or disable access to the offending material. The recitals to the directive do, however, state, in effect, that the 'hosting' safe harbour can only apply in relation to the technical means of making the transmission efficient, seemingly aimed at mirroring the role of telecoms carriers and excluding any kind of editorial involvement.

National variations

EU directives, however, often leave some flexibility in the detailed implementation up to member states, so there is not necessarily complete consistency in the EU within the broad framework of the directive. And the gap may be wider internationally. Whilst the 'pure conduit' element of EU law is broadly matched by US legislation (the Digital Millennium Copyright Act of 1998), the position is more complex with website businesses that have some additional processing role in relation to the data they hold. So, in 2008, eBay won a battle in the USA and lost a battle in France as to its liability for the regular sales of counterfeit products through its online auction sites.

Removal of offending material

ISPs are not obliged either to monitor the information they hold or transmit or to take proactive steps to check for illegal activity, but, if they are specifically advised of infringement, they must act. This advice is typically in the form of a complaint from someone alleging that defamatory material about them has been posted or a formal 'take-down' notice from a trademark, copyright or other intellectual property rights holder, referring to a specific item, asserting its exclusive rights in the relevant territory to that item and requiring the ISP to remove the offending material or message. The ISP must then comply with reasonable speed or face a claim for infringement.

The case of *Metropolitan International Schools* v. *Designtechnica and Google* (2009) is an interesting interim decision – and review of the law – on a case of alleged defamation on the Internet identified through the Google search engine. The judge declined an invitation to create separate protection for search engines and preferred to reach his conclusion by common law principles: that Google was not a 'publisher' of the material in the legal sense, was unaware of the fact that the material may be offending before the complaint was received and, whilst the take-down process may not have happened as quickly as it might, this did not mean – on the facts of the case – that there had been authorization or acquiescence on the part of Google through its employees.

But even removal of the material will not necessarily stop the offender from putting the same content back up again, and they may do so either under their original name or under a new account name. To keep checking and issuing notices in respect of the same offender becomes a hugely time-consuming and ultimately impossible task for the rights holder.

Personal action

Some rights holders believe that it is now better to target the offender rather than the offending material, with the aim of removing the offender from the game. One way of doing this – and discouraging others – is to take direct legal action for rights infringement. But this risks a negative perception of bullying by a major media company and the problem of tracing the offender through only a domain name or e-mail address. The real identity of the offender will presumably be known to the ISP with which they have their Internet connection account, but the ISP will claim that the Data Protection Act restricts such personal information being made available to third parties. So there is another balance between privacy and IP protection to be considered.

Rights holders have responded by pressing for limiting the ISP's immunity where there is regular evidence of infringement. One approach is that, if the abuse continues, the ISP should ultimately be obliged to remove the subscriber's ISP connection. ISPs have been, perhaps predictably, indignant at such proposals. They argue that this is not an issue of national importance, as, for example, the free circulation of terrorist material or even paedophilia might be, but a matter for rights holders. Not only do they not wish to have to debar their own customers, but they also strongly resist any compulsion to do so.

SOCIAL AND CULTURAL ISSUES

Respect for copyright

The arguments as to liability also highlight a cultural issue. Much official rhetoric has encouraged out-of-copyright information being made widely, and often freely, available online, and respect for copyright has often been overlooked and, in other cases, deliberately flouted, leading to the growing (but wholly incorrect) belief among Internet users that if it's available online, it's available to copy. Indeed, the notion of the right to an Internet connection being a human right protected across Europe by the European Convention on Human Rights is gaining ground. The concept of responsibility as the price for even Internet freedom seems slower to emerge.

Many of these issues came to a head in the debates on, and lobbying related to, new EU telecoms regulations during 2008 and 2009, especially around the so-called Bono amendment proposed in 2008 by the French socialist MEP Guy Bono (rather than his U2 namesake). Linked to a debate about the proportionality of offence and sanction, the Bono amendment essentially sought to make it a legal requirement in the EU that, as Internet access is a fundamental human right of freedom of expression and information, anyone seeking to cut off Internet access must get a court order before doing so unless public security is threatened, in which case they can cut off first and seek court approval afterwards. However, the less socialist parts of the actual French government responded to the perceived misuse of the Internet with more traditional Gallic panache. The so-called Olivennes Accord, later brought into French law as the Creation and Internet Law, established an effective agreement between the relevant players in part of the media in France (with the addition of a certain amount of presidential muscle) to introduce the 'three strikes' rule. An infringer will be given two specific written warnings, pointing out the abuse and the consequences. If there is a further abuse, the offender will be 'out', by being disconnected from the Internet. To ensure fair play some form of judicial order will be required before disconnection, as well as some form of registration to ensure that the infringer does not just open an account with another ISP. There have been countermoves to declare this law unlawful under European law, and the position continues to unfold.

In the meantime the so-called *Pirate Bay* case in Sweden in 2009, where the Swedish criminal authorities successfully prosecuted Peter Sunde, Fredrik Neij, Gottfrid Svartholm and Carl Lundström (in a decision announced on 17 April 2009), with the harsh penalty of prison sentences for copyright infringement handed down to the offenders, has sparked a major backlash such that an official 'Piracy Party' was immediately launched and became represented in the European parliament following the 2009 MEP elections. The debate over file-sharing and the matching of rights and responsibilities clearly has a long way to play out.

DRM

Digital rights management (DRM) is the epicentre of another battle. Such controls, embedded in the digital product, may limit the way in which the product can be sold and/or used. The aim is to prevent sales outside permitted territories and to stop action such as copying, pasting and printing of content ('right-click functionality'). Such controls, sometimes coming under the banner of 'technical protection measures' (TPMs), are regarded as essential by many media content providers – a view not shared by all users, especially when the DRM prevents legitimate copyright usage.

Format shifting and interoperability may help here, by permitting end-users to reproduce a purchased digital product in a different format, in order to be able to play that product on the user's other digital devices. This would enable, for example, an electronic game bought by a consumer to be used on the consumer's PC, mobile phone or PDA, so long as it is not copied to someone else.

End-user licence agreement (EULA)

This is the name given to the agreement that a consumer may be required to sign as a condition of purchase; if this is a condition, then the EULA will need to comply and be consistent with the laws applying to consumer sales (see Chapter 10). At the time of writing, many major US companies providing consumer technology, in seeking to impose standard US legal terms on consumers worldwide, seem to be slow in adjusting their policies to comply with English and European law.

Alternative approaches

As technology continuously evolves, alternative approaches are being considered. Improved filtering may help, and methods such as fingerprinting and watermarking digital content may assist in proving unlawful activity, but not necessarily in its detection in the first place. But here again there is tension between the limitations placed on a digital product and the concept that it should be free for a purchaser to use as desired after purchase.

Liability for Internet Content

INCREASED RISK

The joy, and the risk, of the Internet is that communication can be almost instantaneous. Since e-mails and website content are, for most purposes, regarded as equivalent to writing at the point of receipt or download, and many go through little or no editorial process, it follows that the risks of defamation, copyright infringement, breach of privacy/confidentiality/data protection laws and other third-party liabilities are hugely increased by Internet use. There may also be criminal liability for obscenity or public order offences or similar state legislation. These risks in turn raise the questions of who is liable for any claims that result, where they are liable and how, if at all, they can and should protect themselves by contract.

INTERNATIONAL REACH

The case of *Dow Jones* v. *Gutnick* is featured in the next chapter on the international dimension, but needs to be highlighted here because it established the principle – now seemingly gaining widespread international acceptance – that legal liability for content can be created in any country where offending material can be accessed or downloaded. If any offence is judged by local law it follows that the content will be judged by local law, so that even something non-infringing in the home country could give a cause for action in another country where it is downloaded if it is unlawful under local law. It is still something of an open question whether the same principle applies if there is merely a web link on the original site. The legal rules covering many of these issues are different, but there are common themes. For example, as described above, a service provider should not be liable under English law if and to the extent that its role was merely providing the technical conduit for the offending communication and it took reasonable care in dealing with any situation and/or in removing access to the offending content as soon as becoming aware of it. However, even a small element of editorial involvement or 'moderation' of the content could cause loss of the exemption and create the same liability for the service provider as, for instance, a publisher would have, and when the website openly or permissively facilitates infringement, new questions are being raised as to whether the ISP safe harbour provisions do, or even should, apply.

User-generated content (UGC)

Even greater problems arise with networking sites which rely on UGC. These are hugely popular, but have risks attached to those involved. UGC may well be user-generated, but it may not be user-created (user-created content or UCC) if the content was not the original work of the particular contributor. Clips on social networking sites from TV, films, books or even live performances posted by individuals are rarely authorized by the relevant copyright owners. Even if the material is user-created, it might still be infringing; examples would include the recording and broadcasting of a third party's pop song without consent or a video showing the private life of someone who had a reasonable expectation of privacy and had not consented to the use. Similar arguments apply here as with auction sites, and, at the time of writing, major battles are being fought to introduce some effective industry-wide controls, failing which there will be pressure for more legislation.

Personal data

Finally – and the list could go on – there are issues as to the holding and processing of personal data created by all these activities. Posting a video clip including other people on a social network site may well breach the Data Protection Act. At another level, all firms selling through the Web, or their fulfilment companies, assemble a considerable volume of personal data through the order, sales and delivery process – data which will need to be carefully maintained and kept secure and which may well prove commercially valuable. As referred to in Chapter 5 on 'Confidentiality, Privacy and Data Protection', contracts in this area need to be clear as to who has the relevant rights and the responsibility that goes with it.

Common Features in Internet-related Contracts

Apart from the normal and boilerplate provisions of any contract related to the Internet, there are several common features to be considered in relation to any agreement with a strong digital bias. Internet-related contracts will need to consider many of the issues reviewed throughout this book, but with a specific slant. Many licences will be non-exclusive, territory-specific and short-term, renewable subject to ongoing fee payments and compliance with terms and conditions. But there will be exceptions where individual and longer-term rights are likely to be required.

ISP TERMS AND CONDITIONS WITH SUBSCRIBERS

ISPs are subject to a range of possible technical interruptions and other service issues, and will not want to guarantee matters such as continuity of service or freedom from viruses. The same applies to confidentiality; many business Internet and e-mail usage terms expressly remind users that Internet transmissions are, for the most part, not secure and, accordingly, confidentiality cannot be guaranteed. ISPs will nevertheless require contractual protection from subscribers by way of a covenant not to take any action designed or likely to interfere with, or otherwise affect, the ISP's servers or other connections. As discussed, ISPs should be able to remain immune from content claims, but will want direct agreement from the subscriber or user not to store or transmit offensive, sexually explicit or other infringing content, probably coupled with an indemnity in respect of any claim by, or liability to, a third party. This is likely to form part of, or be linked to, an 'acceptable use policy'. ISPs may be advised to seek the contractual right to remove content if they are obliged to, and possibly even if they consider that it may be infringing, and even to suspend the customer's Internet connection, however loath they would be to do so in practice. They are likely to disclaim liability for content that goes astray and remind users to back up their own material. Many ISP terms are still dominated by customer warranties and wholesale exclusions of liability on the part of the ISP, that are potentially invalid or unenforceable under English law, especially with end-user sales. However, some points for the business customer to consider are:

- certainty as to the set-up and ongoing cost
- the extent and speed of Internet access – more especially any limitations on access by time, volume or otherwise
- what service and support functions are available and the extent (or lack) of guarantees of connectivity/permitted downtime
- the level of security features
- cancellation rights on reasonable notice and without penalty if unhappy with the service – or, for any reason, with necessary ISP assistance in the migration
- a clear contact point, not dependent on the Internet if your connection is already down!

DOMAIN NAMES AND TERMS

Domain names were mentioned in Chapter 14 as an important form of intellectual property. More specifically, a domain name is an alphabetical form of a unique IP (Internet protocol) address to enable a computer search to locate the relevant website on the Web, normally through a web browser. Domain name servers translate the (usually) easy-to-remember alphabetical domain name into an IP number. There are various levels of domain names, starting with top-level domain names (TLD) which may either be generic, like .com and .net (gTLD) or country-specific, such as .uk and .fr, with a second level to indicate additions such as commercial usage (for example, .co.uk for business) or other organizations (.org.uk). The unique part of the name is the preceding part – typically the name of the business or individual. Add the appropriate 'http' or 'www' prefix and this becomes the unique locator or URL for that website. At the time of writing, further, potentially wide-ranging, changes in the domain-name regime are being introduced.

ICANN is the Internet Corporation for Assigned Numbers, an international industry body with the remit and power to oversee (as well as delegate, such as to country code managers) the domain name system and determine a range of disputes. Terms and conditions relating to domain name registration will therefore refer any dispute to the relevant dispute resolution processes. There are generally two contracts involved in setting up a domain name: one with the domain name registrar (with the ISP or other party acting as your agent) and the other with the ISP, for additional services such as e-mail. The Web registrar and ICANN have no jurisdiction over the latter contract. Because of its importance, businesses might seek the longest reasonable name registration period they can, and they will need to be particularly vigilant around the renewal period to ensure that what might have become a valuable domain name is not lost at the critical time. Similar considerations will apply to the domain name contract as those set out for contracts with ISPs above, although the domain name terms should be shorter and simpler.

WEBSITE-BUILDING/DESIGN

Many businesses now specialize in website construction and design. What they can offer will vary, but the basics will be a working website with good functionality and design. The developer's standard terms and conditions should not, however, necessarily be accepted without negotiation. One reason for this is to achieve clarity on the ownership or rights to use the key content of the site and to protect confidential information or processes of the client's business.

A typical *website construction agreement* would adapt the principles set out in Chapter 12 on contracts for services and in parts of Chapter 15 on technology contracts, with the client normally wanting a complete job done at a fixed price within an agreed timescale. There will be a specification setting out what the site will do and how it will operate, as the user experience will be important to the site's success. If there is to be ongoing support, the terms and prices for this should be stated. As with software development contracts, the acceptance process will be critical, and the terms should allow for sufficient testing before the site goes live. If the acceptance testing is unsatisfactory, measured against the specification and any other explicit requirements, the contract should set out the process and possible remedies for resolving matters (see Chapter 15). The client will also want considerable flexibility in making changes to the website, both to improve those aspects that are found not to work as well as hoped and to reflect changes in the way in which the site is used and in the clients' own business. The construction agreement should not therefore act as a straitjacket.

Intellectual property ownership in the site construction, design and content is another critical issue. The developer will not want to give away the key technology for building and driving the site, but the client will want to ensure that it can lawfully use that technology and that the site content provided by the client remains fully in the client's ownership. The client may also want the overall look and feel of the site to be unique to it. In many ways, it is the client's digital shop-front and is potentially as important as any other part of its overall brand image. One answer for the client is to identify the elements of the design that are bespoke, in the sense of being created expressly for it, and for the contract to assign or exclusively license these elements to the client. The developer, however, might just wish to consider this further, first to ensure that transfer of the bespoke elements does not include something that is reuseable elsewhere without detriment to the client and, second, as to whether to grant licence, rather than assign, with the grant and exclusivity being limited to that particular website. This would help to ensure both that the client did not 'borrow' the design for another site without coming back to the developer and that the developer could effectively have the design back if the client were to cease using the site. The client then in turn needs to ensure that no element unique to the business, including product or service branding, would ever be transferred or licensed to a third party.

Legal compliance also needs to be planned. If the web developer is also to provide the customer supply and fulfilment technology and content, including sales terms and privacy policy, the developer should warrant that this will fully comply with all applicable consumer or other relevant laws. More often, this is left to the client, who needs to take careful stock of the principles and the latest laws relating to consumer sales contracts.

Web links

Links from one website to another are a regular and essential part of the web-user experience, with the search engine linkage to possible relevant sites being replicated across the Internet spectrum. The casual user may take these links for granted, but the business using web links should have at least a basic understanding of how the technology can be applied and what the legal implications may be. What follows is a brief look at parts of an increasingly complex subject.

WEB LINK OUTLINES

The most straightforward link is probably the hyperlink, an embedded electronic address, normally highlighted, directing the user to another website by way of a single click on the hyperlink. Another type of link acts as a pointer and operates to pull the linked site, or part of it, into the first website. Another type, a deep link, bypasses much of the linked site's homepage content and goes direct to a section of the linked site. What is especially significant about these other types of link is that they do not take the user to the linked website as such, but pull in part of the other site's content, either transparently (where the framework of the linked site can still be seen) or blindly, as in the case of a deep link, by integrating that content – and possibly other third-party content – into the first website. This process can be extended by techniques such as 'page-jacking' by which users are diverted to a wholly different site, which may unrelated and offensive. Clearly web links have the potential to create confusion and raise difficult questions of legal liability.

WEB LINKS – BENEFITS AND RISKS

Branding and reputation are obvious issues arising through the linking process. The law has struggled to keep up with the fast pace of these developments, but does strive to find a remedy where there is both misuse or potential misrepresentation and the prospect of resultant damage. In some cases, links have been embedded in order to ambush the browser seeking one particular product or service into a wholly different site. Legal remedies include a claim for passing-off, where there is a deliberate appropriation of the goodwill of the first business by the second, to unlawful interference with communications. The comparative advertising rules or 2008 Unfair Trading Regulations may also give an effective remedy where consumers are being misled.

Potential problems also lurk for website owners who voluntarily add a hyperlink to their own website. Three examples illustrate this. The first risk is that the link may suggest some association that is not wanted or accepted by the linked site. This could itself give grounds for a passing-off claim by the second site against the first. The second risk is that the link may be held to imply some kind of endorsement of the linked site or its contents. This could be serious if the second site contains material that is offensive or an abuse of third-party rights. In 2008 a French court held a publisher liable for an online article which contained a link though to a story on what was effectively a gossip site which contained material that, at least under French law, infringed the privacy of a well-known French actor (Oliver Martinez). The French court, in *Martinez* v. *Mirror Group Newspapers* (2008), held that adding the link was an editorial decision by the first publisher, who was thus responsible to Martinez for the privacy infringement on the second (gossip) site. This decision has not been followed, and will not necessarily be followed, in all cases or by all national courts, but it does highlight the risk, especially for UK-based media, of being liable for breach of French privacy laws. The third risk is prospective copyright (or even trademark) infringement through using parts of another site as headlines, even if linked back to the other site, as in the *Shetland Times* v. *Wills* case as long ago as 1997.

The following questions should be addressed as a result of these factors:

- Which sites are you thinking of linking to?
- Do those sites have stated terms or policies relating to links?
- Have they taken action against unauthorized links in the past?
- Is your planned linking transparent and not misleading?
- Are there issues relating to trademarks or copyright (protected content)? If so, ideally don't use protected content on your site (especially the trademark of another) and, in any case, make sure that protected content is distinguished and properly attributed on your site so that it does not look like yours.
- Have you entered into a proper linking contract with the third-party site if you can? (See below.)
- Have you included a prominent disclaimer on your site for content on the linked site? It is not foolproof, but may help resist the editorial decision argument that prevailed in the *Martinez* case.

The converse propositions apply to other website owners or operators, who may be advised to monitor links to their site on a regular basis.

A possible disclaimer (but no guarantees given!) might be:

Links are provided in this site to third party websites which may be of interest to readers. Please note that we neither own nor control these third party sites or their content. Accordingly a) we can give no assurance that any information on any such site is correct and up to date; b) we can accept no liability for loss or damage that may arise directly or indirectly from use of such sites or reliance on any content on or referred to in them; and c) such sites may contain content protected by law (such as but not limited to trademarks, copyright, privacy and data protection) which you may not use without appropriate consents.

LINKING AGREEMENTS

As mentioned above, a formal linking agreement is the most secure way of protecting against claims from the linked website operator. These are fairly technical, but some factors to consider (outside the normal contract issues of term, warranties, liability, termination and suchlike) would include:

- the type of link
- the type of content – including what may be and what may not be linked
- framing and visibility of URLs – including above or below the fold (visible screen)
- branding and trademark use
- copyright issues and any specific rights granted
- any development responsibilities and costs
- responsibility for maintenance, response times and security and other service level issues
- password and/or other access requirements
- controls and approvals
- advertising issues
- data protection compliance
- fees, payment and audit
- specific confidentiality provisions.

Content Licensing, Hosting and Reseller Agreements

Beyond simple links, there may be other arrangements between businesses relating to the provision of website content. This section looks at some themes relating to current models and implications.

CONTENT LICENSING AND HOSTING

A digital content licensing agreement is likely to be a further step, and might, for example, permit a retailer or e-tailer to include on its website content from a supplier, such as product and catalogue details and prices. There may be an intermediary third-party supplier of 'middleware' – software which holds and accesses the supplier's information and is capable of processing and responding to customer enquiries. Such an agreement is advisable where there is interplay between the roles of the parties and where there might be any confusion as to respective content ownership or control.

The agreement contents would confirm the ownership of the various IP rights and the respective obligations of the parties. For example, the supplier might specify what content is supplied in what form (and how selective it may be), how it is hosted and indexed and how the search facility is to be provided. The supplier will also want to have the right to withdraw specific content from the site – for example, because there is a problem with it. Then there will be the consumer-facing part of the application with viewing and searching access, technical service provisions and terms and conditions relating to these. The e-tailer will need to maintain the customer website, create a search and enquiry facility compatible with the supplier's, disable right-click functions and track usage and compliance with the supplier's terms and conditions. The supplier needs to remember that an e-tailer in this situation may hold large parts of the supplier's intellectual property in readily usable or transmissible form and will be well advised to approach negotiations with that in mind.

Website advertising is associated with hosting. This area has a fast-developing life and subculture of its own well beyond the general scope of this book. The supplier is well advised, however, to think carefully about the advertising content, the revenue stream and the controls that should reasonably be put in place. One approach is to ensure that the advertising markets the supplier's product rather than anything else. As this may also involve use of the supplier's trademark, care needs to be taken with how and where the content is used.

SAMPLE CONTENT LICENSING AGREEMENT CLAUSES

The following are examples of some provisions that might apply in a content licence. These are, of course, limited and illustrative only of this type of agreement, requiring the normal framework of an enforceable contract to be constructed around them. Each contract needs to be considered on its merits and own facts, and many clauses on these issues are much more complex or far-reaching (whether this is always required or not!)

Definitions (examples only)

Content *means all text, still or moving images, artwork, [watermarks etc], audio or other data or materials related to [type of content to be provided] [together with all digital files and supporting or related information, programs, processes, updates, revisions or new editions] provided by [Content Provider] to [Client] in relation to this agreement.*

Permitted Use *means the ability for the Client to hold, display, run, transmit, translate into different formats or otherwise process or utilize in digital or other form the Content on [or via] the Permitted Website.*

Permitted Website *means the website at the URL [www.[.............] so long as this is owned and controlled by Client.*

Provision of content

Content Provider will provide and update [frequency of update] the Content to Client [set out methodology for this] so that as updated the Content is substantially complete, correct and accurate in relation to its overall subject matter.

Permitted use and limitations

3.1 *Subject to clause 3.2 Content Provider grants to Client during the Term the non-exclusive right to use and integrate the Content for the Permitted Use.*

3.2 *Client may not use or display or otherwise deal with the Content in any way other than the Permitted Use including, but not limited to [set out any specific limitations/ exclusions].*

3.3   Client will not copy [except as to one back-up copy of current Content to be retained by
       Client during the Term only], modify, disassemble, reverse engineer or otherwise separate,
       extract any data from or tamper with the Content [except as strictly required for the
       Permitted Use].

Security measures

Each of Content Provider and Client will use reasonable [industry-standard] technological
security and protection measures [including e.g. encryption etc] to protect Content in its
possession or under its control from unauthorized use or access [or infection].

Proprietary rights

Client acknowledges Content Provider's proprietary rights in the Content [and will acknowledge
such rights in suitable form on each Permitted Website using or displaying any part of the
Content].

WEBSITE RESELLER AND DISTRIBUTION AGREEMENTS

Another stage in the process – possibly implicit if there is a content licensing agreement
– might be some form of reseller or distribution agreement for a supplier's products via
an e-tailer's website. This develops concepts in sales or supply terms and conditions, such
as those discussed in Chapter 9, where the products are in physical form, into the digital
arena.

   Territorial or other restrictions on resale are likely to be an issue (subject to competition
law constraints). Whilst similar issues might arise with physical products, digital sales are
not subject to the restraints of physical delivery and are even more difficult to control
where there is no direct correlation between the number of products manufactured and the
number sold and transmission is so fluid. If the e-tailer holds the product in digital form,
it will have the ability to replicate the product more or less without limit. For example,
consumer books are most often sold on the basis of exclusive territories according to
the publishing rights granted. This in turn may involve appropriate 'metadata' being
supplied to the e-tailer by all relevant publishers. This metadata would specify, among
other things, the exclusive territory in which the relevant edition may legally be sold.
As there may be more than one publisher with the same book for different territories
(typically US and UK publishers for their respective areas), the metadata needs to be
supplied by all publishers and acted on by the e-tailer and all channel partners. Any
breach in that structure is likely to cause inroads into the territorial copyright granted by
the author and is thus likely to be a matter of concern for the publishers concerned, and
also ultimately for the author.

   Channel partners are the third parties linked to the e-tailer – for example, by providing
a linked website through which the digital product may be sold. Channel partners are
unlikely to be parties to the original contracts between the supplier and the e-tailer, but
their compliance is important, especially to territoriality and the thorny issue of security
of the digital product. Earlier comments in this chapter show the importance of some
effective method of protecting digital products against unauthorized reproduction, such

as DRM or another suitable form of encryption. The reseller agreement will want to be as precise as possible on where this responsibility lies.

Other terms

There may also be terms and conditions for the ultimate consumers in the form of an end-user licence agreement (or EULA), as mentioned above, and the reseller agreement will specify whose responsibility this is. For the most part the e-tailer terms will otherwise mirror the terms of the sale of a physical product. Some e-tailers do seek extra warranties, indemnities and other levels of comfort from suppliers. As can be seen from the summaries earlier in this chapter, however, unless the e-tailer takes on some form of quasi-editorial role, it should have no more liability than the equivalent supplier of physical product, and careful consideration should be given before the e-tailers' legal remedies are extended in that area.

Summary and Checklist

In the space of a few years, the technology, know-how and legal processes connected with the Internet have grown exponentially. In the context of the general nature of this work, this chapter can do no more than identify some of the legal issues current at the time of writing and the principles underpinning them, and flag some likely future themes and areas of future legal development.

There is a multiplicity of issues to consider, but the following broad headings may help with an overview.

DEALINGS WITH ISPs

- Are you an ISP or affected by the activities of an ISP?
- Is the ISP business within the safe harbour provisions of the E-Commerce Directive and UK regulations?
- If you are a content provider, do you maintain a watch and issue take-down notices?
- Are take-down notices complied with?

IPRS AND CONTENT RISK

- Do you have a copyright or trademark that is used (or misused) on the Web?
- Are you at risk of liability for Internet content in the UK or elsewhere?
- If so, how are you protected against that liability?
- Have you considered the risk of liability for web links?
- Do you have appropriate disclaimers on your site?
- Do you carefully monitor advertising content and check compliance with consumer and advertising laws and codes of practice?
- Do your practices regarding personal data comply with the DPA?

RELATED CONTRACTS

- Do you have full ownership of your website content?
- Do you have suitable agreements for any web links or other content hosted on, or incorporated in, your website?
- Are you prepared for renewal of your domain name registration?
- Do you have suitable agreements with digital content resellers?
- Do you use DRM or other security measures?
- Is any territorial protection applicable to your business (assuming this is not anti-competitive) carried through into suitable metadata or other territorial controls?

PART V

THE WIDER WORLD, CHANGES AND BREAKDOWNS

17 *The International Dimension*

Introduction – the laws of England, the UK and overseas – The Internet and international law – choice of law and jurisdiction – choice of law (Rome) – international conventions – jurisdiction clauses – other practical issues on choice of law and jurisdiction – arbitration and alternative dispute resolution – international sale and delivery of goods – checklist for drafting contracts with an international element

Introduction

Doing business overseas brings extra opportunities and extra risks, such as:

- the logistics of transport by air, sea or road across international boundaries
- the timing and additional costs involved in delivering overseas
- freight-forwarding documentation
- currency fluctuations and recovery of payment
- VAT (or its equivalents), customs and tax
- different conventions, different laws and different courts in different countries
- political and social risks.

The international dimension can arise as soon as there is some link in the chain of contracts that involves an overseas element – a factor that may give some 'long-arm' jurisdiction in another country or may engage some form of international law. The link principle can apply where the supply of the goods or services originates abroad or is destined to be delivered or received abroad. The overseas element may bring in the terms of relevant international conventions, such as those applicable to carriage by road or by sea, as well as the laws of the other countries involved; the long-arm principle may operate in such areas as competition law, libel or breach of copyright or the supply of technical equipment or other contract obligations that may even constitute criminal offences in other countries, ranging from fraud to hacking into government computers.

'Conflict of laws' or 'private international law' can be highly complex. This chapter therefore seeks to outline some of the issues and lay down some general propositions. The first issue to be aware of is when and how there may be a potentially international nature to the agreement you are dealing with. Having your goods sold on abroad or the fact that your buyer's head office is in another country may be enough to make international law relevant, and, in such cases, even the issue of how and when the contract is formed may be affected. The second issue is that, although it is nearly always worth including choice of law and jurisdiction clauses in your contract, it also pays to understand when you might not want to do this, when your choice may be overridden and what happens if the choice is not made. As the chapter progresses, it will increasingly be seen that, whilst the general principles of law can be followed, high-value or high-risk contracts and international enforcement will require and justify specialist legal help.

The basics of offer and acceptance should not be forgotten and may affect jurisdiction where this depends on where the contract is made. The leading case of *Entores* v. *Miles Far East Corporation* in 1955, followed in later cases, had to contend with offer and acceptance by telex, a new technology at the time. The judges in the Court of Appeal, having exercised themselves as to whether an acceptance shouted across a river, but lost in its noise, would be adequate acceptance if never heard by the person making the offer (a telling approach to international dealings perhaps), decided that a contract between England and Holland was made when the telex acceptance was actually received in England, not when it was sent in Holland. The postal rule (see Chapter 1) was inapplicable to telex, even though there was a gap between transmission and receipt. On that basis the Court held that the English Supreme Court rules could apply so as to enable service of a writ abroad.

The Laws of England, the UK and Overseas

English law is the short name for the law of England and Wales. This book covers only English law, and the laws even of other UK countries may be different.

Scotland and Northern Ireland have their own laws which, whilst similar in many respects to English law, are significantly different in others. For example, real property law is substantially different in England and Scotland, and Scottish legal terminology for court proceedings is very different from that south of the border.

The United Kingdom is the relevant member state of the European Community, rather than its main constituent parts of England, Wales, Scotland and Northern Ireland. However, there is no UK law as such. Where European legislation requires implementation in a member state, this means that the same laws are likely to apply in each UK country. There may, however, be country-specific regulations or other local differences.

Ireland (Eire) is outside the UK and has its own laws. As a member of the EU, its business laws are similar, in many respects, to those of England.

EUROPE

Each member country of the EU has its own law and legal system, and dealing with companies or individuals either of or based in any other country raises the prospect of having to deal with the laws and courts of that other country. These may have very different rules and traditions from English law. The laws of France and several other European countries, for example, are largely derived from, or influenced by, Roman law and based on wholly different principles from English law.

Where it applies, European law prevails over the law of individual member states. With key relationships such as employment, agency and consumers, minimum levels of protection are often made mandatory. European law may therefore well prevail in areas designed to prevent distortion of cross-border trade and economic markets. European regulations have direct effect in member states from the date set out in the regulation, whereas European directives effectively direct member states to bring in appropriate laws in each state by a stated date. In the UK these implementing laws are normally (and perhaps confusingly) called 'Regulations', often passed as delegated legislation. In other cases, European laws, or their mandatory provisions, may be introduced as part of new UK legislation. European law also applies through court decisions, and appeals can be made on points of European law from the highest English court (the Supreme Court from 2009, formerly the House of Lords) to the European Court (or the more junior Court of First Instance). Likewise, the Human Rights Act 1998 brings into force the provisions of the European Convention on Human Rights, and there is an ultimate right of appeal to the European Court of Human Rights. English law then adjusts to take account of the relevant European judgment where the rules are mandatory. English privacy law, for example, has developed in this way and thus effectively becomes a UK law.

THE COMMONWEALTH

English law principles were generally introduced to other countries when they first joined the British Commonwealth and have survived to form the basic or common law of many of those countries since their independence. In dealings with Australia, New Zealand and Canada, for example, similar legal principles are likely to apply to many business dealings, even if the detail of the law and the names of the legislation are different from those in England. Additionally, the Privy Council (a section of the House of Lords) has for centuries been the ultimate appeal court for Commonwealth decisions, which in turn have a persuasive effect on the decisions of lower UK and Commonwealth courts. Commonwealth (especially Australian and Canadian) legal decisions are in turn often as persuasive in the continued development of English law as vice versa.

THE UNITED STATES OF AMERICA

The USA has a dual law, with each state having certain flexibility within the overall framework of US federal law. The USA also takes 'long-arm' jurisdiction over cases where it considers its national or economic interests may be threatened, such as with exports of sensitive technology, even where the US interest is indirect. Similarly, the US Sarbanes-Oxley Act 2002, seeking to establish high levels of internal compliance after the big wave of financial malpractice losses alongside the burst of the 'dot com' bubble, covers even UK-based wholly-owned subsidiaries of US publicly-traded companies.

The Internet and International Law

The Internet massively increases the prospects of business contracts having international reach. There are few border checks in cyberspace and, as yet, relatively few purpose-made laws for the Internet. Some issues that have already arisen, however, are fundamental, such as how to deal with liability for certain types of electronic communication. When looking at the responsibility of ISPs (Internet service providers) is jurisdiction dependent on where the main server is located or where the greatest 'real and substantial connection' with the communication arises? The issue is as yet unresolved, and we can expect much new law in these areas. In the meantime libel law has, for the most part, accepted that electronic communications fall to be judged in the place where they are received or downloaded, not necessarily in the country from which they are sent. So a defamatory statement posted on a website in the USA can be actionable in Australia if the message is received or accessible in Australia (*Dow Jones* v. *Gutnick* (2001)). In that case the further irony was that the message may well have been lawful under First Amendment principles in US law, which gives far more protection to many aspects of freedom of speech than UK and Commonwealth libel tests allowed. More recently, the concern for free speech has caused many US states to pass legislation protecting its citizens from so-called libel tourism claims heard in the UK under English libel laws where the legal tests are different. But the controls to prevent distribution to or access from outside agreed territories are quite limited. Whilst most businesses will (or should) know who they are dealing with via e-mail, the same is not true of open web access. A hasty web posting can thus trigger a liability across the other side of the world when, even if the message appeared inoffensive, the issue may come to concern the logistical problems of fighting a case in another country. There has even already been litigation over property confiscation in *Second Life* in the USA, with the problems of the virtual world being compounded by difficult jurisdictional issues between US states. We clearly have a long way to go in this area.

SUBJECT AREAS AND LIKELY JURISDICTIONS

The rules in this area are complex, but the following principles are a good starting-point for working out in which jurisdiction a claim is likely to be heard:

- contracts for the sale of goods or services to consumers (broadly B2C) – the consumer's home state;
- employment and related contracts – the normal place of employment;
- contracts with commercial agents – where the agent normally carries on business;
- land – where the land is situated;
- IP rights – where the rights are registered or infringed;
- libel and infringement of privacy – where the harm is suffered;
- company constitutions – where the company is constitutionally based;
- negotiable instruments (cheques and so on) – special rules;
- arbitration clauses – likely to depend on the arbitration course chosen;
- insurance – specialist area with special rules.

Choice of Law and Jurisdiction

THE MAIN ISSUES

Where there is a choice, the main issues to consider in this context – all of which interact with one another – are:

- which country's law should apply to the contract (the *'choice of law'* clause);
- which country's courts should have jurisdiction over disputes regarding the contract; (the *jurisdiction clause*); and

- how international disputes should be dealt with (*dispute resolution* – such as litigation, arbitration or mediation).

There may also be major differences according to whether the other counties involved are member states of the EU or are outside that area.

The basic rule is that courts will generally respect the choice of law and jurisdiction made by the parties to a contract. This means that the parties to a contract can have reasonably certainty that the choice they made in the contract will be upheld. This helps to avoid what is known as 'forum shopping', where a one contract party seeks to have the case heard in the country with the law most favourable to its position.

Interrelation of law and jurisdiction

Whilst the choice of law is interrelated with the choice of jurisdiction, the two are not always the same; the fact that one country's law is chosen does not mean that the same country's courts necessarily will, or will have to, hear the dispute. A case may be heard in one country and expert evidence given in that court as to the laws of another country.

Local advice

If the law of another country is chosen, or it seems likely that it may apply, it is always advisable to take early opinion from commercial lawyers of that other country on the relevant implications of local law. This may be especially relevant in relation to issues such as the calculation of damages or the availability of injunctions where these can be material to the kind of redress required.

CONVENTIONS AND REGULATIONS

Principles

Because of potential uncertainty as to which country's courts may hear a case with a cross-border element there are international conventions under which the convention signatories agree to apply common principles.

Rome and Brussels

The cities most closely linked with European conventions regarding choice of law and jurisdiction are Rome and Brussels respectively, but, as time has moved on, the previous conventions are, within the European context, being replaced by regulations. We thus need now to think in terms of the Rome I Regulation, adopted by the EU Council in 2008 relating to choice of law, and the Brussels I Regulation, adopted in 2001 relating to jurisdiction. (Brussels II relates to family law issues.) These replace the old Rome Convention and the Brussels Convention. Where a case involves one of the three 'special cases' – employees, commercial agents and consumers – local law (and courts) are more likely to hold sway because these are essentially local contracts in the place where the employee or agent operates or the goods are purchased. In such cases, contracts are rarely entered into with any kind of equality of bargaining power and the aim is to relieve those affected from having to sue an employer or producer of goods in another country.

The Hague

In addition there are numerous Hague Conventions, such as those on choice of law and choice of court agreements, likely to be of significance outside the EEA. These may regulate, as between those countries who sign the convention, respectively which country's law should apply to a contract or the extent to which an exclusive jurisdiction clause should be honoured by the courts of another country. In general, as stated above, they will respect the choices of the parties made in the contract.

Choice of Law (Rome)

After some period of uncertainty, the UK opted back into the Rome I Regulation, which supersedes the Rome Convention from 2009. The broad principles can be set out with reference to the article numbers of the Regulation:

Article 1 effectively excludes contracts or obligations relating to the 'special cases' mentioned earlier and (less obviously) dealings prior to the contract being created.

Article 3 states that *the parties may choose the law applicable to all or part of the contract* – this will be honoured by European courts except where the law chosen tries to exclude rights that the 'home' state has made non-excludable (such as the 'special cases' above).

Article 4 states that *where the parties have not chosen the applicable law*, the law will depend on the residence (described as the 'habitual residence' of the relevant party), being:

- in relation to sales of goods – where the seller resides;
- in relation to services – where the provider resides;
- in relation to distribution – where the distributor resides;
- in relation to franchises – where the franchisee resides.

If none of the above applies or there is a conflict between the tests, the law should be that of the country where the party required to affect the 'characteristic performance of the contract' habitually resides or, if the contract is 'manifestly more closely connected' with one country than the country selected by either of the previous tests, then the law of that country will apply. If all these tests fail, then the law will be that of the country with which the contract 'is most closely connected'. Failure to choose the applicable law could thus create a considerable degree of uncertainty, which is another good reason for choosing the applicable law.

Article 5 relates to *conditions of carriage* – of goods and, separately, of passengers. With goods, if both carrier and consignee reside in one country, the laws of that country apply but, if not, the law is likely to be that of the country where the goods are to be delivered.

Article 6 relates to *consumer contracts* – this is will be the law of the country where the consumer resides.

Articles 7 and 8 cover specific aspects of *insurance and employment contracts* respectively.

NON-CONTRACTUAL OBLIGATIONS

The principles

The Rome II Regulation, adopted in 2007 and fully effective across EU member states from January 2009, covers choice of law regarding obligations that arise outside the terms of the contract. Rome II is therefore the applicable regulation for claims for civil wrongs (or 'torts'), such as negligence. In addition to pure contractual rights, many of the 'special cases' are also outside the scope of Rome II.

The applicable law is likely to be the law of the country where the damage occurs, or is likely to occur. This is where the harm is felt, even if the cause is somewhere else (as opposed to the English law principle of where the events causing the damage occurred). Rome II is therefore somewhat analogous to the Internet libel principle mentioned earlier that liability arises where a communication is received, even if it is sent from the other side of the world. Different rules may apply where the parties habitually reside in the same country or where the damage is caused by a product, breach of competition law or infringement of intellectual property rights, or the claims relate to insurance or subrogation.

'Non-contractual' obligations may be more important to contracts than would at first appear. A problem in the operation of a contract might produce a cause of action in tort quite apart from the right in contract. Examples would include negligence in the performance of contractual duties which might give rise to claims outside the contract, giving the risk that separate cases on the same set of events could be litigated in different countries.

Rome II, article 14 enables the parties to choose the applicable law for many such non-contractual obligations, provided they are engaged in some form of 'commercial activity', with the choice being freely made and not imposed. Business contracts may therefore specify, but need to make it clear, that the same law will apply to the parties' obligations within and outside the contract – but the choice is then binding.

Jurisdiction Clauses

Jurisdiction clauses set out which courts should deal with disputes and the enforcement of the contract. In England, the relevant court will normally be the High Court of England and Wales. In the USA, with its federal constitutions, the state or city of the court is often specified. The intention is that, if there is exclusive jurisdiction, only the courts of the named country or state may deal with any disputes. If jurisdiction is non-exclusive, the courts of a named country may deal with a dispute, but other courts are not precluded from doing so. Where all parties are in Europe, the Brussels I Regulation of 2001 will most likely apply.

BRUSSELS I

The principles

- As with contracts, the general rule is that the parties can agree on the jurisdiction or forum in which the case is to be heard and that choice will be respected, provided the convention rules do not require exclusive jurisdiction, as summarized below.
- Unless otherwise agreed, a defendant is generally to be sued in the courts of the country in which they are domiciled – usually the country where they normally live.
- In the case of contract disputes there is the option of suing the defendant in the courts of the country where the contract (or the principal obligation under it) was due to be performed. With supply of goods, this is presumed to be the country where the goods were, or should have been, delivered.
- The special cases already mentioned have their own rules. With consumer contracts, the consumer has the option to be sued in their own country, but may sue the supplier in the supplier's own courts if this gives the consumer greater rights. This principle (article 15) is taken to cover Internet selling also.
- In the case of torts (civil wrongs) the defendant may be sued in the courts of the country where the harmful event occurred or is likely to occur (a principle followed in Rome II relating to the applicable choice of law).

First to court

Despite these rules there is also the principle that the court where an action is first filed (sometimes known as 'first seised') will generally have the right to continue with the case and that any other country's courts should decline involvement. This principle is more likely to apply where there is doubt as to which country's courts do have jurisdiction.

Jurisdiction clauses

'Non-exclusive' jurisdiction may leave the matter open. English courts will still, where appropriate, seek to uphold the contract choice unless there are strong reasons otherwise. The mere fact that it would be more convenient for another country's courts to hear the case will not be a compelling reason if those factors were known about when the contract was negotiated (see *Hit Entertainment* v. *Gaffney* (2007)).

A *judgment* in one EU member state is generally to be recognized in all other member states provided that it is not against public policy or inconsistent with existing laws of that country. Judgment is then enforced in the same way as any other judgment in that country.

Other International Conventions

THE HAGUE CONVENTIONS

There are many Hague Conventions especially relevant to international trade outside the European Union, and, in appropriate cases, a check will need to be made as to whether the relevant states have signed up to the appropriate convention and whether any of the exclusions or exceptions applies. The two conventions most likely to be relevant to business contracts are summarized by their titles: the Convention on the Law Applicable to Contracts for the International Sale of Goods (1986) and the Convention on Exclusive Choice of Court Provisions in Business to Business Agreements (2005). For example, if the parties have not made the choice themselves, the applicable law will be that of the state where the seller has his place of business at the time the contract is concluded. There are, of course, exceptions, and the law will be that of the state where the *buyer* has his place of business when the contract is made if: a) negotiations were held and concluded in that state; or b) the contract expressly requires the seller to perform his obligation to deliver the goods in that state; or c) the contract terms were effectively set out by the buyer as part of an invitation to tender (ITT). In addition, if the contract is clearly more closely connected with some other law, the contract will be governed by that other law.

UN CONVENTIONS

In most other parts of the world the UN Convention on Contracts for the International Sale of Goods (1980) (CISG) sets out the basic terms for sale of goods contracts. It was created under the auspices of the United Nations Commission on International Trade Law (UNCITRAL). Significantly, it has not been ratified by the UK where it seems to have been opposed by many major trade organizations. The CISG sets out a series of rules for the international sale of goods that aim to avoid many of the issues of choice of law and jurisdiction and often work well with dispute adjudication by arbitration. The rules may apply where the country whose law has been chosen has ratified the Convention or where there is arbitration under the rules of the International Chamber of Commerce, so a contractual choice of a law other than English may mean that the CISG will apply by default. The Convention sets out rules for the formation of sale of goods contracts across national borders, the obligations of seller and buyer in relation to the sale, breach provisions, the passing of risk, remedies and limitations on remedies. The USA and most European countries are signatories, with the UK, Brazil and India being significant absentees.

OTHER CONVENTIONS

There are many other conventions with wide-ranging ratification, such as the New York Convention on the Recognition and Enforcement of Arbitral Awards, which may be relevant to cross-border litigation. See also the International Sale and Delivery of Goods section below.

Practical Issues on Choice of Law and Jurisdiction

COURT APPROACHES

Conflict

Despite all these rules, one party to a contract may apply to its home courts, even where there is a jurisdiction clause giving exclusive choice of court to another country. English courts will generally uphold the regulations and conventions, but may take the case if they consider that English jurisdiction was selected on a fair and freely chosen basis and if proceedings in another country were calculated to subvert or frustrate the English action. (See, for example, *Standard Bank plc* v. *Agrinvest International Inc.* (2007).)

Factors supporting the contractual choice include:

- The country chosen is a convenient place to hear the case.
- The relevant actions were due to be carried out or completed in the chosen country.
- The damage is suffered in the country chosen.

Factors against the contract provisions include:

- It would be far more difficult in practice to hear the case in the country chosen.
- The country chosen has little relationship to where the parties were due to perform their obligations.
- The case concerns consumers, employees or agents – where the case will normally need to be heard in the country where they habitually reside or work.
- The claim relates to issues such as libel, breach of privacy rights or intellectual property. Under these circumstances, the case will normally need to be heard in the country where the rights arise or are infringed.

DRAFTING AND NEGOTIATING CHOICE OF LAW AND JURISDICTION CLAUSES

Choice of language

If there is more than one language being used, it may be sensible for the contract to provide which is the official language of the contract (in addition to which law applies) and that all notices under the contract must be served in that language.

Jurisdiction clause

A jurisdiction clause may state that the choice of courts (but not the choice of law) is exclusive or non-exclusive. A non-exclusive choice means that the parties may take action in the chosen court but does not necessarily preclude a claim, or a defence, in another jurisdiction.

Disputes on negotiating jurisdiction clauses

When deciding which state's courts to choose, have regard to the speed, predictability and cost of the alternatives available. You may find that the other party with whom you are negotiating wants to make it as difficult as possible for you to sue them if anything does go wrong. If the wish to make it difficult for the other to sue is mutual, you might each accept that any proceedings you bring must be in the courts of the other party. This increases the costs and logistical difficulties of bringing a case, but gives the home player the comfort of knowing the issue is going to be serious if the away team is prepared to come over to take action. It also means that neither of the parties can be forced to use foreign courts except to enforce their own rights. This 'stand-off' approach is not ideal, but may avoid a dispute before the contract is even signed.

Disputes on negotiating choice of law clauses

A similar split choice of law clause should be avoided (probably at all costs) because it will be almost impossible to know with any certainty which law will apply and thus how to interpret the contract, or even whether there is a valid contract at all. How, then, can you broker a deal on choice of law? One way would be to choose the CISG (see p. 317) where there is a straight sale of goods, but the implications of this would need to be very carefully considered as they may impact on the norms of doing business. Another would be to look at the principles of Rome I and seek to apply those as a litmus test. For example, Rome I would have, as a default position, the law of the country where the seller of goods or the provider of services habitually resides. After all, the suppliers need to be clear on what it is they are supplying, based on their national laws. But with distribution or franchise agreements, the applicable law would be the country where the distributor or franchisee resides. By extension, in a contract for licence of intellectual property, such as trademarks or copyright, the proper law would logically be the law of the country where the rights are created or established, because the extent of the rights depends on that law. If these tests fail, then try the Rome I tests to determine where the party required to effect the 'characteristic performance of the contract' habitually resides or the country which is 'manifestly more closely connected' with the contract (article 4).

Planning

In planning the contract, consider:

- the extent of the international aspect and which countries might be involved;
- whether the contract is one of a series where consistency is important;
- what parts of the contract have to be performed where;
- whether the other parties are likely to accept your choice of law;
- whether the courts of the other countries are likely to accept your choice of law;
- whether, by using the law or courts of another country, the CISG might apply;
- how easy it would be to enforce the contract if you had to;
- whether to seek local legal advice and, if so, when (highly advisable if the law is that of another country of which you have little experience and where the risk or remedies may be very different from English law).

Drafting

In drafting the contract:

- do include a choice of law clause – it is nearly always better to do this than not;
- do include a jurisdiction clause – normally (but not always) best made exclusive;
- don't make that choice artificial – it may fail if the country chosen has no relationship to where and how the contract is to be performed;

- try to ensure that all other contracts related to the same subject have the same choice of law and jurisdiction clauses;
- consider adding (in non-consumer sales) the same choice of law for non-contractual obligations – and pre-contract dealings;
- remember that where local law gives greater protection to residents, such as employees, agents and consumers or other special cases mentioned above, the contractual choice may be overridden.

Other general considerations

- Consider whether and where other countries may claim 'long-arm' jurisdiction if fulfilling the contract might cause harm in that other country, such as infringement of personal or intellectual property or economic rights.
- Consider the possible impact of e-mail, Internet access and other electronic communications, where the risk of creating a liability in another country is much greater.

Arbitration and Alternative Dispute Resolution

There has been a major growth in alternative dispute resolution (ADR) as opposed to settling contentious issues by court proceedings, especially in an international context. ADR may include arbitration, but also extends to non-binding mediation where the parties put their case to a mediator who will attempt to negotiate a resolution between them. Mediation is generally non-binding, at least under English law, and UK courts will often require the parties to have attempted mediation before proceeding to trial. In international contracts much may depend on the legal systems of the parties' respective states. Even the home party may sometimes prefer a neutral venue for dispute resolution. It is best not to make uninformed assumptions and it is worth checking with lawyers familiar with the law of the other party's country as to what conventions apply in that country and the extent to which issues may or may not be suitable for settlement in that jurisdiction.

ARBITRATION OR EXPERT DETERMINATION

The parties need to decide what they want. If they want someone who will listen to, and weigh up, all the arguments on all sides in a quasi-judicial way before arriving at a reasoned conclusion based on the evidence supplied, they might want to choose an arbitrator. Alternatively, if they require someone who is an expert in the field in question and able to make an informed judgement on such matters as valuations of products or businesses or even the extent of losses, they might prefer an expert.

ARBITRATION OR LITIGATION

Nature of issue

Arbitration and expert determination are normally seen as alternatives to litigation, but they may be used within the same contract. A contract may provide for specific specialist issues to be subject to arbitration but for others to be left open to the normal litigation process. Neither party should, however, be forced to go through an unnecessary arbitration where the issue is simply the enforcement of a delivery or payment obligation and there is no other substantive issue to be resolved.

Certainty

The UK courts will normally uphold an agreement to submit to arbitration or expert determination. Challenging the decisions of experts is normally limited to evidence of 'manifest error' (which does need to be something very wide of the mark). There is normally no appeal if the expert's decision is perceived to be wrong, and the parties have to be open to this risk in deciding to appoint an expert. In extreme cases there may be a claim in negligence against an expert, but this is liable to be fraught with difficulties itself, so the best approach is to accept that the decision of an expert might give certainty but that certainty might not suit either of the parties. Appeals against an arbitrator's decision are equally difficult and are really limited to instances where the arbitrator can be seen to have misunderstood or misapplied the law. Expert determination is often quite fast but arbitration is less so; however, as the agony of appeals can prolong matters for years, both can bring certainty faster than litigation.

Cost

Cost is also a factor. Some High Court cases in London come before a judge much faster and at less cost than they used to, whereas a complex arbitration may cost more and take longer than a full court hearing. With less chance of appeal, however, arbitration can give more control over costs in the long run. It can also be easier to have an arbitration award enforced in some other countries than a court judgment.

Privacy

There is also the issue of publicity. Arbitration is normally a private affair, conducted in chambers, whereas High Court litigation can attract great media attention, and the reports and even the detailed witness statements are open to all.

ISSUES IN DRAFTING ARBITRATION CLAUSES

Choice of forum

Where the parties to an international contract opt for arbitration, they will probably adopt one of the international arbitration procedures. A prime candidate in Europe is the International Court of Arbitration of the International Chamber of Commerce (ICC), based in Paris, which is internationally recognized and prides itself on speed and cost-effectiveness. The London Court of International Arbitration (LCIA) operates even closer to home, but has a more international scope than its name suggests and is strong in mediation. The American Arbitration Association (AAA) administers international arbitration proceedings through the International Centre for Dispute Resolution (ICDR), with offices including New York City, Dublin and Mexico City. In many cases, the Arbitration Rules of the United Nations Commission on International Trade Law (UNCITRAL) mentioned earlier are adopted. The parties can also choose a neutral forum, and there are several strong candidates in Europe. These bodies all have their own recommended wording for suitable clauses. Some countries are even rumoured to offer tax concessions if chosen as an arbitration venue!

Other options

Even then, there are decisions to be made. Are there to be three arbitrators or just one? Where will the arbitration be? What language will it be conducted in? Each of these decisions has potential cost and time implications. The English Arbitration Act 1996 adopts many of the UNCITRAL rules, but tries to streamline the procedures where possible and defines the duties and powers of the arbitrator and the relationship between the arbitration and the role and powers of the courts. Reference to the 1996 Act is common in English contract arbitration clauses.

International Sale and Delivery Of Goods

Other rules may apply where goods are sold and delivered overseas. The CISG has already been mentioned as an alternative basis for contractual obligations when dealing overseas. One or two other factors to consider are set out below, in outline only, as different businesses tend to have their own rules and terms. Care should nonetheless be taken where a set of terms is incorporated by reference, as those terms may affect a carefully prepared risk/benefit structure.

Incoterms

Incoterms are a set of definitions of certain terms used in international trade. The best known traditionally are probably EXW (ex works), FOB (free on board) and CIF (cost – or carriage – insurance and freight). The effect of these terms is as follows: EXW is broadly that that buyer takes the cost and risk of delivery from the time that the goods leave the seller's premises or warehouse; FOB means that risk is taken when the goods are delivered and loaded to a specific ship in a specific port; and CIF means that the goods are delivered to the ship, and the seller arranges and covers the cost of the shipment and insurance to the point of delivery to the buyer's home port. In these examples the cost to the buyer increases progressively as the risk to the seller increases. Incoterms are devised and published by the ICC and are updated regularly. The current reference at the time of writing is *Incoterms 2000*, but is likely to be revised before long. Although English is the original and official language of Incoterms, endorsed by UNCITRAL, Incoterms have the advantage of being officially translated into some 31 languages. They are copyright of the ICC, which advises reference to the precise terms set out on its website rather than summaries elsewhere! (See www.iccwbo.org and www. iccwbo.org/incoterms.)

CMR conditions

These are derived from the Convention on the Contract for the International Carriage of Goods by Road (CMR). The abbreviation CMR is derived from the French official version of the rules. This is another UN Convention and one that will be critical to any contract involving international road haulage.

Bills of lading

Bills of lading, which have long has a major role in shipping and other international transport, have increasingly given way to various forms of commercial invoice able to be delivered electronically. The issues to be covered are to show evidence of title/the right to possession of the goods and a receipt for them (and their condition), combined with a set of terms of carriage. Whatever the documentation used, it needs to show that the bearer has the right to take delivery. This is a specialist and developing area where specific trade and local customs may dictate the process and comments used. These will need to be researched and followed in individual cases.

Checklist for Drafting Contracts with an International Element

Faced with this range of complexity, what steps can a business take to make the best decisions? Here are a few suggestions, mostly picking up on points raised above:

INTERNATIONAL ELEMENT

- Is there a predominantly English or only a minor international element?
- Is there sale of goods across international boundaries?
- If so, do the laws of the other party apply so as to bring in the CISG? If so, is this appropriate?
- Are there international transport issues involved such that Incoterms and/or CMR conditions or other convention terms might apply?
- If payments fall to be made in a foreign currency, consider the potential effect of currency fluctuations, which can turn comfortable profit into painful loss in a brief time. Hedging may be wise but expensive. Consider alternatives such as:
  - a fixed exchange;
  - a smoothing mechanism to level fluctuations over a period of, say, three or six months; and/or
  - the right to terminate future commitments if the rate falls outside a predetermined band.

CHOICE OF LAW (IF THERE IS A MATERIAL INTERNATIONAL ELEMENT)

- What is the ideal choice of law for the contract? If it is English law, provide for this in the contract with the exclusive jurisdiction of the English courts, but if you might want to enforce the contract overseas, you may want to make jurisdiction non-exclusive.

- If there are aspects where different local laws will or might prevail (see above) check or get your lawyer to check with lawyers in that jurisdiction how the contract will be affected.
- If you may need to enforce the contract in the other country, take advice pre-contract as to the 'best buy' in terms of dispute resolution and enforcement in that country.
- If the other law is likely to play a major role in the contract, consider how much work would need to be done to amend the contract to be consistent with that other law, but try to avoid a major 'cultural' redraft unless this is really necessary.
- If choice of law or jurisdiction is becoming a bone of contention, step back and look at the issues and how critical they really are in terms of your objectives, the rewards of the contract and the risks of non-performance. Then review the law and jurisdiction issue again, but do avoid a split choice of law.

DISPUTE RESOLUTION

- Is there likely to be a technical or factual issue better decided by some independent reference, such as a future price? If so, consider whether this would be best decided by an arbitrator acting in a judicial way or by an expert seeking evidence and then coming to a professional opinion. Specify the issue clearly and which body should nominate the person concerned if you cannot agree on a choice up-front or at the time.
- If proceedings seem to be looming, consider claiming first in your home courts to try to avoid the other party going to its local court before you take action.

18 *Transfers, Changes and Problem Contracts*

Introduction – transferring contracts – change of control, variation and novation – problem contracts – incomplete contracts – defective and unenforceable contracts – disputed terms: is the contract correct? – changes by actions after the contract is agreed – summary and checklist

Introduction

The question of whether and how contracts can be transferred or delegated may be of considerable significance because such changes are likely to bring a new party into the contractual equation. This chapter deals first with transfers and subcontracting, then reviews the effect of takeovers on contracts and finally considers many 'problem' contracts, where there may not be a contract at all or where the terms of that contract are unclear.

Transferring Contracts

The general rule is that most contracts may be freely assigned (that is, transferred) to another party unless the contract prohibits this. The main exception is the 'personal contract'.

THE GENERAL PRINCIPLES OF TRANSFER AND ASSIGNMENT

Assignment

'Transfer' in law mostly refers to something physical, such as goods, whereas 'assignment' indicates the transfer of legal rights and obligations, such as an agreement for services, a trademark licence or an agreement for the sale of goods, as opposed to a transfer of the goods themselves. The basic rule with contracts is that, whilst you can assign or pass on your rights (or benefits) under a contract, you cannot assign your obligations (or burden) on their own unless the other party agrees. If the 'benefit and burden' of the contract is assigned – for example, if a buyer assigns a sales contract to a sub-purchaser, requiring the sub-purchaser in turn to pay the seller for the goods – this does not of itself relieve the buyer of the obligation to pay the seller if the sub-purchaser does not. The only way for the buyer to be relieved of the obligation is by being expressly released from the contract by the seller. A good way of doing this is typically for the contract to be novated, which requires the consent of each of the seller, buyer and sub-purchaser. This covered further in 'Novation' below.

Personal contracts are the exception to the general rule of assignability, being those contracts where the services are essentially personal, such as an employment contract, or where the identity of the parties is regarded as critical to the deal. In a contract for services, for example, the client would not expect Ben Brown to turn up instead of Adrian Andrews if the client has specifically contracted for Andrews. Similarly, a contract for creative work, such as authorship or composition, is personal for both parties, since the identity of both author/composer and publisher/recording company is regarded as a key factor. Personal contracts *cannot* therefore be assigned without the consent of the other party unless the written contract says otherwise, whereas most non-personal contracts *can* be assigned unless the contract says otherwise.

Form of assignment

A legal assignment needs to be in writing and signed by the assignor, with notice of assignment being given (see below). Without these formalities there may still be an equitable assignment, but enforcement of the contract would then require the cooperation of the assignor, which might be problematic at a later stage.

Subcontracting

Subcontracting is an alternative approach, being effective delegation. Take a contract for a range of services. The service provider (head contractor) may want to delegate some services to a specialist subcontractor. The subcontract would set out the details and terms of that arrangement as between service provider and subcontractor, leaving the head contract (and the liabilities of the parties under it) unaffected.

Consent to subcontracting may be required under the head contract. So, if a service provider wishes to subcontract a specialist part of the contract for services, the contract would probably require that the client's written consent first be obtained. The client would probably have complete discretion, because having unknown subcontractors, especially if there were several of them, could be a logistical problem. The client, as a condition of consenting, might also require an express undertaking from the subcontractor to perform the subcontracted duties. This gives the client the chance to establish a link to the subcontractor, which the client could enforce directly if need be, while retaining its rights against the service provider as head contractor. The head contractor would remain liable for any failures in the performance of the head contract (but not necessarily for any other defaults of the subcontractor unless the contract provided for this).

The subcontractor may be happy with this, provided the head contractor honours its obligations, but would still be at risk if, say, the head contractor became insolvent or lost the head contract through breach. The subcontractor could then be left with no contract and a possible unsecured claim for any amounts owed to it by the head contractor.

Sub-licensing

Sub-licensing involves similar considerations, being a specialist subcontract under which the sub-licensee is given the power to exploit certain rights, such as copyrights, trademarks or technology. In such cases, it helps the rights owner to have direct recourse against the sub-licensee if there is any breach of the express contract terms. For example, the owner of a trademark (licensor) may grant a licence to a company (licensee) which is strong in production and marketing to produce and sell goods which carry the trademark. If, however, the licensee grants a sub-licence to a third party to manufacture and sell the same products in another territory, the licensor will have no direct control as to what the sub-licensee does. The licensor might therefore either bar any sub-licences without consent, and negotiate specific terms when requested, or require, in the main licence, that any sub-licence is in equivalent terms to the main contract with a direct covenant by the sub-licensee in favour of, and directly enforceable by, the licensor.

THE EFFECT OF BREACH OF RESTRICTIONS ON ASSIGNMENT OR SUBCONTRACTING

Consent to assign or subcontract

Always check whether the contract requires the consent of the other party (not always the client) to assignment, subcontracting or delegation of functions. If it does require this and consent is not obtained, that may be an irremediable or fundamental breach of the contract, which could lead to termination and a damages claim. If there is no restriction, personal contracts may not be assigned, but others can. If consent is required, check whether the other party may unreasonably withhold (or delay) that consent. If the wording is not there, the other party can potentially be as difficult as they like in refusing consent. References to consent 'not being unreasonably withheld' mean what they say – requiring a standard of reasonableness that can be objectively judged – and can therefore make an enormous difference to the respective bargaining power of the parties.

Implied consent may, however, arise if one party does assign the contract, even in breach of the need for consent, and the other continues to deal with the assignee (the transferee) in place of the previous party. For example, if an assignee tenders payment or goods that were due under the contract anyway and the other party accepts that payment or those goods without protest, consent to the transfer may be implied, even though it was prohibited by the contract. So, care needs to be taken in responding in such circumstances, as the wrong move could accept an assignment and even create, or lose, a damages or even termination claim.

Declaration of trust is a mechanism sometimes used to circumvent non-assignment provisions. The 'assignor' does not assign but declares that the benefit of the contract is held in trust for the 'assignee'. This has been upheld by the courts (see *Don King* v. *Warren (No.1)* (2000)), and requires a specific prohibition in the contract to prevent it – something rarely seen in pure business contracts.

Automatic transfer is rare but can arise by operation of law. An example here is TUPE, which provides for employment contracts to pass *automatically* on a TUPE transfer, unless *the employee* (not the transferor) objects.

Change of Control, Variation and Novation

Takeovers and change of control clauses are considered in some detail in other chapters. A change of control can amount to a form of *de facto* assignment because, although the contracting parties remain the same, control of one of them passes to a third party. The fact that the contract contains a non-assignment clause will not prevent the change of control taking place nor invalidate the contract. This requires a specific change of control clause (see Chapter 4).

Handling a change of control: an object lesson

If a change of control occurs, it is critical to look at exactly what the clause says, to plan carefully and to act within the wording of the clause, as seen in one notable case in which former clients of mine were involved. Our client had a contract with a smaller company to provide specialist trade counters at the other company's stores. The contract contained a change of control clause, especially to cover the risk of the smaller company being taken over by a rival of our client. When there was indeed such a takeover, everything hinged on a telephone call made by a senior executive of the rival to our client. In effect, the rival jumped the gun by claiming that our client had exercised its rights to terminate under the change of control clause in that conversation, whereas our client's evidence, believed by the court when the case came to trial, was that the rival had acted unilaterally in terminating the contract and effectively throwing our client's equipment and trading operation out of the relevant stores. The significance was that the operation was a profitable one for our client, who might have been prepared to accept the takeover and continue the arrangement, as this might have suited its purpose as well as making a useful profit contribution. In the event, the rival, by trying to pre-empt the decision, had to pay substantial damages for breach of contract to compensate for our client's lost profit in respect of the remaining period of the agreement.

Variation

Variation of a contract may take place informally, as seen below, or formally by means of an express agreement. Obviously such an agreement is best confirmed in writing, especially if the contract contains a 'no variation' clause seeking to prohibit variations unless made in writing and signed by the parties. Beyond that, no great formality is required, but there are two aspects that are easily overlooked. The first is that further payment or the promise of something new in return is generally required, since the consideration in the original agreement will then be 'past'. Some exceptional cases notwithstanding, even a signed variation agreement may be unenforceable if there is no consideration, unless, of course, it is signed as a deed. It is obviously also wise for any change to an existing contract to be specific as to the contract and the clauses changed, and it is sensible to confirm expressly that the rest of the agreement will remain in full force. The second easily overlooked point is to check whether there are any third-party beneficiaries of the contract (see 'Contracts for the benefit of third parties' below). If there are, variations prejudicing their entitlement under the contracts cannot be made without their consent. They should therefore be made parties to any variation agreement.

Novation

Novation (literally meaning 'new act') is similar to assignment except that it is a three-way arrangement. Assume that: 1) A has a contract with B; 2) B wants to assign that contract to C; but 3) A wants a full covenant from C to abide by the contract; and 4) B wants A to release B, so there is no comeback on B if C defaults. In a novation the incoming party, C, will take over all rights and duties of the party it replaces (B), and B will be fully released from the contract. In effect, a new contract (novation) is created between A and C, and B drops out of the picture. This is the ideal position for B, but will only be possible if A and C agree (C really has nothing to lose, but A might be reluctant to novate if C is financially weaker than B) or, quite exceptionally, if the contract provides for novation. Novation may also occur informally, but this is not a principle best relied on without a written novation agreement.

Assignment and Subcontracting: Practical Issues

Alienation clause is the name given for the clause restricting assignment, subcontracting or the like. The issues that such clauses raise may require careful thought and planning. Set out below are some reminders and further points of detail and practicality.

- *Assignments* should always be explicit and in writing.
- *Notice of assignment* in writing should be given by the assignee (C in the example above) to the other party to the original contract (A), whether the contract specifies this or not and even if consent to assignment has been given. Only when it receives that notice can A safely deal directly with C. Consider the alternative case of assignment of a loan. The lender (A in this case) wants to assign to C the right to receive repayment from the borrower (B). C needs to notify B of the assignment since, otherwise, B will (and will be entitled to) repay A as the original lender and C as assignee could lose out. C should give written notice of assignment to B and ask for B to acknowledge that notice. There is, of course, a trap for the borrower here; if, having received notice of assignment to C, B mistakenly pays A, the debt is not discharged, and if A fails to pay C, B will have to pay C the money all over again.
- *Action or inaction* can imply consent or waiver of the right to object, even if there is no formal written consent. If your consent is required and you don't agree, you need to make this clear as quickly as possible since delay could compromise your position.
- *Assignees should check* (before taking an assignment) that there are no outstanding *breaches of contract* (by either party) or allow for how any breaches will be dealt with, preferably taking an indemnity from the assignor for any outstanding defaults on its part. Conversely, outstanding breaches will usually be a good reason for the other party to refuse consent to the assignment if consent is in fact required.
- If the *identity of the other party* matters to you, make the original contract personal and prohibit assignment and subcontracting. You can always consent to specific cases when they arise.
- If the *ability to assign or subcontract* your part of the agreement is important to you, ensure that you have the power in the contract to do so.
- If *you agree to the principle of assignment and sub-contracting* consider adding a clause requiring that the assignee or subcontractor enters into a direct deed with you to fulfil the terms of the contract. This will be a deed of adherence in the case of an assignment or deed of covenant in the case of a subcontract.

- If the *financial strength or identity* of the other party is important to you, and you do agree an assignment clause, don't agree that the other party should be automatically released on a permitted assignment (but try to negotiate such a provision for yourself if you want to assign),
- Might you be affected by a *change in the control or ownership* of the other party? If so, include a change of control clause, but leave yourself the option as to whether or not to terminate, since automatic termination might work against you.
- When dealing with a *group of companies*, consider how far up the group the change of control might occur and check that your definition covers this.
- When *dealing internationally*, remember that other countries may have different conventions and laws which may apply, even on issues not dealt with in the contract. There may also be different expectations in other countries on the part of those with whom you are dealing.

PROBLEM CONTRACTS

In the field of business contracts, things are not always what they seem. Arrangements or negotiations which seem to fall short of the requirements of a valid contract may be found to have legal effect, and those which appear sound may turn out to have defects that wholly or partly undermine them. To seek a path through the complexity, problem contracts are now considered under three broad sections set out below. Inevitably there will be some overlap between these groups, but the distinctions should help identify what legal arguments may exist both to support and counter your desired position. The final two chapters of this book look first at the remedies that may be available for breach of contract and then at contract termination and its effects.

- *Incomplete contracts* – those where the requirements for the creation of a complete contract have never actually been fulfilled.
- *Defective contracts* – those which appear to be complete, but which have some basic legal flaw or defect in them that may cause them to be partly or wholly ineffective.
- *Disputed terms* – where it is accepted that there is a contract, but the meaning or terms of that contract are disputed.

Incomplete Contracts

WERE ALL THE KEY POINTS AGREED?

Many contracts are not finalized and signed before work starts and a dispute arises. The question then is whether there is a contract and, if so, what its terms are. Answering this may involve going back through the negotiations to discover whether and when offer and acceptance matched on all material points. Often there is a mass of potentially conflicting correspondence and notes of telephone conversations, but even worse may be reference to meetings and phone calls without any clear record of what was said or if anything was agreed. The construction industry, which should know better in view of its annual expenditure on legal fees, has been a major offender over the years, and similar problems often arise with IT contracts because of pressure to get on with the job in a belief that 'the paperwork will catch up' (see Chapter 15, 'Jumping the Gun', p. 276).

VHE CONSTRUCTION PLC V. ALFRED MCALPINE CONSTRUCTION LTD (1997)

Background

This case was mentioned briefly in Chapter 1 and is a classic study of this type of situation. Despite lengthy negotiations between the head contractor and a subcontractor on a building project there was no composite written contract. A dispute arose because the soil conditions were unusual, making foundation works much more complex and costly. The subcontractor had access to a soil report during the course of negotiations, but had not studied it. Had it done so, the substantial amount of extra work required would have become apparent. On discovering the true position the subcontractor wanted to be paid on a *quantum meruit* basis, which allows a fair rate for the work actually carried out, rather than the fixed price previously discussed. *Quantum meruit* is, however, available only where there is a contract without a fixed price.

The decision

After a detailed analysis of the facts, the judge concluded that a contract had indeed been entered into at a late stage of the negotiations, finding that all the contract fundamentals described in Chapter 1 (matching offer and acceptance, certainty on all relevant major terms and an intention to enter into a legally binding commitment) were present at a particular point in time. He identified the precise time that agreement was reached on the last outstanding item during a specific telephone conversation between managers on each side.

The implications

Once a contract is formed, what happens afterwards is irrelevant to understanding and implementing the terms of that contract. The contract that had been created during negotiations was for a fixed price, so that both parties risked the work being more or less than expected. Moreover, because the soil report had been available to him before the contract was created, the subcontractor was deemed by the judge to have knowledge of the circumstances described in it, whether he had read it or not. The subcontractor accordingly had to absorb the major additional costs of the foundation work.

IS THERE A CONTRACT? – AN OUTLINE CHECKLIST

- Is there a signed and exchanged contract? If so, has this been signed by all parties and dated? If so, consider whether:
  a) the contract may already have been terminated in some way - for example by expiry of a fixed term, by agreed form notice, for breach or by mutual consent; or
  b) whether the apparent contract is defective in some way (see next section).

- Were terms agreed 'subject to contract'? As previously seen, 'subject to contract' generally prevents a binding obligation arising until a formal contract is agreed and signed by all parties. If there is no signed contract, and it's clear that negotiations throughout have continued to be 'subject to contract' and neither party has acted in some irretrievable way in reliance on the other, there is unlikely to be a binding contract.

- What terms were agreed in negotiations? If there is no signed contract and no binding exchange of offer and acceptance, look at all the correspondence/e-mail exchanges that have taken place and any meeting notes. Look for things you do not want to see, as well as those you do! Looking at all the evidence, is there a point at which all the material financial and other commercial terms were actually agreed, even if this was over a period of time and several exchanges?

- Is there an agreed but unsigned contract? If the evidence is that the terms of a detailed written contract were agreed between the parties, even though the agreement was never finally signed, the court will generally enforce that contract (see *Grant* v. *Bragg* (2009), where an e-mail expressly agreed the terms of a contract negotiated between the respective lawyers and indicated willingness to complete the transaction).

- If there was apparently no settled agreement was there nevertheless, at some point, evidence of a mutual commitment to a deal (such as action by one party accepted by the other), even before the formal contract was signed? Payment (and acceptance) of an advance sum or starting work on a project could be such an event from which there is really 'no turning back'. In such cases, the law is reluctant to permit one party to take advantage of another where the first has encouraged or permitted the second to believe that a binding agreement exists. If, as a result, the second party acts to its own detriment, such as by carrying out work or spending money, and cannot easily go back to its original position, there may be a legal remedy under the principle known as *part performance* because the second person will have partly performed the contract which the first (wrongly) encouraged them to believe existed. This applies even if there has been no express promise or consideration provided by the second party. The part performance doctrine is generally available only as a defence, not as a means of attack, and is not an absolute legal right.

- Have things changed subsequently? Assuming at this point that there appears to be a binding commitment on identifiable terms, it then pays to run through the headings below to check that there is not some defect in the contract and that its terms have not been changed or waived or, indeed, that the contract has been terminated already.

Defective and Unenforceable Contracts

The law may intervene if the circumstances of a case fit into an established category of legal remedy, but the court's view will depend on all factors. As explained in Chapter 1, the law distinguishes between *void* (the contract is deemed never to have existed), *voidable* (the contract is capable of being set aside) and *unenforceable* (the contract is valid, but all or some part of it cannot be enforced). For example, a restriction would be unenforceable to the extent that it breached competition law, but the rest of the contract would remain valid unless the unlawful element was so significant as to 'taint' the whole contract.

LEGAL DEFECTS

Signature defects

When a contract query arises, first check the original contract – it is notable how often either the date is left blank or one of the parties has not signed. This will at least raise questions. It could be that there never was final agreement at all. On the other hand, if the circumstances suggest that a contract was in final form and treated as agreed, then lack of a date and all signatures will probably not invalidate the agreement, if the written terms encapsulate everything that had been agreed and the parties acted on that basis (see *Grant* v. *Bragg* above).

However, such defects are more serious with *deeds*, where execution requirements are strict. A deed is likely to be invalidated by incomplete signatures on or delivery of the same document. This may not affect the enforceability of any underlying agreement, but it could prevent the parts requiring execution as a deed from being effective. In a tax case, *Mercury Tax Group* v. *HMRC* (2009) the parties had – as sometimes happens – extracted the signature pages of a deed, had these executed on their own and then bound them into the relevant deeds. The additional problem was that the signature pages were from an earlier draft of the deed, which was later changed. The court held that this was not an effective execution of the deed. In principle, a scanned copy of a duly executed and witnessed deed delivered by e-mail with the authority of all should be acceptable, but the practice of signing execution of pages separate from the main document should be avoided.

Total failure of consideration

Even if there appears to be a binding contract, have you or the other party done at least something that you or they promised to do? If not, there may what is called a 'total failure of consideration'. This means that the party seeking to enforce an obligation on the other has totally failed to do anything they promised to do (and should by then have done), so that the essential contract requirement of valuable consideration has completely failed to materialize. In that case, courts might treat the entire contract as void.

Condition precedent

Does the contract include a condition that needs to be satisfied before the rest of the contract comes into effect? Typical examples are the requirement for some form of third-party consent, such as consent to assignment of a contract. There should always be a time limit for this third-party action and there may need to be a process as to what, if anything, the parties should do, first, to achieve the objective and, second, if the condition is not satisfied – for example, if a request for consent is refused (see also Chapter 4, 'Best/reasonable endeavours', p. 54. In general, if the condition precedent is not satisfied, the rest of the contract terms will fall away, except for certain general clauses, such as those relating to confidentiality which may continue to apply if the contract so provides.

No right to sell (you can't give what you don't have)

In law you cannot sell or transfer a better right of ownership of something that you have yourself. This is known by lawyers as the *nemo dat* rule (*nemo dat quod non habet* – no-one can give what they do not have). Even buying the goods in daylight in one of the long-established London markets will not now rectify bad title. If the goods are stolen, they must be handed back to the rightful owner. There are slight legislative variants of this rule in relation to motor vehicle finance arrangements.

Gifts

By their nature, gifts are, at least in theory, given freely and, as such, are not part of an enforceable contract (unless part of a bargain with a third party – see 'Contracts for the benefit of third-parties' below – or given in a document executed as a deed). Sometimes, however, it is difficult after the event to tell what the intention originally was, and it is all too easy to mistake a loan for a gift. With alleged gifts of money this can be even more difficult. It is worth checking and confirming assumptions in good time. Even if it is embarrassing to request it, a written confirmation of the intent to make a gift might save much heartache later.

Illegality/provisions contrary to public policy

The courts will generally refuse to enforce a contract which contains key terms that are illegal or contrary to public policy. This is because the civil law does not wish to support criminal activities or even activities contrary to that most difficult of standards to judge – public morals. Thus a contract to pay fines for criminal offences would be unenforceable, although the actual payment might be legal. This point should be kept in mind by those who deal with governmental regulations where these contain criminal sanctions for breach and contracts which, for example, attempt to evade tax or VAT laws, support bribery or which might contain transactions that are illegal under company law. Where the illegal provision is a minor term only, the courts will be more inclined to regard that term only as unenforceable but hold the rest of the contract to be valid.

Breach of competition law is worth singling out as it is a material risk in many business contracts and can have disastrous effects. Quite apart from the risk to the liberty and pockets of those involved, such breaches may undermine critical terms of the contract or even, in extreme cases, make the whole contract illegal and void. Even the threat of arguing breach of competition law can be a powerful negotiating tactic. Chapter 8 sets out further guidance.

Gambling contracts and debts

For public policy reasons the law will generally not enforce the recovery of a gambling debt. Gaming, especially online, has taken this into a different arena as the activity is at a distance and some of those involved are regarded as needing protection from exploitation. Online gaming has been a major growth industry and has attracted heavy regulations which are outside the scope of this book.

Contracts with those under age

Check whether all parties were over 18 at the time the contract was made. Contracts for anything (except for so-called 'necessaries') entered into by individuals under the age of 18 are not enforceable against them unless the minor adopts the contract after reaching the age of 18 (see Chapter 1).

Corporate incapacity

Has the correct company name been used and are there any company or insolvency law issues affecting the company? (See Chapter 6.)

Actual and apparent authority

Does the person you are dealing with have the authority to commit their company to the deal? This is also covered in Chapter 6 and may be an issue if people do not have the status they claim (such as director or partner). Some employees have actual authority to deal with third parties on behalf of their company, either because the law says so (as with directors) or because the board of the company has expressly authorized them to that effect. Others are put in a position by their company where they have apparent – or ostensible – authority to make commitments on their company's behalf. This will generally include managers and people with senior executive titles which indicate their authority when acting in the course of their normal work but not, for example, a junior office assistant. If the person who agrees the deal has neither the actual nor the ostensible authority to do so, the agreement will not bind their company, although it might bind the individual, unless the company actually adopts or approves it. Bear in mind also that if you sign a contract for someone else and cannot show that you have the authority to do so, you could be sued personally on the contract, so it pays to have your authority clearly set out and signed by those authorizing you.

BEHAVIOURAL ISSUES

Fraud

English law has always been ready to try to find a remedy where someone's interests have been damaged by the fraudulent behaviour of others. Fraud therefore can invalidate any contract where there has been an intention to deceive or a deliberate concealment of relevant facts which misleads the other party. Fraud is, however, extremely hard to prove since it requires evidence of intention on the part of the fraudster, and even alleging fraud is, of course, highly contentious. There can be a fine line between encouraging someone to believe what they might want to believe and deliberately misleading them. Claims for actual fraud are therefore very limited and more likely to be brought under the misrepresentation laws (see below).

Duress

Duress can invalidate a contract, but how much duress would need to be proved? Fear of imminent physical danger is likely to be accepted by the courts. At the other extreme, mere timidity or general fear of circumstances is unlikely to suffice. In general, the courts will require a fairly high level of proof that the obligation is one that would not have been undertaken but for the pressure that had been exerted. This in turn will depend on the nature and vulnerability of the person alleging duress. Due to their very nature few cases of duress have ever come to court.

Undue influence

Some people are in a position of particular trust or responsibility, such that the law recognizes that those relying on that trust must be protected. Thus if someone has 'undue influence' over another, they must not abuse that influence so as to benefit themselves or unfairly disadvantage the person relying on them. This may arise in family situations where one relative, especially if elderly, relies on another person, whether relative or not, for business advice. Solicitors and doctors who, for many years, have acted for clients who have come to rely on them in making decisions or taking action are in a potential position of being able to exercise undue influence over their elderly or infirm clients. Accountants and directors of family companies could play a similar role in relation to their clients and shareholders, and the courts will be especially harsh on any professional person enriching themselves at the expense of others. The onus in practice may be on the professional to prove that the benefit was indeed intended and granted by someone fully aware of what they were doing, so those in such positions are recommended to get a second, independent, opinion as to the intention and sound mind of the person granting the benefit.

MISTAKE IN CONTRACTS

This is a complex area where it is essential to understand what the mistake is and how it has occurred in order to follow the legal implications.

Mistake as to identity (knowing who you are dealing with)

The legal textbooks are full of fascinating examples of how one person can enter into a contract with another on the basis of mistaken identity. If this happens, the apparent contract may well be void (and thus ineffective), but in business such events are rare. It is more likely that the mistake relates to what the other person has to sell or spend, what their authority is or what they can deliver. Where there are cases of mistaken identity, the dispute is often between two innocent parties because 'the rogue' will have disappeared or become insolvent. Simply giving an alias is unlikely to be grounds for avoiding the contract, unless the identity of the person was critical to the bargain. To set aside a deal you will normally need to show that the rogue is impersonating a particular person, namely the specific person with whom you thought you were conducting business. With regard to companies, the key issues are covered in Chapter 6.

Mistake as to the nature of the transaction

Sometimes someone will be handed a document to sign and will be told (or will infer) that it is a particular type of document, whereas it is really something entirely different. For example, a trusted PA might pass the company boss an apparently normal document that is in fact a transfer of the company's freehold property to the PA's nominee company. What the boss believes is being signed and what is in fact being signed are entirely different documents. In such cases, the legal principle of *non est factum* (not my deed) might save the day if all else fails. The transaction would be void at the request of the person duped, even if there was no actual misrepresentation. But this is a very limited remedy for exceptional cases.

Mistake as to content or commitment

The law will not enable business people to escape from a bad bargain unless there is fraud, misrepresentation, mutual mistake or similar circumstances, as outlined above. The law expects those in business to take care with the commitments they are undertaking and the documents they are signing and will not permit them to escape from an obligation simply because it turns out to be onerous. Thus the fact that you simply did not read a contract before signing, and did not realize its obligations, will be no defence against an action by the other party to enforce those obligations.

CONTRACTS FOR THE BENEFIT OF THIRD PARTIES (SEE ALSO CHAPTER 4)

The general rule is that only the actual parties to a contract may enforce its terms. If two (or more) parties agree to confer a benefit on a third party, and that third party is not a signatory to the contract, it used to be the case that the third party could not enforce the contract. The Contracts (Rights of Third Parties) Act 1999 changed that position so that, since 2000, a third party can enforce a contract under which it obtains a benefit provided that it can show (in broad terms) the nature *and extent* of the benefit to which it is entitled. The sting in this particular third-party tail is that if there is such a third-party benefit, the named parties to the contract may not vary or cancel the contract in a way which prejudices the third party without the consent of that third party.

Disputed Terms: Is the Contract Correct?

If there is a dispute as to the meaning of a contract, it is sensible to consider first whether there is a more basic defect in the contract or in events leading up to it, as set out in the previous section. Assuming that the contract does seem valid, the next stage may be to consider whether it is a true representation of the bargain actually agreed between the parties. Sometimes there may be other terms that had been understood by the parties, but were not actually included in the contract. Sometimes the contract may be clear and correct, but may be unfair in the sense that it conflicts with consumer law. What follows may serve as a checklist to work through before electing to treat the written contract terms as complete and enforceable. (See also Chapter 2 on issues such as the 'construction' of contracts.)

THE 'PAROL EVIDENCE' RULE

The principle is that the English courts will generally refuse to look behind the terms of the final written contract to bring into account previous negotiations, especially terms supposedly agreed orally ('parol evidence'). The oral terms are deemed to have been absorbed into the actual written terms. The principle makes good sense in that it avoids what might otherwise be claims on many contracts, but, like every legal rule, there are exceptions. The main exception is where the written terms are themselves unclear and evidence of earlier dealings is necessary to explain them; under these circumstances, external evidence may occasionally be allowed to clarify the intended meaning.

MISREPRESENTATION

The old common law produced many cases concerning whether false representations by salespeople gave rise to legal remedies, such as the classic claim that a Bugatti (almost a Formula One racer of its day) would be a 'good general touring car'. These days a buyer who is able to show a court that a seller misrepresented a product to induce its purchase would have a good chance of being able to claim compensation and perhaps to walk away from the contract.

The Misrepresentation Act of 1967 provides that a misrepresentation may give rise to legal action even if the misrepresentation was made innocently and even if the failure was simply an omission to update a buyer – for example, if a previous statement had subsequently become untrue. Assuming that it could be proved as to what was actually said (which is rarely simple), there could be three possible types of misrepresentation in B2B transactions:

1. *sales spiel* – general statements extolling the virtues of the goods or services, but not intended to be relied on by a reasonable sensible buyer (curiously known by judges over the years as 'mere puffs') – *no sanction*; or
2. *actual representations* – false statements preliminary to the contract as to quality, performance or some other factor specifically designed to encourage or comfort the buyer in the choice of product or in its suitability, sufficient to induce the buyer to purchase or fail to make enquiries that would otherwise have been made – *likely to be actionable misrepresentation,* unless actually and fairly excluded by the contract itself; or
3. *actual terms of the contract* – likely to be *actionable as breach of contract* except, again, so far as fairly excluded by the contract itself.

Rescinding the contract

Misrepresentations of the second and third kinds may entitle the buyer to rescind the contract (treating it as void from the outset) and/or to claim damages. Nevertheless, the right to rescind for misrepresentation can easily be lost if: a)the buyer, knowing of the falsity, affirms the contract expressly or by behaviour; or b) the buyer delays unreasonably (even a few weeks may be enough); or c) the parties can no longer be restored to the position they were in before the contract was made.

Damages depend on the type of misrepresentation. If the representation was fraudulent or negligent, the innocent party might achieve rescission *and* damages, but, if innocent, the buyer may rescind or claim damages but not both. The courts will not readily accept that minor misrepresentations justify the potentially extreme remedy of rescission. The level of damages may also depend on the circumstances. Generally, damages are assessed on the same basis as in tort – the cost of putting the innocent party is the position it would have been in if the misrepresentation had not occurred. This follows the principle of rescission in treating the contract as void and trying to restore the innocent party to its pre-contract position. In some cases, the innocent party may, however, be better off by not claiming rescission but rather claiming damages for loss of bargain if the representation could be treated as an effective warranty of a state of affairs that should have existed, so careful thought may be required before a set course is chosen.

A *negligent misstatement* is a form of negligence similar to a misrepresentation, and the duty not to make such statements runs alongside duties in contract law. The duty exists where a person making a statement knows that the listener is likely to act on the basis of the statement. Where the listener does act as encouraged, the duty may be broken and a claim in tort may arise (see *Hedley Byrne* v. *Heller* (1964)). The onus of proof here is tougher for the innocent party than in misrepresentation.

Consumer protection regulations (see Chapter 10) now give an even broader range of remedies for such actions in B2C transactions and will probably be a more direct route for redress for disappointed consumers.

Exclusion and limitation clauses, together with entire agreement clauses, may be invoked to seek to exclude any representation itself or to exclude or limit any liability for its effects, but will be subject to the unfair terms provisions of UCTA (see Chapter 7).

DECEIT

Occasionally an innocent party deceived by another may have a better claim in 'deceit' if able to show that there was some dishonest element to the misstatement. If deceit is established, it is effectively punished as fraud, and the defendant may be liable for whatever loss flows from the deceit without the limitations that the loss must be foreseeable, as in simple breach of contract law claims.

COLLATERAL CONTRACTS

In their struggles to find acceptable legal solutions for unfair situations the courts also discovered the 'collateral' contract, which is a side agreement running alongside the main terms. This may be useful where the terms in question were not part of the main contract, but were part of the basis on which the parties agreed to do a deal. There is sometimes a fine distinction between a representation and a collateral contract, but it is worth noting that a collateral contract which, on its own, would be unenforceable for lack of consideration may in fact be binding simply because it is itself additional consideration for the main contract. A collateral contract might also be a remedy for a third party acting in reliance on a collateral statement. An instance of this was *Shanklin Pier Ltd* v. *Detel Products Ltd* (1951) in which a paint supplier assured a pier owner as to the right type of paint to be used for the pier. The pier owner engaged decorators to use the paint, and it proved unsatisfactory. The court held that, although the issue arose out of the redecorating contract, the paint supplier was liable to the pier owner under an enforceable collateral contract.

RECTIFICATION

Rectification is the legal process of having a contract amended to reflect the real intentions of the parties, but it is a difficult remedy to achieve. There are two broad grounds on which rectification may be sought. The first is that both parties made a mistake such that the contract as signed did not reflect their joint intentions. The second ground is that there was a clear mistake by one party on which the other party unconscionably relied. The type of situation that can arise in this second case is where party A becomes aware that party B has overlooked or forgotten something that had been discussed and agreed in principle (or possibly would have readily been agreed). It is necessary for B to show that A was actually aware of the omission *and* acted unconscionably either by not drawing it to B's attention or unfairly refusing to amend the contract afterwards. There is therefore either, in the first case, a mutual mistake in omitting a term that had clearly been agreed or, in the second case, an element of bad faith by A which prejudices B – a very tricky area indeed to negotiate through the courts.

Changes by Actions After the Contract is Agreed

This section covers the possible legal effects of actions by the parties *after* the contract comes into existence, which may affect the status of the contract or the responsibilities of the parties under it.

VARIATION, WAIVER, ESTOPPEL AND RELEASE – HAVE THE TERMS CHANGED?

Informal variation

As time passes, what the contract says and what the parties are actually doing may turn out to be very different. If this happens, it is best to consider whether the parties have, by their words or actions, mutually agreed to vary the contract, despite what the contract may say. Points to consider are as follows:

- A suitable 'no variation' clause in the contracts may prevent informal variation but is not conclusive, especially if the result could be manifestly unfair to one party.
- Any variation is likely to need new consideration (or part-performance linked to the variation) or be signed as a deed to be effective.
- Any variation or release of the original contract can automatically discharge the obligations of a guarantor unless suitable wording is included in the guarantee.
- If there is a third-party beneficiary of the contract, that third party must consent to the variation if the variation affects their rights.
- To be effective, anything relating to land may need to include all relevant terms, be in writing and be signed.

Waiver

Waiver can likewise arise by conduct or inaction, where the evidence suggests that one party has implicitly accepted a breach of contract by the other. Waiver can operate without writing or consideration, so care is required. If there is a breach, the 'innocent' party has a reasonably short time to decide whether or not to take action. If it does not, this may be deemed a waiver of that breach (although probably not any repetition of it). But, once the innocent party has elected and communicated a course of action, it will be bound by that election. If a decision is made to release a claim, this should be clearly documented so that it is clear what has been released and what has not.

This is often also a good opportunity to restate the bargain and the commitment to go forward, such as by serving a formal default notice, waiving it on this occasion but making it clear that further breach will lead to action. Waiver can still apply despite the existence of a non-waiver clause, as the Post Office discovered to its cost in *Tele2 International Card Co SA* v. *Kub 2 Technology Ltd* (2009). Tele2 had to give the Post Office a parent company guarantee by 24 December each year, and the contracts stated that its failure to do so would be a material breach entitling the Post Office to terminate the contract. One year Tele2 failed to give the guarantee, but the Post Office took no action until it finally decided to exercise its right to terminate nearly a year after the guarantee should have been delivered. This was far too late, said the Court of Appeal, as the Post Office had abandoned its right to terminate on that ground, effectively affirming the contract by its inaction.

Estoppel

Estoppel is a variant of waiver, such that the 'innocent' party has acted in some way so as to prevent their later claiming breach of that term. There are various types of estoppel, and the issue can become quite abstruse, but examples would be positive encouragement towards the 'defaulting' party to take the action that is later complained of or openly standing by and letting it take that action without objecting. Estoppel is only available as an equitable defence to protect the party in question if the breach is later alleged against them.

Release

Release is normally a formal recognition that a party has been released from all or certain obligations, either going forward or in relation to past periods. It is advisable for anyone seeking to rely on the principle to have the release in writing and signed as a deed, unless there is some new consideration being provided, such as revised payment arrangements for the future, when there may be less need for a deed.

Reversion

Reversion is the process of transferring rights back to the original rights holder. For example, in publishing, an author may be able to revert the copyright in a work if the work goes out of print for any period or sales fall below stipulated minimum levels. Reversion does not of itself terminate the contract, but has a similar practical effect for the work in question.

Frustration

Frustration of a contract or the long-term impact of force majeure are actions outside the control of the parties and are dealt with in Chapter 20.

Tax

Changes of this nature to a contract, especially if they result in an effective transfer of ownership or rights, may have VAT and tax implications.

REPUDIATION – REFUTING THE EXISTENCE OF THE CONTRACT

Parties to a contract need to continue to honour the terms of that contract, even if they do not particularly like the terms any more or one party thinks that the other may not be honouring those terms. Phrases such as 'I don't care what the contract says, what I need/demand is...' could amount to repudiation of the contract because the statement or action either denies that the contract exists or ignores its terms. Both show an intention not to be bound by the contract. This issue is covered further in Chapter 20 in relation to the importance of making the right choices in seeking a remedy for breach of contract. Specialist legal advice is essential at an early stage if the stakes are at all high.

Summary and Checklist

Businesses need to be on the lookout for changes in the identity or constitution of the other party to a contract. The relevant issues should be understood and any required action taken quickly. There is no harm, and potentially much advantage, in checking the situation with the other party first since action based on misunderstandings can be both prejudicial and self-defeating. Points to consider include the following.

TRANSFERS AND SUBCONTRACTS

- Is there a transfer or a proposed transfer (assignment)?
- Is this permitted by the contract? Does it require consent?
- If so, has consent been requested – and received in writing?
- Has notice of assignment been given and received/acknowledged?
- Is subcontracting permitted? If so, the same issues apply.
- Should there be a novation (for transfers) or a direct covenant (for subcontracts)?
- Are all parties adequately protected?

CHANGE OF CONTROL/VARIATION ETC

- Is there a (proposed or actual) takeover of one of the parties to the contract?
- Is there a change of control clause in the contract? If so, does it cover the situation?
- What rights has the other party got under the change of control clause?
- Are they likely either to be prejudiced by it or to want an excuse to terminate?
- Are you clear as to what is actually happening?
- Has the way in which the contract is being operated changed so as to amount to variation?
- Has either party waived or released (or be likely to be estopped from insisting on) its rights?
- Has there been any possible repudiation?

INCOMPLETE, DEFECTIVE AND OTHER PROBLEM CONTRACTS

- Is the contract complete and signed by all?
- Were all parties aged 18 or over when they signed?
- Were all signatories authorized to sign?
- If not, have all the terms actually been agreed – and, if so, are they still subject to contract?
- Has there been part performance?
- Has either party totally failed to do what they undertook to do?
- Are there any conditions precedent?
- Are there any possible breaches of competition law?
- Is there anything else that might be illegal or contrary to public policy?
- Has there been any misrepresentation or any collateral contract?
- Has there been any fraud, deceit, duress or undue influence?
- Was there any major mistake in identity, nature of the transaction or basic content?
- Were there any beneficial third-party interests? If so, have appropriate consents been given?
- Are the terms of the contract clear? Does it say what was intended?

19 *Contract Disputes and Remedies*

Introduction – the contract review: being ahead of the game – some likely problem areas – legal actions open to an unpaid contract party – remedial action – injunctions and similar orders – damages – arbitration and alternative dispute resolution – economic torts –summary and checklist

Introduction

How often have people said at the end of lengthy contract negotiations: 'Let's put the contract in a drawer and never look at it again'? To do so would be to miss much of the contract's value, since in practice the signed agreement may be merely one point in the overall management of the business relationship. The prior planning will have defined the rules and should have improved the relationship's chance of success, but how those contractual promises are performed is even more important. With planned longer-term relationships the negotiation process may also have highlighted where the stresses and strains might be likely to arise, in terms of both subject matter and attitude. People have different aspirations and different approaches, and they can change, both in their jobs and in themselves. How well will the contract bear, and help manage, the resultant strain?

The Contract Review: Being Ahead of the Game

As with employees and business plans, any ongoing contract should be reviewed regularly against both pre-agreed milestones or broad objectives and the changing business landscape. Revisiting the contract also helps you judge whether those objectives do remain the same, whether they are being achieved, what could be done better and what revisions should now be made. This may lead to suggested revision of the contract itself.

KNOWN CHANGES

There are likely to be some real triggers for a review which should not be missed. Rapid changes in the business world mean that it can become expedient to 'lose' contract commitments originally intended for the longer term. Financially, whole markets can shift as fortune's wheel turns. There may be new management with different views. A takeover may change both ownership and direction of a business radically. Some, but probably not all, of these factors might have been anticipated in the contract drafting.

ACTING BEFORE THERE IS A DISPUTE

There are good legal reasons for reviews, too. If there is a dispute later, the parties involved will review the contract, but there will be a much lower prospect of resolving any areas of uncertainty once battle lines have been drawn. If errors are spotted early, the chances of resolving them and amending the contract before they become an issue are far higher than doing so when disagreement has already arisen.

One simple precaution is to look at the term and termination provisions of current contracts. What are the key terms and how might these be invoked – or resisted? Even as this chapter was being written I was asked to look at a contract which had a rolling renewal clause, one where the contract term rolls forward from year to year unless terminated by written notice. In this case, the notice had to be given at least a year before each contract anniversary date and there was a built-in 15 per cent annual price escalation provision if the contract continued – a major burden in a recession. The anniversary date had, of course, just passed. The person who had negotiated the original contract had since moved on, and the new manager was left unable to change what had now become an onerous contract for another year. A month earlier the clause might have been spotted in time.

WHAT'S GOING WRONG?

Basic human instincts rapidly suggest that, when things start to go wrong, someone else must be to blame. When reviewing contractual relationships it's important to be honest and assess your own position as well as that of the other party involved. Have you really performed beyond any reproach? An excessive belief in the righteousness of your own case can reap unpleasant consequences down the line, so it's vital to assess the weaknesses of your case as much as its strength and the weaknesses of the other party's case before launching into battle.

SOME LIKELY PROBLEM AREAS

Every problem is slightly different, but four main themes commonly occur. These are summarized below and then discussed in turn.

- *payment problems* – failure to pay or to pay on time;
- *delivery or service problems* – failure to deliver on time or as agreed;
- *relationship problems* – causing a change in the approach or level of commitment;
- *external events* – where the unexpected (or unplanned for) happens.

PAYMENT PROBLEMS

The first signs of problems vary. One party may not pay on time, may not be able to pay generally or may simply refuse to pay. There may be unauthorized set-offs or deductions – often the case with complex and ongoing stock deliveries – or there may be more general fears, such as that the other party is overcharging or about the recoverability of future payments.

Cash flow difficulties may be anything from a temporary receipts blip to an irreversible slide into insolvency, with creditors increasingly sucked into the mire by being encouraged to continue supplies or credit to keep their customer afloat. But are you being told the truth? Does the debtor even really know what is happening? Might precipitate action cause the collapse feared, or is this the time for decisive action?

A creditor faced with the cash flow story should consider some gentle detective work. To test the story, both for honesty and to see if the debtor really is in control of its business, you might request up-to-date management accounts and a balance sheet. If these are not rapidly forthcoming, either they don't exist, which means that the debtor is guessing (probably optimistically), or they are being deliberately withheld, which may mean that your debtor knows that the position is bleaker than is being claimed. Will they show you evidence of the major orders claimed to have been received that will turn the business around? If so, can you be sure that these are legal commitments? Will they show you a total or even a list of other creditors to show how many are in the queue? Creditors can make a renewed credit check and visit the debtor's place of business to check that they are still in operation. Look out for activity and stock levels and even a possible change of name on the door!

Confidentiality may be an issue, but not an insurmountable one. Certainly, directors of companies in financial difficulty need to be careful, where there is a risk of insolvency, to avoid becoming personally liable if the company trades beyond the point of no return. But they should be receiving sufficient professional advice to find a way of presenting creditors with enough relevant information to consider whether to grant financial support.

Debtors should, on the other hand, be very wary of overextending or putting personal liability and assets at risk unless they are very confident that this is the right course of action. The blind belief that everything will turn out all right in the end is, sadly, usually not matched by experience.

Legal action for non-payment is considered below.

DELIVERY OR SERVICE PROBLEMS

Perhaps the second most common contract problem (after failure to pay) is one relating to the quality of timeliness of delivery or service. This may in turn impact on payment, with the customer withholding payment if sufficiently dissatisfied. At this point, the seller or service provider will really take notice and a simmering problem can become a major dispute.

For convenience, *delivery* in this section refers to both goods and services unless indicated otherwise.

The first step is to look at the delivery or service obligations in the contract and see whether these are date-specific. If the due date for performance has passed, check the correspondence to see whether any delay has effectively been accepted (as is often the case). Phrases which might imply agreement to wait are 'Thanks for keeping me updated – I look forward to hearing from you' or 'Please do what you can to deliver by the end of March' or even 'I see that the contractual delivery date has now passed. Please let me know when I can expect the [products]'.

Very late delivery may suggest that the contract has been abandoned, if there has been no intervening correspondence effectively agreeing to wait. This is rare, and the outcome can be uncertain if the issue is contested.

Time of the essence

If an agreed date has passed, consider serving formal notice making 'time of the essence'. This means giving a realistic date, which will depend very much on the circumstances (a few days for urgent or sensitive supplies, but longer in other cases), and a statement to the effect that if delivery is not completed in that time, you have the right to terminate the contract. This is a clear statement of intent, but should not be mixed with any message suggesting that it is 'just' a precautionary measure or similar. An example of a 'time of the essence' letter would be:

> *Further to [our recent e-mails/your letter of ...], as you know the contractual delivery date for your [product] has [long] passed. I am accordingly writing to give you formal notice that we require delivery [of the products – or as appropriate] as per the contract by no later than [date]. Time is of the essence in respect of this date, which means that if we do not have delivery by [date] we may terminate our contract with you [in respect of [the products]] with immediate effect.*

If delivery has still not taken place by the date specified in a notice making time of the essence, check the contract again and serve notice of termination immediately if that serves your purpose. The contract should then be at an end. If you wait, this may be regarded as acceptance of further delay.

Quality of goods

Contract terms may require that any claim as to any defects in the products or delivery must be notified within a stated period. If there are any such claims, they should be dealt with quickly lest they infect the relationship or become an excuse for non-payment or an unnecessary obstacle to recovering the debt.

Quality of services

Quality of services can be more difficult because the issue is more likely to be a matter of individual, and sometimes subjective, judgement. A service-level agreement (SLA) should help in specifying objective standards to be reached, but even here issues are unlikely to be clear-cut.

Dispute escalation clauses

Any dispute escalation clause should be checked as to whether it is applicable and, if so, that it has been properly used. Disputes and litigation over whether the quality of services meet contractual levels are, even with clear contracts, likely to be messy and have unpredictable results If there is the chance of a sensible resolution this should be taken, possibly with a rewriting of the relevant part of the contract to cover the future. In other cases, it soon becomes apparent that something has gone more fundamentally wrong, and disengagement with damage limitation is the only realistic way forward. In that case, it may be necessary to move directly to contract termination as set out in the next chapter.

RELATIONSHIP PROBLEMS

Changes in personnel or new management or simply human disaffection can rapidly lead to a wholly different approach to management of the contract. There might be a remedy under the contract, such as a change of control clause in the case of a takeover, but more often the problem is handling the effects of the change rather than the cause. The legal solution may not be straightforward because there may be human issues involved or power battles in a changing corporate structure, so the challenge may be to discover which person to approach to seek to resolve matters and what accommodation might be available.

Market power is a phrase from competition law, but it serves as a useful reminder that tactics have to depend not just on the strength of the contract, but also on the nature of the business partner who may now become your opponent. And, of course, market power is probably the ultimate factor in attitudes to negotiation. How much does each party need the other now and in the future, and how much damage could each do to the other in legitimate market trading?

EXTERNAL EVENTS

Harold Macmillan famously defined the most difficult thing about politics as being 'events'. Events are those things that happen around you while you are busy getting on with life – or business. When planning contracts there is always the question of how far to try to plan ahead and how far to stick to essentials only, responding to events as they arise. In one-off supply contracts there is probably little point in planning for too many contingencies in the future. If things change sufficiently, you can change arrangements. Conversely, the longer the contract term, the greater is the need to think about what might happen and to build in contingency plans. Events may trigger a force majeure situation, such as the unexpected inability to obtain supplies of a necessary material or a sudden embargo preventing trading. But a force majeure clause may not assist where there has been lack of foresight or plain error.

The financial crisis that erupted in 2008 – and its effect on business after that – is a case in point. Sudden loss of liquidity is unlikely to qualify as force majeure, but its impact is potentially catastrophic. Unless the contract expressly provides for some form of adjustment mechanism, even a huge swing in currency values will not entitle the damaged contract party to relief, despite the possible corresponding benefit to the other party. It follows, however, that, just as one party may be congratulating itself on benefiting from the exchange rate swing, it might be faced with the potential insolvency of the other party as a result. So the letter of the law might need to be tempered with the spirit of good sense in order to try to salvage a revised arrangement that may keep both parties afloat for the longer term.

Legal Actions Open to an Unpaid Contract Party

An efficient credit control system should detect payment irregularities quickly. The sales team may need to be instructed to stop selling and the service or transport people from providing more services or supplies to a defaulting customer while a way forward is found. Legal options open to a supplier in this situation include:

- *giving written notice of breach* to the customer, especially if the contract is for a longer term;
- making *time of the essence* for payment, if not already so specified, especially where failure to comply could trigger a valid termination notice;
- *exercising a right of set-off* – the rules are quite complex, with different types of set-off available at law. In general, only amounts actually due, and not amounts to become due in future, can be set off against sums due and payable the other way. If the other party is potentially insolvent, it is important to exercise any available right of set-off before the onset of insolvency, which has its own technical definition. Once the insolvency process has started it will be too late, with the solvent party probably obliged to pay the whole of the debt due to the insolvent party (via its administrator, liquidator or other insolvency practitioner) and then seeking to recover the amount it is owed in return as an ordinary unsecured creditor;
- *withholding goods ordered* as an unpaid seller under s. 38 of the Sale of Goods Act;
- *claiming interest* under the contract where the late payment of debts law or the contract terms permit you to do so (see below) – the debtor might be encouraged settle promptly if a debt is incurring interest;
- *issuing court proceedings* for non-payment – a powerful lever in many cases, but beware the professional litigator ready to tie you up in protracted litigation, taking advantage of the system to put off debts and then lever a low settlement;
- *serving a 'statutory demand'* for payment, being a notice in specified form under s. 123 of the Insolvency Act 1986 (often called a 'section 123 notice') requiring payment within 21 days – a useful process, on which you should get legal advice, but only available where the amount due is not disputed and in excess of £750;
- *issuing a winding-up petition* against a company which has failed to meet a clearly defined payment obligation, either following a court order or a section 123 notice (as above) where the debt has not been paid within the due period.

WINDING-UP

The threat of a winding-up is very potent to a substantial company, but must not be used improperly and will tend to bring in all the other creditors. It could thus actually accelerate a winding-up where the company might just have been able to trade through. Insolvent winding-up also leads to potential recovery action by a liquidator against the directors of the insolvent company, which might make the directors even more risk-averse. Creditors also need to remember that, if they succeed in getting in ahead of other creditors, such a payment might amount to a 'preference', with the one creditor being paid in preference to others where there are insufficient funds to pay all. A future liquidator of the company making such a payment may be able to set aside such a payment and demand repayment from the creditor paid preferentially. (See also Chapter 6 on directors' duties.) The law does, however, accept that some suppliers of essential goods or services can impose tough terms as a condition of continued supply.

Remedial Action

CONTRACTUAL ASPECTS

Check the contract first

Sometimes an over-hasty action can fatally undermine the case or lock a party into expensive legal proceedings where the cure becomes more serious than the disease. The key is to react quickly by reviewing the contract terms and overall position carefully and looking at the options open to you, including potential legal remedies and their likely effects. Only then can a sensible decision be made, even if the decision is to do nothing for now.

Urgency may, however, be required in certain cases. If urgent action is required, this should be implemented quickly in an informed and strategic way. One instance where you need to act with all speed is if you wish to preserve the right to seek an injunction (see below). Another point to watch, in international disputes, is the possible advantage, if the case is going to be litigated, of getting to your own national courts first, in order to prevent the other party from applying to their courts first, even if there is a jurisdiction clause in your favour (see Chapter 17).

Limitation periods

At the other extreme there are time limits within which legal proceedings must be issued, running from the date of the cause of action, which is generally the date of breach of the contract or the date when a loss is first sustained in the case of negligence. These are three years for personal injury claims, six years for contract and negligence and 12 years in the case of agreements signed as a deed or for claims relating to land. These limits may be extended where the defect (or fraud/mistake) was not apparent at the outset. There are also a number of remedies which are equitable and are thus at the discretion of the courts and which they are unlikely to exercise in favour of those who delay unreasonably.

BEHAVIOURAL ASPECTS

According to some scientists and behavioural analysts, *fight, fright or flight* are the three likely alternative responses of the reptile (or even dinosaur) brain that (even today) directs many of our reactions. The principle can be seen at work in the legal process.

The *fighter* will immediately threaten to sue and may even issue a writ first and explain afterwards, tending to regard the whole exercise as a trial of strength and willpower and being reluctant to discuss or compromise even when the odds are overwhelmingly adverse. Nothing less than total surrender of the other party may be acceptable, and sometimes litigation is inevitable if the fighter is surrounded and advised by like minds.

Those who *take fright,* on the other hand, will freeze and do nothing – graduates of the Ostrich School of Management. There will be no response to letters before action or the writ. The first action may come after default judgment when the bailiffs are sent in. Some claimants will, indeed, have given up by then, but taking fright and doing nothing is unlikely to deter a determined claimant.

Taking flight is a variant of fright, based on the premise that to run away is to reduce the risk of being caught. The 'flighter' will probably have limited assets (at least in any local jurisdiction) and a history of starting again. Insolvency may even be seen as one means of escape.

All three styles tend to become a way of life, and the signs may be there at the outset. If so, it pays the other party also to recognize these styles and plan for them at the outset. To expect a fighter to be prepared to compromise and act reasonably at the outset is probably as unrealistic as expecting the 'flighter' to engage with the merits of the issue before they are pinned in a corner. The signs may all be there in the pre-contract negotiations!

PRACTICAL STEPS

Many contracts enable certain steps to be taken without court action. For example, where the other party has paid a deposit, the contract may permit you to forfeit this. Alternatively, where the other party defaults and payment or performance is still due from you (as the innocent party), you may be entitled to withhold that payment or performance. This is normally fairly certain to bring matters to a head! Repossession of goods sold under a valid retention of title has already been mentioned and, where the contract or circumstances permit, goods may be stopped in transit. These steps are always worth considering before legal proceedings are taken, although both the entitlement to take them and the effect of taking them need to be carefully thought through. It is essential that the steps are fully authorized by the contract and that all necessary prior warnings or notices are served first. If you take action which is not authorized by the contract or under the general law, you may find yourself be in breach of contract – a breach that may be irremediable or repudiatory, thus not only undermining your right to take the action, but exposing you in turn to loss of the contract and a damages claim.

SETTLEMENT

Most litigation is settled before the case reaches court, but the timing of offers and negotiations, and the ways in which this may be approached legally, is a complex exercise best handled by those with the relevant skills and experience. If you do manage to reach a settlement, you should give the terms almost as much consideration as you would give the drafting of a complex agreement from scratch. This is a contract that has already failed, so the prospect of further hostilities cannot be that remote. It is advisable to look back to the original contract to check that everything that has gone wrong so far has been covered and then to look forward to see what other issues should now be covered. As ever, it is easier to resolve these at the stage when there is agreement than later.

LEGAL REMEDIES

If all else fails, the parties will need to look to their rights at law. This book is more a manual for negotiating and drafting business contracts than a detailed guide to litigation, which is a specialist subject, so the remedies normally available are reviewed here only in general terms. Even then, two caveats should be made loud and clear. First, each case depends on its own merits. No two circumstances are ever the same and no two contracts are ever the same, so parallels with other circumstances or reported cases have to be made with care. Second, whilst law suits now *can* be relatively speedy, decisions can often be appealed, so the experience still has the potential to cause breakdown and the financial effects can match the worst nightmares.

Legal advice at an early stage can and should provide a clear and testable structure for likely opposing viewpoints. But, when seeking legal advice, be prepared to hear what you don't want to hear. There is always doubt, because truth is an intangible commodity. It is only when live evidence is heard in court and tested by cross-examination that the truth begins to emerge, and even then imperfectly. Anyone who believes that they could withstand detailed questioning in a witness box with equanimity is unlikely to have undergone the experience! The real object of getting good advice is to marshal the facts and the arguments and to present or respond to a claim in the best possible way. The process should help to sort out the strengths and weaknesses of the respective cases. If litigation becomes inevitable there should at least be the knowledge that every reasonable effort has first been made to avoid it.

LOOKING OUT FOR DEFENCES

Don't assume that your claim (or your defence) will be simple. There may be questions of potential illegality, unfair exclusion clauses or contract terms, breach of competition law or some of the other issues considered in earlier chapters which might bar or limit the claim. Any claim is also quite likely to bring counter-claims, especially where relationships have seriously deteriorated. If any of the terms are potentially illegal, it might be better to settle on reasonably advantageous terms at the outset rather than to risk all against a determined defendant. If there are risks under competition law, consider offering a modified and more restricted form of non-compete undertaking that will serve your commercial needs. Before going too far down the litigation line think carefully as to how the other party might choose to counter-attack.

Injunctions and Similar Orders

OBTAINING AN INJUNCTION

An injunction is a court order (generally) prohibiting a named person or business from doing something. There are certain types of injunction that are orders actually requiring someone to do something, but these are much less common. In some circumstances, such as a potential disposal of disputed property or planned publication of material infringing privacy rights, an injunction can be obtained the same day, even over the weekend.

Specific performance is like a positive injunction in that it requires a party to a contract specifically to carry out their obligations under that contract. It will not, however, be ordered to require a person to perform a personal task, such as employment or even opera singing (*Lumley* v. *Wagner* (1852)), although an injunction may be granted to prevent them performing the same job for anyone else for a suitable period. The judge may also refuse an injunction if this might require close court supervision over a period or if it seems likely that third-party rights will be prejudiced by the order.

Injunctions and specific performance are *equitable remedies* which will only be granted if the circumstances justify it. Parties seeking such orders will also need to show that they themselves performed as they should have done under the contract and that they have not acted improperly. This is known graphically as 'coming to the court with clean hands'. The court has a wide-ranging discretion as to whether to grant the order or not and, if so, on what terms, and potential claimants need to think hard before rushing into injunction proceedings without careful consideration of the possible outcomes. Substantial costs may be involved, as well as the risk of paying damages and the defendant's costs (as in most litigation) if the application is unsuccessful.

To obtain an injunction you will normally need:

- a clear legal cause of action against the other party (defendant)
- a summons or claim form (formerly called a 'writ') setting out the claim
- a strong initial (prima facie) case of material breach of contract by the defendant – or occasionally the imminent risk of material breach
- to have acted with all reasonable speed to protect your position
- to maintain the status quo until the case is fully heard.

OTHER TESTS

Even if you have a good prima facie case, there are other hurdles to jump. The court will be mindful that it will only have heard part of the story. An injunction is a temporary remedy pending full trial of the case, and only at full trial will witness evidence be heard and cross-examined. To grant you an injunction may therefore cause considerable distress and/or damage to the other party which would be completely unjustified were you ultimately to lose the case. The judge hearing the injunction application will therefore normally make the order only if:

- satisfied that damages would not be an adequate remedy for you (or that the defendant might not be able to honour a damages award so that you would go uncompensated); and
- you (as claimant) give (and would be able to honour) an undertaking to pay the defendant damages for the loss and disruption caused to the defendant by virtue of the order if an undertaking is granted against the defendant and subsequently discharged on further hearing; and
- it appears that more damage would be done to you by refusing the injunction than would be done to the defendant by granting it (sometimes known as the 'balance of convenience', or even the 'balance of inconvenience', test).

FURTHER PROCEEDINGS

An injunction is, in theory, only the first stage of full proceedings which will conclude at trial (or even at final appeal three or four courts later on), so a full set of proceedings must be prepared with the obligation to file a detailed statement of claim and continue with all other requirements of a litigation claim. In practice, however, the outcome of the injunction application will often decide the whole case. If the injunction is granted, the defendant will rarely continue to contest the action since the first objective will have been lost. If the injunction is refused, the claimant will have come away with the litigation equivalent of a bloody nose and may have lost ground in a fully contested action. In other cases, the court may make orders to preserve specific property and assets until trial, to prevent the defendant disposing of the cause of action or a valuable asset.

Protecting intellectual property rights and the confidentiality of information (such as that held by an employee planning to join a competitor) are situations where injunctions may be especially appropriate. In some cases of extreme urgency there may even be a first interim injunction hearing, often at short notice and sometimes without the defendant present, to decide whether an injunction should be granted to preserve the situation as it is pending the second stage, which is a fuller hearing, with both parties present and able to provide full statements, as to whether an injunction should be granted pending trial or should be discharged. The claimant must be careful not to mislead the court in those circumstances as the court will rely on the information supplied under oath on the claimant's side alone.

Damages

The basic measure of damages in a claim for breach of contract is the cost of putting the innocent party in the position in which they would have been if the defaulting party had properly performed the contract. (The principles are explored in some detail in Chapter 7.) The damages are therefore likely to reflect the loss of bargain or expectation, being the difference in value between what the innocent party *should have* received under the contract and what they *actually* received. In sale of goods cases there may be an additional right to special damages under s. 54 of the Sale of Goods Act 1979 where the circumstances were known to the party breaking the contract. Occasionally, the claim may be for 'reliance loss', where loss of bargain is difficult to establish and where the damages are based on reimbursing the innocent party for the expenses incurred in entering into the contract. When considering damages for loss of profit in breach of contract cases the general rule is that there may be recovery for loss of any contracts which were actually in force and known about by the parties at the time, but not for loss of general goodwill or potential future contracts, even with the same customer. Such loss of profits or consequential loss, and how liability for it may be excluded or limited, is explored further in Chapter 7 on exclusion and limitation clauses.

Deposits and advance payments are treated differently, the former being liable to be forfeit on termination for breach (provided the deposit is not really a penalty) and the latter capable of being recovered subject to being set off against any damages claim.

BREACH OF DUTY OF CARE

In some situations claims will exist both for breach of contract and in negligence for breach of the duty of care. The duty of one of the parties to the others may be greater in negligence than in contract and the possibility of an alternative claim should always be considered by both potential claimants and defendants. The implications may extend to whether any exemption clauses in the contract cover liability in tort (civil wrong) as well as contract, whether the measure of damages would be the same and whether the limitation period for bringing proceedings would be the same.

LIQUIDATED DAMAGES

The advantages of liquidated damages clauses, which give a predetermined level of compensation for certain breaches have been looked at earlier (for example, in Chapter 4), together with the importance of ensuring that such provisions are unlikely to be construed as unenforceable penalty clauses. A liquidated damages clause will ideally avoid the problems of identifying what loss has actually been caused, but may also limit a claim.

DAMAGES FOR DISAPPOINTMENT OR DISTRESS

For the most part, although damages may be awarded for mental distress which has reached clinical levels, they will not be ordered for loss of enjoyment or disappointment where there is no other actual loss. There are exceptions to this general rule, including employment contracts where emotional distress may be a direct factor in the compensation awarded and also contracts, such as those for a package holiday, where pleasure and relaxation are the main purpose of the agreement (see, for example, *Jarvis* v. *Swan Tours* (1973)).

Loss of opportunity may be a valid head of damages – for example, if the contract could have been likely to lead to greater things. This could potentially arise in the arts, sports or celebrity fields, where the relevant 'talent' has the opportunity to enhance reputation, with corresponding financial benefit. These elements do have to be foreseeable within the normal damages rules, and a fairly high level of proof may be needed to establish additional loss on this ground.

MITIGATION OF LOSS

Innocent parties may not just stand idly by and let the potential damages escalate. They have a duty to mitigate their loss. For example, if a distributor's contract is terminated on short notice, the distributor should nevertheless act promptly to try to replace the lost business during the rest of the notice period. They would then need to reduce their claim by the profit they earned or would have earned if they had followed up possibilities properly (probably the gross profit if the overheads would be incurred anyway) by way of reduction in their overall claim. This does not need to involve taking financial risks or legal action against a third party, but if a third party, or even the 'guilty' party, makes a lesser offer than set out in the contract, this may have to be considered to avoid the innocent party having its damages reduced by the 'lost' value of that offer.

ACCOUNT OF PROFITS

The position is different in many intellectual property matters where the aggrieved party may be entitled to choose between a claim for damages and a claim for an account of profits. In the latter case the claim will be related to the benefit to the wrongdoer, who may be required to account for the whole of the profit derived from the unlawful act, even if that profit appears excessive in relation to the loss caused to the claimant. The issue is explored further in relation to IP claims in Chapter 14.

INTEREST AND COSTS

Interest

It's worth considering whether there may be a claim for interest at the high levels fixed under the Late Payment of Commercial Debts (Interest) Act 1998, as mentioned in Chapter 4. In any case, once a court claim is issued, the claimant may also claim interest on the amount due at the rate of interest specified from time to time as applicable to judgement debts, together with the legal costs involved in the proceedings.

Costs

The costs will be calculated on a fixed-scale basis in relation to undefended proceedings and otherwise will be assessed according to the further work done in the case. A losing claimant will generally have to pay the defendant's legal costs. The amount recoverable is normally in the region of 60 per cent of the actual costs incurred between the solicitor and client, so that even in a case of supposed full recovery, the claimant may still be out of pocket for the irrecoverable balance of costs. If, however, the case is fought on the basis of a conditional fee agreement (CFA), the scales may be tipped towards the claimant with the CFA. This is a hotly disputed area with media lawyers in particular and likely to be subject to some form of court or legislative restriction at some point.

Other costs

The real costs in management time should also be considered, both those directly involved in dealings with the potentially complex documentation and evidential requirements of a case and those arising from the disruptive and even emotional aspects of court proceedings. None of these should be underrated.

RECOVERING DAMAGES

Winning the case may be only part of the battle, the question then being whether the successful party can actually get paid. Although weapons such as bailiff action and charging orders on property do exist, there is always the risk of the defendant becoming insolvent. Even the apparently well-off defendant can prove to have no assets by the time the case comes to trial. This is all the more reason, therefore, for would-be claimants to evaluate other ways of resolving disputes more cleanly and quickly.

Protective steps

Where a defendant has most of their assets outside the UK, there may be concern that the UK-based assets will be removed from the jurisdiction and be unavailable to the claimant if the claimant wins the case. To deal with this, the courts have developed certain specialized injunctions whereby the defendant will be ordered not to dispose of, or remove, any assets while the case is live. Another specialized form of injunction permits claimants and their advisers, supported if necessary by the police, to enter premises of potential defendants without prior warning and to seize and retain incriminating evidence or actual counterfeit property which is found there. The courts may also, in very limited cases, make orders against either impecunious or non-resident claimants ordering them to provide security for the costs which the defendant will incur and might be unable to reclaim if the claimant effectively disappears.

Arbitration and Alternative Dispute Resolution

LITIGATION OR ARBITRATION?

As can be seen throughout this book, litigation may be lengthy, costly and uncertain. In some cases, the main issues are sufficiently clear-cut to be suitable for arbitration. The choice between litigation, arbitration and expert determination, and some of the contract drafting issues involved, was reviewed in outline in Chapter 16 on contracts with an international dimension, and the principles largely hold good for UK issues too.

The Arbitration Act 1996 introduced a customer-conscious arbitration system, whose declared aims were to provide for the fair, speedy and cost-effective resolution of disputes by an impartial tribunal. As a result, arbitrators were expressly given certain powers to make interim orders previously only available to judges. But the process is still not cheap or necessarily speedy.

ADR

Given the problems of litigation, formal arbitration and expert determination, there has been considerable growth in alternative methods of resolving commercial differences. Alternative dispute resolution (ADR) brings in a neutral third party to mediate. A mediator's role is to find and build on common ground and to seek consensus, whereas an arbitrator is asked to make a judgement and an expert is asked to make a decision. ADR is not mutually exclusive with litigation or arbitration, and parties to high court proceedings are generally required to confirm that they have actively considered mediation before going ahead with court action. The leading ADR contact in the UK is the Centre for Effective Dispute Resolution (CEDR) in London, and many industries also have their own mechanisms for resolving contractual disputes between or affecting their members.

Quick tests

In considering which, if any of these options to adopt, the following points are worth bearing in mind:

- Arbitration may be no cheaper or quicker than litigation – and could be even more expensive.
- Arbitration may be less suitable where witness testimony and cross-examination is likely to be critical.
- Arbitration can generally be kept private and confidential.
- Arbitration will be binding if the contract so provides, or if all parties agree to enter into binding arbitration.

- It is very difficult to appeal against an arbitration decision, so the ruling is likely to give greater certainty.
- Courts often require mediation to be considered.
- Mediation is non-binding; you may spend the time and effort but still not reach a conclusion.
- Mediation can help flush out some key issues early on, which may be a benefit or not, depending on your case.
- When mediation fails, there can be problems about confidentiality of arguments and privilege of without prejudice proposals.

See also the comments in Chapter 17 on arbitration and expert determination, especially where there is an international element.

Economic Torts

Case law has now established two so-called 'economic torts' – unlawful causation of loss and inducing a breach of contract – which can be regarded as ancillary to contract law.

UNLAWFUL CAUSATION OF LOSS

This is a tort, or 'delict', rather than a claim in contract. A claimant needs to show that the defendant a) *intended* to harm the claimant in some way and b) used *unlawful* means to do so (see *OBG Ltd* v. *Allan* (2007)). In the same year was the House of Lords decision in *Douglas* v. *Hello!* *OK!* magazine had agreed a scoop with Catherine Zeta-Jones and Michael Douglas for their wedding pictures. *Hello!*, its arch rival, published a spoiler. In addition to underlining their approval of the development of privacy law, the Lords held that loss of sales to *OK!* was an inevitable consequence of *Hello!*'s actions, which were designed to enrich itself by publishing the spoiler, knowingly breaching the confidentiality and exclusivity given to its rival and drawing sales away from *OK!* as a result. *Hello!* knew that this was unlawful and were liable for the resultant loss.

INDUCING A BREACH OF CONTRACT

Here, a claimant needs to show: a) *intent* – the other party knew it was inducing a breach (or was reckless about whether it did so or not); and b) *effect* – that the action was intended to procure the breach that actually occurred. The principle has been seen at work in the field of football management, where players or managers may be encouraged to move from one club to another, and employment, where employees may be encouraged to break their existing contracts and move to a competitor. In such cases it is important to assess whether there is an encouragement to *break the existing contract* or merely a request to join another team or company once the first contract has been properly brought to an end. If, for example, an employee on 12 months' notice was encouraged by a competitor to leave their existing employment and join the competitor immediately, this would entitle the existing employer to sue the competitor for damages for the loss of the employee's services (net of remuneration) for the notice period. To make matters more serious, if two or more parties jointly plan to induce a breach of contract, the interference then becomes a criminal conspiracy with a potential custodial outcome. The better course for the competitor, if it wishes to pursue this slightly risky path, is to make an offer with a start-date arising when the individual is legally free to join, expressly recognizing the validity of the notice, but letting commercial logic dictate the result.

Summary and Checklist

It is quite likely that a problem will arise at some stage in the implementation of a contract, especially a longer-term agreement. The best approach is to take notice of all the signs, enquire and pursue the enquiry as to the cause of the problem in order to find its source and pursue your case firmly and consistently, being realistic as to the options open, the risks which may arise and the best practical outcomes. Be as objective as possible and take advice to reinforce that objectivity and the options open to you. As well as the points covered in the previous chapter's checklist, points to consider include those listed below.

CONTRACT PREPARATION AND REVIEW

- In preparing the contract, be clear as to what level of performance is required in each case, avoiding, for example, references to 'acceptable standards' and similar general expressions.
- Review your ongoing contracts regularly to check that they are still appropriate and that you are still getting the level of performance you expected.
- Recognize the fact that if another party changes the rules, and you accept the situation, you are not only tacitly accepting their breach (or waiving your rights in legal terminology), but you may also be effectively agreeing to a variation of the contract itself.
- Don't delay in seeking redress if your rights might be prejudiced as a result.
- Beware interfering with someone else's contractual rights.

CLAIM AND COUNTER-CLAIM

- Check exactly what the contract does say and ensure that you are on firm ground. if you are not, modify your strategy accordingly and try to strengthen the weaker areas.
- Beware giving the other party cause to make counter-claims against you.
- Where you consider the other party is falling short, tell them about it as quickly as possible, letting them know what you expect, and follow it up immediately in writing so that there is a clear 'paper trail' if matters ever come to court. (Whether people settle litigation or the terms on which they settle is often determined by the strength of the incidental paperwork.)
- If you elect to negotiate, make it clear that you do so on a 'without prejudice' basis.
- Consider whether you are taking – or giving – the opportunity to mitigate the loss.
- Be realistic about your prospects of success and the costs and risks of litigation before committing your business to it.

- If you agree settlement terms, ensure that these deal with all outstanding (and consequential) issues, are clearly set out in writing and signed and that there is adequate consideration to make the agreement or release binding.

INJUNCTIONS AND SPECIFIC PERFORMANCE

- Ensure that you perform your part and keep 'clean hands'.
- Act quickly and openly.
- Consider any sensible offer, even if only in potential mitigation of loss (you are not obliged to accept less than you are entitled to).
- Consider the balance of convenience and whether damages would be an adequate remedy.
- Watch confidentiality.

ARBITRATION, MEDIATION ETC

- Do you want a clear decision, even if you may not agree with it?
- Is this a case for an arbitrator to weight up the arguments or for an expert to decide?
- Do you want to reduce the chance of an appeal?
- Do you want to 'have your day in court'?
- Is publicity or privacy more important?
- How will your witnesses feel about being cross-examined?
- Would you be prepared to try mediation and, if not, why not?

20 *Termination and Afterwards*

Introduction – no-fault termination – termination for breach – serving termination notices – other grounds for contract termination – after termination – some dos and don'ts – summary and conclusion

Introduction

A contract for the sale of goods will be completed by delivery and payment. Other contracts will involve ongoing commitments and may be for a longer term, but, in both cases, the contract obligations will be expected to continue until each party has done everything it had promised to do. There may also be express terms applicable after termination, such as the sale of surplus stock and other winding-down arrangements. And if there have been any defaults, the innocent party will not want to lose its right of redress. To avoid compromising the legal position or any claims that may exist, care needs to be taken as to when and how a contract is brought to an end. A distinction should then be made between: 1) contracts that expire automatically; 2) termination on no-fault notice; and 3) termination for fault. But before taking (or defending) any action, review the circumstances and the issues set out in the previous two chapters. After all, terminating a contract is affirming that it validly existed in the first place.

No-Fault Termination

A fixed-term contract will, by definition, usually come to an end automatically – by 'effluxion of time'. In such cases, no notice or prior warning need be served. If you review your contracts regularly, this should not come as the surprise it may be if you do not! If there is no fixed term, the contract will require positive action to terminate, usually with a specified period of notice. That notice must comply strictly with the terms of the contract but, once validly given in accordance with the contract, the die is cast and, unless there is enforceable agreement to the contrary between all parties, the contract will terminate when the notice runs out.

During the notice period the parties need to continue to perform as before, but attitudes may have changed if notice effectively means the end of their business relationship. The point should be considered even at drafting stage. Ideally, the notice period will be long enough for each party to make the necessary adjustments and find new people to deal with (if, indeed, they have not already done so), but no longer than that. Factors to be considered include disposal of remaining stock, availability of spare parts or maintenance for goods already sold, and a possible sensible moratorium on direct competition, all considered below.

REASONABLE NOTICE

If, most unusually, the contract is for an indefinite period with no provision for termination, the courts will be reluctant to presume that it was intended to carry on indefinitely and may treat the agreement as terminable at any time by either party on reasonable notice (see the comments in Chapter 4 as to what may be reasonable notice). Courts will have regard to the period that the arrangement has been in force, the capital and other investment put into the relationship, and the period which the parties would reasonably need to bring their relationship to an end.

DECIDING WHICH COURSE TO TAKE

To terminate or not to terminate?

Sometimes there is no material breach, but one or both parties feel that things have changed to such an extent that they cannot continue working together. In such situations, even if there is actually a mutual wish to terminate, the attitude and first approach can make all the difference to whether an amicable parting of the ways can be achieved. Once the decision is made to try to terminate on the grounds of breach, it can be very difficult to go back on it, and the emphasis may switch to blame and recrimination, attack and defence. Ultimately, if one party is unable or unwilling to fulfil its contractual obligations, the agreement is probably doomed to failure, so, unless there are manageable compensating mechanisms built in, it may make little sense to give the relationship artificial respiration. Some form of compromise by way of agreed resolution may turn out to be preferable to lengthy and uncertain litigation, but this does require both parties to engage in constructive and realistic dialogue.

Tactics can become important where these issues are raised. When there is breach the innocent party should follow up quickly and doggedly if necessary. Sometimes the mettle of the other party is tested to see just what they will and will not accept. There is also no viable substitute for a clear paper trail setting out each default and requiring its remedy in a reasonable defined period, whether termination is proposed or not. The idea is that, if the issue ever does come to court, it will be abundantly clear to the judge as to where justice is best served.

NO-FAULT TERMINATION ON NOTICE – AN EXAMPLE

> *This agreement will continue in force for a period of two years from the Commencement Date and thereafter until either party serves not less than three months' written notice of termination on the other, such notice to expire on or at any time after the initial two-year term.*

Note that if the clause had concluded '… such notice to expire on any anniversary of the Commencement Date' (or words to that effect, the notice would have to be for at least three months and would have to expire on an actual *anniversary* of the Commencement Date (the capital letters indicating that this is a defined term which needs to be checked).

The idea is that once nine months of a contract period had passed, the parties would have the certainty of working together for at least another year.

Termination for Breach

TERMINATING A CONTRACT

No express default clause

At common law the 'innocent' party may lawfully terminate a contract on the grounds of breach by the 'defaulting' party if the breach is sufficiently material to the performance of the contract overall. Even if the contract does not contain an express breach clause, therefore, the right still exists unless the contract states otherwise, but the breach does have to be serious enough either to constitute a material breach or repudiation, as seen below.

Express default clause

Most business agreements with ongoing obligations contain specific default provisions, such as the following:

> *Either party may terminate this agreement at any time by serving written notice on the other party if the other party is in [material] breach of this agreement, and [if such breach is capable of remedy] fails to remedy the breach within [14/21] days of written notice specifying the breach and requiring its remedy.*

Comment on example

As indicated by the square brackets there are a few options here. It is certainly worth thinking about, and possibly negotiating, what would be a reasonable maximum length of time for any likely breach to be remedied. Note that the time period is sometimes expressed as working days, and the difference may be critical. The right to remedy may be limited to situations where the breach is capable of remedy, such as a delayed delivery or failure to pay on time. Failure to remedy the default within the stated period will then give the innocent party (being the party serving the breach notice, even if they are not entirely 'innocent' in other respects) the right to terminate the contract. Depending on the contract wording, the termination may be automatic or it may require a second and final termination notice.

    Specifying breaches incapable of remedy can be useful, where there are major issues, and has been upheld in some cases. Examples at common law include assignment to an unrelated third party without consent, in breach of an express requirement for consent in the contract, as there is then no going back.

Decided cases

To follow the trail of reported judgments, and the word games of some judges, on the issue of what level of breach is required to justify termination of a contract is like walking through a labyrinth. It would be possible to cover the entire length of this book on the subject and still not escape the maze. This comment should be warning enough, but unfortunately contracts do get broken and businesses need to know what they (and the other party) can do about it. So this is designed as a practical summary designed to assist drafting and broad understanding, but with the caveat that early and specialist legal advice is highly advisable before any final decision is made to terminate a contract. If you get it wrong, you may be liable to the other party for the loss that ensues, which might be more than they owe you by way of damages for breach in the first place.

Quick tests

Bearing in mind the warning above, suggested initial tests are:

- whether there has been *substantial performance* of the contract by the defaulting party, rather than concentrating on its *lack of performance*;
- whether the 'innocent' party is being *deprived of the real benefit* that they signed up for; and
- whether *termination is really necessary* or whether damages could possibly be an adequate remedy.

MATERIAL BREACHES AND MATERIAL TERMS

Material breaches

The breach notice procedure may be limited to material breaches, but what is a material breach? There are several conflicting cases, but no single fully reliable legal test, and a material breach is likely to be more obvious at the time it occurs than when trying to define it beforehand. As a guide, a breach is likely to be material if it gives the innocent party substantially less in relation to the contract as a whole than they would have been entitled to if the contract had been properly performed. It may often be easier to decide when a breach is not material. If the breach can be remedied, it is probably not material. Some drafting contracts prefer to refer to breach of a material term, which ultimately is likely to lead to a similar result. (Some go even further and refer to material breach of a material term, which may be a step too far.)

Persistent breaches can be another problem. Some businesses, by inattention or design, keep on breaking the contract in ways that individually are minor, but which cumulatively become a real burden on the other party. Persistent delays in payment, for example, or persistent delays or shortages in delivery or lateness of response to service calls all start to take their toll. Taken together, they can become material if, to borrow another phrase from employment law, they undermine the relationship of trust and confidence between the parties. Some contract clauses therefore refer to persistent breaches as grounds for termination, in addition to material breaches. Care then needs to be taken where there are fine lines, such as failure to seek approvals for minor issues, where the approval may easily be overlooked without real detriment, or service levels which are compensated for by specific payments or refunds written into the contract.

REASONABLE TIME AND TIME OF THE ESSENCE

Reasonable time

The ubiquitous word 'reasonable' was considered in Chapter 4. In *Astea (UK) Ltd* v. *Time Group Ltd* (2003) an IT supplier had a 'reasonable time' to perform its obligations. The trial judge had to decide if that time had been exceeded so as to justify termination by the client. He analysed the situation overall, including how long the supplier was expected to take, how far that time was likely to be exceeded and why the delay occurred (especially whether anyone else was to blame). His test ultimately was similar to that for material breach above (and, to some extent, whether the delay went as far as repudiation – see below). If considerable work had been done and there was no flat refusal to continue, the client was likely to receive substantially the value for which it had contracted, and it would be a rare case that would justify termination in such circumstances. The client would, of course, still be entitled to seek damages if there was a breach, without necessarily needing to terminate.

Time of the essence

Time of the essence clauses reduce this flexibility, provided they are properly followed up. Any extension of time beyond the contractual date should either be offered on the basis that it is without prejudice to the innocent party's rights or expressly on the explicit basis that time is of the essence of the deferred date.

BEING CLEAR

Ideally, the issues identified in planning and drafting the contract will clarify the courses open when there is breach and suggest the best course for the objectives of the innocent party. One example would be where a liquidated damages clause is included in the contract. This needs to be considered alongside the overall effect of any exclusion or limitation clauses in the same contract before a decision is made to pursue that remedy and/or termination. You need to consider all the relevant clauses before making a decision as to which to operate, including any dangerous 'sole remedy' clause, which seeks to exclude all other claims including the common-law right to damages if a particular course is taken, even for a major breach. The somewhat complex case of *Stocznia Gdynia SA* v. *Gearbulk Holdings Ltd* (2009) repays study in this connection and in relation to care in drafting appropriate clauses in the first place.

Serving Termination Notices

The template example clause, Example 1 from Chapter 4 (p. 59), reads:

> *This agreement is for an initial term of two years commencing on [Commencement Date] and will continue in effect after that period unless and until terminated by either party on six months' written notice to the other, such notice to expire on the second or any future anniversary of the Commencement Date.*

The template trademark licence in Appendix D reads:

9.1   Either party may terminate this agreement at any time by serving written notice on the other party if the other party:

    9.1.1   is in [material] breach of this agreement and fails to remedy such breach within [14/21] days of written notice specifying the breach and requiring its remedy; or

    9.1.2   becomes insolvent or unable to pay its debts as they fall due.

The notice clause states:

Notices: Any notice or other communication given under this agreement must be in writing delivered personally, or sent by first-class post, or sent by e-mail with a delivery receipt, to the relevant party's address specified in this agreement or to such other address and e-mail address as either party may have last notified to the other. Any notice or other communication is deemed to have been duly given on the day it is delivered personally, or on the second day following the date it was sent by post, or on the next working day following transmission by e-mail.

Comment

So this contract requires written notice served personally or by first-class post (some clauses require recorded or other special delivery) or, if sent by e-mail, a delivery receipt must be requested and obtained, and in either case the last notified address must be used. If the correct method is not used, the notice may be ineffective and a vital termination option or date may be lost.

SAMPLE NO-FAULT TERMINATION

To Company B [full name – ensure that the correct names are used]
[Correct address for service]
Attention: [see note below]

Dear Sirs

We refer to the agreement dated […] between [our respective companies – or as appropriate] relating to [subject matter of agreement, in case there is more than one] (**agreement**). In accordance with clause [8.1 or as appropriate] of the agreement we give you notice terminating the agreement as at [… – specify a day at least the required number of months distant – but see below]. Please note that in accordance with clause […] of the agreement we will require you to [deliver up stock, provide accounting etc as per agreement]. We would also respectfully draw your attention to the provisions of clause […] of the agreement regarding [e.g. confidentiality/future dealings with our competitors etc].

Please acknowledge receipt.

Yours faithfully

Director, For and on behalf of A Ltd

SAMPLE NOTICE REQUIRING BREACH TO BE REMEDIED TO AVOID TERMINATION

> We refer to the agreement dated [...] between [our respective companies – or as appropriate] relating to [subject matter of agreement, in case there is more than one] (**agreement**). Clause [...] of the agreement requires you to [specify as appropriate]. In breach of the provisions of that clause you have failed [set out details in sufficient clarity with reference to any previous reminders]. In accordance with clause [9.1 or as appropriate] of the agreement we give you notice requiring these breaches of the agreement to be remedied no later than [... – specify date for remedy according to contract, excluding date of service of the letter – see below]. Please note that in accordance with clause [9.2] of the agreement if you fail to do so we will [be entitled to terminate the agreement/ regard the agreement as terminated – as appropriate] with immediate effect.
>
> Please acknowledge receipt and confirm your intention to remedy as required.

Such notices are best served on the senior manager responsible for the contract, but copied to the company's managing director or company secretary to give the notice the best chance of being taken seriously at the highest level.

Other Grounds for Contract Termination

Alternative remedies for bringing a contract to an end should at least be considered before the termination notice is served, although some of these are, in their way, potentially even more contentious than a fault termination notice and are only likely to be available in exceptional cases.

RESCISSION

Examples of circumstances in which a court may order rescission (rescinding of the contract altogether) are:

- *misrepresentation* – where the party would not have entered into the deal if the true facts had not been misstated;
- *failure of a condition precedent* – where the performance of the rest of the contract was dependent on some earlier condition which was not fulfilled; and
- *total failure of consideration* – where the other party had completely failed to perform their part of the bargain.

With rescission the courts seek to restore the parties to their original position *before* there was a contract, so far as it is possible to do so. This is different from the normal calculation of damages for breach of contract, which is compensation for the loss of the benefits that the innocent party would have obtained if the contract had been duly performed. Damages for breach of contract may, however, also be awarded. If you believe that you have been the victim of a misrepresentation, you should consider carefully whether you might be better off seeking damages for breach of the contract, with the representation being treated as a term of the contract in that case, or seeking to rescind and claim damages on that basis.

Breach of condition or representation may justify rescission under English law, whereas breach of a warranty alone will not. This is also a point for negotiation and it is generally worth challenging references to conditions and representations, if you are being asked to give them, to undertakings and warranties respectively. This is a perennial issue with contracts originating in the USA where US lawyers take some convincing to part with their beloved 'reps and warranties'.

RESTITUTION

Restitution is an equitable remedy requiring that someone is restored to their previous position. This might involve the return of property – or its value – sold or given away on a false basis, such as through the improper exercise of undue influence. The right is based on an assumed understanding of fairness between parties to an arrangement, whether there is a formal contract or not.

A similar remedy applies to *unjust enrichment* where, for example, one person receives a windfall benefit at the expense of another. The principles of equity may then order restitution to the innocent party of what they have lost and the other has unfairly gained. Again, this can arise outside of any existing contract. In some cases, entitlement to restitution of goods can even be traced through to their proceeds of sale but, as with other equitable remedies, there is a delicate balance between legality, procedure and overall fairness to be established.

REPUDIATION

Repudiating a contract involves showing that you are not prepared to honour the original deal, or, in extreme cases, even accept that a binding contract exists.

The effect of repudiation is that the innocent party can choose *either* to accept the breach and keep the contract in existence *or* to treat the contract as actually terminated. In either case, the right to damages for any loss caused by the breach and/or early termination is preserved. This choice is significant because, if the circumstances really do amount to repudiation, the innocent party terminating the contract can avoid any further obligations (such as being automatically discharged from any restrictive covenants). But if the original action did not in law amount to repudiation, claiming repudiation will itself amount to repudiation by the party alleging it. The converse proposition then applies and the 'guilty' party will suddenly have avenging powers!

The choice, or election, needs to show clearly what the decision is and be communicated in an effective way. Even conduct can suffice, but the party accepting the repudiation and treating the contract as over must do so unequivocally.

AN EXAMPLE OF REPUDIATION AND THE OPTIONS AVAILABLE

Consider a distribution contract between a manufacturer and a distributor for three-year exclusive distribution rights in Norway (assuming no competition law impediments). Assume that the manufacturer has covenanted not to sell competing products direct into Norway during the contract term, but actually does so. On its own, this action would be a breach of contract. If the distributor requests the manufacturer to adhere to the contract and not sell into the distributor's exclusive territory, but the manufacturer blatantly refuses to do so, the distributor would have the choice to:

1. remonstrate with the manufacturer to try to persuade it to restore the distributor's exclusivity; or
2. claim breach and seek a court injunction preventing the manufacturer from selling direct or through anyone else during the contract term; or
3. claim the manufacture's refusal to adhere to the contract as repudiation and treat the contract as terminated. If repudiation is established any post-termination restrictive covenants on the distributor would fall away and the manufacturer would not be able to prevent its now ex-distributor from dealing with a competitor immediately; or
4. claim material breach and terminate the contract on that ground, after a remedy notice if appropriate.

Implications of the choice

The distributor would need to decide quickly. Continuing to order from the manufacturer as before, even under protest, may be deemed to be acceptance of the breach and affirmation of the contract. There would also be no absolute certainty that a court would see the manufacturer's action as repudiation, although point-blank refusal to adhere to a contract is very strong evidence. If the distributor failed to justify its claim, its own action would itself be repudiation, with the distributor potentially bound by the restrictions and liable for breach of contract damages. Good legal advice is essential here.

INSOLVENCY

In the absence of a clause to that effect, the insolvency of one party does not automatically terminate the contract. Many contracts, including the samples in this book, either provide for automatic termination on the insolvency of one of the parties or give the other party the right to terminate in that event. The solvent party will, in most cases, want to terminate as soon as it can, without waiting for a future liquidator to disclaim the contract or a receiver or administrator to seek some advantage from the trading position. In the absence of any insolvency clause in the contract, the solvent party should be alive to any breach, such as non-payment, and act quickly to require remedy or termination.

TERMINATION BY FRUSTRATION

'Frustration' at common law applies where, through no fault of the parties, it becomes no longer possible for the parties to complete their bargain. The situation is, in fact, remarkably uncommon and is not to be confused with situations where one of the parties has agreed to bear a particular risk or type of risk or is at fault in some way. If a manufacturer agrees with a wholesaler to sell and deliver products direct to a third-party retailer and the products are stolen and lost en route, it is unlikely that the contract would be frustrated. The issue would be as to which of manufacturer and wholesaler had agreed to bear the risk, either under the contract or by virtue of terms implied by law.

A force majeure clause is a safer option than relying on the uncertainties of the doctrine of frustration, and can also be used to specify the period during which the parties' obligations may be suspended before either could bring the contract to an end.

DEATH

Post mortem

Death of a contract party will not necessarily terminate the contract unless the contract becomes impossible to perform, in which case the contract is likely to end by frustration, as described above. When planning contracts, although the subject may seem off-limits, it may be worth considering the point and how it might be covered in the agreement. For example, with a publishing agreement, the death of the author before the manuscript is finished would probably frustrate the contract, unless, exceptionally, both publisher and the author's estate agreed to someone else completing the work. But, on frustration, the advance paid on signing the publishing contract would technically become repayable. If, however, the author were to die after finishing and delivering the manuscript, there is no reason for the contract not to continue unless there were, for example, critical ongoing publicity or similar personal obligations. The benefit of the contract, being the right to receive royalties and a share of sub-rights income, would then pass to the author's estate.

The estate

On someone's death, their estate falls to be dealt with by their executors (if they left a valid will) or by their administrators (if there was no valid will). Until there is a grant of probate (where there is a valid will) or the grant of letters of administration (where there is no valid will) no one has the legal right to deal with the estate. Anyone who does so runs the risk of becoming personally liable for what they do. This interim period, which could be many months, can therefore be a problem because performance of the contract is in hiatus. Once a grant of representation (probate or letters of administration) has been granted, the appointed personal representatives (the executors or administrators as appropriate) have authority to deal with the estate. They can then deal with, and vary, any subsisting contracts to which the deceased was a party as may be agreed with the other party. Anyone dealing with the personal representatives should request and retain a certified copy (certified by the probate registry or a solicitor as a true copy of the original) of the relevant grant or representation (probate or administration) as proof of the representatives' right to act for the estate.

The surviving spouse or partner of the deceased will often want to able to handle these matters, but they will have no legal authority to do so unless and until they are formally appointed under a grant of representation. There is no certainty that they will be appointed in all cases, especially if (as happens only rarely) the estate is in any way contested. Any dealings with them should therefore be made strictly conditional on their due appointment.

After Termination

CARRYING ON AS BEFORE

Termination of a contract is not necessarily the end of a business relationship. The parties may simply carry on working together in the same way, but, if they do, there could be some uncertainty as to the legal relationship. They may be regarded as continuing the original agreement. If so, will the original obligations and notice provisions still apply? Or they may be regarded as entering into a new arrangement, from project to project but without any formal structure? The vexed question of trading terms could then arise all over again. For all these reasons, it is best that terms are agreed and recorded in writing as to the basis of the continued trading.

POST-TERMINATION OBLIGATIONS

There is a legal presumption that all the terms of a contract are fulfilled on completion. Accordingly, many contracts contain a 'non-merger' clause that states which provisions are intended to remain in force after completion of the parties' primary obligations. Many contracts also specify particular obligations that apply after termination of the contract. Clause 10.4 of the sample trademark licence in Appendix D, for example, sets out a series of provisions to take effect after termination. There are also many clauses mentioned in relation to outsourcing agreements in Chapter 13. A typical clause will cover such matters as:

- restrictive covenants applying after termination (see also comments on restrictive agreements in Chapter 8)
- provisions as to the compulsory sell-off of remaining stock (or stock bearing the licensed trademark)
- cessation of use of a licensed trademark
- change of company name to a name not using part of a licensed trademark
- ownership and use of intellectual property
- continuation of confidentiality undertakings
- transfer of staff (see comments on TUPE in Chapter 13).

Some Dos and Don'ts

Do:
- review the contract careful before you serve formal notice;
- make sure you look at all the clauses, not just the obvious ones;
- check carefully the timing on any notices to terminate;
- consider adjustments, variations and even compensation short of termination;.
- look at the circumstances and options open to you;
- try to leave some option for the other party rather than leaving them forced into a corner;
- distinguish between breach and termination;
- watch clauses and limitations about damages before deciding what to do;

- check what happens (and what you will need) after termination;
- ensure that your language and notices are clear and follow your rights under the contract;
- stick to the essentials;
- check the notices clause in the contract and serve notice strictly in accordance with that clause;
- act promptly – not just follow the timescales in the contract – to preserve your rights;
- brief the rest of your team and ensure that they follow suit;
- refer to any follow-on action and timescales that are covered by the contract.

Don't:
- mix a formal notice with a justification that is not required by the contract;
- add insults or get angry;
- avoid or confuse the issue by trying to be too nice;
- make your notice conditional on something else (unless you really mean to);
- make any defamatory remarks about the other party or anyone else that could cause a libel suit;
- make any claims that you are unable to substantiate;
- make any demands that are not justified under the contract;
- refuse to honour the contract in a way that could amount to repudiation.

Summary and Conclusion

DRAFTING

Good drafting, and the time it takes, may make all the difference when there are problems. Contracts need to be drafted with a view to what might go wrong and what should happen if it does. Like a good set of board minutes, a contract should be a record of what has been agreed, how it is to be achieved and a reminder of the action required to fulfil those promises.

ANALYSIS

When problems arise, a thorough analysis should be undertaken, the facts should be separated from fiction and emotion and a sensible, but flexible, strategy should then be worked out. That strategy should be regularly reviewed in the light of events. Practical solutions should be considered alongside legal redress and the longer-term objectives and risks analysed. Care needs to be taken not to interfere with the contacts of other businesses and, equally, not to fall into any traps laid by the other party. The party who was your partner may now be your opponent, but they may be in no greater rush to start litigation than you. Communication is worth preserving and informal or even formal mediation might avoid the worst aspects of a dispute.

LITIGATION

If you feel that litigation is becoming inevitable, sit down with your lawyer and carefully evaluate the potential costs, risks and rewards before taking action, but, once committed, be prepared to put your efforts behind the action to maximum advantage while recognizing that enormous patience, time and a deep pocket may be required!

DON'T BE AN OSTRICH

Above all, when things need to be done, don't bury your head in the sand and pretend that everything is fine with the world or that it is not fine but you can't do anything about it. It is normally better to make an informed choice – even an informed choice to wait until something changes – than to do nothing out of fear of doing something.

Appendix A: Archaic Language and Suggested Alternatives

(See also Chapter 2.)

by reason of	because
each and every	all
expiry/expiration [of agreement]	end
for the avoidance of doubt	[avoid – see Chapter 2]
hereafter/hereby/herein	from now on/[omit]/in [clause x]
hereof/hereunder	[omit in each case – or] in this agreement/below
in the event that	if
inter alia	among other things
mutatis mutandis	with any necessary changes
notwithstanding	[omit – or] although/despite
null and void	of no effect
per se	by itself/on its own
prior to	before
procure	obtain/ensure
pursuant to the provisions of	under/in accordance with
save that	except [that]
the said	[omit or define term]

the same	[restate or refer specifically]
thereafter/thereunder	after[wards]/in clause [x]
thereof	[omit – or] in that clause/agreement
with the exception of	except

Appendix B:
Example (Short-form) Product Sale Agreement

(See also Chapters 2 and 9.)

Agreement dated ....20...
Parties
Smith (Computer Supplies) Limited (Company number ....) of .... (**Seller**)
Braby Business Machines Limited (Company number ....) of .... (**Buyer**)

Introduction
Seller has agreed to sell and Buyer to buy fifty (50) F502/zt. computers (**Products**) for the sum of four hundred and sixty-five pounds each (exclusive of VAT and delivery) (**Price**).

1 **Delivery**

    1.1   Seller will deliver the Products to Buyer at the Buyer's premises at [...] or elsewhere within England as Buyer may direct the Seller in writing within seven days of the date of this agreement (**Delivery**).

    1.2   Seller will ensure that Delivery takes place no earlier than [...] and no later than [...]. [Time will be of the essence in respect of the later date.]

2 **Price and payment**

    2.1   Buyer will pay the Price plus VAT at the prevailing rate to Seller in full by direct bank transfer to Seller's bank [bank details] no later than 30 days from end of the month in which Delivery takes place and Seller delivers a formal VAT invoice for the Products to Buyer.

    2.2   Seller may charge and Buyer will in addition to the Price pay for any additional third-party costs of Delivery resulting from Delivery taking place more than fifty miles from Seller's distributors' premises at [....].

    2.3   If the Price remains unpaid seven days after the due date Buyer will in addition pay Seller interest on the amount unpaid at the rate of three percentage points per annum above [...] Bank plc base rate for the time being in force, such interest being payable before and after any judgment for sums unpaid.

    2.4   [The Seller's terms and conditions of business (last revised October 20...) will apply as if set out in this agreement. Where there is any inconsistency between those terms of business and the terms of this agreement, the latter will prevail.]

Comment: See Chapter 9 for more on terms of business. Note that the agreement might vary the standard terms of business and that the buyer would need to check all other terms and their suitability to this transaction. The reference to which terms prevail may be necessary as the agreement contains terms as to payment which may well conflict with those in the seller's TOB.

3 **Commissioning of Products** [*Note comments on this area in Chapters 9 and 12*]

    3.1   Seller will at Seller's cost provide a suitably competent person to assist Buyer with installation and commissioning of the Products on not more than two half-days at mutually convenient times within the two weeks following Delivery. [*Consider whether travelling expenses should be charged, especially if installation is more remote than 50 miles.*]

    3.2   Seller will not be responsible for any defects or errors relating to the Products except to the extent that these are identified and reported in writing to Seller within [21 days] after Delivery.

    3.3   Products are sold on the basis as specified in the Seller's product descriptions and, except for the Products not complying with Seller's specification or defects in manufacture reported as set out in clause 3.4, Seller's liability to Buyer for non-compliance with specification or defect in manufacture promptly reported under the provisions of this clause 3 is limited to refund of the Price or replacement of the Products as Seller may decide.

    3.4   [*Other limitation of liability provisions – see especially Chapter 7.*]

4 **Boilerplate clauses** [*if applicable – see Chapter 4.*]

Signed by [Sidney Smith]	**Signed by** [Ben Braby]
For and on behalf of Smith (Computer Supplies) Limited	**For and on behalf of Braby Business Machines Limited**

Appendix C:
The Contract Planner/Rolling Memorandum

(*Note:* This is an example of the planner/rolling memorandum as referred to in Chapter 3.)

Order processing software contract planner – last revised [...] March 20...
Contract team: SB (lead), FW (technical), IM (finance)

Issue	Initial	Response/update	Action/comment	Current
Subject	New software system to handle order processing – designed externally to our requirements (schedule attached).	Issues on 3.2 and 3.3 in schedule.	FW following up (by 31.3)	
Object	Effective order processing measured by: a) ability to handle current volumes of [...] customer orders with expansion up to [...] orders with.	a) They won't guarantee numbers.	a) Need to check our data. (IM)	
	b) average 24-hour maximum turnround on average staff complement of three accounts staff.	b) No guarantee.	b) Check training lead times. (IM)	
	c) 99.9% accuracy – initial measure after 4 weeks' operation and regular reassessment each quarter.	c) They will offer 95% maximum commitment – do we agree?	c) Set up review process – build into contract? (FW)	
Benefits	Ability to process customer orders within three working days and invoice immediately, leading to greater customer satisfaction and average invoicing one week earlier than current levels, giving improved cash flow and ability to negotiate early payment discounts with suppliers.	Not part of contract – we will have to be certain that operating standards will achieve that result.	a) Ensure implementation team fully up-to-date. b) Build in trial process before full acceptance to identify any issues. c) Check redress under contract if key benefits are not achieved.	

Issue	Initial	Response/update	Action/comment	Current
Cost	Fixed cost (budget figure £x) to satisfactory implementation with annual support and maintenance contract with guaranteed 24-hour response (budget figure £y).	Caveats on commissioning costs if interfacing problems – otherwise OK.	Retain fixed cost for basics but negotiate contract provision for maximum extra costs (£x).	
Risks	a) Choosing wrong supplier b) System non-compliant or fails implementation. c) Delays caused in commissioning process. d) Failure after implementation – workable but not to specification. e) Failure after implementation – non-workable – need to terminate f) System works but maintenance poor – need to find a new maintenance provider (will anyone else have the knowledge?) but not to lose system.	a) Let's see how reliable they are in negotiations. b) Build in resilient testing and adequate timescale. c)/d) As b) with minimum acceptable contractual requirements (watch limitation clauses!). e) Suitable termination clause + damages. f) Ensure we can terminate maintenance contract on reasonable notice without terminating software licence.	a) IM to conduct due diligence in finances, FW on technical – review at next meeting. b) FW by 31.3. c) SB to flag to legal to review. d) SB to pursue in negotiations + review insurance. e) IM to work out possible loss/cost to us; SB to flag to legal. f) SB to follow up in negotiations/flag to legal.	
Effects	Ensure we have follow-up plan for long term.	In discussion.	Seek indefinite/renewable term + required upgrades.	
Tolerance	Ensure we have sensible timescale.	(Confidentially) build in some slippage time.	SB to negotiate payment schedule, but consider reasonable period for possible delay to go-live and possible compensation mechanism.	

Appendix D:
Sample Trademark Licence

(*Note:* Apart from being especially relevant to IP rights (see Chapter 14), this document is illustrative of many of the typical general and boilerplate clauses and concepts referred to in this book.)

Trademark Licence
Dated [...]
Brand Owner [name, business address and (if appropriate) company number]
Licensee [ditto]

Comment: The names 'Licensor' and 'Licensee' are typical in many licences, but easily cause confusion, as there is a difference only in the last two letters. Accordingly, I have preferred the definition 'Brand Owner' here.

Introduction

The Brand Owner is the owner of certain trademarks [which are currently registered/the subject of applications for registration in the UK/the European Community/elsewhere] in classes [...] by virtue of the Registration [*or* Applications] and has agreed to license the use of these trademarks to the Licensee on and subject to the terms of this agreement.

Comment: This is an example of a recitals clause (see Chapter 2) that establishes some of the basic facts but could be dispensed with. Alternatively, it could be used as the basis for fuller explanation if this would assist immediate understanding of the background to the document.

1   **Definitions and interpretation**
         1.1   In this agreement:
                  Accounting Period means the period from [1 January to 31 December] in each year of the Term or such shorter period as consists of the period from the Commencement Date to 31 December next or 1 January to the Termination Date.
                  Associated Company means a company which Controls or is subject to Control by another or is under common Control with another.
                  Claim means a claim or challenge by a third party to the validity of the Brand Owner's rights and entitlements to the Marks [and Registrations] or a claim that the Licensee's use of the Marks in accordance with this agreement infringes any registered or unregistered trade mark or brand rights of any third party together with all proper legal costs and expenses of such third party.
                  Commencement Date means [...]

Control means the legal or beneficial ownership of [50% or more/more than 50%] of another entity or the power to direct the affairs of another entity.

Comment: This is a wide definition of control – see Chapter 4, 'Change of control clause', and Chapter 6, 'Companies and contracts'.

Infringement means an infringement or alleged infringement by a third party of the Marks in the Territory or any attempt by a third party to pass off its products as those of the Brand Owner or Licensee in the Territory

Licensee's Turnover means the total amount [received/receivable] by the Licensee in each Accounting Period from sales or licensing or other dealings by or on behalf of the Licensee with the Products [bearing the Marks] after [third-party commissions/returns and [fair provision for] bad debts in that period].

Comment: This is a critical definition to be clear on as regards amounts receivable or actually received, which could be a material difference, and the ability of the licensee to deduct third-party commissions or returns or other sums where products are liable to be returned by customers. Sometimes the definition 'Net Receipts' is preferred.

Marketing Materials means all promotional, marketing or sales materials together with all website or other online content produced by or for the Licensee which in any way describe, advertise or promote the Products.

Marks means the [registered trademarks [...] and [...], further details of which are set out in the schedule.

Comment: Sometimes there will be a separate licence to use the name of the brand owner in generic form – for example, as part of the trading name of a division selling the licensed products, as distinguished from the registered trademarks themselves.

Permitted Use means the production, marketing, sale and distribution of Products [specify permitted channels or other limitations].

Products means the [...] and [...] [to be] produced, marketed and sold by [or on behalf of] the Licensee.

Registrations [or **Applications**] means the registrations [or applications for registration] of the Marks, further details of which are set out in the schedule.

Royalty means a royalty of [...] per cent of the Licensee's Turnover.

Term means a period of [five] years from the Commencement Date or until earlier Termination.

Comment: Note that the length of the agreement is in this case set out in the definitions clause. In other cases it could be stated in clause 2 or in a separate clause specifying the Term, cross-referred

to in the definitions section. See also comments under clause 2 below on the relationship between term and the period of trademark registration.

Termination means the actual termination of this agreement in accordance with its terms.

Termination Date means the date on which Termination takes effect.

Territory means [the world – *or define countries*].

1.2 In this agreement:

1.2.1 all references to a statutory provision include references to any statutory modification, consolidation or re-enactment of it, whether before or after the date of this agreement, for the time being in force, all statutory instruments or orders made pursuant to it, and any statutory provision of which that statutory provision is a re-enactment or modification;

1.2.2 the singular includes the plural and vice versa; any gender includes all genders; and 'person' includes corporations, partnerships, other unincorporated bodies and all other legal entities and vice versa;

1.2.3 unless otherwise stated, a reference to a clause, party or a schedule is a reference respectively to a clause in or a party or schedule to this agreement;

1.2.4 the clause headings are inserted for ease of reference only and do not affect the construction of this agreement; and

1.2.5 if there is any inconsistency between this agreement and [insert name of appropriate document], the terms of [this agreement] will prevail.

Comment: If the definitions are extensive, they might go better in a schedule or a glossary (see Chapter 2). The definitions can be built up as the draft progresses but, for ease of reference here, they are commented on in the text as they appear. Those set out above are likely to be the basics only. The definitions should be carefully checked for any consequential changes as the draft is amended in negotiations.

2 The Marks

2.1 The Brand Owner is the owner of the Mark [and will use reasonable endeavours at its own cost to [obtain the Registrations] [and ensure continuation of the Registrations from the date of expiry of the Registrations for a further ten-year term].

2.2 The Licensee acknowledges to the Brand Owner that:

2.2.1 all rights in the Marks belong to the Brand Owner;

2.2.2 the Licensee will not acquire any rights to the Marks except to the extent and by virtue of this agreement;

2.2.3 all goodwill in the Marks generated by their use under this agreement [(as opposed to the business of the Licensee by virtue of the Permitted Use) – *these words will not be offered by the Brand Owner but might be added by the Licensee to protect its rights in the goodwill of the business it runs*] will belong solely to the Brand Owner.

Comment: The marks will be as referred to in the definitions section and may also cross-refer to a distinctive style or logo which will match that of any registered trademark and will probably then be set out in a schedule to the licence agreement. If there is such a distinctive style or logo, the licensee will be obliged to follow it exactly. The definition of registrations ties the mark to the public protection and flags the possible need to be clear about at least one renewal, especially if the original registration term is near to its end. TM licences may run for shorter periods, possibly subject to a renewal option. The licensee will want a reasonable period to exploit the marks, but the brand owner may not want its hands tied to renew registration in the same format and classes. See also comments on 'reasonable endeavours' in Chapter 4.

3   Grant of rights

Comment: Clauses 3, 4 and 5 can be considered together. The first sets out the rights granted, but does so expressly subject to clause 4 as to how, when and where the marks can be used and clause 5, which deals with approval of the way in which the marks are to be used on products and marketing materials. The level of control by the brand owner will vary according to the circumstances and the popularity of the trademark. The draft distinguishes between those rights which are exclusive and those which are non-exclusive – a key distinction for both parties. The licensee will probably want to be the only one entitled to use the marks in relation to products of the kind it deals in, but the brand owner will not want to grant any exclusivity in relation to broader uses, such as part of a trading name or on general marketing materials. For more detail on exclusivity see especially Chapter 8.

Subject to clauses 4 and 5 the Brand Owner grants to the Licensee the following rights throughout the Territory during the Term:

3.1   the exclusive right for the Licensee to use the Marks for the Permitted Use; [together with the exclusive right [for any Associated Company of the Licensee to use the Marks *or* to sub-license the Marks to Associated Companies of the Licensee] for the Permitted Use for periods of up to five years during and no longer than the Term];

3.2   the non-exclusive right to use the Marks as part of its trading name for that division or part of its business involved solely in the Permitted Use (and so as not to be used for any other part of the Licensee's business [subject to – *set out any further conditions*]);

3.3   the non-exclusive right to use the Marks on the Marketing Materials and websites for promotional and marketing purposes in relation to the Products in a way that clearly distinguishes the Marks as applying only to the Products and Permitted Use and for no further or other purpose connected with the Licensee.

4   Use and conditions of use of the Marks

4.1   The rights set out in clause 3 are expressly subject to the Licensee complying with the requirements of clauses 4 and 5, except as otherwise agreed in writing in advance by the Brand Owner.

4.2   The Licensee will prominently and consistently display the Marks on all Products and Marketing Materials [together with the symbol ®] with a statement that the Marks are the [registered] trademarks of [Brand Owner name] and are used under licence.

4.3   The Marks may be used as a trading name only in conjunction with the word […] and will not be used jointly with any other trademark or trading name of the Licensee or any third party.

4.4   The Marks will on all occasions be used in precisely the form, style and colour set out in the [Registrations/Applications] [schedule 1].

Comment: The brand owner may want to make provision also for any future amendments to the trademarks.

4.5   The Licensee will in its use of the Marks act consistently with the Brand Owner's brand values of [e.g. quality, value for money and innovation] [and in compliance with the Brand Owner's trademark guidelines as notified to the Licensee from time to time].

4.6   The Marks will not be used [actively to seek sales of Products bearing the Mark outside the Territory nor in any other way] except as specifically authorized in clause 3.

Comment: The words in square brackets need care. On 4.2 see the comments on falsely claiming registered trademark status in Chapter 14. In 4.6 the extra words will clearly only apply where the territory is less than worldwide, but see Chapter 8 on the relevance of competition law and the distinction between active and passive sales, especially Internet sales.

4.7   The Licensee will not during the Term use, register or apply to register any trademark, domain name or e-mail address which is the same as or colourably similar to any of the Marks and will on request and without consideration transfer to the Brand Owner any such registration as the Licensee may nevertheless make.

4.8   The Licensee will not use the Products or the Marketing Materials or otherwise take action relating to them in a way which might reasonably be expected [materially] to damage the reputation or goodwill of the Brand Owner or otherwise bring the Marks into disrepute.

4.9   The Licensee will provide such further details as the Brand Owner may from time to time request as to the extent and frequency of the Licensee's use of the Marks.

5   **Product quality and approval**

5.1   The Licensee will submit to the Brand Owner for its written approval full details (including, without limitation, the shape, dimensions, colour and design of the Product and all proposed Marketing Materials relating to it) of any new Product to be developed or marketed by the Licensee in good time before its first sale or marketing and will not promote, market or sell such new Product without such prior written approval from the Brand Owner, such approval not to be unreasonably withheld or delayed.) [*Add obligation to supply sample Products if appropriate.*]

5.2   All Products produced and sold by or for the Licensee bearing the Marks will be of good design and quality, produced and marketed to a high standard in accordance with all applicable product safety and other laws and regulations.

5.3   The Licensee will promptly withdraw from production and sale any Products or marketing/promotional literature which the Brand Owner, acting reasonably, notifies the Licensee in writing to be non-compliant with the terms of this agreement.

5.4   In order to ensure compliance by the Licensee with the requirements of clauses 4 and 5 the Licensee will immediately prior to their marketing or sale and on written request by the Brand Owner at any time during the Term supply the Brand Owner with [two] free [copies/samples] of each [new] Product together with all packing and Marketing Materials relating to it or any amendment to such Products, packaging or Marketing Materials.

Comment: Clause 5.4 may apply in addition to the approval requirement under clause 5.1, the intention being to ensure that the products have not changed since first approved by the brand owner.

6   Brand Owner's rights and obligations

6.1   [The Brand Owner undertakes with the Licensee during the Term not itself to use or license [or permit] any third party to use the Mark anywhere in the Territory in relation to products which are similar to [and/or] may be sold in competition with or substitution for the Products.

Comment: This sub-clause is only likely to be relevant where the licensee has exclusivity in certain territories as set out in clause 3 (and see 4.6). See note to clause 3 and generally below.

6.2   The Brand Owner may by reasonable notice (having regard to the circumstances) to the Licensee require the Licensee to cease the use of the Mark on and in relation to for one or more specified Products in the event of a Claim as to such use or if it appears that such use of the Marks is the cause of or may lead to a Claim.

6.3   [The Brand Owner will not [knowingly] do or permit anything to be done in relation to the Marks or otherwise take action relating to them in a way which might reasonably be expected [materially] to damage the reputation or goodwill of the Marks or otherwise bring the Marks into disrepute.]

Comment: Clause 6.1 is a basic provision which effectively means that where the brand owner has offered exclusivity in a defined area for use of the mark it should not permit anyone else to use that mark for similar products within that area. Clause 6.2 is also not as inoffensive as it first looks and would normally need to be resisted by a licensee, as it makes the licensee potentially suffer for breach of the brand owner's warranty in clause 7.1 below. There may, however, be exceptional circumstances where something along these lines is appropriate. Clause 6.3 is the counterpart of clause 4.8 and may be something for the licensee to consider, especially if there is any minimum royalty-type arrangement and the licensee could be locked into a deal that commercially no longer works. See also the termination provisions.

7   **Warranties, [Indemnities], Claims and Infringements**

Comment: These are relatively short-form provisions dealing with a complex area, as warranty and indemnity clauses are rarely, if ever, simple. The principles in relation to such clauses are considered in more detail in Chapter 4. As set out in the definitions clause (1) 'Claim' here is a challenge by a third party to the brand owner's rights to the mark whereas 'Infringement' is a third party's actual or apparent infringement of the brand owner's rights in the mark. See also the note at the end of this clause.

7.1   The Brand Owner warrants to the Licensee that the Brand Owner:
    7.1.1   is the sole legal and beneficial owner of the Trademark;
    7.1.2   is not aware of any Claim or Infringement;
    7.1.3   is fully entitled to enter into this agreement, grant the rights granted in it and perform its other obligations under it.
7.2   The Licensee warrants to the Brand Owner that it is fully entitled to enter into this agreement and able to perform its obligation under it.
7.3   If either party becomes aware of a Claim or Infringement:
    7.3.1   the party first becoming so aware will immediately notify the other party of such detail as it has of the Claim or Infringement;
    7.3.2   the parties will liaise as to what (if any) action to take to defend the Claim or in respect of the Infringement;
    7.3.3   the Brand Owner may (but will not be obliged to) at its own cost and for its own benefit solely take such action as it considers fit in relation to any Claim or Infringement; [*or*
    7.3.4   if the Brand Owner fails to take or defend any action in respect of an Claim or Infringement the Licensee may do so at its own cost and for its own benefit in its capacity and for its benefit as Licensee of the Marks in the Territory only (but not as Brand Owner);]
    7.3.5   a party taking action in respect of an Infringement or defending a Claim under this clause 7 may request the other party to provide reasonable assistance in connection with any such legal action or defence at the cost of the initiating or defending party [but without obligation to take action which would or might reasonably be expected to damage or prejudice its reasonable commercial interests].

Comment: These clauses are variable and the first draft clause from a brand owner may well seek to go further than this – and without the comfort of the second part of the clause.

7.4   The Licensee will indemnify the Brand Owner against any third-party claim (including legal costs and expenses) arising out of the Licensee's use of the Mark otherwise than strictly in accordance with this agreement.
7.5   The Brand Owner will indemnify the Licensee against any third-party claim (including legal costs and expenses) arising out of the Licensee's use of the Mark strictly in accordance with this agreement.

Comment: Clauses 7.4 and 7.5 will be matters for negotiation. Most trademark licences will include an indemnity clause similar to 7.4, but licensees should avoid open-ended indemnities or liabilities which are not the result of breach of a specific licensee warranty or obligation. Similarly brand owners increasingly seek to limit their own risk and may be reluctant even to warrant or give indemnities in respect of third-party claims or even licensee losses, requiring licensees instead to make and rely on their own searches. Brand owners may also seek to limit the amount of any liability (as discussed further in Chapter 7). Trademark owners often take a fairly inflexible line in relation to any changes to their agreements, but the issues raised here are all matters of analysing and negotiating risk against cost and benefit – one of the key themes of this book.

8   Royalties

8.1   The Licensee will within [60 days] from the end of each Accounting Period prepare and sent to the Brand Owner a statement showing details of Licensee's Turnover for that Accounting Period.

8.2   Within 30 days from the date of the statement under clause 8.1 and in any event within 90 days from the end of each Accounting Period the Licensee will pay the Brand Owner the Royalty for that Accounting Period.

Comment: there may need to be specific invoicing arrangements referred to here, tied in with VAT accounting as set out below.

8.3   The Licensee will keep all appropriate records of Licensee's Turnover during the Term to verify the statement produced to the Brand Owner and will supply to the Brand Owner (under conditions of confidentiality) such further information as the Brand Owner may reasonably request relating to the Licensee's Turnover and will, if so requested by [and at the expense of] the Brand Owner [no later than two years after the end of any Accounting Period], obtain and forward to the Brand Owner a certificate from the Licensee's auditors verifying that the amount of the Licensee's Turnover for that Accounting Period has been correctly calculated in accordance with this agreement.

Comment: Many audit clauses will be more specific and may give the party relying on the information (in this case, the brand owner) the right, by itself or through a third-party auditor, to inspect the appropriate records of the licensee. If the inspection indicates a misdeclaration there will then be provision for any deficiency to be made good immediately and, where the misdeclaration exceeds a stated percentage, such as 5 per cent, the costs of the inspection will then be for the account of the party making the misdeclaration – here the licensee. Such audit provisions are now becoming more and more significant and detailed where royalties or other payments (such as a pure percentage of receipts from resales) rely on a declaration system as to sales by the party making the payment.

8.4   The Royalty is calculated net of VAT. If VAT (or its equivalent) is or becomes payable in respect of the Royalty the Licensee will pay such VAT to the Brand Owner at the applicable rate within 14 days of production by the Brand Owner of a suitable VAT invoice.

8.5   All amounts payable under this agreement must be paid by the Licensee net of any deduction or set-off of any kind.

Comment: Some clauses also require the licensee to make good – or gross up – any deductions from royalty payments required by the laws of the licensee's home country – for example, in the form of withholding tax, as many countries require tax to be deducted from royalty payments being made to recipients outside the country.

8.6   The Licensee will pay the Brand Owner interest calculated on a daily basis at [two] percentage points above […] Bank PLC's base lending rate from time to time on any sums paid [14 days or more] late under this agreement.

9   Termination

9.1   Either party may terminate this agreement at any time by serving written notice on the other party if the other party:

9.1.1   is in [material] breach of this agreement and fails to remedy such breach within [14/21] days of written notice specifying the breach and requiring its remedy; or

9.1.2   becomes insolvent or unable to pay its debts as they fall due.

9.2   The Brand Owner may terminate this agreement by serving written notice on the Licensee if the Licensee challenges the validity or ownership by the Brand Owner of the Marks or its entitlement to use or license any of the Marks.

9.3   [Either party/ the Brand Owner] may terminate this agreement at any time by serving written notice on the [other party/the Licensee] if the [other party/Licensee] undergoes a change of Control.

Comment: These are short-form clauses only, but contain the key issues to be thought about. It is unlikely that brand owners will offer a change of control clause as affecting them, but this may be relevant to a licensee if the ownership of the brand by a reputable group is regarded as key for the licensee. In that case the licensee may also wish to add the right to terminate if the marks are brought into disrepute (except by action of the licensee itself), even without a change of control – see also, on this issue, clauses 4.8 and 6.3 of this document and the comments on IP contracts in Chapters 14 and 20 respectively.

10   Effects of Termination

10.1   On and immediately as from Termination, subject to clause 10.2, the Licensee will:

10.1.1   cease use of the Marks and [as soon as practicable/within … months of Termination] remove all representations or signs or materials containing the Marks from any place of business of the Licensee or any Product or Marketing Materials or destroy any such from which the Marks cannot be removed; and

10.1.2   change its [corporate and trading name] to a name not including the Marks or any name using the words '[…]' and/or '[…]' either separately or in conjunction or any colourable imitation of the or any of the Marks.

10.2   The Licensee may for a period of [12 months] only from Termination:

    10.2.1   continue to sell such Products as were in existence or in the course of production at Termination and during such period use Marketing Materials for such (but not new) Products; and

    10.2.2   continue to use the Name as part of its [corporate or business] name [and during such period the Brand Owner will not license the use of the Marks to another licensee in relation to products which are the same as or competitive with the Products].

10.3   Termination will be without prejudice to:

    10.4.1   the obligations of the Licensee to continue to pay Royalties and observe the terms of clause 8 in respect of all periods prior to and after Termination;

    10.4.2   the requirements of confidentiality in clause 11 which will continue as set out in that clause [*add reference to any other specific clauses intended to apply after Termination – see Chapter 20*]; and

    10.4.2   the rights of either party accrued due up to the date of Termination.

11   Confidentiality

11.1   Each party agrees to keep confidential the [financial] provisions of this agreement and the negotiations leading to it together with all information relating to the business or affairs of the other party and not to disclose any such information except:

    11.1.1   with the other party's prior written approval;

    11.1.2   where required by law or by a regulatory body having jurisdiction over it (and then after prior notification to the other party so far as the law allows); or

    11.1.3   to its own professional advisers on a 'need to know basis' and on terms of strict confidentiality.

11.2   The provisions of clause 11.1 will continue to apply during the Term and for a period of [two/five] years after Termination, but will not apply to any information that is or comes into the public domain where this does not occur through breach by either party of the provisions of this clause or apparent breach of a duty of confidence owed to any third party.

12   General provisions

12.1   *Notices*: Any notice or other communication given under this agreement must be in writing delivered personally, or sent by first-class post, or sent by e-mail with a delivery receipt to the relevant party's address specified in this agreement or to such other address and e-mail address as either party may have last notified to the other. Any notice or other communication is deemed to have been duly given on the day it is delivered personally, or on the second day following the date it was sent by post, or on the next working day following transmission by e-mail.

12.2   *Entire agreement*: This agreement and the documents referred to in it constitute the entire agreement between the parties, and supersede all other agreements or arrangements between the parties (whether written or oral, express or implied), relating to the subject matter of this agreement.

12.3   *Force majeure*: Neither party will be liable for any failure to perform or delay in performing any obligation under this agreement by reason of any circumstance beyond its reasonable control provided that it promptly notifies the other party of such circumstance and uses its reasonable endeavours to mitigate the effect of such circumstance on any affected obligation. If such circumstance continues to prevent performance for more than 60 days, either party may terminate this agreement on 30 days' written notice.

12.4   *Assignment*: Except as otherwise specifically permitted under this agreement, neither party may assign or transfer or sub-license its rights or obligations under this agreement without the prior written consent of the other party, such consent not to be unreasonably withheld or delayed. This clause will not prevent the assignment or transfer of rights or obligations to an Associate. Subject to the above, this agreement is binding upon each party's successors and assigns and personal representatives, as the case may be.

12.5   *Severability*: Any provision in this agreement which is held by any competent court or tribunal to be illegal or unenforceable will to the extent necessary be regarded as omitted from this agreement and the enforceability of the remainder will not be affected.

12.6   *Waivers*: No party will be affected by any delay or failure in exercising or any partial exercising of its rights under this agreement unless it has signed an express written waiver or release.

12.7   *Variations*: No variations of this agreement are effective unless made in writing signed by the parties or their authorized agents.

12.8   *Right of third parties*: The parties intend that no term of this agreement may be enforced by any person who is not a party to it.

12.9   *Law and jurisdiction*: This agreement will be governed and construed in accordance with the laws of England and Wales and the parties submit to the jurisdiction of the English courts.

Comment: See Chapter 4 in relation to such 'boilerplate' clauses.

Schedule (details of Marks [(and current Applications/Registrations)]

[Complete as appropriate with the precise permitted form of the use of the marks and current applications or registrations; check correlation with definitions in clause 1.]

Signed for and on behalf of
XYZ Limited by [...]
in the presence of :

Signed for and on behalf of
XYZ Limited by [...]
in the presence of :

Appendix E:
Sample Technology Agreement Checklist

There is, of course, no definitive list of all the issues, but the project checklist below encapsulates many of the technology contract issues considered in Chapter 15. In this checklist 'ITP' means IT provider. 'System' includes software, but not hardware unless both are to be provided under the contract.

Scope of the Agreement

Clarify whether there is agreement for services or a new system or both:

- What is to be provided?
- By whom?
- For how much (and when payable)?
- Within what timeframe?
- Are there penalties for missing a time or stage?
- Is there to be provision for a second stage if required?

If there is to be a new system, is the system is to be acquired/developed:

- wholly bespoke?
- wholly common platform/third-party proprietary?
- partly a mix of the two?
- partly open-source?

Is the system to be:

- bespoke and exclusive to the client? (If so, does it include any third-party components and/or open source code?)
- completely non-bespoke?
- partly exclusive? If so, how?

Is the agreement to cover:

- software only? (If so, is specific third-party hardware to be used?)
- hardware only?
- a mix of software and hardware? (If hardware, who chooses the hardware?)

Criteria:

- What is the system meant to achieve?
- What benefits does the client expect from it?
- How is the system to be installed?
- What are the performance criteria?
- How/to what extent is performance to be guaranteed by the ITP?
- How is performance to be measured?

Main risks/potential business impact of failure:

- wrong supplier
- system fails to achieve requirements
- delay
- major failure after go-live
- persistent minor failures
- future maintenance
- other (specify).

Go-live:

- What is the proposed go-live date?
- How critical is this date/is there tolerance?
- Is alpha and beta testing required? (If so, who will carry this out when and where?)
- What are the acceptance procedures?

Financials

Services element:

- Min/max days of services to be provided?
- Is the day rate specified?
- Is the rate guaranteed for any further stage?
- What, if any, expenses are to be paid additionally?

System element:

- Fixed overall fee?
- If not, what variables will apply?
- Is there a cap on the total?

Payment terms:

- for services
- for the system
- retentions.

Warranty:

- Performance warranty/extent?
- How long?
- Any extra costs in warranty work?

Maintenance/support/updates etc:

- Maintenance agreement?
- How long?
- What service-level provisions will apply?
- Cost and when payable?
- Terms for termination before/after that period?
- Is renewal price guaranteed – for how long?
- Upgrades/new versions?
- Bug-fixes/troubleshooting updates?
- Upgrades/new versions/editions?

Rights granted and limitations

Which companies in the client's group or otherwise are entitled to use the system? Are there any limitations on client's use of the system in terms of:

- location?
- number or type of users?
- activities/types of business?
- territories?

Are there any limitations on ITP use of same/similar system?

- For example, area/timescale/client's competitors etc.

Escrows

- Is there to be an escrow agreement with a trusted third party (for example, NCC) to ensure that the source code is available following future possible breach or insolvency of the ITP?
- Is there to be a financial escrow account to cover such risks?

Agreement

- Who will draft?
- Will there be one agreement or several? (Watch conflicts between agreements.)
- Check full and correct company names etc.

- *Governing law* – Which law will govern the agreement? (Consider where the installation is located, any sub-licences, implied legal obligations, whether consumers are affected, the need to retain overseas lawyers and costs involved.)
- *Technical information* – Have definitions and any technical schedules been double-checked?

Stop Press!

Times, tide – and, these days, new law – wait for no man. As the text of this book was being finalised, new developments were incorporated where possible, but a line had to be drawn for the book to reach print. This section therefore aims to bring the position as up-to-date (as at the end of October 2009) as possible. As with the main text, and given the daily outpouring of new law and legal comment, what follows has been inevitably selective. In some cases it updates developments already presaged in the text; in some it gives further examples of principles already set out; in a few cases, however, there are genuine surprises. Case law, like everything else in life, can take a dramatic shift along unexpected paths, and sometimes expected paths with unexpected consequences. This update, which also picks up a couple of slightly older cases which seem to have especial relevance, follows the main scheme of the five parts of the book, with cross-references where applicable.

Part 1: Creating and Writing Contracts

The question of when *an exchange of emails and phone calls* evidences a binding contract was considered in Chapter 1 (see especially the VHE case summarised on p. 16) and Chapter 2 (in the build up of the Braby/ Smith exchanges from p. 20 onwards). The principles summarised in those chapters were affirmed in *University of Plymouth v European Language Center* [2009] EWCA Civ 784, where the Court of Appeal overruled the County Court in holding that a contract had *not* been created in the particular circumstances of the case. Although an expectation might have been created (as to the number of beds available for an ELC course at the University), ELC (the claimants) failed on at least two main grounds. First they had trouble showing exactly when and how the alleged contract had been created, especially in failing to prove that they communicated their supposed acceptance of the University's supposed offer. Second, the court observed (para 25) that 'the parties were even at the [sic] late stage still negotiating with a view to reaching a final agreement on terms.' In these circumstances there could be no binding contract.

    Cantor Index v Thomson ([2008] EWHC 1104) examined the classic problem of accepting part payment of a debt. A creditor (Cantor), having rejected the proposal of a debtor (Thomson) to pay by instalments (by Cantor making a counter-offer), then paid in a cheque received from Thomson with a further counter-offer. On the facts the court concluded that, by paying the cheque into its bank account, Cantor had accepted the offer in Thomson's accompanying letter and was bound by Thomson's terms, even though those terms differed from Cantor's previous offer of settlement and even though the cheque bounced. This is a reminder of the dangers of accepting partial payment without prior agreement as to the terms of doing so.

    What level of commitment may be required to obtain third party consent, when this is required, and when might it be reasonably or unreasonably withheld? (See Chapter 4,

p. 54 on and Chapter 18, transfers, p 237.) In *CEP Holdings v Steni* [2009] EWHC 2447, a distribution agreement was incompletely assigned. The decision is a useful review of case law both on whether there had been effective assignment or novation of the agreement, showing the challenges of proving implied consent, and on the true interpretation of an obligation in the agreement to use 'all reasonable endeavours', where the court allowed some flexibility but did require some real action to have taken place. A different standard appears to apply where there is a fiduciary type discretion, rather than a withholding of consent. The decision in *Bank of New York v Montana Board of Investments* ([2008] EWHC 1594) upheld the principle that in such cases discretion must be exercised in good faith and neither capriciously nor arbitrarily.

Part 2: Key Legal Issues Affecting Contracts

The issue of *what is confidential* and how far it should be kept confidential (see Chapter 5) is not only one of the great social and political issues of our age but occupies more and more legal attention. Parliament itself, the ultimate creator of new law, has at the time of writing, become embroiled in the scandal of MPs expenses, raising issues about when someone handling essentially secret financial information is morally and legally entitled to disclose that information to public scrutiny. As in the old maxim 'who guards those who guard', disclosure of confidential information raises not just the issue of whether the disclosure is justified but who receives it and for what purpose. Members of the House of Lords themselves became angry at the use by the press of the Freedom of Information Act to obtain what the Lords believed was personal information, their lordships uncovering in the process a power under the Data Protection Act to seek disclosure of the recipient of such information.

Also in October 2009 came the attempt by a leading firm of libel lawyers acting for international oil traders, Trafigura, to seek to impose restrictions on what appeared to be genuine reporting of parliamentary debate. There were two additional factors involved here, one concerning the use of so-called 'super-injunctions' effectively banning publication of material that may breach *confidentiality or privacy* before the issue has been fully tested, and the other being the furious backlash bringing together MPs, The Guardian newspaper and the public, orchestrated through the medium of 'Twitter', itself a means of rapid electronic communication of very recent origins.

Similarly, the power of the blog has continued to grow, raising questions about *privacy* and anonymity. In October, in *Author of a Blog v Times Newspapers* ([2009] EWHC 1358), a leading privacy case, the judge permitted the identification of a previously anonymous blogger who had written various critical comments regarding police matters. The blogger, who sought an injunction to prevent The Times newspaper unmasking him, turned out to be a detective constable, identified by a reporter from information already available on the Internet. The judge held that the blogger had no reasonable expectation of privacy; even if he had had such a reasonable expectation, this would be outweighed by the public interest in favour of free expression by the newspaper. The judgment suggests that blogging must be assumed to be a public, not a private, activity. The public interest was engaged and made paramount by the blogger's role in the police and the breach of the police rules of conduct.

At a more detailed level *Imerman v Tcheguiz* ([2009] EWHC 2024), whilst fascinating for many other reasons, is worth noting for the proposition supported by the court that there is a powerful case to say that any information stored on a firm's computer systems may be regarded as *confidential information* by virtue simply of being *password protected*, whatever its actual content.

At the statutory end of the same debate, *data protection* continues its inexorable march. New guides are expected during 2010 – an ICO Guide and a Personal Information Online Code of Practice. We face a new DPA acronym as 'Binding Corporate Rules' (BCRs) are likely to become more prevalent. The long arm of the criminal law also threatens to reach further into the data protection field. Not content with the Information Commissioner's higher registration fees and the powers of the ICO and the FSA to fine companies for data protection breaches, the Ministry of Justice has published a consultation paper suggesting potential custodial sentences for those involved in selling or offering to sell personal data that has been unlawfully obtained.

Meanwhile the European Court of Justice has re-emphasized the risk of *competition law* breach by holding that a *single meeting* (in this case between mobile phone operators) could form the basis for a cartel. The issue was not the number of meetings but the opportunity the parties had to take account of the information obtained in order to co-ordinate their behaviour.

Exemption clauses – the case of *Lobster Group v Heidelberg*, mentioned under Part 5 below, confirms many of the principles set out in Chapter 7 and shows again how much care needs to be taken both in drafting and defending exemption clauses of various kinds, as well as the risks of terminating a contract improperly.

Part 3: Contracts for Sales and Services

Consumer fairness – The name and logo of *Foxtons*, the estate agents, is familiar to home hunters in London; the firm has a strong business in both residential sales and lettings. Some landlords who had let their properties through the firm later sold the property to their erstwhile tenants but then found that Foxtons' letting terms included a clause requiring them to pay a substantial commission on the sale as well as on the letting that preceded it. Some landlords complained to the Office of Fair Trading, who finally took Foxtons to court under UTCCR (see Chapter 10). The issue was first whether Foxtons' terms were expressed in 'plain and intelligible language' and second whether business landlords were 'consumers' so as to come within UTCCR at all. On the second point, the court held that whilst many landlords were not consumers, others who had acquired one or two properties as an alternative form of pension could reasonably be regarded as such. Further, the provisions as to commission on a possible future sale was not part of the core bargain between the parties, which related to the letting, so would not have received much attention from the consumer, had not been specifically drawn to their attention when agreeing to instruct Foxtons and moreover were hidden away in the small print. Even once moved in location they were too vague to be regarded as 'plain and intelligible'. (*OFT v Foxtons Ltd* [2009] EWCH 1681.)

On the *consumer regulatory* front the new *Provision of Services Regulations* will (by order of European directive) come into force by the end of 2009. These are mainly concerned with encouraging cross-border European trade by ensuring customers know who they are dealing when buying services, requiring clear information disclosure on complaints handling and establishing official bodies with powers to oversee implementation. Easy electronic access will suffice for the purpose of providing the information. Services are widely defined, including professional services that may have their own regulators, but some have their own rules, such as in banking and finance, where many of us will already have been deluged with new terms and conditions from the new payment services regulations. So terms of business for providing services will need to be reviewed (again!) but website terms following the principles set out in Chapter 10 should be well placed.

The government published in late 2009 a White Paper proposing changes to many *consumer regulations,* many relating to consumer finance but some changes can also be expected to the Sale of Goods Act together with new measures against those who abuse consumer trust through the Internet. Assuming that the government's own department can keep up with this pace of change further up-to-date guidance should be available from the BIS/ BERR website.

Moving on to services generally, what happens if a client signs a major contract in the belief that a particular individual, whom they know and trust, is leading the team and the client then finds that the person in question had resigned, even before the project contract was signed? This was the central issue in *Fitzroy Robinson v Mentmore* Towers ([2009] EWHC 1552). The architects in question did not tell their client that the team leader (Jeremy Blake) had submitted his resignation, and that he would at most work one year on a three year project, apparently because the architects feared they would lose the contract. The evidence showed that Mr Blake was expressly named – held out in effect - as the team leader in the project brief and the architect's chief executive dishonestly failed to correct the effective representation that Mr Blake would be available for the project. The court decided that this was a conscious decision, amounting in law to fraudulent misrepresentation and deceit. Even so, damages were not easy to assess, as no delay was ultimately caused and it was difficult for the client to show financial loss. Potentially the client might even have had the ability to rescind the contract on the grounds of misrepresentation (see p. 338). This situation, in some ways a very human one, shows the importance of not misleading another contract party during negotiations. Whilst the architects could not really commit to Mr Blake being available for the full project duration, the court decided that they deliberately withheld the information of his resignation. If Mr Blake was that critical to the project, however, the client could have insisted on the right to terminate if he left or, at the least, could have negotiated to right to be consulted immediately if the architects became aware of his decision to leave and to be consulted as to his replacement.

Part 4: Technical contracts

Copyright – To re-enforce concerns about a common lack of understanding of the UK fair dealing rules, a recent European Court of Justice decision held that copying as little as eleven words of a news article (not in UK) could amount to breach of copyright. Perhaps ironic then that a survey by Consumer Focus and the Open Rights Group has relegated UK to having the worst (that is, most restrictive) copyright rules, by far. This relates to many of the provisions of our main copyright law, dating from 1988, not reflecting the realities of the modern electronic, multi-media and multi-device world, an issue that is being steadily addressed but which opens up the apparently ever-widening divide between copyright owners and licensees and those who take the view that essentially everything published on the Internet should be accessible and usable.

One of the key battlegrounds in this area is of course that of unlawful *Internet file-sharing*, where much has been happening to no great effect as yet. The French 'three strikes rule' (see p. 295) took a knock when the French Constitutional Council declared in mid-2009 that the French Creation and Internet Bill 2008 giving effect to the rule was itself unconstitutional. The UK government, alongside progress on the Digital Economy Bill, has been using at least stronger language than before in its own apparent determination to address the problems of P2P file sharing when this constitutes blatant copyright infringement. The government has set a target of a 70 per cent reduction in illegal P2P file sharing, failing which it will expect Ofcom to step in and apply appropriate technical measures, but 2010 elections may yet affect the timing of any new rules. At the same time the pendulum continues to swing as to the requirement for, and extent of, a judicial (and possibly appeal) process before disconnection of offenders from their Internet accounts. On a parallel issue in Europe Commissioner Reding has pledged a modern set of rules encouraging the digitization of books and a registry to ensure fair returns for authors and publishers, but again political considerations – and possibly even the views of authors and publishers - may affect the extent and timing of the detail.

On the business marketing side the issue of what has become known as *'behavioural advertising'*, using cookies, 'web beacons' and other technology to track not just the buying habits but potentially also the interests of individuals as shown by their Internet browsing (also relevant to Chapter 10 on website sales) is receiving close scrutiny from a personal data and privacy perspective. This challenges the interpretation of both the DPA (for example as to how far IP addresses in themselves may be protected personal data, which may depend on whether they actually identify the individual) and the Privacy and Electronic Communications Regulations 2003 ('PECR'). The broader issue may lead to new regulations spelling out the need for individual users to have opt-in rights based on full disclosure of how and where the tracked information may be used. Firms accordingly need to keep a close eye on changes to PECR and their electronic privacy policies under close review.

Somewhat against the trend of armour-plating the consumer, a recent Court of Appeal decision suggests that website disclaimers may be more effective and need to be less conspicuous than previously thought to achieve their objective.

Part 5: The Wider World, Changes and Breakdowns

Execution of deeds – The Mercury tax case decision on defective execution of a deed featured on p. 333 has been criticised as being incompatible with modern commercial practice. A Joint Working Party (JWP) has been set up through the aegis of the Law Society, setting out guidance as to best practice if all parties are not present and able to execute completed documents.

Guarantees, misrepresentations and their effects continue to cause problems and the case of *Lobster Group v Heidelberg Press* [2009] EWHC 1919 is recommended study for those who are considering refusing payment or even claiming the right to terminate a contract for misrepresentation or un-remedied breach. The facts were quite complex but, in essence, Heidelberg, major manufacturers of printing presses, supplied a press to a company who hired it to Lobster Press, as it then was. There was a 12-months guarantee limited to repair or replacement and a damages exemption clause. After problems arose with the press which the hirer was unable fully to resolve, Lobster terminated the hire payments and returned the press. The court held that, on the facts (as must always be stressed), there was no misrepresentation. A clause providing for repair or return was reasonable as was the 12 months' limitation period for repairs or replacement, but the only material failure had not in fact been reported within the 12 months' period. Exclusion of consequential loss was acceptable in this case, but not the purported exclusion of damages for immediate loss, increased costs and direct damage. However, Lobster had failed to show what loss it had really suffered, apart from costs of rectifying certain defective printing. Its losses were therefore limited to those costs; the defect in question did not justify withholding payment, which the contract terms precluded, nor entitle Lobster to a rebate of hire charges, nor was it so serious as to be a repudiatory breach justifying termination, making Lobster's termination of the agreement itself wrongful.

Finally on p. 366 the issue was raised of the ability of an innocent party to terminate a contract for *persistent, but not individually material, breaches*. The decision in *Alan Auld Associates v Rick Pollard Associates* ([2008] EWCA Civ 655) supports the argument that such cumulative breaches may show an intent not to be bound by the contract at all. This becomes a repudiatory breach, even if the individual breaches might not have been material. This especially applies if the breaches are 'persistent and cynical', such as those described by the court in that case.

List of Cases Cited

Page references at the end of each case refer to where the case appears in this book.

Hotel Services v. *Hilton Int. Hotels* [2000] 1 All ER (Comm.) 750, see p. 129
Imageview Management v. *Jack* [2009] EWCA Civ. 63, see p. 206
Imerman v Tcheguiz ([2009] EWHC 2024), see p. 400
Inntrepreneur Pub Co. Ltd v. *East Crown Ltd* [2000] 2 Lloyd's Rep. 611, see p. 130
Internet Broadcasting Corporation Ltd (t/a NETTV) v. *MAR LLC (t/a MARHedge)* [2009] EWHC 844 (Ch), see p. 131
Investors Compensation Scheme v. *West Bromwich Building Society* [1997] UKHL 28, see p. 30
Irvine v. *Talksport* [2003] EWCA Civ 423, see p. 258
Jackson v. *RBS* [2005] UKHL 3, see p. 77 & p. 129
Jarvis v. *Swan Tours* [1973] 2 QB 233, see p. 356
Koufos v. *C. Czarnikow Ltd (The Heron II)* [1969] 1 AC 350, see p. 115
Lobster Group v Heidelberg Press [2009] EWHC 1919, see p. 403
Lonsdale v. *Howard & Hallam* [2007] UKHL 32, see p. 209
Lordsdale Finance v. *Bank of Zambia* [1996] QB 752, see p. 62
Lumley v. *Wagner* (1852) 42 ER 687, see p. 353
McQuire v. *Western Morning News* [1903] 2KB 100, see p. 53
Martinez v. *Mirror Group Newspapers* 2008 (French court decision), see p. 301
MCA Records v. *Charly Records (No. 5)* [2001] EWCA Civ. 1441, see p. 104
McKennit v. *Ash* [2005] EWHC 3003 (QB), see p. 85
Mercury Tax Group v. *HMRC* [2008] EWHC 2721, see p. 333 & p. 403
Metropolitan International Schools v. *Designtechnica and Google* [2009] EWHC 1765, see p. 294
Millam v. *The Print Factory* [2007] EWCA 322, see p. 104
Mosley v. *Group Newspapers Ltd* [2008] EWHC 1777 (QB), see p. 85
Murray v. *Big Pictures (UK) Ltd* [2008] EWCA Civ. 446, see p. 85
OBG Ltd v. *Allan* [2007] UKHL 21, see p. 359
OFT v Foxtons Ltd [2009] EWCH 1681, see p. 401
Pereira (J) Fernandes v. *Mehta* [2006] EWHC 813 (Ch), see p. 11
Prenn v. *Simmonds* [1971]1 WLR 1381, see p. 31
Proforce Recruit Ltd v. *Rugby Group Ltd* [2007] EWHC 1621 (QB), see p. 31 & p. 34
Proform Sports Management v. *Proactive Sports Management* [2006] EWHC 2903 (Ch), see p. 12
Prudential v. *Ayres* [2008] EWCA Civ. 52, see p. 66
Quest 4 Finance v. *Maxfield* [2007] EWHC 2313 (QB), see p. 131
Rackham v. *Peek Foods* [1990] BCLC 895, see p. 54
Regus v. *Epcot Solutions* [2008] EWCA Civ. 361, see pp. 128–9
Reklos v. *Greece* [2009] EMLR 16, see p. 85
Rhodia Int Holdings v. *Huntsman Int* [2007] 2 Lloyd's Rep. 325, see p. 54
Sam Business Systems v. *Hedley* [2002] EWHC 2733 (TCC), see p. 128
Shanklin Pier Ltd v. *Detel Products Ltd* [1951] 2 KB 854, see p. 339
Sheffield District Railway v. *The Great Central Railway* (1911) 27 TLR 451, see p. 54
Shetland Times v. *Wills* [1997] SC 316, see p. 301
Simkins Partnership v. *Reeves Lund* [2003] EWHC 1946 (QB), see p. 124
Six Continents Hotels v. *Event Hotels* [2006] EWHC 2317 (QB), see p. 131
St Albans City and District Council v. *International Computers Ltd* [1996] 4 All ER 481, see p. 46, p. 124 & p. 127
Stabilad v. *Stephens & Carter* [1999] 2 All ER (Comm.) 651, see p. 45
Standard Bank plc v. *Agrinvest International Inc.* [2007] EWHC 2595 (Comm.), see p. 318

List of Relevant Legislation

Page references at the end of each piece of legislation indicate where the legislation is referred to in this book.

Index